THE ALLURE OF MATTER

Edited by
ORIANNA CACCHIONE
and WEI-CHENG LIN

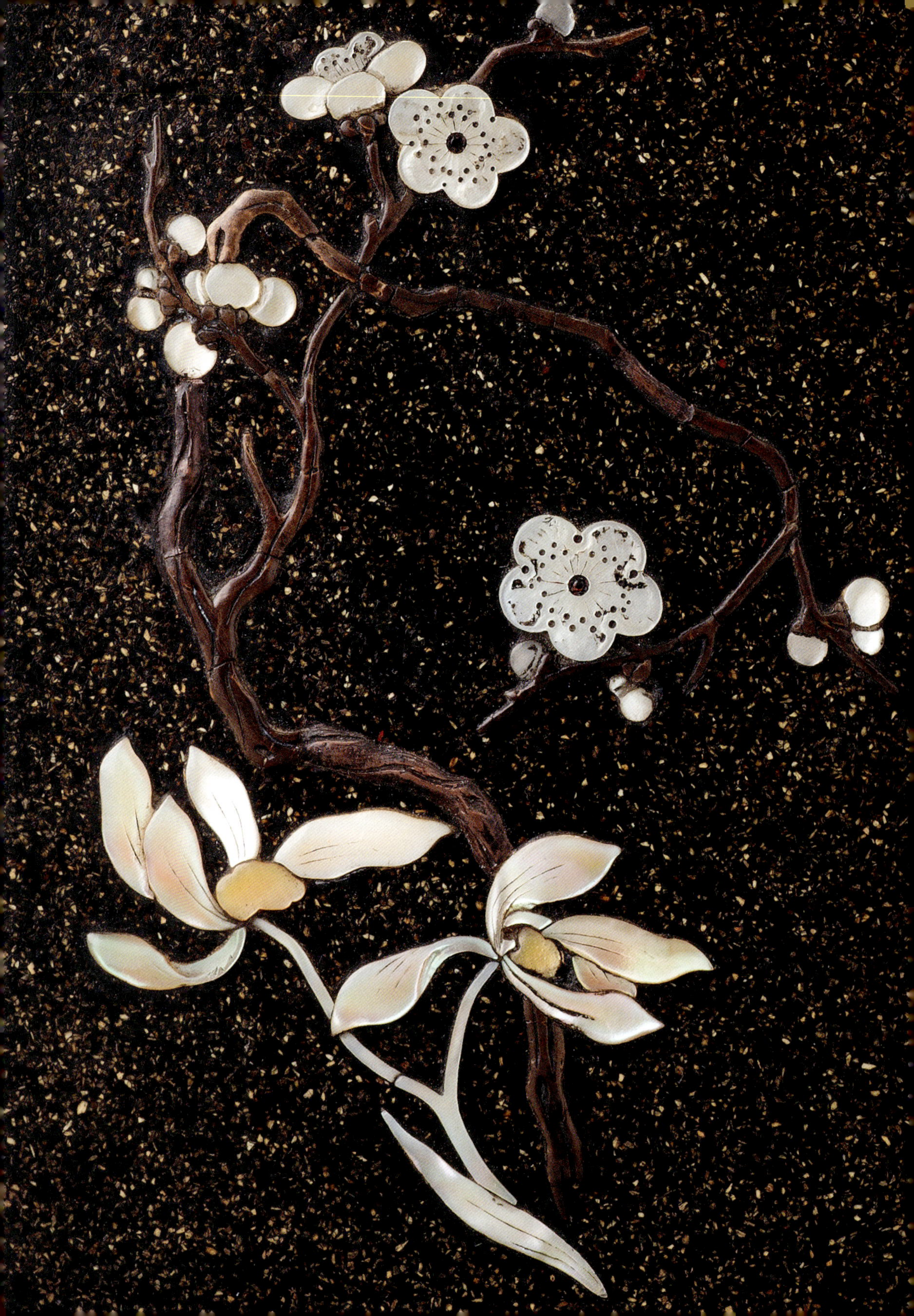

THE ALLURE OF MATTER

MATERIALITY ACROSS CHINESE ART

Edited by
ORIANNA CACCHIONE
and WEI-CHENG LIN

PUBLISHED BY THE UNIVERSITY OF CHICAGO'S
CENTER FOR THE ART OF EAST ASIA AND SMART MUSEUM OF ART

This publication was produced by the Smart Museum of Art and the Center for the Art of East Asia, The University of Chicago, in conjunction with the "Art and Materiality" symposium, organized by the Smart Museum of Art and the Center for the Art of East Asia, The University of Chicago, February 6–8, 2020. The symposium was held on the occasion of the opening of the exhibition *The Allure of Matter: Material Art from China*, curated by Wu Hung with Orianna Cacchione.

The Allure of Matter: Materiality across Chinese Art was supported by a grant from the Robert H. N. Ho Family Foundation, with additional funding from a Yuen Research Grant, Ralph Wanger, and the Center for the Art of East Asia, The University of Chicago.

何鴻毅家族基金
THE ROBERT H. N. HO FAMILY FOUNDATION

Library of Congress Control Number: 2021912763

 Distributed by the University of Chicago Press.

ISBN: 9780935573640

Publication Managers:
Gail Ana Gomez, Simone Levine
Copyeditor: Timothy Johnson
Indexer: Gerald Van Ravenswaay
Proofreader: Natalie Haddad
Design and production:
Jena Sher Graphic Design

Printing and binding: BALTO Print, Lithuania

Front cover image: Cai Guo-Qiang, *Black Peony*, 2008. Gunpowder on porcelain, 66.83 × 37.31 x 5.72 cm. Photo: I-Hue Lee. Courtesy of Cai Studio.
Back cover image: Glass lobed elliptical bowl, Tang dynasty. Glass, height: 2.9 cm, diameter at lip: 5.5–5.9 cm. Found in silver jar, Hejiacun Hoard. Xi'an, Shaanxi province.
© Shaanxi History Museum.

SMART MUSEUM OF ART
THE UNIVERSITY OF CHICAGO

Smart Museum of Art
The University of Chicago
5550 S. Greenwood Avenue
Chicago, Illinois 60637
773.702.0200
smartmuseum.uchicago.edu

CENTER FOR THE ART OF EAST ASIA
THE UNIVERSITY OF CHICAGO

Center for the Art of East Asia
The University of Chicago
5540 S. Greenwood Avenue
Chicago, IL 60637
773.834.1060
voices.uchicago.edu/caeatest

CONTENTS

DIRECTORS' FOREWORD

This book, *The Allure of Matter: Materiality across Chinese Art*, is a testament to the incredible intellectual depth, rigor, and interdisciplinarity for which the University of Chicago is known. It grew out of the groundbreaking scholarship that was presented at the "Art and Materiality" symposium, which was organized on the occasion of the Smart Museum of Art's spring 2020 exhibition *The Allure of Matter: Material Art from China*. From the start, the exhibition, symposium, and now this volume exemplify the collaborative spirit of partnership at the University of Chicago. We are elated that the Smart Museum of Art joined with the Center for the Art of East Asia to co-publish this volume; the Center's faculty expertise in premodern Chinese art perfectly complements the Smart Museum's trailblazing history of introducing contemporary Chinese art to American audiences. Together, Orianna Cacchione, Curator of Global Contemporary Art at the Smart Museum, and Wei-Cheng Lin, Associate Professor of Art History and the College, have augmented the longstanding relationship between the Smart Museum and the Department of Art History at the University of Chicago. Museum staff and art history faculty have produced decades of exhibitions, programs, and catalogues together, notably *The Allure of Matter: Material Art from China*, which was curated by Wu Hung with Orianna Cacchione. Nonetheless, this book establishes a new chapter in the Museum and Department's partnership across the shared courtyard of our Edward Larrabee Barnes buildings—this is the very first time an art history faculty member and a Smart Museum curator have produced a stand-alone volume of scholarly essays.

Following the success of and critical enthusiasm for the "Art and Materiality" symposium, this volume advances further exploration of the themes that emerged at the conference and provides an essential reference for teaching of this previously little-studied topic. Importantly, the contribution this volume makes to the fields of Chinese and global art histories is twofold: first, it fortifies the importance of materials across centuries of art in China, and second, it enables materiality to rise as an elegant theme that activates Chinese art's resonance with a global lexicon for art history. The scholars who Orianna Cacchione and Wei-Cheng Lin have brought together expand this publication's sphere of contributors far beyond the University of Chicago (as far as the United

Kingdom and even Australia). We are thrilled to publish the work of these contributors and to welcome voices from so many institutions in this volume: Alex Burchmore, University of Sydney; Orianna Cacchione, Smart Museum of Art; Anne Feng, Boston University; Yuhang Li, University of Wisconsin–Madison; Nancy P. Lin, The University of Chicago; Wei-Cheng Lin, The University of Chicago; Sara A. Moy, independent conservator; Rachel Rivenc, Getty Research Institute; Catherine Stuer, Denison University; Wu Hung, The University of Chicago; and Yusen Yu, University of Oxford. We commend these contributors for the rigorous research and original lines of inquiry with which they have shaped the chapters of this volume. Their findings not only join our research here at the University of Chicago, but, even more critically, advance scholarship within the broader field of art history that we share.

We are immensely grateful to our supporters for recognizing and joining in the collaborative spirit and broad impact of this volume. First and foremost, we thank the Robert H. N. Ho Family Foundation, which, from its position in Hong Kong, so enthusiastically adapted a grant to support this volume and empowered our ability to make an impact in the midst of the COVID-19 pandemic. We are also thankful for Ralph Wanger's support for this project and his commitment to the Center for the Art of East Asia, without which this publication would not have been possible. Furthermore, we sincerely thank the Alphawood Foundation and Wrightwood 659 for their enduring partnership and support of *The Allure of Matter* exhibition and this volume. With consideration to any University endeavor, we are grateful for the support of our colleagues across campus, especially the visionary leadership of Provost Ka Yee Lee and UChicago Global, which further enabled the geographic reach of this volume as part of their worldwide efforts at the University. We are grateful for a Yuen Research Grant from the University of Chicago that bolstered this project in its final months. We deeply appreciate the steadfast partnership of UChicago Arts. We are also grateful for our supporters of *The Allure of Matter* exhibition, especially the Andy Warhol Foundation for the Visual Arts, the E. Rhodes and Leona B. Carpenter Foundation, and Lorna Ferguson and Terry Clark.

Finally, we want to thank the staff of the Smart Museum and the Center for the Art of East Asia for making this volume's publication possible. We are honored that the publication continues the broader efforts of Wu Hung, Harrie A. Vanderstappen Distinguished Service Professor of Art History and the College, Director of the Center for the Art of East Asia, and Smart Museum Adjunct Curator. From curating *The Allure of Matter* exhibition to lending his expertise to this volume, Wu Hung has made invaluable contributions to this publication and the field at large. We also want to recognize Katherine Tsiang, Associate Director of the Center for the Art of East Asia, for partnering with us. The collaboration has been truly transformative for both the Center for the Art of East Asia and the Smart Museum of Art and has allowed us to continue to expose Chinese art to broader audiences in Chicago and around the world. We are all extremely appreciative of our Development Department at the Smart. And, last but certainly not least, we express our deepest gratitude to Orianna Cacchione and Wei-Cheng Lin for gracefully working together as co-editors and publishing a volume of such exceptional caliber.

Amina Dickerson
Bill Michel
Co-Interim Directors
Smart Museum of Art, The University of Chicago

ACKNOWLEDGMENTS

This book builds upon the scholarship presented at the "Art and Materiality" symposium at the University of Chicago on February 6–8, 2020. Held as part of the celebrations surrounding the opening of the exhibition *The Allure of Matter: Material Art from China* at the Smart Museum of Art and at Wrightwood 659, the symposium took the exhibition's focus on materiality in contemporary Chinese art as its point of departure to examine the importance of materiality in both premodern Chinese art and global contemporary art. Mirroring the two halves of the symposium, this publication documents and augments the original event as it further aggregates a transhistorical body of scholarship. At the same time, the publication follows *The Allure of Matter* exhibition and its catalogue in developing materiality into a powerful lens to analyze Chinese art within global narratives that have remained woefully inactivated in art history—until now.

Such a transhistorical undertaking necessitated collaboration, and the critical breadth that this publication embodies would have been incomplete without all who contributed their expertise to its development. We are grateful for all of the speakers at the original "Art and Materiality" symposium, whose insightful research inspired this undertaking, and especially for the essayists who expanded their original presentations for this volume. Our thanks are due to Anne Feng, Yuhang Li, Catherine Stuer, and Yusen Yu for each applying their expertise to present a well-developed arc that underscores the importance of materiality across premodern Chinese art. We are equally grateful to Rachel Rivenc, Sara A. Moy, Alex Burchmore, and Nancy P. Lin for contributing their interdisciplinary perspectives to our pioneering volume and illuminating materiality in contemporary Chinese art. Above all, we are deeply grateful to Wu Hung, whose scholarship forms the larger umbrella under which this publication figures itself. We are honored that this volume expands the pioneering foundation Wu Hung, the Smart Museum of Art, and the Center for the Art of East Asia have established for the study and exhibition of Chinese art.

We are tremendously grateful for the generous and enduring support of our sponsors and supporters. The Robert H. N. Ho Family Foundation provided steadfast and sustained support of the original symposium and the volume you read today. Without their dedication this project would not have been possible. We also express sincere gratitude to Ralph Wanger for providing support to the

Center for the Art of East Asia at the University of Chicago. We graciously acknowledge the generous support we received from the University of Chicago's Yuen Research Grant. We would be remiss to not acknowledge the ongoing commitment and unwavering enthusiasm of the Alphawood Foundation and Wrightwood 659. The Foundation provided essential support for *The Allure of Matter* exhibition and this publication and continues to support the Center for the Art of East Asia as we work together to cultivate the future of the field.

We owe our deepest thanks to the many colleagues at the University of Chicago, the Center for the Art of East Asia, and the Smart Museum whose essential cooperation made this volume possible. This volume is an example of the type of scholarship that can only be germinated at a university art museum. It has been an extraordinary joy to watch scholars, curators, and conservators come together to share their knowledge and contribute to the new modalities for research highlighted in this book. We are indebted to this intellectual community. The Center's Director, Wu Hung, and Associate Director, Katherine Tsiang, along with the Smart Museum's former Interim Director, Jill Sterrett, and current Co-Interim Directors, Amina Dickerson and Bill Michel, championed this project and encouraged us at every step in the process. We are grateful for their insightful leadership and ongoing support. The Center's organizing assistance helped to bring the publication to fruition, and we are grateful to have the first opportunity to contribute scholarship on contemporary Chinese art to the Center's illustrious publications program. We are fortunate to have worked with the Smart Museum's development team, led by Lisa Abel and Sara Arnas. We appreciate beyond words their unwavering advocacy and endorsement of this project. We are also indebted to C. J. Lind, who promoted the exhibition and this book with fervor. Like an exhibition, a publication requires hard work, dedication, and the backing of an entire museum team, and we are exceedingly grateful to all of our colleagues at the Smart.

Our most emphatic gratitude and admiration is due to the publication's production team, which enabled us to produce this extraordinary volume. We express our warmest thanks to Jena Sher, whose publication design masterfully handles a wide historical arc of subject matter and illustrations in such a way that activates their material nuances while turning a fresh perspective upon them. We also thank Simone Levine, Curatorial Research Assistant for Global Contemporary Art, for shepherding this publication from start to finish. Without Simone's commitment to detail and enthusiasm, this volume would not have been possible. Special thanks also goes to Gail Ana Gomez, the Smart Museum's

Exhibitions and Publications Manager, for lending her expertise and more broadly overseeing this publication's production. We were honored to have worked with editor Timothy Johnson, who meticulously refined each text and importantly contributed his own expertise on Chinese art. We appreciate the diligence that Gerald Van Ravenswaay brought to his work indexing this volume. We are also grateful to Natalie Haddad for her precision in proofreading the final galley. Additional thanks goes to Smart Museum intern Catherine Grace Lyons for her essential role in organizing the images, image captions, and rights information, and to Caroline Otter at the Center for the Art of East Asia for providing administrative support.

We must also acknowledge our partners at the Los Angeles County Museum of Art, Seattle Art Museum, and Peabody Essex Museum, who initially came together to co-organize *The Allure of Matter* exhibition. Although the full national tour was cut short due to COVID-19, we are eternally grateful for the advice, support, enthusiasm, and camaraderie of the organizing curators at each museum: Stephen Little, Catharina Manchanda, Ping Foong, Trevor Smith, and Susie Ferrell.

Finally, we are thankful for all involved in this publication for their commitment to this project in the wake of a global pandemic. We deeply appreciate your contributions during this unprecedented and challenging time, and we are indebted to you for recognizing this publication's potential to make a lasting contribution.

Orianna Cacchione
Curator of Global Contemporary Art
Smart Museum of Art, The University of Chicago

Wei-Cheng Lin
Associate Professor of Art History and the College
The University of Chicago

Preface

Wu Hung

This volume has a dual significance: it is an independent study of *materials* in Chinese art that encompasses premodern, modern, and contemporary periods; and it also marks a new stage in a large research and publication project centered on *The Allure of Matter: Material Art from China* exhibition.

Initiated in 2014, this project began by investigating the innovative use of unconventional materials by several generations of experimental Chinese artists. After a number of presentations and panel discussions, all organized by the Smart Museum of Art at the University of Chicago, it became clear that this was indeed a highly significant phenomenon in Chinese avant-garde art since the 1980s, a trend that also resonated with some crucial movements in global contemporary art in both the East and the West. A decision was then made to organize a major exhibition to showcase and interpret this phenomenon.

The ensuing preparation followed two directions: research and organization. Consisting of archival investigation, studio visits, artist interviews, and contextual studies, a series of focused research programs were conducted to trace the history of Material Art (*caizhi yishu*) within contemporary Chinese art, and in this process to identify its representative artists and key works, as well as its emergence and historical development. Another aspect of this research was to explore the symbiotic relationship between contemporary Chinese art and global contemporary art. While connecting Material Art with earlier avant-garde art movements such as Arte Povera (Poor Art) in Italy and Mono-ha (School of Things) in Japan, the in-person contacts between pioneers of Material Art and other contemporary art scenes in the 1980s and 1990s defined a specific topic in the investigation.

On the organizational front, the Smart Museum took the lead and formed an ambitious, multi-institutional collaboration: the exhibition was to be co-organized by five institutions, the Los Angeles County Museum of Art, the Seattle Art Museum, the Peabody Essex Museum, Wrightwood 659, and the Smart Museum. The Smart Museum also took on the responsibility of compiling a scholarly catalogue with a threefold purpose—namely, to provide detailed documentations of the works and artists in the exhibition, to present a historical narrative of Material Art and define its major characteristics, and to situate this art in a global context both synchronically and diachronically.

Many people contributed to these two undertakings. I was fortunate to have Dr. Orianna Cacchione as my co-curator to oversee the entire operation. Collaboration was the key: in addition to the partnership between the five participating institutions, colleagues in European art and American art wrote learned essays for the catalogue; the entire Smart Museum staff was involved in the preparation and realization of the exhibition; several branches of the University of Chicago, such as UChicago Arts under the Provost's Office, the Department of Art History, and the Center for the Art of East Asia, also provided support. Our graduate students, on both PhD and MA levels, constituted a vital force and engaged in interviewing artists, composing catalogue entries, and assisting the project's organization.

The exhibition opened in Los Angeles in 2019 and in Chicago in 2020, accompanied by a beautiful, substantial catalogue with the same title. The Chicago opening had an additional significance in introducing the second phase of the overall project, to expand the scope of the project beyond contemporary art. A symposium organized in conjunction with the exhibition opening defined this new initiative as studying the significance of *materials* over the entire course of Chinese art. Scholars in both premodern Chinese art and modern/contemporary art presented papers; their wide-ranging topics helped define a new field of art historical inquiry.

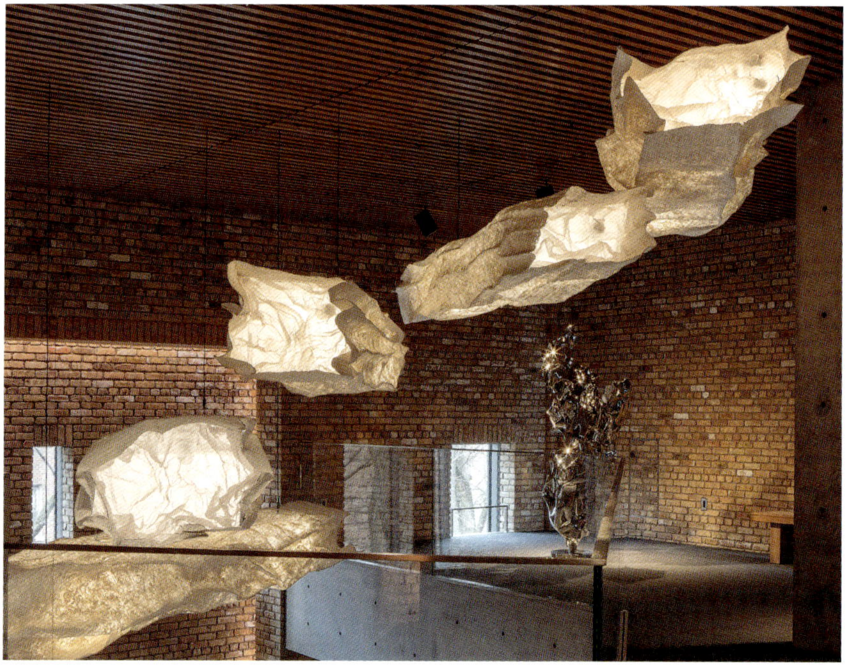

Figure 1 Installation view, *The Allure of Matter: Material Art from China*, Wrightwood 659, 2020. Courtesy of Wrightwood 659.

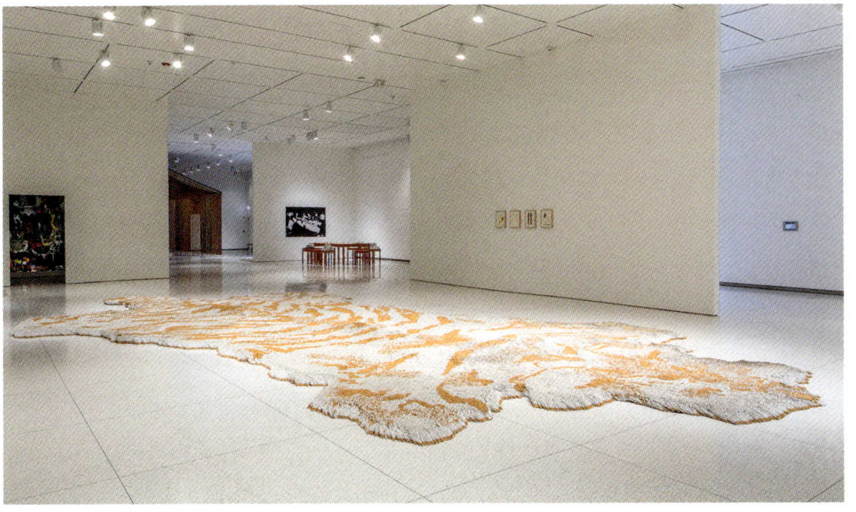

Figure 2 Installation view, *The Allure of Matter: Material Art from China*, Smart Museum of Art, The University of Chicago, 2020. Courtesy of the Smart Museum of Art.

As the two editors of this volume state in their introduction, until very recently, the concept of "materiality" has mainly been theorized through European and American art and art history, naturally prioritizing cultural and artistic experiences in the West. This volume strives to create a better balance in art historical scholarship. Presenting a group of well-researched cases in Chinese art, it reveals important ways in which materials act, operate, and mediate in a major non-Western art tradition. By covering the broad historical periods from the early first millennium CE to the present, it also seeks to find the crossovers between premodern, modern, and contemporary practices. I very much appreciate the editors' diligent work in compiling the volume, and hope that its publication will facilitate the studies of both Chinese art and global art.

The Allure of Matter

Materiality across Chinese Art

Orianna Cacchione
and Wei-Cheng Lin

In the catalogue for the exhibition *The Allure of Matter: Material Art from China*, curator and art historian Wu Hung describes a new art form, based not on representational, iconographic, stylistic, or even geographic conventions but instead on the materials used in its making. For Wu, "Material Art" (*caizhi yishu*) is a "type of art [that] entails an artist's consistent use of unconventional materials to produce works in which *material*, rather than image or style, is paramount in manifesting the artist's aesthetic judgment or social critique."[1] Material art emerged in China in the 1980s, as artists began to incorporate unconventional materials into their artworks, breaking from past artistic styles, most importantly, socialist realism. Huang Rui (b. 1953) made small collages that included paper and fabric. Huang Yong Ping (1954–2019) amended canvases with everyday and found objects, making what he would call "material object collage reliefs" (*shiwu pintie fudiao*) and "readymade object collages" (*xianchangpin*

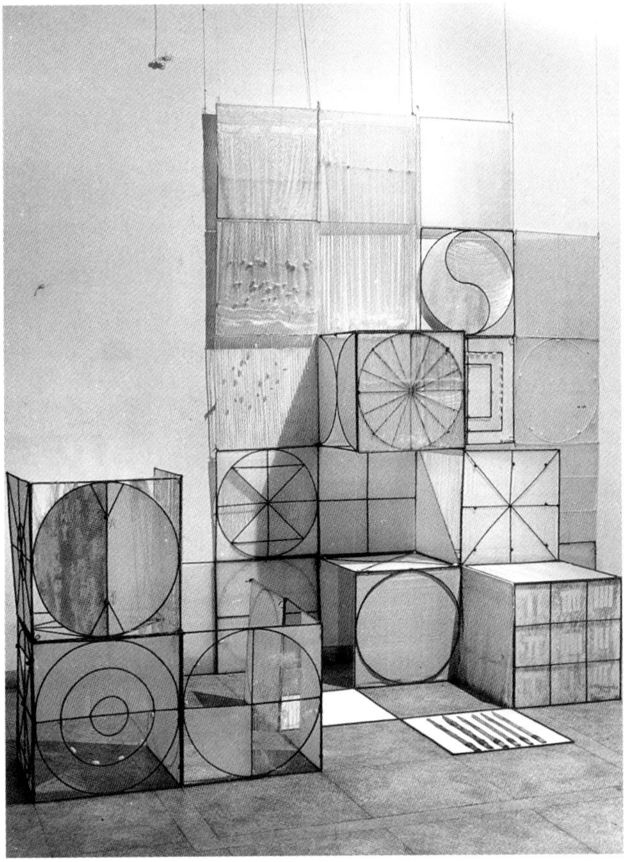

Figure 1 Liang Shaoji, *Yi Series No. 1–Magic Cube*, 1988. Silk fabric, dried silkworm cocoons, rice paper, and metal, dimensions variable. Installation view, *China/Avant-Garde*, National Art Museum of China, Beijing, 1989.
Courtesy of Liang Shaoji.

pintie). Gu Dexin (b. 1962) experimented with plastic, melting, molding, and forming scrap pieces into abstract sculptures. Shen Yuan (b. 1959) filled a plastic "bed" with water and fish. Liang Shaoji (b. 1945) first threaded together raw silk into an installation of cubes (fig. 1), but quickly abandoned fabric to instead train silkworms to spin raw silk directly upon various supports. Around the same time, Shi Hui (b. 1955) began working in tapestry. Perhaps best known, Cai Guo-Qiang (b. 1957) used fireworks and gunpowder to innovate a new form of drawing. In the 1990s and continuing today, these material explorations proliferated to encompass materials as diverse as water, *xuan* paper, cement, raw meat, pig brains, the human body, yak butter, human fat, honey, porcelain, incense ash, and pantyhose, to name a few. Radical in its conception, Material Art pushes readings of contemporary Chinese art beyond the now staid reliance on political ideology, history, or cultural exchange too often found in American and European scholarship into an interpretive format that prioritizes the work of art itself and reconnects to the "material turn" globally. This volume expands the scope of Material Art to broader practices of China's material culture by including analyses of premodern artifacts alongside contemporary works. The objective is not to forge or propose a continuous sense of history, but rather to better observe the extent to which contemporary Material Art in China is connected to, or informed by, its premodern antecedents.

Throughout history, materials have factored considerably in the development and significance of Chinese art. Examples such as jade scepters (fig. 2), bronze vessels, stone statues, glassware, lacquerware, timber furniture, gold-sprinkled paper, inkstone, etc., all find their ways into modern Chinese art collections. Yet these artifacts are also historical material objects, revealing cultural practices over time of the Chinese in their dealing with various materials and ways in which objects made of those materials mediated their self-expressions, social and societal relations, and understandings of the world around them. The general "material turn" in several academic fields during the 1980s also shifted art historians' attention in their inquiries from a focus on aesthetic and principally visual and iconographic qualities of art to its material reality and multivalent significance.[2] Many argue that we can no longer dismiss material aspects of art as secondary—for they also played an indispensable and participatory role in the production of artistic values and ideologies. Instead, the ways in which materials *affect* artistic production must be taken into account beyond considerations of which artists used what, in order to see the potential of matter.[3] New trends of material cultural research in Chinese art history, including works

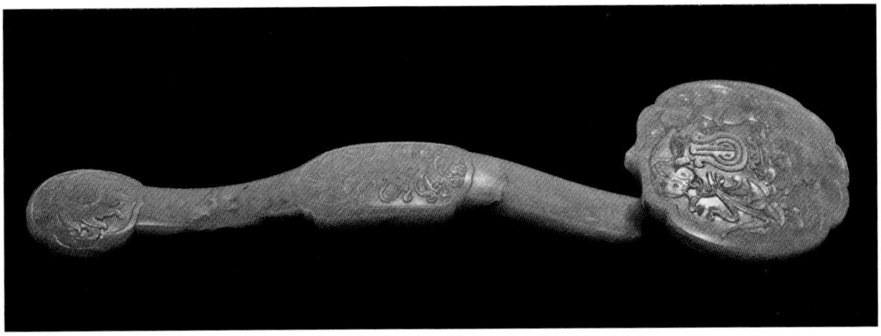

Figure 2 Ruyi scepter, eighteenth or nineteenth century. White jade, 40 × 13 × 5.4 cm. Collection of the Smart Museum of Art, The University of Chicago, The Brooks McCormick, Jr. Bequest, 2015.1422.

by Craig Clunas, Wu Hung, and Jonathan Hay, among others, are exciting and welcoming, but scholars have thus far engaged mostly finished artworks rather than the materials of which they are made.[4] Certainly, one cannot expect to find "Material Art" from premodern China exactly as defined by Wu Hung. However, a focus on the materiality of art suggests that materials themselves contribute to the creation and meaning of an artwork as much as the artist or maker. Methodologically, the "material turn" demands that art historians take into account the role, agency, potentiality, and constraints materials have on artists and artworks, not just impacting the final artwork but deeply informing the process as well. To come to terms with the importance of materials proposed here, this volume nonetheless calls to refocus our objects of inquiry on the materials that artists, artisans, and craftspeople use, the histories they have, and the vibrancy or agency they possess from a historical perspective.

Today, in the research of art history, especially that in modern and contemporary art, the "material turn" is not just applied in some specific regional studies but has become increasingly transnational with global appeal. The theoretical approaches and methodologies developed in the studies of materiality are diversified, fast expanded, and necessarily interdisciplinary. Beyond asking what a material is, this volume seeks to ask what does a material do, what does it mean, and how does it provide a novel interpretative framework that can connect different historical periods and places from around the world. For our purposes, this introduction is intended to provide an overview of some essential theoretical positions of materiality to foreground the ten chapters included in this volume, each discussing specific materials utilized in artistic productions from either premodern or contemporary China.

THEORIZING MATERIAL

Materials are not always in the purview of art historical inquiries.[5] Conventionally, art historians are more concerned with issues arising from visual representation, persistently privileging the idea revealed in images over that materialized as a thing. When materials are looked at, they are treated as physical carriers, or media, of some profound ideas or immaterial beliefs. Divides between high and low art, fine and decorative art further encourage a prioritization of the former for art historical research while delegating the latter to material cultural studies. Recently, scholars across disciplines have slowly come to see art as possessing not just visual qualities, but also physical and sensual ones.[6] As such, art cannot be reduced to its materials; neither can materials be sublated to the inert, reticent, or inanimate substance of art. Most recently, scholars and conservators have taken on materials of all kinds—as tenuous as bubbles and clouds and as amorphous as dirt and water—as topics of analysis.[7] They are concerned less with the style of art than with its substances, inquiring into issues such as the properties and behavior of materials, their acquisitions and new technologies needed to treat them, and contexts in which materials are valorized with geopolitical, historical, and ecological meanings.

More relevant to our discussion is a shift in the very conception of the role of materials that has been underway from the phenomenological encounter to the ways in which histories, stories, and agency are directly embedded in materials. Anthropologist Tim Ingold argues, "to understand materials is to be able to tell their histories—of what they do and what happens to them when treated in particular ways—in the very practice of working with them."[8] These material histories, activated through their use, connect premodern art forms to contemporary practices. Materials carry with them not only the long histories of the varied ways artists and artisans have worked with them across time and culture, but also the ways in which they bear witness or document historical events. Perhaps the most obvious example in contemporary Chinese art is the way Ai Weiwei (b. 1957) destroys antique ceramics and reconfigures centuries-old wooden furniture and beams, pillars, and rafters scavenged from demolished or neglected temples into new abstract structures. Ai Weiwei's iconoclasm and alterations of these objects evoke the materials' histories and also materialize history.

The vitality of materials has been theorized by Jane Bennett as the "capacity of things—edibles, commodities, storms, metals—not only to impede or block the will and designs of humans but also to act as quasi agents or forces with trajectories, propensities, or tendencies of their own." As Bennett observes, "things do in fact *affect* other bodies";[9] they provoke responses in other objects and in people—a sense of being repelling, a smell, perhaps even a memory—in which the object itself "makes things happen, to produce effects."[10] British anthropologist Alfred Gell was one of the earliest scholars to identify this agency, describing "objects as active participants, not merely passive signifiers."[11] Implicit within this theorization is the reciprocity in subject formation, where objectification becomes "the circular process by which everything we create also creates us."[12] This vibrant or vital materiality presents a radical shift in subject/object duality and imbues our study with new ethics that must take into account the object as other. As Karen Barad has argued, matter thus "is understood as a dynamic and shifting entanglement of relations rather than as a property of things."[13]

Material relations implicate not just the medium but the subject as well, whereas "relational materiality thus recognizes the reciprocity between artefacts [sic] and people and acknowledges that the formation of any knowledge about the material world is dependent on that network."[14] The material is a connective substance; for Giuliana Bruno, material is "an intertwining matter through which impressions are conveyed to the senses, a medium is a living environment of expression, transmission, and storage."[15] Although Bruno's work is directed at the screen, she reactivates the materiality of practices that are often assumed to be virtual or immaterial.[16] Bruno argues that materiality is not just about materials, but rather "of activating material relations." As she has written, "For us, materiality involves a refashioning of our sense of space and contact with the environment, as well as a rethreading of our experience of temporality, interiority, and subjectivity. Rethinking materiality in this sense, then, means fostering new forms of connection and relatedness."[17] Materiality, thus, reconnects not just to the object, the thing, the medium, but to the environment, state, and subject as well.

The exploration of material agency and the remapping of material relations also help invigorate an interest in the process of production, built upon scholarship about craft that flourished in the 1970s.[18] There has been a renewed emphasis on artisanal knowledge as the basis of an appreciation of the meaning, function, and operation of a historical object. More than an intellectual engagement, this knowledge of craftsmanship—made up of skills, experiences, and tacit intelligence—is directly tied to the artisan's use of tools and dealing with materials, not only cognitively but also physically. More recently, sociologist Richard Sennett has proposed to view the maker's relations with her or his materials in a more engaging and humanistic light, advocating what may be termed material thinking: we think when working with our materials, which allure, seduce, and implore us into making something.[19] It is through the intuitive manipulation of materials as such that the artisan and artist invest materials with ideas, meanings, and values.

THE ALLURE OF MATTER

THEN AND NOW

The Allure of Matter: Materiality across Chinese Art picks up on these themes and stretches its view into premodern Chinese art in order to reconnect with contemporary counterparts. Thus far, materiality has largely been theorized through European, American, and, to a lesser extent, Japanese art and art history, prioritizing a so-called Western understanding of material, its use, and its possibility for phenomenological encounter or signifying capacity.[20] Even in recent texts written about Chinese art, materials and their materiality are rarely referenced, let alone explicitly emphasized, as the subject of inquiry.[21] This volume shifts these paradigms to focus instead on the ways materials act, operate, and mediate works of Chinese art from the early first millennium CE to the present day and seeks to find the crossovers between premodern, modern, and contemporary practices. This volume considers not just the ways that contemporary artists have revisited, reused, and repurposed so-called traditional materials, but also the ways that reading premodern materials impacts our understanding of the contemporary, and vice versa, in order to find continuities and divergences across time.

An interesting example of contemporary material art, though it did not catch our attention until the production of this edited volume, is worth mentioning here as it well explicates what this publication is intended to accomplish. *Ice Buddha* (*Bingfo*) is a site-specific performance created in 2006 by Ga De (b. 1971), a Tibet-based contemporary artist. In the performance, a Buddha image sculpted out of a large block of ice was pushed into the Lhasa River (fig. 3), and as the ice Buddha began to melt, it slowly sank deeper until it vanished completely without a trace—a process captured in a series of photographs.[22] *Ice Buddha* is inspired by an annual ritual performed in Tibet to commemorate the Buddha's nirvana, a euphemism for his death, by dipping a Buddha statue into the river. *Ice Buddha* recalls a few other contemporary Chinese performances created at the Lhasa River, most notably *Stamping the Water* (*Yin Shui*, 1996) (see fig. 5 on page 261) by Song Dong (b. 1966), capitalizing on spiritual implications of the sacred river. What separates *Ice Buddha* is its literality, which derives from the sculpting of a real Buddha statue with all its iconography, yet using ice, an unconventional material for making sacred images, to tease out the religiosity of Buddhist icons in a drastically different manner from tradition. Translucent and reflective, ice is unstable and transformative: while ice materializes the moment of Buddha's nirvana in his physical form, the ice Buddha also quickly melts and becomes immaterialized as part of the sacred river. The question of what materiality means in the conception of Buddhist icons—a perennial polemic in Buddhism as discussed in Wei-Cheng Lin's chapter in this volume—is revisited in a new light through this transhistorical view, which is also localized in a specific time and space.

As *Ice Buddha* demonstrates, materiality connects contemporary and premodern Chinese art in unexpected ways, provoking new questions about the continuous use of materials throughout Chinese history and also illuminating

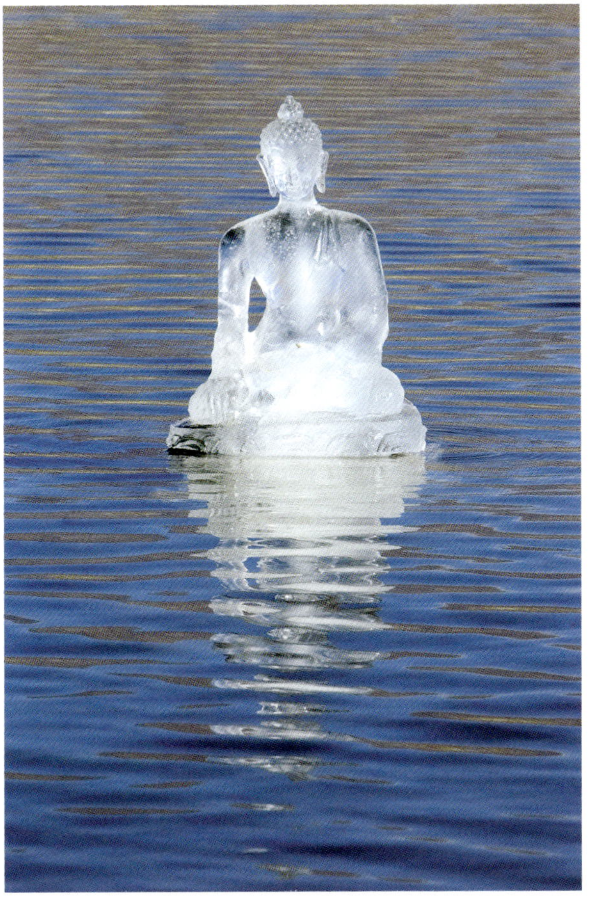

Figure 3 Ga De, *Ice Buddha (Bingfo)*, 2006. Site-specific performance with Buddha made of ice, dimensions variable over time. Courtesy of Ga De.

the ways Chinese philosophic and religious traditions continue to impact nontraditional materials. How have traditional artistic materials—from jade to *xuan* paper to porcelain—in China been transformed by contemporary artists while still embodying the past? How have the characteristics of materials—translucence, opacity, viscosity, immateriality, and plasticity—been employed, exaggerated, and manipulated by Chinese artists throughout history? How have Chinese philosophic traditions, including Buddhism, impacted the ways in which materials are conceptualized and mobilized, connecting premodern and contemporary art practices through intellectual traditions? This volume takes a transhistorical view and also incorporates the perspectives of art historians, curators, and conservators to offer new perspectives on the ways materials work in Chinese art.

MATERIALITY IN PREMODERN CHINESE ART

The first part of this volume comprises five chapters that deal with art and its materiality in premodern China. Although each author approaches her or his materials distinctively from each other, the five papers together make explicit that Chinese art historians need to engage issues of materiality far more than we have previously, and that the shifting focus on materiality is not only welcome in the field but has also helped explore questions that have hitherto not been productively interrogated.

Many scholars in Buddhism consider materiality as the second order of religion after spirituality. In his chapter, Wei-Cheng Lin challenges this general consensus by looking into the various materials of which Buddhist icons from medieval China were made. Canonically, Buddhist theology was centered upon the critique of materiality, rendering all materials equal, especially in the context of making sacred images. In reality, a wide range of materials was used to produce and replicate Buddhist icons, and the choice of one material over any others, Lin argues, was deliberate in accordance with a system of Buddhist materiality. Investigating the process of making, Lin sketches a matrix of materials that is based on the availability of materials, their material qualities and capacities, required manufacturing technologies, and involved labors and craftsmanship. In this matrix, it becomes clear that Buddhist sacred icons are as much spiritually empowered as they are materially conditioned.

Wisdom has been accredited to those who claim that physical qualities of materials are informed chiefly by tactile experience. Anne Feng's chapter, which investigates rock crystal and glass, rebuffs such a claim. Imported into China during the medieval period, objects made of crystal and glass were most often described as shimmering, fiery, icy, liquescent, otherworldly, and unfathomable, rather than with the physical qualities that characterize most other materials. The transparency of rock crystal and glass, instead, was conducive to extraordinary visual experience and visuality. In religion, this effect of transparency was further translated into the experience of divine manifestation and became an essential vehicle for visualizing sacred power. Ultimately, Feng suggests that this materiality of transparency gave rise to new possibilities in medieval China to rethink visual culture and the ontology of pictorial space.

In his chapter, Yusen Yu discusses a unique corpus of Persian manuscripts scribed on gold-sprinkled paper imported from Ming China—a topic that considers materiality in a transregional context. The gold-sprinkled paper in question was made of plain paper finely decorated with abstract patterns of gold flecks or figural motifs painted with gold powders. The finished paper is visually glossy and exuberant but physically heavier and less absorbent; thus it was primarily used for a handscroll's frontispiece and, to a lesser extent, for painting and calligraphy. Once traveling across regional boundaries, the gold-sprinkled paper was perceived variably. To be used for Persian manuscripts, the paper was cut into smaller pieces, onto which the text was scribed directly regardless of decorative patterns or pictorial motifs on the paper or their positions. Yu submits that, more than the Chinese, Persian scribes and readers were attracted to the materiality of the paper—its weight, gloss, exuberance—to appreciate its very thingness that aggrandized the text scribed on it.

Catherine Stuer's chapter focuses on lacquer as material for the crafting of objects and images in early nineteenth-century China. Because of its plasticity, lacquer could be used to make objects of various types for both daily and scholarly purposes. This metamorphosis of lacquer into different forms, Stuer contends, was provoked by the material's affectivity, which arouses the mind of the maker to the creation of objects more than any other stimuli of creativity or pragmatic reasoning. Using lacquer work by Lu Kuisheng (d. 1850) as the central piece of discussion, Stuer analyzes how lacquer was creatively applied across different type-forms; how new modes of lacquering were created to mimic different materials and the objects they shape; and how decorative variations in ground and pictorial décor were reinvented across different lacquer surfaces. In short, it was the craft practices derived from materials that played a central role in promoting a rethinking of normative conceptions of creativity and materiality in visual and material art toward the end of China's imperial era.

Also focusing on late imperial China, Yuhang Li's chapter investigates objects made of a very different material, paper—more specifically, *zhizha* (lit., tied-together paper), often translated as "pasted-paper objects" in English and comparable to papier-mâché. As early as the seventh century, *zhizha* was made to substitute for objects made of any materials and burned at funerals as a way to transform and transfer them to the other world. In this context, paper is concurrently the (spiritual) medium and material because of its ephemerality and flexibility when covering over an armature to mimic real objects. In other words, *zhizha* can take any form of real objects while negating their qualitative differences, since all *zhizha* objects possess exactly the same thingness irrespective of social, gendered, and aesthetic hierarchies of the real objects and their actual materials. Toward the late imperial era, a shift in the practice was seen from an ideology of universal equality enabled by *zhizha* objects to the spectacle of the burning of those objects in a flame. In an ironic turn, Li concludes, spectacles in effect promoted a new mode of social hierarchy not anticipated by *zhizha* objects destined invariably to be reduced to ashes.

MATERIAL ART IN CONTEMPORARY CHINESE ART

The second part of this volume shifts the focus of inquiry to the ways in which materials operate and are operable in contemporary art made in China since the 1980s. Combining the research of scholars and conservators, these chapters reinforce the important role materials have played throughout the history of Chinese art while also problematizing the stability of definitions of materiality. The authors in this section demonstrate how contemporary artists have favored the contingency, agency, impermanence, and transformation of materials in their work. Furthermore, these chapters demonstrate the important and often overlooked connections between contemporary art practices, materials, and their premodern antecedents, suggesting new modes of comparison and lines of inquiry.

In her chapter, Orianna Cacchione traces the transformation of materials in Huang Yong Ping's practice from the radical intervention of the 1983 *Five-Person Modern Art Exhibition* through his book-washing methods of the late 1980s and 1990s. As a founding member of the artist group Xiamen Dada, Huang banded together with other artists in the early 1980s to first experiment with unconventional artistic materials (such as animal bones and plaster molds) in what Cacchione explains was a rejection of representational art. In 1986, Huang and other members of Xiamen Dada shifted to employing and even burning nontraditional materials and found objects as they more radically challenged standard practices of viewing and institutional conventions. As Cacchione argues, following these early experiments, nontraditional materials took on a new ontology in Huang's practice when he developed his "wet method" of washing texts in washing machines so as to empty materials of any meaning.

In her chapter, Rachel Rivenc discusses the artist Cai Guo-Qiang's use of gunpowder—his signature artistic material—across the arc of his career. Drawing upon the findings of a four-year research project at the Getty Conservation Institute (GCI) and extensive interviews with the artist, Rivenc combines reports on the elaborate techniques and chemical properties of Cai's artworks with the artist's interpretations of the power of explosive material. Beyond merely incorporating gunpowder in his drawings, Rivenc demonstrates how Cai activates the agency of the material itself to go beyond the control of his hand. For Rivenc, Cai's recent return to painting has allowed the artist to interrogate painting's basic tenets, and push the boundaries of material experimentation. As she concludes with the conservation issues at stake for Cai's gunpowder works, she poignantly connects his paintings' potential to change over time with the artist's interest in entropy, chaos, and instantaneousness.

Conservator Sara A. Moy similarly addresses issues at stake in conserving artworks made with unconventional materials through her own research on artworks made by artist Gu Dexin. Known for his adamant critiques of art sales, collection, and display, Gu famously relinquished control over his works of decaying materials—burnt plastic and raw meat—from the moment an exhibition opened. Having been previously tasked with conserving Gu's works, Moy addresses the larger challenges of how to care for and oversee Gu's works that are actively decomposing and deteriorating. Analyzing not just the material constraints of the works but also the principles and definitions of artmaking that Gu developed, Moy argues that stakeholders must take into account these principles when making decisions about how to extend the life of an artwork—or even relinquish it, ultimately allowing for its destruction.

Focusing on the practice of Song Dong, Nancy P. Lin locates shared themes, particularly ephemerality and impermanence, that emerge across Song's works with the material of water and the artistic media of photography and video. As Lin argues, Song not only bridged video art and conceptual photography with his fascination with water as a material, but also combined these three elements so as to underscore what he calls their shared "immaterial" (*feiwuzhi*) qualities. From filming water's evaporation to making works of conceptual photography, Song pursued the gamut of "immateriality" that emerged as themes of transience and ephemerality in the intermedial combinations of water, photography, and film. Lin also unpacks the site and cultural specificity with which Song approached making a series of works in Lhasa in Tibet and the themes of intimacy and touch he explored across works from the late 1990s to 2011. Ultimately, Lin finds Song's pursuit of the immaterial across water, video, and photography to be in fact deeply concerned with visuality's inextricable connection with materiality.

Alex Burchmore considers porcelain in works by Ai Weiwei, Liu Jianhua (b. 1962), and Cai Guo-Qiang as a distinctively contemporary material while connecting to the history embodied within the material itself. He charts the arcs of each artist's use of porcelain, reclaiming many of their porcelain works beyond the physical or phenomenological characteristics of the material. Burchmore takes a "fugitive" approach that activates porcelain's ability to permutate and transform its own representation as it escapes straightforward categorization. Looking beyond the "Chinese-ness" of porcelain on the art world's global stage, Burchmore repeatedly locates ways in which these artists manipulate or exploit the materiality of porcelain and its material histories in their works. In each material aspect of porcelain that he finds the artists to activate, Burchmore also underscores the artworks' subtle interrogations of porcelain's exoticization, authentication, and commodification.

NOTES

1 Wu Hung, "Material Art from China: An Introduction," in *The Allure of Matter: Material Art from China* (Chicago: David and Alfred Smart Museum of Art, 2019), 15.
2 See, for example, Jules David Prown, "Mind in Matter: An Introduction to Material Cultural Theory and Method," *Winterthur Portfolio* 17, no. 1 (Spring 1982): 1–9.
3 Sarah Posman, et al., "Matter on the Move," in *The Aesthetics of Matter: Modernism, the Avant-Garde and Material Exchange* (Berlin: De Gruyter, 2013), 7.
4 Craig Clunas, *Superfluous Things: Material Culture and Social Status in Early Modern China* (Honolulu: University of Hawai'i Press, 1991); Wu Hung, *The Double Screen: Medium and Representation in Chinese Painting* (Chicago: University of Chicago Press, 1996); Jonathan Hay, *Sensuous Surfaces: The Decorative Object in Early Modern China* (Honolulu: University of Hawai'i Press, 2010).
5 For a good discussion in this regard, see Michael Yonan, "Toward a Fusion of Art History and Material Culture Studies," *West 86th: A Journal of Decorative Arts, Design History, and Material Culture* 18, no. 2 (Fall-Winter 2011): 232–48.
6 See for example, Sally M. Promey, ed., *Sensational Religion: Sensory Cultures in Material Practice* (New Haven: Yale University Press, 2014).
7 For instance, the Getty dedicated its 2019–2020 scholarly program to the theme art and ecology, focusing not on ecologic objects but on various materials that constitute ecology.
8 Tim Ingold, "Toward an Ecology of Materials," *Annual Review of Anthropology* 41 (2012): 434.
9 Jane Bennett, *Vibrant Matter: A Political Ecology of Things* (Durham: Duke University Press, 2010), 3. Emphasis our own.
10 Bennett, *Vibrant Matter*, 5.
11 Ruth M. Van Dyke, "Materiality in Practice," in *Practicing Materiality* (Tucson: The University of Arizona Press, 2015), 14.
12 Van Dyke, "Materiality in Practice," *Practicing Materiality*, 8.
13 Petra Lange-Berndt, "Introduction: How to Be Complicit with Materials," in *Materiality*, Documents of Contemporary Art, ed. Petra Lange-Berndt (Cambridge, MA: The MIT Press, 2015), 17.
14 Hanna B. Holling, Francesca G. Brewer, and Katharina Ammann, "Material Encounters," in *The Explicit Material* (Leiden: Brill, 2019), 5.
15 Giuliana Bruno, *Surface: Matters of Aesthetics, Materiality, and Media* (Chicago: University of Chicago Press, 2014), 5.
16 Bruno, *Surface*, 8.
17 Bruno, *Surface*, 8.
18 Pamela H. Smith, "In the Workshop of History: Making, Writing, and Meaning," *West 86th: A Journal of Decorative Arts, Design History, and Material Culture* 19, no. 1 (2012): 4–31.
19 Richard Sennett, *The Craftsman* (New Haven: Yale University Press, 2008), 1–15.
20 This is perhaps nowhere more apparent than in the *Materiality* volume, which almost exclusively focuses on the voice of American and European artists, scholars, and curators, with the exception of two lone Japanese contributions.
21 Two notable exceptions include David Clarke, "The Watery Turn in Contemporary Chinese Art," *Art Journal* 65, no. 4 (2006), and Mary Bittner Wiseman, *A Grand Materialism in the New Art from China* (Lanham, MD: Lexington Books, 2020).
22 We thank Ga De for sharing initial ideas and conceptions of this performance with us.

PART I
PREMODERN CHINESE ART

Materiality of Buddhist Icons in Early Medieval China

Wei-Cheng Lin

In 2004, an underground crypt located outside present-day Xi'an was uncovered, revealing five large stone Buddha statues.[1] All five statues are standing Buddhas dressed in traditional monk's garb, sharing stylistic characteristics that date them to the late sixth century. The dating is confirmed by the only inscription found in the crypt, engraved on the base that supports one of the standing Buddhas (fig. 1). Missing its right arm and part of its nose, the Buddha statue

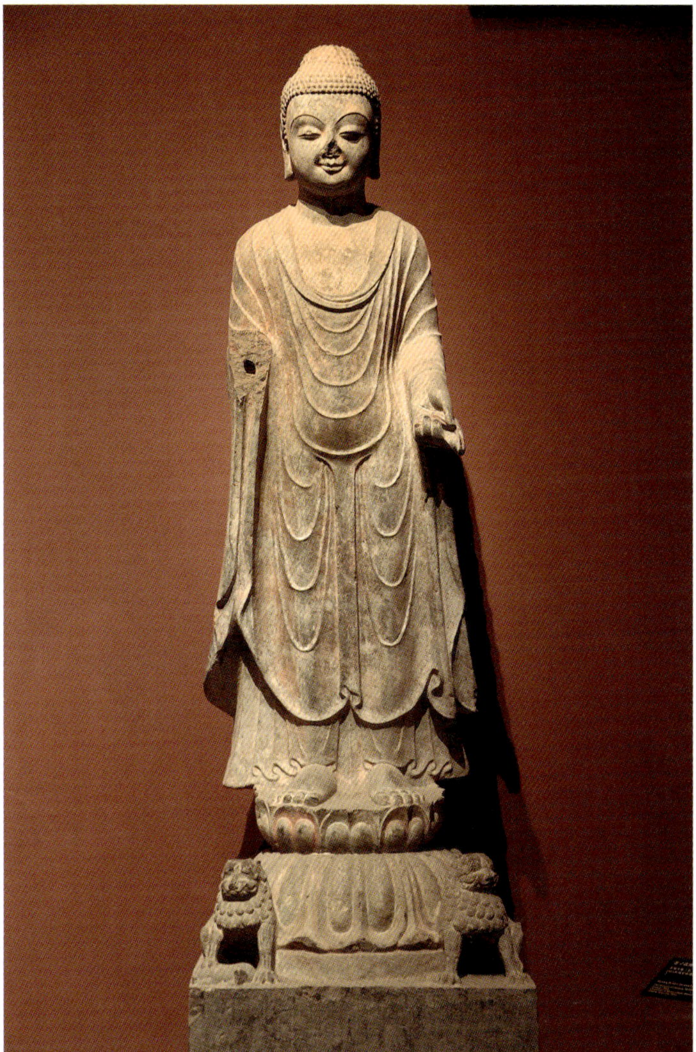

Figure 1 Standing Buddha, 580. Limestone, height of Buddha: 195 cm, base: 43 × 73.5 × 75 cm. Beiling Museum, Xi'an. Photo: Wei-Cheng Lin.

(measuring 195 centimeters high without the base) is otherwise in good condition, making it one of the largest and finest freestanding Buddhist statues from this period.[2] According to the inscription, a layperson named Zhang Ziwen commissioned the statue in 580, during the final years of the Northern Zhou dynasty (557–581), in order to earn spiritual benefits on behalf of his parents and ancestors of the past six generations. The text recounts the following about the statue and its making:

> The stone was quarried from famous mountains. Skilled artisans were hired for their inexhaustible designs . . . thereby I respectfully commissioned this *jade statue* of Śākyamuni Buddha. Its posture and presence are brilliant and luminous such that the statue appears no different from the Buddha's true presence.[3]

The inscription yields the only information we know of about the commission and production of this specific statue. However, one would be surprised to learn that while the inscription explicitly describes the standing Buddha as a jade statue (*yuxiang*), the modern excavation report clearly identifies the material as limestone. More precisely, it is a specific kind of limestone known as *qingshi* (lit., blue/green stone) in Chinese that can still be found in Fuping, which is to the north of Xi'an. The limestone there has a hard but finer, granular texture; when polished, its gray surface appears glossy, a quality described in the region as *moyu*, literally "ink jade."[4] Is it possible then that the devout patron chose the particular material for its make-believe appearance as jade, a more precious material than limestone, perhaps in order to maximize the devotionalism? We may never be able to find out whether that was the case, nor if the "trick" actually worked or not. For our purpose, what is certain is that a system of Buddhist materiality must have existed in medieval China to justify and make sense to the Buddhists of the time the deliberate choice and expression of the material for the sacred image. If so, what was this system like?

Answering this question is not easy. Arriving in China around the late first century, Buddhism—then also known as *xiangjiao*, or "religion of images"—came with practices of sacred images that decisively enriched the Chinese tradition of iconic worship that had developed until then. By the fifth century, the term *xiangjiao* was further used to remark on the fact that ritual engagement with icons had become an essential characteristic of the religion.[5] Accordingly, the adoption and use of Buddhist icons for ritual purposes did not appear problematic to the Chinese during the first centuries after the introduction of Buddhism. The exact material of which an icon was made, however, seems to have eluded the attention of both canonical and historical records. Buddhist canons contain few explanations with regard to what icons are or how they work, let alone the materials and techniques used to create them. Accounts about the debate between Buddhist apologists and opponents over the ontology of icons (i.e., their relationships with the deities they represent) that first appeared in the late fourth century actually provide us with elaborations on the nature and religious functions of Buddhist sacred images.[6] Yet even in the most ferocious anti-Buddhist rhetoric against sumptuous spending on Buddhist image making, no arguments addressing the (mis)use of specific materials were advanced. In an anecdotal case, a Tang Chan master named Danxia Tianran (739–824) was recorded to have burned a wooden Buddha statue as firewood, an act considered sacrilege that shocked many believers. The Chan master explained that his action was meant to "cremate" the Buddha statue for its relics. When people questioned how one could expect to obtain relics from a statue made of wood, the master replied by asking, "If that's what you believe, why should people be upset with me?"[7] All in all, though the ontology of icons remained polemic, there seems to be a general inclination in early Buddhist discourse to divert people's attention from the material aspects of sacred images.

Indeed, in theory, the question about the material of which an icon was made seems to be a moot point, insofar as the icon is efficacious. In practice, however, Buddhist icons were made of a variety of materials—bronze, stone, jade, wood, clay, lacquer, and more—each of which would have entailed a specific technique and process of production that necessarily determine how an icon is to be made and its sacred practice conceptualized. The availability of materials would be a factor, but the choice of one material over any others must have also been a deliberate decision, as illustrated by the Buddha statue discussed at the outset. In this chapter, I argue that Buddhist sacred icons are as much spiritually empowered as they are materially conditioned. To put it differently, the sacred practices in medieval China that enlivened and animated the sacred icon were also necessarily conceived, configured, and constricted by the materiality of the icon. To see this, instead of focusing on one single material, this chapter proposes some contextual frameworks in support of the argument for the materiality of Buddhist icons as it took shape during China's medieval period.

WHAT IS A BUDDHIST ICON—MATERIALLY?

Icons belong to the most important category of sacred objects in Buddhism, and they were indispensable for transmitting the religion across East Asia. What an icon is, however, remained under debate throughout most of the religion's history. The basic rationale for making Buddha images is to bring to mind the presence of the Buddha, who could no longer be met in person.[8] This can already be observed in one of the earliest extant sutras in China, the *Scripture of Cultivating Wisdom* (*Daoxing bore jing*), translated in 179. In the conversation between two bodhisattvas, Dhamōdgata first states that it was after the Buddha entered nirvana that believers started making his images. He further explains how the images are used:

> When they see these images, there is not one of them who does not bow down and make offerings. These images are upright and handsome, perfectly resembling the Buddha. When men see them, they all rejoice and revere them with flowers and incense.[9]

Dhamōdgata then turns to his disciple Sadāprarudita and asks: "Would you say that the Buddha's spirit is in the image?" The answer from the disciple was an emphatic no, as he replies: "It is not there. The image of the Buddha is made only because one desires to have men acquire merits."[10]

This understanding of Buddhist icons is resonant with what was put forth in the earliest known sutra that specifically addresses issues about the making of Buddha images. Translated before the end of the Eastern Han dynasty (25–220), the brief text, the *Scripture on the Production of the Images* (*Zuo fo xingxiang jing*), narrates the conversation between the young protagonist, King Udayana, and the Buddha. As the story goes, King Udayana was so enthralled by the dignity of the Buddha's appearance that he requested that the Buddha allow him to make an image of his likeness after the Sage's passing into nirvana, so that he could continue to behold his visual presence. The Buddha was delighted by the request, and in the remaining part of the sutra he went on to enumerate the abundance of spiritual benefits promised to anyone who produces and transmits such an image.[11] Accordingly, the making of sacred images was encouraged by the Buddha to assist believers when engaging their practices amid the sacred presence and to receive merits, insofar as the image resembles the Buddha perfectly, but was not to be confused with the Sage himself.

This canonical stance on the ontological status of Buddha images evolved over the next few centuries in response to the rising criticism toward the use of Buddhist icons.[12] One piece of evidence for this changing stance can be found in the legend of the so-called first Buddha statue, which was allegedly commissioned by none other than the aforementioned King Udayana. Several versions of this legend existed in China from the third through seventh centuries.[13] In the fuller version of the story, the narrative is embellished with additional details that betray the evolving understanding of the Buddha image during this early period. According to the later versions, the Buddha once went away, spending a summer in heaven to preach to his deceased mother, Lady Māyā. The absence of the Buddha devastated King Udayana, causing him to wish to have a statue of the Buddha made to help him recall the likeness of the Sage. He hence implored Maudgalyāyana, a disciple of the Buddha, to transport a piece of sandalwood to heaven along with thirty-two skilled artisans, each carving one of the Buddha's thirty-two perfect bodily features. After the wooden statue was completed, King Udayana was overjoyed, venerating the statue no differently than he did the Buddha. When the Buddha finally returned from heaven, the statue miraculously rose up to greet and pay homage to him. The Buddha in turn stated: "To educate and enlighten sentient beings in the time when I am no longer here, I indeed rely on you."[14]

In these later accounts, the Buddha image is *not* the Buddha; however, since the image was made by faithfully portraying the likeness of the Buddha, it also partakes in its very sacredness. The icon made as such could not only perform miracles, but it could also serve as the object of veneration as if it were the Buddha. More specifically, insofar as the icon is accurately made with the Buddha's thirty-two perfect bodily features, it could be just as real as the Buddha's "true presence," an English translation of the Chinese term *zhenrong* (or *zhenxing*, meaning "true form"). In medieval China, *zhenrong* was used to refer to any sacred, miraculous icon, and more specifically, the allegedly first Buddha statue, that could exert or evoke the Buddha's true presence.[15] This idea of "true presence" is most often associated with the so-called thirty-two perfect bodily features (*xiang*, or *lakṣaṣa* in Sanskrit), referring to physical characteristics—such as cranial protuberance (*uṣṇīṣa*) and white curls between the eyebrows (*ūrṇā*)—present on the body of virtuous men, especially that of the Śākyamuni Buddha, as the karmic result of countless eons of effort on the path to either worldly or spiritual perfection.[16] In Buddhist literature, a Buddha image that demonstrates all thirty-two perfect bodily features is further described as *xianghao juzu*, literally "[with] complete, perfect bodily features," considered the prerequisite for a Buddha image to be viewed as the true presence of the Buddha.

However, despite the fact that the precious material, sandalwood, is named in the King Udayana legend, none of the accounts addresses the issue of material. In fact, in the later rendition of the *Scripture on the Production of the Images*, which also includes the account of King Udayana's commission of the first Buddha statue, the text unequivocally downplays the importance of the material of which Buddha images are made. The relevant passages read:

> One will gain merits by doing the following things: embellish icons with varied decorations; make icons by melting gold, silver, copper, metal, lead, or tin; sculpt icons from sandalwood; embroider icons with pearls and fine threads; and build icons with mud, plaster, or wood. One should make Buddhist icons based on one's abilities as long as they show the Buddha's esteemed appearance, even if the icon is as tiny as a finger.[17]

Accordingly, not only material, but dimension and size are also outside major concerns of making Buddha images. On the contrary, the sutra warns about severe consequences if a Buddha image were made without bearing all thirty-two perfect bodily features.

In this light, there seems to be a predilection in these texts for undermining the role of materiality in the production of the Buddha image, and so the spiritual rewards one garners can be articulated. Yet, as Buddhist apologists and believers placed stronger emphasis over time on the ritual and spiritual functions of the image to reveal the truth, the canonical dismissal of material's role became less attainable, particularly outside strict Buddhist doctrinarism. For example, a dedicatory inscription dated to 562 that accompanies a Buddhist image thus opens: "When the true presence [*zhenrong*] of the Buddha hid its splendor [after his nirvana], the true doctrine ceased its reverberation. Vast emptiness is distant and expansive—without images there is no way to manifest its truth."[18] Making Buddhist images is about more than collecting spiritual benefits, since they are also indispensable to both representing the divine's "true presence" and reviving the true doctrine. The material of which a Buddha image was made, it appears, was chosen deliberately to ensure that the true presence can be physically and visually represented and transmitted in its very materiality. Let's recall the dedicatory inscription of the Northern Zhou statue in Figure 1: "Its posture and presence are brilliant and luminous. The statue appears no different from the Buddha's true likeness." Its material may not be what the inscription claims, but jade is evoked to suggest an animate quality conveyed through the local limestone. Another inscription dedicated to a now-lost stone Buddha statue puts it even more explicitly: "This stone statue of Śākyamuni was reverently made. It is adorned and carved gracefully and as elegant as a gilt bronze statue. The beauty of its perfect bodily features is exactly the same as that of the Buddha's true presence."[19] In a sense, material is applied positively as a critical means, whereby the true presence of the Buddha could be perceived.

Once the material to be used was decided upon, there was still one unsolved issue. Although it was a required mandate that a Buddha image must bear all of the Buddha's perfect bodily features, no texts from our period of interest provide exact instructions for transcribing them in painting or sculpture.[20] The issue obviously did not deter artisans from making Buddha images. On the other hand, one would be hard pressed to find *any* extant Buddha statue that was truly made with all thirty-two perfect bodily features. It seems, therefore, the exactitude of an icon in portraying the Buddha in terms of bodily features (i.e., *xianghao juzu*) should not be taken literally, at least not to artisans from medieval China. Instead, the use of "models" seems to have been the key.

In one version of the Udayana legend that was widely quoted in Buddhist texts, the sandalwood Buddha was recorded to have eventually been brought to China from India at the request of Emperor Ming (r. 28–75) of the Eastern Han. After having acquired it, the emperor treasured the statue so much that he further ordered painters to produce exact copies modeled after it.[21] This additional detail was doubtlessly fabricated to forge a lineage of sacred icons in China that could be traced back to the first Buddha statue and to the birthplace of the religion. The method of copying by using an authentic model was nonetheless relevant to the actual production of Buddha images. In particular, as the Udayana legend was available in several versions and widespread in the fourth and fifth centuries, this method must have been considered a sanctioned mechanism whereby copies of Buddha icons could be reproduced accurately in order to transmit the authenticity of their prototypes.

Dai Kui (c. 331–396), one of a handful of artisans from this early period whose names are known to us, was famous as the most talented master of his time for making Buddhist statues.[22] In an early seventh-century account, Dai was recorded as an exceptional sculptor in both bronze casting and stone carving; as the text states: "Dai's Buddha images matched the measurements of their models without even one slightest error, recreating the intensity of the sheen

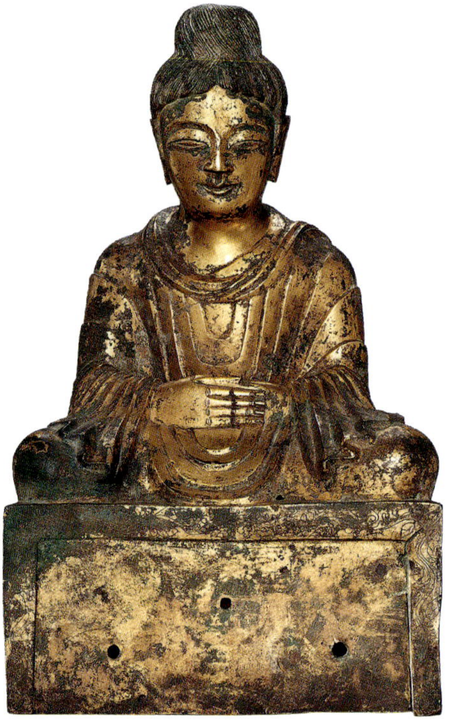

Figure 2 Buddha, 338. Bronze with gilding, 40 × 24.1 × 13.3 cm. Hebei province, China. Collection of the Asian Art Museum of San Francisco, The Avery Brundage Collection, B60B1034. © Asian Art Museum of San Francisco.

and color accurately."[23] None of Dai's work survives for us to fully comprehend his art and method of production; but it is clear that even with the best-known early master in history, the merits of his Buddhist statues were gauged less by his genuine creativity than by his masterful skills to replicate models exactly.[24] In this light, I shall argue, Chinese artisans were put in a position to consciously devise new techniques of replication in order to work with different materials. In this case, not only were Buddhist icons produced in a system of materiality, but their productions, as well as meanings arising from the process of production, were also necessarily conditioned and constricted by it.[25]

MATERIALITY OF BUDDHIST ICONS IN PRACTICE

Claims that the Udayana Buddha statue eventually made its way to China during the late fifth and sixth centuries are noteworthy. Except for the textual accounts, no material evidence corroborates the actual transmission of the first Buddha statue to China.[26] These historically unverifiable claims nonetheless suggest that Buddhist communities in medieval China took a great interest in the "lineage" of sacred icons. To a great extent, these claims also reveal the anxieties Buddhist communities had about the image-making affairs and the

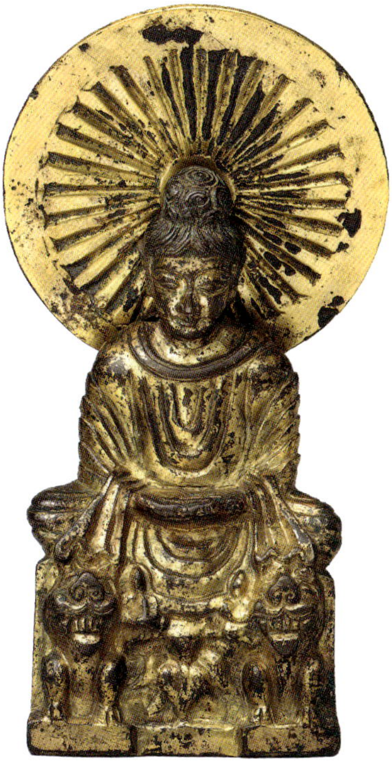

Figure 3 Seated Buddha, probably Shakyamuni (Shijiamouni), late fourth to early fifth century. Gilt bronze, piece-mold cast, 16.5 × 7 × 3.5 cm. Collection of the Metropolitan Museum of Art, Purchase, Arthur M. Sackler Gift, 1974, 1974.268.8a-c.

authenticity of the copies produced in China. However, while all purportedly traceable lineages of Buddhist images were largely forged through legends, most existing Buddhist images do not have a reliable provenance that can help one ascertain the prototype to which each of them could be traced in history. Dedicatory texts of Buddhist statues are often either completely reticent or ambiguous about their formal origins. Instead, authors of these texts deemed the process of production more important, and they dedicated most of their writing to recount the great effort and collaboration organized to replicate Buddhist images perfectly and to thereby seamlessly transmit the divine presence.[27] It is then not coincidental that the earliest extant Buddhist statues from the fourth and fifth centuries in China are gilt-bronze statues (*jintong xiang*) of relatively small sizes, made by using a mold (*mo* or *fan*).[28]

China's earliest datable Buddha image is a gilt-bronze statue (fig. 2), dated to 338 by inscription. At 39.4 cm in height, it depicts the Buddha seated in yogic posture with overlapping hands that rest on his lap. He wears a long, close-fitting monastic shawl covering both his shoulders. A tang projecting from the back of the head suggests that a now-missing halo was originally attached to it. Another gilt-bronze Buddha (fig. 3), dated to the late fourth and early fifth century and now in the collection of the Metropolitan Museum of Art, preserves the gilt halo and a copper pin that attaches it to the statue.[29] These two statues look almost identical in their treatment of the Buddha's posture and garment, except for the hands and the pedestal, or throne. The physical characteristics present in the two statues would relate them to the style in the ancient region of Gandhara, present-day Pakistan and Afghanistan.[30] Indeed, a third gilt-bronze Buddha of the identical style (not illustrated here), dated also to this general period and reportedly uncovered in 1979 near present-day Xi'an, was found with an inscription in the Yuezhi *kharoshthi* language, which originated in the region to the north of the Indian subcontinent.[31] The epigraphical evidence thus points the origin of the style to that general region. In fact, at least more than sixty other gilt-bronze Buddha statues of this style—all dated to the fourth and fifth centuries—have been found in China (mostly in north China, with some in the south), varying only in size, minor details, and attachments, or lack thereof. In short, at least some prototypes of this particular Buddhist image type must have transmitted through the Silk Road and were faithfully preserved in these Chinese "copies."

Their physical differences, regardless how slight, also suggest that these statues could not have been cast from the same mold. Still, the method of casting reveals that the production of each of the statues was executed with the goal to replicate its model as accurately as possible. In the Gandharan region, Buddhist artifacts made of bronze, including figural sculptures, were cast using the lost-wax method.[32] The flexibility of wax allows artisans to make objects of desired shapes and score elaborate details to enhance naturalism. Since the wax needs to be melted out—leaving the space for molten metal to be poured in—and the mold has to be broken to separate the bronze from the mold, the method produces only one single, unique bronze in each cast.[33] In China, this more straightforward method was not used; rather, the group of gilt-bronze statues under discussion were cast using piece-molds, a method and technology that had been developed since the pre-Shang Bronze Age (c. 2100–1600 BCE) mainly for weapons and vessels.[34] Unlike the lost-wax casting method, in which the artisan could work the wax directly into shape, piece-mold casting starts with creating molds from an existing or pre-made model.[35] As seen in Figure 4, the front and back piece-molds can be made directly from the model to produce a clay replica, which is then shaved down to make the core and the bottom. These three pieces are then reassembled with metal spacers (indicated by the red rectangles) inserted to keep the core and the mold assembly apart. After each cast, the piece-molds are broken to reveal the statue, but the mold can simply be remade from the same model. In other words, the piece-mold casting technology provides a method that facilitates the direct replication of the model to manufacture multiple, precise copies—without artisans' starting from scratch in each cast.

The major drawback to this method, however, is the constricted stylistic expression of the cast object. To make it easier to remove the mold from its model, for instance, statues made using piece-molds often appear blocky, lacking undercuts to portray elaborate drapery or minute details such as hand gestures (*mudrā*). Some scholars attribute the stylistic adjustment from the more naturalistic and dynamic outlook of the Gandharan images to the rather stiff and rigid form observed in these early gilt-bronze statues to Chinese taste.[36] It is, however, more probable that this Chinese style was not created by choice but as a result of the material and casting method. In the biography of the eminent monk Dao'an (312–385), a foreign-looking gilt-bronze Buddha statue, likely similar to the gilt-bronze Buddhas discussed here, was criticized as "antiquated and weird" (*guyi*), and in a style apparently at odds with people's taste then.[37] In other words, the use of molds to faithfully replicate the model as closely as possible was prioritized in the production of Buddhist images at the expense of artistic preference or perfection.

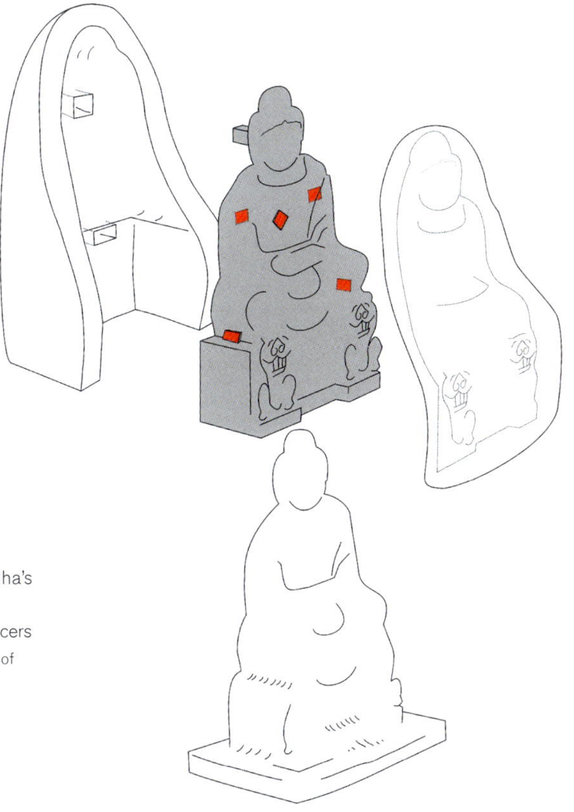

Figure 4 Expanded view of Buddha's conjectured piece-mold sections and core, with locations of metal spacers shown as red rectangles. Courtesy of Donna Strahan.

It is also unlikely that the less-refined qualities were due in part to the level of the bronze-casting technology in medieval China. Although no foundry for producing Buddhist icons has ever been located, textual records about oversize or life-size gilt-bronze statues are many. A colossal Śākyamuni Buddha of thirteen meters, for example, was recorded to have been cast in gilt bronze in Pingcheng (present-day Datong, Shanxi), the Northern Wei (386–534) capital. A more sophisticated technology must have been developed to cast gilt-bronze statues in such a scale, and it is little wonder that the project was commissioned under the imperial auspices.[38] In fact, by the sixth century, when the lost-wax method was also deployed to produce Buddhist statues, the piece-mold technology continued to dominate their production. In many cases, the mold, after being created from the model, would be further carved manually for casting finer and more intricate details that could better imitate, for instance, folds of draperies previously only seen in statues produced with the lost-wax method.[39] To that end, the production process could perceivably be more laborious, and yet the effort also demonstrates how artisans managed to be more innovative and creative with the material and its production procedure within the restriction of replication as the chief goal.

Early Buddhist statues can be divided into a few basic types by either their posture or the identity of the deity represented. While scholars take the limited taxonomy as a reflection of the relatively uniform religious practices that revolved around a few Buddhas and bodhisattvas during the first centuries of Buddhism's history in China, the use of piece-molds must have also contributed to the limitation of the existing types and their transmission. In regions that lack sources of bronze, Buddhist communities resorted to other materials and production techniques available locally to achieve the same goal. In 1955, for example, at the ancient site of the Xiude Monastery (Xiudesi) in Quyang, Hebei, more than 2,000 Buddhist statues (ranging between 20 and 50 cm in height) were uncovered, all made of local white marble, or *baishi*.[40] The majority of the statues are dated to the sixth and seventh centuries, commissioned by local monasteries and Buddhist societies. Interestingly, many of the statues share the exact same stylistic features as gilt-bronze ones, as shown in Figures 5 and 6. Both are standing Buddhas with identical postures and hand gestures—another major type of Buddha image during this early period. The gilt-bronze statue (fig. 5) found in an underground pit located in present-day Boxing, Shandong, was made using piece-molds. The Buddha and the mandorla-shaped halo were cast together. A tang projecting from the bottom was then tapered to fit snugly into the lotus base cast separately.[41] The marble statue (fig. 6), in contrast, was carved in one piece, including the lotus base—now serving as a decorative feature—as well as the plinth. It is evident that the marble statue was carved modeling after a gilt-bronze counterpart.[42] This material-crossing copying from gilt-bronze to stone is particularly conspicuous when the number of stone statues produced just became greater. The majority of them are also found with traces of gilt used to decorate the face and lines or areas carved in low relief, testifying to an intention to capture the shimmering and metallic quality of their gilt-bronze models.

Without using a mold, stone sculptors would be required to have a high level of artistry and experience to accurately reproduce models available to them manually. No historical texts yield precise information about the training of sculptors or methods utilized to produce exact stone (or wood, for that matter) copies of an existing model. Interestingly, when the replication of sacred images relies primarily on the virtuosity of talented masters, Buddhist literature finds ways to undermine the role of human agency. In a seventh-century account, it is said that a Buddha statue (presumably carved by Bodhisattva Maitreya) that portrays the moment of his enlightenment "with complete perfect bodily features" (*xianghao juzu*), was enshrined in the Mahābodhi Temple in Bodhgayā, India.[43] The "true presence" (*zhenrong*) of the statue attracted a slew of believers to copy it, but none were successful upon returning home. A Chinese official, Wang Xuance (fl. 641), led a delegation to the temple for the same purpose; as many before them, Chinese artisans also failed at the task. Finally, the artisans performed ritual circumambulation, confession, and repentance for days, and only after all that was a picture bearing the "perfect resemblance" of the holy icon successfully made and brought back to China. When the delegation returned to the Tang capital Chang'an with the "model picture," the account continues, "the religious and laymen vie with one another to copy it."[44] Today, more than twenty Buddha images whose origins purportedly can be traced back to the Indian prototype in the Mahābodhi Temple survive in China. A discussion of these extant Buddha images will take us afield, but suffice it to note that the task of artisans, in fact, was to minimize their intervention, making their work seem as unnoticeable as possible, such that the replication of the model would appear seamless and miraculous, as if achieved through the divine power.

Another material that entails exceptional skills and a laborious making process is lacquer. According to research on the few extant lacquer Buddha

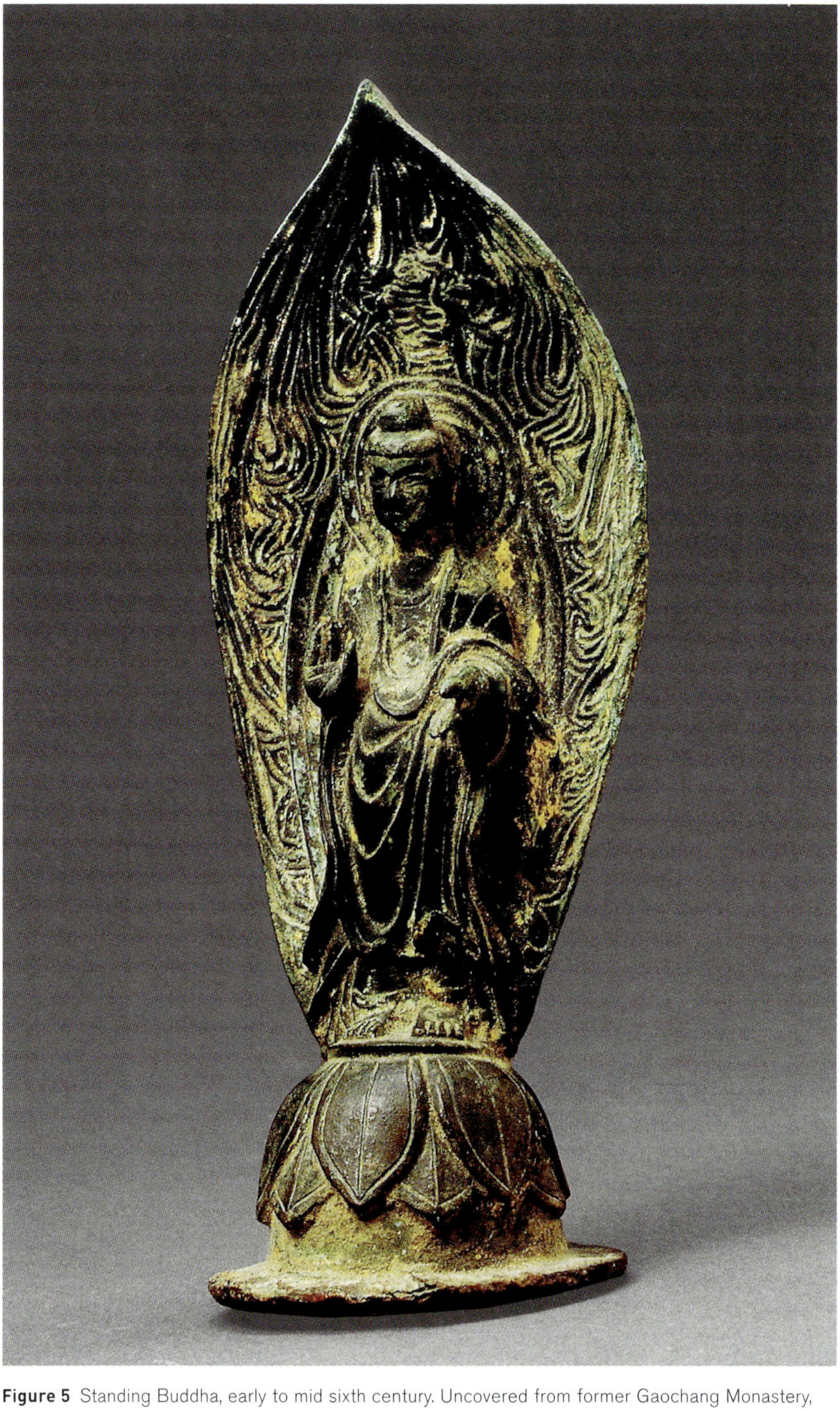

Figure 5 Standing Buddha, early to mid sixth century. Uncovered from former Gaochang Monastery, Boxing, Shandong. Gilt bronze, height: 15 cm. Courtesy of Zhang Shumin.

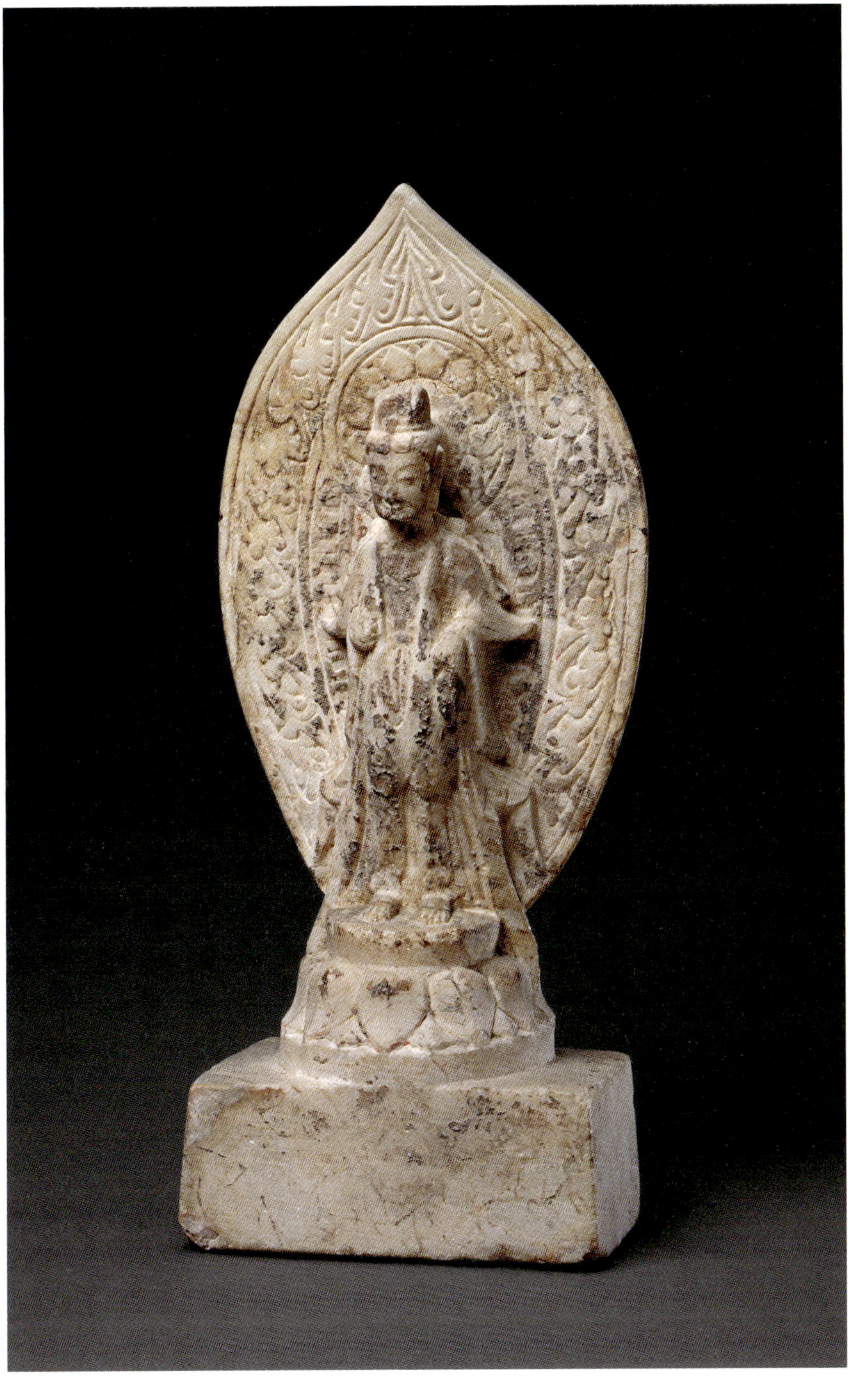

Figure 6 Standing Buddha, 528. Uncovered from the former Xiuding Monastery, Quyang, Hebei. Marble, height: 29.5 cm. Provided by the Palace Museum.

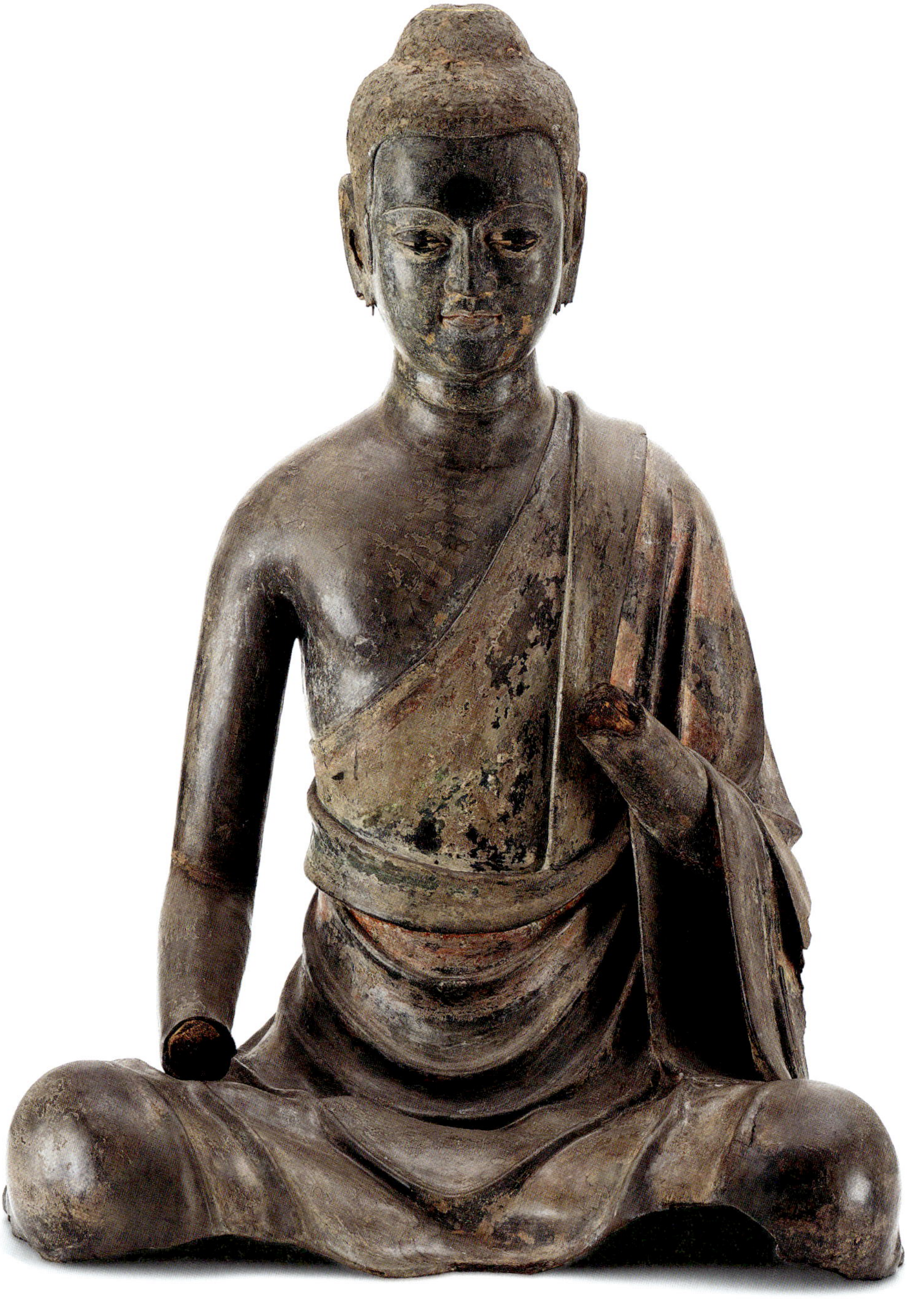

Figure 7 Historical Buddha, late sixth or early seventh century. Hemp cloth, lacquer, wood, metal wire, and glass with traces of pigment and gilding, 99.5 × 72.5 × 56.7 cm. Collection of the Freer Gallery of Art, Smithsonian Institution, Washington D.C., Purchase—Charles Lang Freer Endowment, F199.46.

statues, including the one now in the collection of the Freer Gallery of Art (fig. 7), the production starts with building a core structure, made of either wood or clay, onto which multiple layers of fabric soaked with lacquer are applied to fashion the surface into the form of the statue.[45] The core is decisive and likely made after an existing model (or model picture) since it dictates the shape, posture, proportion, and measurements of the statue even before the lacquer is applied. Once the lacquer is dry, in the case of clay core, the statue will be hollowed out by removing its core, a procedure that gives the dry-core lacquer statue the name "hollow-core statue," or *tuokong xiang* in Buddhist literature.[46] Here, the emphasis on the procedure of *tuo*, referring to the action of removing the core, suggests the intimate formal relationship between the core and its lacquer layers. The lacquer layers allow the artisan to build or sculpt more realistic details and depict more sensuously the physical appearance of the Buddha image; yet it is the core that leaves the imprints of the model's physical presence literally *inside* the statue through the production process (fig. 8).[47]

Unlike Buddhist statues made of other materials discussed thus far, records about lacquer ones are limited. In all likelihood, the comparatively small number of lacquer statues is due largely to the material cost, as well as the elaborate and meticulous process of production. Raw lacquer resin is toxic, which increases the difficulty of production, and layers of lacquer applied to the core that could only be laid one at a time after the previous layer is dry also made the production a labor-intensive task. One thus finds records of lacquer statues only from accounts of imperially sponsored monasteries or major Buddhist establishments in local regions that could afford to commission such precious icons. The trade-off is both practical and religious. Lacquer statues are insect impervious, since the material is toxic; but more importantly, the lacquer surface appears waxy and reflective, evoking the animate quality of sacred images associated with the potency of the divine they were made to represent. Furthermore, because of its light weight, the dry lacquer hollow-core statue became a popular choice for performing a ritual procession (*xingxiang*) held during Buddhist festivals to receive reverence and offerings outside the monastery.[48] Indeed, in the sixth century, a lacquer statue was recorded to have come to life nightly to perform ritual circumambulation;[49] separately, another lacquer statue was described glowing with divine radiance frequently.[50] The liveness and mobility accorded to lacquer statues that seemingly negate materiality and gravity would have solidified the belief in the divine nature shared by the statues and transmitted by the model through the production process.

It may not be practical, however, to expect the growing number of Buddhist communities across medieval China would all be able to commission Buddhist statues that required material resources, financial sources, elaborate procedures, and competent artisans. A much easier manufacturing method that utilizes a more malleable and economical material was developed alongside Buddhist statues made of other materials. Starting from the late fifth century, at least several Buddhist centers in present-day Shandong utilized a similar way to manufacture small, low-fired clay images (fig. 9).[51] These clay statues, ranging 10–25 cm in height, were made by manually pressing clay into a half mold, rendering them only a half image with a flat back. A tang projecting from the bottom was tapered and wedged tightly into a separately made base to appear like a statue in the round. Indeed, the low-fired clay statue—comprising also the halo, lotus base, and plinth—is meant to imitate the stone statue with its granular surface, which was also originally colored and gilded just like those made of stone (see fig. 6). Yet, unlike their stone counterparts, these clay statues made using a mold could be reproduced in great quantities much faster to meet the needs of the monastics and local lay believers. The mechanical process of production

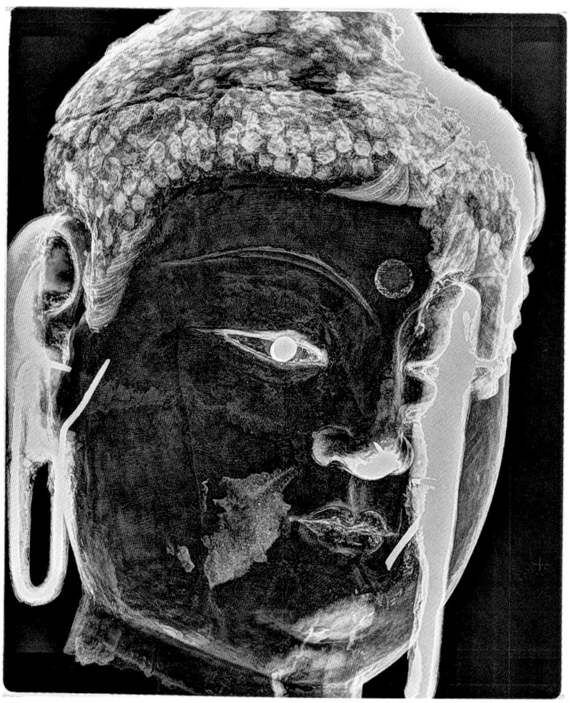

Figure 8 Bodhisattva head, eighth century. Hollow-core dry lacquer. X-radiograph showing the top section of the head attached above the forehead after the inner core was removed. Courtesy of Donna Strahan.

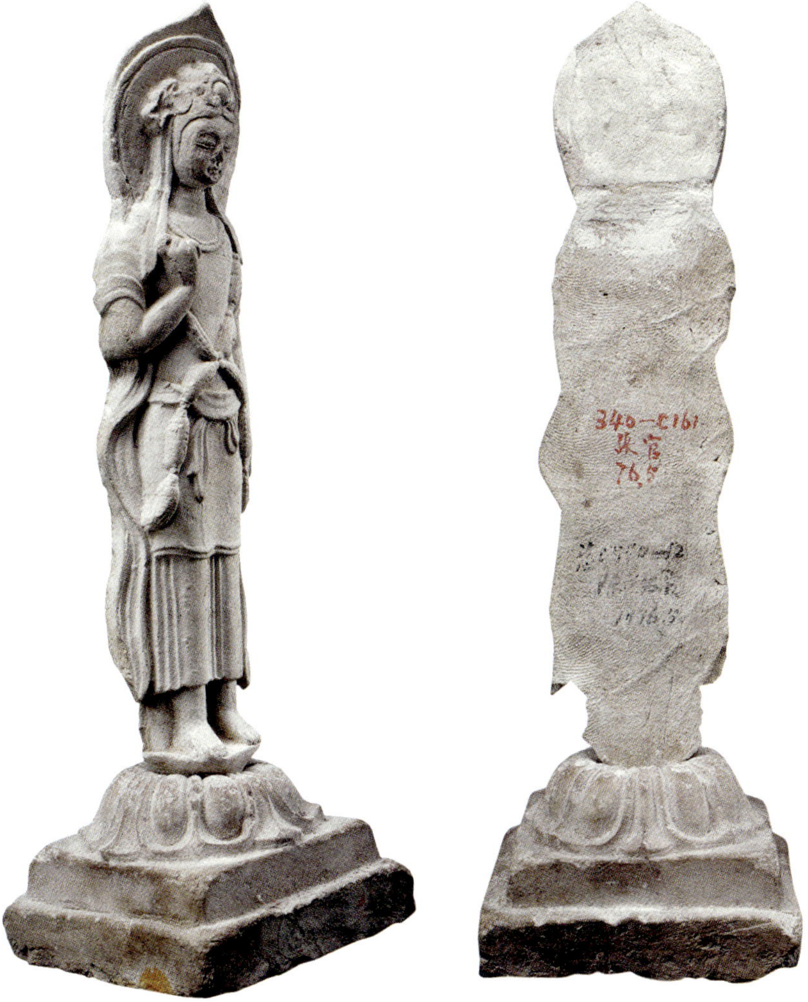

Figure 9 Standing bodhisattva, mid-sixth century. Uncovered from Boxing, Shandong. Low-fired clay, height: 22.2 cm. Three-quarter and posterior views. Courtesy of Zhang Shumin.

necessarily minimizes the intervention of the maker, while ensuring an accurate transmission of the model to its copies without human errors.

Clay, an inexpensive and readily available material in most parts of China that had been used to mold figural images, is not a surprising choice. In fact, the making of clay statues, baked or unbaked, using a mold might have been inspired by the manufacturing of tomb figurines that used the same material and employed exactly the same, if not a more complicated, method.[52] The application of clay was further validated during the early Tang when the Indian method of making Buddhist clay images, called *tuomo nixiang* (literally, "press-mold-clay image"), was transmitted to China.[53] The "imported" method provides Buddhist communities in China with religious justifications for utilizing the seemingly unworthy material for sacred images.

A great number of small votive tablets made of baked earthenware said to have replicated this Indian method were excavated from sites of former major monasteries in the Tang capital near present-day Xi'an. Typically, an image of a Buddha triad is depicted on one side of the tablet; and among surviving examples, a group of identical tablets also shows an inscription of twelve characters in relief on the reverse (figs. 10–11). The inscription reads: "The marvelous body of true reality is achieved by the meritorious deeds of pressing clay. [Noted in the] Great Tang."[54] Here the "marvelous body of true reality" refers to the figural form of the Buddha that could materialize the absolute truth. Such a sacred form of the Buddha, according to the inscription, could be achieved by anyone who simply presses clay into a mold to make exact copies of the image, an act considered a meritorious deed. We don't know the exact quantity of such tablets made from this time, but the practice must have been widespread since examples of such tablets are also found in Japan and Southeast Asia.[55] Also, as a meritorious deed, the more one makes such an image by pressing clay into a mold, the more merits one accumulates. Both the material and the production method facilitate the possibility of multiplying the sacred image in a great number quickly, giving the tablets an alternative name, "*juzhi xiang*," meaning an image that could be replicated for ten million copies.[56] Indeed, number matters in Buddhism, at least in the image-making context of sacred icons.

The importance of number can also be observed in a ritual that involves making ten thousand Buddha images in sand. The earliest canonical text that instructs such a large-scale image reproduction with sand is dated to the early eighth century, but the ritual, known as "Ritual of Stamping Sand Buddha Images," or *Yinsha fohui*, was not formalized and did not become popular until the ninth century, especially in the Dunhuang region in present-day Gansu province.[57] The ritual was performed by individual Buddhist devotees, who recite prayers orally while pressing a stamp that bears the Buddha image into sand to make identical impressions of the image. The use of sand as the ground for a profusion of Buddha images deliberately invites their disappearance after the ritual is concluded. As the "impression of the sand Buddha" (*yinsha fo*) is necessarily short lived, the surviving stamp (fig. 12) becomes the only evidence of the now extinguished images and a reminder of their ephemeral materiality.[58]

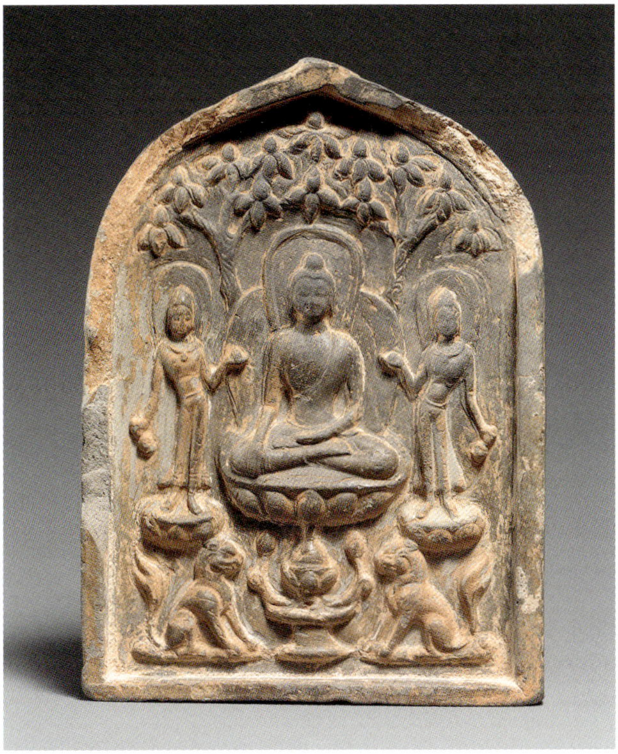

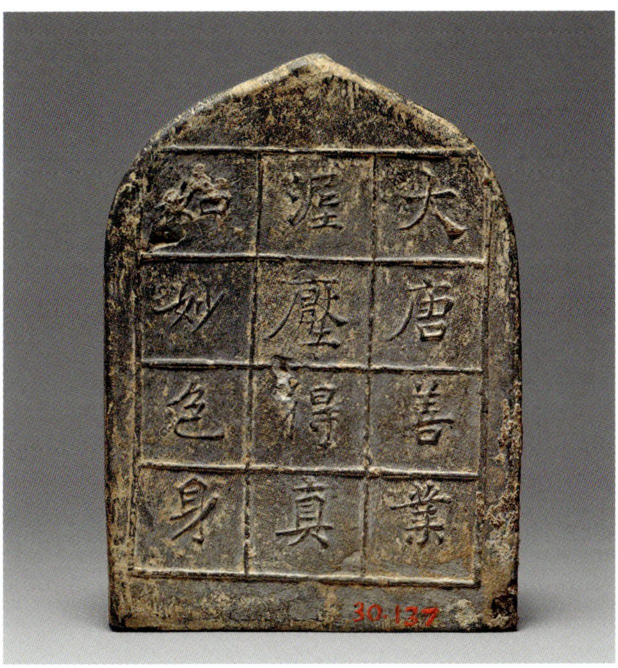

Figures 10–11 Votive tablet with Buddhist Triad, seventh century. Earthenware with traces of pigment, 14.6 × 10.8 cm Frontal and posterior views. Collection of the Metropolitan Museum of Art, Rogers Fund, 1918, 18.56.29.

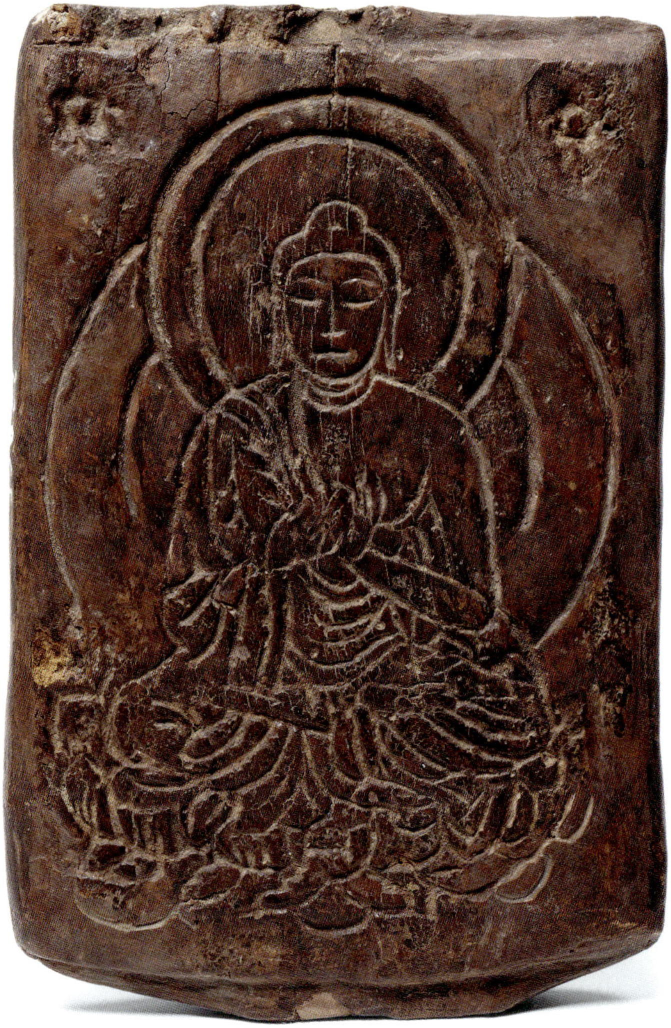

Figure 12 Printing block with image of the Buddha. Seated Buddha with his hands forming the mudra dharmachakra, eighth to ninth century. From Cave 17 (Pelliot, niche annexed to Cave 163, Mission Paul Pelliot, 1906–1908). Wood, 15.4 × 10.2 × 0.1 cm. MG23965 © RMN-Grand Palais / Art Resource, NY.

MATERIALITY AND RELIGIOSITY OF BUDDHIST ICONS

It should be clear by now that regardless of the material employed, the ultimate goal of making Buddhist icons had been to faithfully replicate the model, such that the truth, power, and efficacy of the original could be transmitted to its copies. Each copy is then an "authentic replica" that extends the holiness of the divinity, whose image (i.e., *zhenrong*) the first icon bears, a notion already made explicit in the King Udayana legend. In practice, Buddhist practitioners and artisans on the ground who worked with different materials were put in the position of devising methods of replication that could meet the challenge. The deployment of techniques such as casting or shaping an icon using a mold (*tuo*) or making impressions of a Buddhist image with a stamp (*yin*) should be examined in this light. As for statues made of materials that do not require a mold or stamp, the role of the artisan became quintessential, yet not in terms of their ability to create, but instead to replicate the model accurately to such an extent that their intervention was taken only as a means necessary to achieve the divine work.

However, as each material has a different visual and material quality and capacity that require a particular production procedure to achieve the goal, some materials were more preferable than others, for one reason or another. For instance, there was a great emphasis on the metallic and illuminating quality associated with the radiance of the Buddha as the "golden man," or *jinren*, as described in early texts.[59] This explains why the earliest extant Buddhist statues are all made of gilt bronze, which in Buddhist literature could be called either *jintong xiang* ("gilt-bronze statues") or simply *jinxiang* ("golden statue").[60] The pursuit of the same quality must have also promoted the use of limestone for its fine, smooth, and reflective surface rather than sandstone, which tends to have a grainy and coarse texture. In this regard, marble was also deemed superior to limestone, even though the former is less pliable. The same reasoning would have also prompted the application of gilt despite the virtually guaranteed additional cost. Likewise, lacquer is not the most cost-effective choice due to its labor-intensive and time-consuming process of production. If preserved properly, lacquer lasts longer than wood, and yet, like wood, it is also vulnerable to fire and intense heat, which might explain why only a handful of lacquer Buddhist statues survived from the early periods. Lacquer's capacity to enhance the realistic and sensuous quality of Buddhist icons, however, justifies the resources that certain Buddhist patrons would lavish over such a costly commission.

Indeed, the choice of materials was also inextricably tied to their patronage, as well as their intended functions. Stone, metal, and lacquer—materials not as readily available and more difficult to work with—were inherently the purview of individuals and Buddhist clerics of a higher social status. Such a commission would stipulate the resources, skills, techniques, and wealth required of such an endeavor. Buddhist statues made of these more durable materials also took a more prominent position in ritual and in the religious space where they were seen. In addition, size also made a difference. Oversized bronze statues were much rarer because of their cost and resource availability, and thus were commissioned only through state sponsorship. By comparison, small bronze statues were more likely produced by laity for various devotional purposes.[61] Similarly, as suggested by dedicatory inscriptions, patrons of small stone statues belonged to social groups of the less privileged, while larger ones were mostly commissioned by local Buddhist societies, wealthy patrons, and major monasteries.[62] In contrast, low-fired clay statues and earthenware tablets, largely excavated from former monastic precincts, were made by monks, nuns, or lay believers for the purposes of special Buddhist events, rituals, or karmic benefits.[63] They could be manufactured in great quantity much more easily, but concurrently they are less enduring. Sand, the least durable material, is also least conditioned by availability of resource, labor, and time, making it the most ideal material for large-scale image production.

In summary, predicating on the premise of replication, I propose that any material used in the making of Buddhist icons during China's medieval period should be gauged by cost-efficiency, endurance, and multiplicity as the major criteria in the matrix of materiality (fig. 13). Icons made of materials located toward the right side of the chart are more challenging to (re)produce or multiply and thus more expensive, but they would be unique and more durable. Conversely, icons made of materials located toward the left side of the chart are much easier and economical to replicate in greater quantity through the use of tools such as molds and stamps, but they are also more perishable. Taking notes on how one material might have been used versus others, it is fair to claim that medieval Chinese Buddhists explored proactively the materiality of Buddhist icons to articulate and express their sacrality, rather than being restrained from speaking about material specificities of icons. Also, accounts about icons made of more durable but less reproducible materials, such as those in the right side of the chart, dominate medieval Buddhist texts. Yet one suspects that images made of clay, mud, or sand made using a mold or stamp must have outnumbered those made of durable materials, and that it was those images, made of less durable materials, that actually helped establish Buddhism as a "religion of images," though most of their material evidence no longer exists. In short, artisans/makers of Buddhist icons had multiple materials at their disposal and their choice, or choices, would be indicative of religiosity of Buddhist icons reframed in such a matrix of materiality.

Although Buddhist icons cannot be reduced to their materials, the material choice matters in our understanding of their religiosity. To take the doctrine of karma as an example: making of Buddha images is a sanctioned meritorious act that brings the practitioner innumerous spiritual benefits. As discussed previously, "number" makes a difference in this context; that is, the more images one makes, the more merits one accrues. In reality, however, durable and precious materials do not lend themselves conveniently to any large-scale image production and thus would not be ideal for expediting one's accumulation of merits. In other words, despite that Buddhist texts and apologetics repeatedly downplay the importance of material and render all materials equal, not all of them are compatible in the ways that each material fulfills its religious role and functionality. Durable materials are often taken as the medium that could literally materialize the meaning of the dharma body (*fashen*, or *dharmakaya* in Sanskrit), or "true body," that is, the absolute existence of the Buddha, which is imperishable and eternal.[64] On the contrary, clay, mud, or sand Buddhas are meant to be ephemeral and transient, expounding the chain of causation in the phenomenal world, including Buddhist images. Also, in the "Ritual of Stamping Sand Buddha Images," one reads: "[We] make holy images using a mold at the

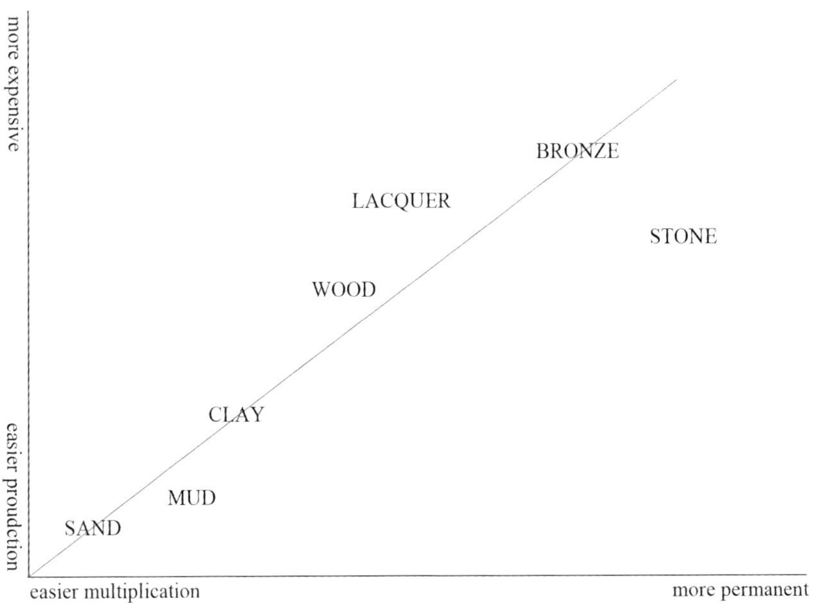

Figure 13 Chart showing the matrix of materiality for the productivity of Buddhist icons during China's medieval period. Chart by Wei-Cheng Lin.

shore and print [the Buddha's] golden presence with a stamp as numerous as the sands of Ganges."[65] Sand, indeed, by facilitating the image-making process in the quantity that other materials cannot, offers an opportunity to visualize the immeasurable and otherwise unpresentable power of the Buddha—a divine manifestation simultaneously not to be bound by the material.

Returning to the standing Buddha dated to 580 in Figure 1, the statue was commissioned during the first few years after the massive religious persecution leveled against Buddhism in 574 and 578 during the reign of Emperor Wu (r. 561–578) of the Northern Zhou. Buddhism was subsequently revived under the auspices of Emperor Jing (r. 579–581) and enthusiastically advocated by his prime minister, Yang Jian (541–604), a devout Buddhist who later became the founder of the Sui dynasty (581–618).[66] As the inscription dedicated to the statue notes: "Without the illuminous virtues of the emperor and wisdom of the prime minister, how could we have retrieved the extraordinary religion and re-established it from its previous extinction?"[67] It is most likely that in this post-persecution context, Buddhism witnessed a new surge of financial supports around the capital area, making the commission of this oversized stone statue possible. The local limestone, or *qingshi*, prized for its smooth and glittering surface when polished, was acquired intentionally to materialize the "brilliant and luminous" quality associated with the true presence of the Buddha. Even more important, it is called a "jade" statue to evoke not just the green luster of jade but also its hardness for the Buddha statue—and by extension, his teaching, or dharma—to "endure for eternity" (*qiongjie bujin*), as supplicated in the inscription. We may never know whether this "material trick" works or not, but I contend, it is in the materiality of Buddhist icons that the trick was taken literally as a physical means to materialize the icon's sacrality and religiosity.

NOTES

1. Zhao Liguang and Pei Jianping, "Xi'an dongjiao chutu Beizhou fo lixiang" [Standing Buddha statues of the Northern Zhou excavated from the eastern outskirt of Xi'an], *Wenwu* 9 (2005): 76–90.
2. See Wei Zheng and Ma Mingyue, "Yetan Fojiao zaoxiang de Chang'an moshi" [Revisit the Chang'an model of Buddhist statues], *Dunhuang yanjiu*, no. 3 (2020): 1–13; Zhongguo shehui kexueyuan kaogu yanjiusuo, ed., *Gudu yizhen: Chang'an cheng chutu de Beizhou fojiao zaoxiang* [Remaining treasures of the ancient capital: Buddhist statues of the Northern Zhou excavated from the city of Chang'an] (Beijing: Wenwu chubanshe, 2010).
3. *Gudu yizhen*, 80. Emphasis added by the author.
4. See Yu Chun, "Chang'an Xiwei Fojiao zaoxiang tezheng jiqi yuanliu kaocha" [On the characteristics and origins of Buddhist statues from Chang'an during the Western Wei], *Xibu kaogu* 15 (2018): 168.
5. Eric M. Greene, "The 'Religion of Images'? Buddhist Image Worship in the Early Medieval Chinese Imagination," *Journal of the American Oriental Society* 138, no. 3 (2018): 455–84. I thank Eric Greene for sharing his research with me.
6. See Kwi Jeong Lee, "Shaping the Formless: Debates Over Buddhist Images in Medieval China, ca. 300–700" (PhD diss., Princeton University, 2018). I thank Kwi Jeong Lee for sharing her dissertation with me.
7. See Takakusu Junjirō and Watanabe Kaigyoku eds., *Taishō shinshū daizōkyō* [Taishō edition of the Buddhist canon] (Tokyo: Taishō Issaikyō kankōkai, 1924–1935) (hereafter *T.*), 2076, 51: 310c13–c16. For further discussion of the anecdotal case, see Gregory P. A. Levine, *Long Strange Journey: On Modern Zen, Zen Art, and Other Predicaments* (Honolulu: University of Hawai'i Press, 2017), 54–74.
8. How to make the absent Buddha present through the making of the Buddha image was already an issue in Indian Buddhism before its transmission to China; see Robert DeCaroli, *Image Problems: The Origin and Development of the Buddha's Image in Early South Asia* (Seattle: University of Washington Press, 2015).
9. *T.* 224, 8: 476b17–20. Translation is after Lewis R. Lancaster, "An Early Mahayana Sermon about the Body of the Buddha and the Making of Images," *Artibus Asiae* 36, no. 4 (1974): 289.
10. *T.* 224, 8: 476b21–22.
11. *T.* 692, 16. For this scripture, see Robert H. Sharf, "The Scripture on the Production of Buddha Images," in Donald S. Lopez Jr., ed., *Religions of China in Practice* (Princeton: Princeton University Press, 1996), 261–77.
12. If, as explicated in those early texts, the divinity was not to be contained in, nor manifested through, the mundane and transitory material of which icons were made, why should Buddhists exhaust wealth and resources to produce them? As Kwi Jeong Lee argues in her dissertation, this question might have actually prompted Buddhist apologists to invest greater religious significance in the understanding of icons to justify the ritual use of them. See Lee, introduction to "Shaping the Formless."
13. The version that became the basis of later renditions is from the Chinese translation of the *Ekottaragama* (*Zengyi ahan jing*), translated in the late fourth century; see *T.* 125, 2: 705c28–706a18. On the different versions of the legend, see Sun-ah Choi, "Quest for the True Visage: Sacred Images in Medieval Chinese Buddhist Art and the Concept of *Zhen*" (PhD diss., University of Chicago, 2012), 61–72.

14. This is based on the legend recorded in Xuanzang's (602–664) *Da Tang xiyu ji*, or the *Great Tang Records of the Western Regions*, compiled in 646; see *T.* 2087, 51: 898a15–16. An earlier version of the legend that also concludes the story with the Buddha encountering his image can be found in *Guanfo sanmei haijing*, or the *Scripture of the Sea of Samadhi of Visualizing the Buddha*, translated in the early fifth century; see *T.* 15: 643.678b7–23.

15. Sun-ah Choi, "*Zhenrong* to *Ruixiang*: The Medieval Chinese Reception of the Mahābodhi Buddha Statue," *Art Bulletin* 97, no. 4 (2015): 364–87.

16. See Robert E. Buswell Jr. and Donald S. Lopez Jr., *The Princeton Dictionary of Buddhism* (Princeton: Princeton University Press, 2013), 1950–51.

17. This later version has a slightly different title, the *Scripture on Merits [Accrued through] the Production of the Images* (*Dacheng zaoxiang gongde jing*), translated into Chinese in 692; see *T.* 694, 16: 793b25–c1.

18. See Hou Xudong, *Wu liu shiji beifang minzhong Fojiao xinyang: yi zaoxiang ji wei zhongxin de kaocha* [Buddhist beliefs among common people in northern China during the fifth and sixth centuries: an investigation centered on dedicatory inscriptions about making images] (Beijing: Zhongguo shehui kexue chubanshe, 1998), 236; translation after Greene, "Buddhist Image Worship in the Early Medieval Chinese Imagination," 463.

19. See Hou, *Wu liu shiji beifang minzhong Fojiao xinyang*, 238.

20. In fact, not all texts that include the list of the Buddha's thirty-two perfect bodily features agree with each other. See Buswell and Lopez, *The Princeton Dictionary of Buddhism*, 1950–51.

21. See *T.* 2015, 52: 397b25–c13. Kwi Jeong Lee discusses the incorporation of the legend of the Udayana Buddha into the tale of the first Buddha image brought to China in Lee, "Shaping the Formless," 164–76.

22. Like other famed artists of this time, Dai Kui's artistic achievement is known to us through limited textual sources rather than his art. Scholars have argued that not all the recorded accounts about Dai Kui are credible, but it is still instrumental to see how his art was assessed and received even if some details are apparently fabricated. For textual sources about Dai Kui, see Yin Lixin, "Dai Kui 'shanzhu foxiang ji diaoke' zhiyi" [Questions about Dai Kui's specialization in "casting and sculpting Buddhist statues"], *Meishu guancha*, no. 12 (1997): 55–57.

23. See Daoshi (d. 683), *Fayuan zhulin* [Jade grove of the dharma garden], *T.* 2122, 53: 406b1.

24. This should not be taken as to deny the importance of genuine creativity or disregard any artistic decisions made by artisans, since, indeed, given the common goal of replication, stylistic differences did exist among different regions and periods. The point I wish to make here is that historical texts and Buddhist literature explicitly put more weight on accuracy than on artistic characteristics or value.

25. Donna Strahan provides an excellent overview of the production of Chinese Buddhist statues from a technical perspective in her article, "Creating Sacred Images of the Buddha: A Technical Perspective," in Denise Patry Leidy and Donna Strahan, *Wisdom Embodied: Chinese Buddhist and Daoist Sculpture in the Metropolitan Museum of Art* (New York: Metropolitan Museum of Art, 2010), 27–45.

26. For a discussion of these accounts, see "Youtianwang zhantan ruixiang liubu Zhongguo kao" [A research on the miraculous icon, the sandalwood Udayana statue, and its proliferation in China], *Lishi yanjiu*, no. 2 (2012): 163–73.

27. The most comprehensive study on the concept and practice of "replication" in early Chinese Buddhism is Hsueh-man Shen, *Authentic Replicas: Buddhist Art in Medieval China* (Honolulu: University of Hawai'i Press, 2019).

28. For a study of early gilt-bronze Buddhist statues, see Li Jingjie, "Zaoqi jintongfo puxi yanjiu" [A research on the lineages of early gilt-bronze Buddhist statues], *Kaogu*, no. 5 (1995): 451–65.
29. See the entry written by Denise Patry Leidy in Leidy and Strahan, eds., *Wisdom Embodied*, 48–50.
30. See Denise Patry Leidy, "Buddhism and Buddhist Sculpture in China," in Leidy and Strahan, eds., *Wisdom Embodied*, 3–25; Su Bai, "Buddha Images of the Northern Plain, 4th–6th Century," in James C. Y. Watt, et al., eds., *China: Dawn of a Golden Age, 200–750 AD* (New Haven: Yale University Press, 2004), 79–87.
31. See the entry written by Angela F. Howard in Watt, et al., eds., *China: Dawn of a Golden Age*, 134.
32. See Harry Falk, "'Buddhist' Metalware from Gandhara," *Bulletin of the Asia Institute* 26 (2012): 33–60; Chandra L. Reedy, "Appendix: Technical Analysis," in *The Crossroads of Asia: Transformation in Image and Symbol in the Art of Ancient Afghanistan and Pakistan*, ed. Elizabeth Errington and Joe Cribb (Cambridge: Ancient India and Iran Trust, 1992), 246.
33. See Anna Bennett, "Lost-Wax or Piece-Mould Casting," *Arts & Cultures: Antiquity, African, Oceania, Asia, Americas* (2006), 268–71.
34. Scholars, both in China and elsewhere, have done a great deal of research on this topic; see Robert W. Bagley, "Shang Ritual Bronzes: Casting Technique and Vessel Design," *Archives of Asian Art* 43 (1990): 6–20; Lukas Nickel, "Re-Thinking Bronze Casting Technology in Ancient China," *Artibus Asiae* 66, no. 1 (2006): 5–39.
35. A detailed and useful discussion of the piece-mold cast for the early Chinese gilt-bronze Buddha statues is Donna Strahan, "Piece-Mold Casting: A Chinese Tradition for Fourth- and Fifth-Century Bronze Buddha Images," *Metropolitan Museum Studies in Art, Science, and Technology* 1 (2010): 133–53.
36. See Marylin Martin Rhie, *Early Buddhist Art of China and Central Asia* (Leiden: Brill, 2002), vol. 2, 254–60.
37. Huijiao (497–554), *Gaoseng zhuan* [Biographies of eminent monks], *juan* 5; *T.* 2095, 50: 352b17–22.
38. See Yang Xuanzhi, *Luoyang qielan ji* [Record of the monasteries of Luoyang], *juan* 1; *T.* 2092, 51: 1000a14–16. For textual records on Buddhist gilt-bronze statues, see Li Jingjie, "Jintongfo de wenxian kaocha" [An investigation of textual records about gilt-bronze Buddhist images], *Gugong bowuyuan yuankan*, no. 1 (1995): 51–57.
39. See Yu Chun, "Chang'an diqu Beichao jintong foxiang xingzhi yu zhuzao jishu tezheng" [The formal and bronze-casting characteristics of gilt-bronze Buddhist statues of the Northern and Southern Dynasties from the Chang'an region], *Wenbo*, no. 3 (2016): 37–44.
40. Luo Fuyi, "Hebei sheng Quyang xian chutu shixiang qingli gongzuo jianbao" [A brief work report on the stone statues excavated from Quyang county, Hebei], *Kaogu tongxun*, no. 3 (1955): 34–38. See also Yang Wenhui, et al., eds., *Quyang shidiao yishu ji lishi wenhua yanjiu* [A research on the history and culture of the stone-carving art from Quyang] (Baoding: Hebei daxue chubanshe, 2009).
41. See Li Shaonan, "Shandong Boxing chutu bai yu jian Beiwei zhi Suidai tong zaoxiang" [More than one hundred bronze statues of Northern dynasties and Sui excavated from Boxing, Shandong], *Wenwu*, no. 5 (1984): 21–31.
42. The stylistic connection between the marble statues with gilt-bronze statues, including those from the Shandong region, is discussed in Li Jingjie and Tian Jun, "Dingzhou xi baishi foxiang yanjiu" [A research on the marble Buddhist statues of the Dingzhou style], *Gugong bowuyuan yuankan*, no. 3 (1999): 66–84.

43. The earliest record about this famous statue at the Mahābodhi Temple, also known as *puti ruixiang* ("sacred icons under bodhi trees") by the end of the seventh century, is from Xuanzang's *Da Tang xiyu ji*, *juan* 8; *T.* 2087, 51: 916.

44. See Daoshi, *Fayuan zhulin*; *T.* 2122, 53: 503a7–11.

45. See online essays published in tandem with the exhibition *Secrets of the Lacquer Buddha*, held December 9, 2017, through June 10, 2018, at the Freer and Sackler Gallery of Art. "Practice and Production: Four Life-Size Chinese Buddhist Sculptures," National Museum of Asian Art, accessed March 3, 2021, https://asia.si.edu/exhibition/practice-and-production-four-life-size-chinese-buddhist -sculptures-in-american-collections/.

46. The term *tuokong xiang* is used interchangeably with *jiazhu* in Buddhist literature. See Huilin (fl. 810), *Yiqie jing yin yi* [Sound and meaning of all sutras]; *T.* 2128, 54: 808c16.

47. See Donna Strahan and Blythe McCarthy, "Construction from the Inside Out: Early Chinese Lacquer Buddha Fabrication," National Museum of Asian Art, accessed November 23, 2020, https://asia.si.edu/essays/construction-from-the-inside-out-early-chinese-lacquer-buddha-fabrication/.

48. The ritual procession involving lacquer statues in China may be traced to as early as the sixth century. See Jiang Jiahua, "'Luoyang qielan ji' xingxiang yanjiu" [A research on "ritual processions of Buddhist images" as seen in the Record of the Monasteries of Luoyang], *Qiushi*, no. 2 (2013): 84–86.

49. Yang Xuanzhi, *Luoyang qianlan ji*, *juan* 4.

50. Daoxuan, *Xu gaoseng zhuan* [Extended biographies of eminent monks], *juan* 25; *T.* 2060, 50: 661a29–b1.

51. Zhang Shumin and Xiao Guitian, eds., *Shandong baitao Fojiao zaoxiang* [Low-fired clay Buddhist statues from Shandong] (Beijing: Wenwu chubanshe, 2011).

52. This is not conclusive, but a kiln located in the Tang capital, Chang'an, was uncovered with clay molds used to produce both tomb figurines and Buddhist images. See Shaanxi sheng kaogu yanjiuyuan, ed., *Tang Chang'an Liquan fang sancai yaozhi* [A kiln for baking tricolor artifacts found in Liquan Ward of Tang Chang'an] (Beijing: Wenwu chubanshe, 2008).

53. The practice was recorded in Yijing's (635–713) travel diary, titled *Nanhai jigui neifa zhuan*, or *A Record of Buddhist Practices Sent Home from the South Sea*. Yijing traveled to India during the late seventh century. See *T.* 2125, 54: 225c15–17. See also Shen, *Authentic Replicas*, 107–22.

54. Translation after Shen, *Authentic Replicas*, 108.

55. Shen, *Authentic Replica*, 123–36.

56. *Juzhi* is a Chinese transliteration of the Sanskrit term *koti*, meaning an enormous number, and can be understood as ten million, one hundred million, or more. See Hagihara Hajime, "Genjō hotsuga 'jūguchizō' kō—'sengyōdei' senbutsu wo megutte" [On *juzhi* images made according to Xuanzang's vow: about clay Buddha images known as *shanye ni*], *Bukkyō geijutsu* 261 (March 2002): 80–100.

57. See *Cishi pusa luexiu yuqie niansong fa*, or *The Rite for Reciting Maitreya Bodhisattva's Spiritual Cultivation of Yoga Practice*, in *T.* 1141. For more on the "Ritual of Stamping Sand Buddha Images," see Wang Sanqing and Wang Yayi, "Dunhuang wenxian yinshafo wen de zhengli yanjiu" [A research and compilation of ritual texts related to stamping sand Buddha images from Dunhuang Manuscripts], *Dunhuang xue* 26 (2005): 45–74.

58. A discussion of the surviving stamp can be found in Neville Agnew, Marcia Reed, and Tevvy Ball, eds., *Cave Temples of Dunhuang: Buddhist Art on China's Silk Road* (Los Angeles: The Getty Conservation Institute, 2016), 242–45.

59. The term *jinren* is used in the story of the dream of Emperor Ming. It is recorded that Emperor Ming of the Eastern Han once dreamed of a golden man with a halo, flying in and out of his court. He later learned that the golden man in his dream must be the Buddha in the land west of China. The story was well documented and circulated during the period of our discussion; for an example, see Huijiao, *Gaoseng zhuan*, *juan* 1; *T.* 2059, 50: 322c20–28. In some other cases, *jinren* could also refer to gilt-bronze statues.
60. See Li, "Jingtongfo de wenxian kaocha," 51.
61. This can be observed from the dedicatory inscriptions included in Zhang Shumin, ed., *Shandong Boxing tong foxiang yishu* [The art of gilt-bronze Buddhist statues from Boxing, Shandong] (Taipei: Yishujia, 2005), 151–53.
62. See Li and Tian, "Dingzhou xi baishi foxiang yanjiu."
63. Shao Guitian, "Baitao fo yu tuofo kao" [Low-fired clay Buddhist icons and Buddhist icons made using a mold], in Zhang and Xiao, eds., *Shandong baitao Fojiao zaoxiang*, 36–49.
64. I discuss the significance of stone in manifesting permanence and eternity of the Buddha body in Wei-Cheng Lin, *Building a Sacred Mountain: The Buddhist Architecture of China's Mount Wutai* (Seattle: University of Washington Press, 2014), 64–80. See also Robert E. Harrist Jr., *The Landscape of Words: Stone Inscriptions from Early and Medieval China* (Seattle: University of Washington Press, 2008).
65. The passage appears in many renditions of the ritual text discussed in Wang and Wang, "Dunhuang wenxian yinshafo wen de zhengli yanjiu."
66. See Lan Jifu, *Suidai fojiao shi lunshu* [On the history of Buddhism during the Sui dynasty] (Taipei: Taiwan Shangwu, 1993), 5–10.
67. Zhao and Pei, "Xi'an dongjiao chutu Beizhou fo lixiang," 80.

Luminescent Visions

Transparency and Transformation in Medieval China

Anne Feng

Painters in medieval China started to explore the optical effects of transparent materials with innovative techniques. One of the earliest examples of this process can be found in a seventh-century cave at Dunhuang. A standing bodhisattva gently holds a transparent bowl in his right hand (fig. 1).[1] The contours of the vessel have been limned with thin ink outlines and filled in with a light wash. The translucent quality of the vessel is further accentuated by the position of the deity's hand: the viewer can see, through the object, the silhouette of his thumb and index finger. The portion of the hand behind the vessel is shown in a lighter color than the rest of the palm. Through this superimposition of forms, the opacity of the hand renders the bowl transparent.

The shape of the vessel in this visual template—one widely used in religious painting at Dunhuang and beyond—closely resembles glass and rock crystal bowls and cups that were imported into China in the medieval period.[2] The mural

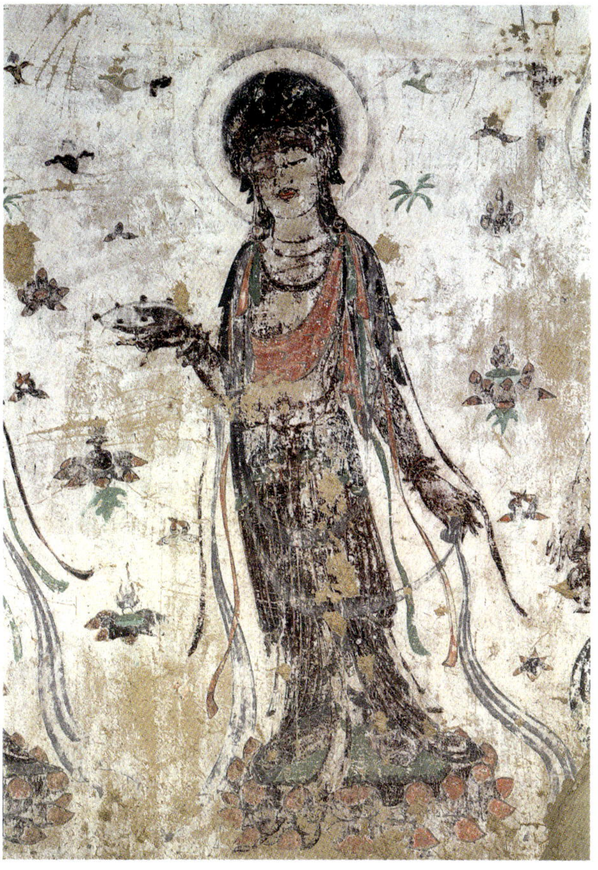

Figure 1 Bodhisattva holding a glass bowl, early seventh century. Cave 401, Mogao Grottoes, Dunhuang, Gansu province, China. © Dunhuang Academy.

painter's composition can be understood as evidence of this influx of exotic objects *and* as a sophisticated attempt to capture the phenomenal experience of viewing a transparent thing. Transparent materials, the vessel attests, engendered new optical experiences and profound shifts in material culture and painting in Sui-Tang (581–907) China.[3] Modern conceptions of transparency are often tied to advancements in industrial technology and the imagination of utopian social forms.[4] In the ancient world, however, the question of seeing through crystal and glass elicited interpretive ambiguities and epistemological challenges.[5] Transparent things remind us to think twice about what we see. I argue that, by the seventh century, the ambiguity of such optical experience is harnessed to form a new type of imagination that is generative—one that opens up the possibility for supramundane transformations. Divine presence could, artifacts discussed throughout this essay suggest, be lodged in the qualities of translucent matter, which visualizes the instability of material form, thus allowing for a reconceptualization of what constitutes pictorial space.

This chapter investigates how the inflow of exotic rock crystal and glass objects in medieval China inspired a newfound interest in the experience of transparency. Rock crystal and glass were often used as metaphors to describe what translucency meant for medieval subjects. This materiality of transparency in medieval China should be understood, in Michael Ann Holly's terms, as "the meeting of matter and imaginations, the place where opposites take refuge from their perpetual strife."[6] Art historians have argued that the classical idea of media emerged from the see-through quality of rock crystal in ancient Greece and the Roman Empire.[7] In China, however, I contend that medieval writers and painters saw transparency less as a stable material property than as a "transformative force." Transparency was not an innate or essential feature of a thing, but a state that an object could assume and occupy temporarily; dissolving distinctions between inside and outside, solidity and emptiness, the transparent state consequently created new possibilities for thinking about the ontology of pictorial space in medieval China.

DESCRIBING TRANSPARENCY

A translucent object transmits and reflects light at the same time, allowing things behind the object to become visible, while the object itself attains a certain luminance.[8] From a medieval perspective, what one took to be transparent, however, was qualitatively different from our experience of gazing through a camera lens or the window of a modernist office building. Across the ancient

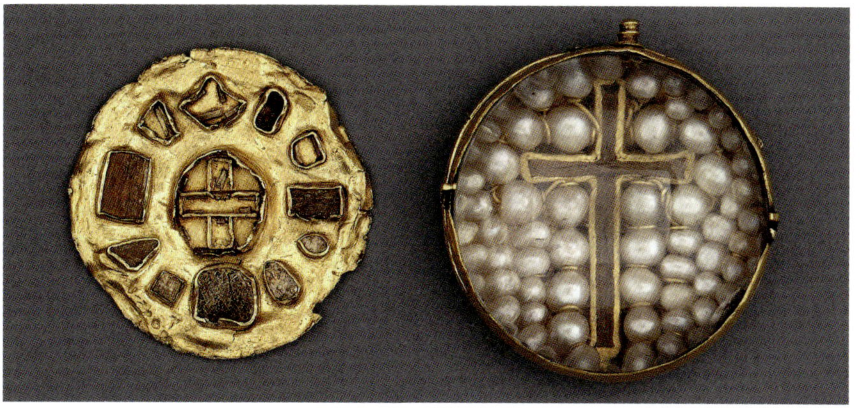

Figure 2 Reliquary pendant, c. 1200. British Isles. Gold, wood, rock crystal, pearl, 54.5 × 5.2 × 2.6 cm. 1946,0407.1. © The Trustees of the British Museum.

world, thinkers were acutely aware of the contingencies of vision, as transparent objects posed philosophical questions about matter, form, and perception.[9] Archaeological findings show that rock crystal and glass objects circulated widely across the Eurasian continent, from the Roman world to South and East Asia.[10] Rock crystal and glass vessels arrived in China mostly as exotica from the Roman and Sassanian empires, and later in the Islamic world. Flows of craft knowledge and natural resources accompanied the expansion of diplomatic gift giving and luxury trade, while the two materials accrued poetic and religious associations of purity and the fantastic as they passed through the hands of the social elite. Rock crystal and glass were often paired together and wedded with Chinese ideas of alchemy and immortality, while materializing Buddhist notions of emptiness.[11] Taken as optical things, they also magnified the fragmentation and subjective nature of visual experiences. In medieval China, what was central to the visual force of translucent and transparent things was their capacity to collapse distinctions between outside and inside, surface and substance, form and matter. To say something is transparent, medieval writers would often describe how the object is "shining thoroughly inside and outside" (*neiwai tongche*) and turn to glass and rock crystal as key metaphors—it was "glass-like" (*ru liuli*) or "crystal-like" (*ru shuijing*).[12]

As a type of gemstone, rock crystal is a transparent variety of crystalline quartz (SiO_2).[13] From the Greco-Roman world to Mesoamerica, colorless quartz was treasured as rare, petrified ice that was imbued with magical qualities for healing and divination.[14] In medieval Europe, rock crystal was regularly used as a type of lens that could magnify, obscure, or distort images behind it. In this

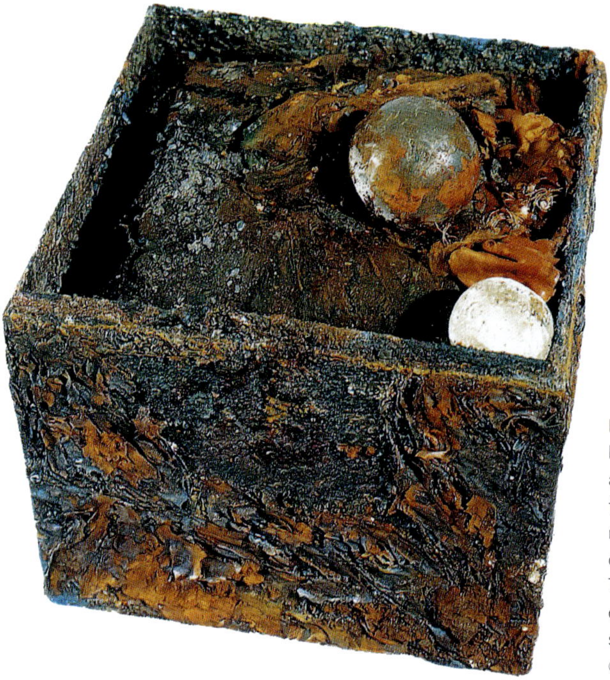

Figure 3 Two crystal orbs found between the fifth iron casket and fourth silver casket of the five-fold reliquary found in the secret niche of the Famen Monastery relic crypt, Shaanxi province, China, Tang dynasty (618–907). Rock crystal, large orb, diameter: 5.2 cm, smaller orb, diameter: 3.9 cm.

thirteenth-century pendant reliquary (fig. 2), a rock crystal dome is used to magnify the cross and pearls beneath it. Artisans took advantage of the optical qualities of the gemstone to encourage tactile experiences of devotional objects.[15] Chinese historical texts note how rock crystal was abundant in Persia, Gandhara, and the Byzantine Empire.[16] The Roman world was described as a place where people used crystal food containers and dwelled in palaces with crystal pillars.[17] Together with glass vessels, crystal cups entered China through the tributary system. The most common objects found in elite tombs or relic crypts are drinking vessels, rosary beads, and small pieces of jewelry.[18] The Chinese called the stone *shuijing*, which can be translated literally as "water essence" or "water germ."[19] Gandharan emissaries brought crystal cups to the Tang court in 619,[20] while burning lenses were also imported into China in the form of crystal orbs. Transparent spheres of pure rock crystal could refract sunlight and set things on fire. This function imbued rock crystal, something originally associated with ice and water, with a paradoxical association with the sun and heat, and was at times called *huojing* or "fire essence."[21] In 621, the ruler of ancient Vietnam, Linyi, sent so-called fire orbs (*huozhu*) to the Tang court. The fire orbs were each "the size of a chicken egg. They were round, white, glimmering, and emitted light of several *chi*-feet."[22] There are in fact two crystal orbs inside the famous Famen

Monastery five-fold casket that contain the True Body relic of the Buddha.[23] The diameter of the larger crystal orb is 5.2 cm—approximately the size of a chicken egg (fig. 3). These crystal balls were perhaps similar to the fire orbs that circulated at court in the seventh century.[24]

Glass, on the other hand, has a far more complicated history in China, which has continued to puzzle philologists and archeologists alike.[25] Colored glass beads have been created in China since the Warring States period (481–221 BCE) (fig. 4), and early glass, which was mostly opaque, was molded through processes of casting to imitate jade.[26] Blown vessels of clear glass were widely produced in the Mediterranean world and Central Asia, but the Chinese lacked such technology and mainly obtained glassware through import.[27] Glass cups and bowls were used during banqueting as prized possessions for Chinese aristocrats, while skilled craftsmen were recruited for palace workshops to develop glassmaking technology locally. The naming of glass also demonstrates the complexity of how this foreign substance was domesticated in Chinese culture.

Although frequently listed together as distinctly different materials, glass and rock crystal were both treasured for their translucent qualities.[28] Glass is often referred to as *liuli* (sometimes *boli*), a phonetic translation from the Sanskrit term *vaidūyra*, which denotes beryl. Another similar term is *biliuli*, which might have come from the Persian word "*belur/bylwl*," which means rock crystal.[29] In some cases, the Chinese term *liuli* is associated with lapis lazuli in Buddhist texts.[30] The term *liuli* itself opens up a far wider constellation of material associations, from transparent glass to colorful gemstones. This means that the Chinese term *liuli* encompassed two distinct yet interrelated visual effects—when opaque, it could achieve an iridescent quality like colored glass or jewels,

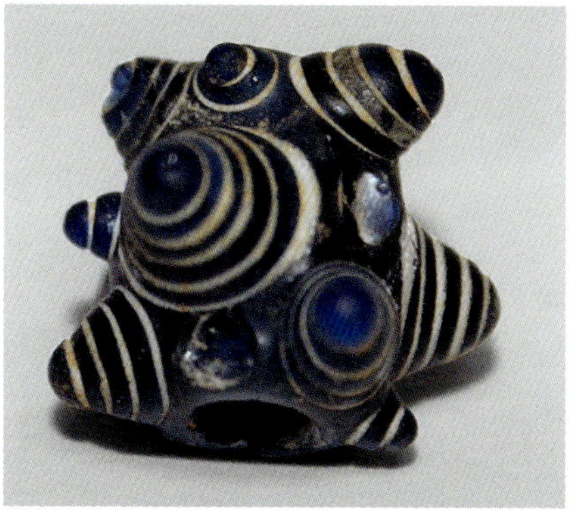

Figure 4 Bead, 600 BCE–200 CE. China. Blue glass, diameter: 2.08 cm. 1940, 1214.34.

while, on the other hand, it could also be transparent, like rock crystal. These two visual effects appear to be the opposite from each other; however, in the medieval period, when one took something to be transparent, she/he saw it as being both colorful and colorless at the same time.

We can trace a gradual conceptual alignment between glass and rock crystal in China, when Chinese craftsmen began to manufacture glass objects domestically. The Daoist master Ge Hong (283–343) tried to distinguish rock crystal from glass by examining their means of production:

> Foreign countries make rock-crystal bowls, but in fact [these bowls] are made by melting a mixture of five different types of ashes. Now there are several people in Jiao[zhou] and Guang[zhou] who know how to *forge* [*zhu*] this material. Today, if you speak of this to commoners, they will not believe you. They would say, rock crystal is originally a substance of nature, it is a type of gemstone.[31]

Rock crystal was usually shaped through processes of cutting and polishing, while ancient glass was created by shaping the molten form of silicon dioxide combined with different chemical substances. Guangzhou has been a major port city of south China since the Eastern Han period (25–220), and unearthed glass materials from the region show high percentages of soda lime. Chemical analysis demonstrates that these specimens were created by glassmaking technology development in the West, which may have reached China via India through maritime trade.[32] The writer laments how glass is mistaken for rock crystal, but this passage also shows how glass manufacturing was associated with alchemy and metalwork, for glass was "forged" [*zhu*] from combining different substances. Rock crystal is a type of stone created by nature, while glass is forged by the human hand.

By the Tang (618–907) period, the terms *liuli* and *shuijing* that designate glass and rock crystal were used almost interchangeably.[33] This semantic misperception is evident in the Hejiacun hoard, which was buried in the Tang capital, Chang'an, in the eighth century and contained over a thousand pieces of luxury items that were associated with palace workshops and the imperial treasure house.[34] In one silver jar, archeologists discovered a glass bowl and a crystal cup. The glass bowl was likely manufactured in the Gandharan region, while the uniquely Chinese shape of the crystal cup suggests that it is a domestic product. Ink inscriptions on the lid of the jar, however, list "one *liuli* cup and one *liuli* bowl" among its contents (figs. 5–7).[35] This means that the crystal cup was also understood as a *liuli* vessel.

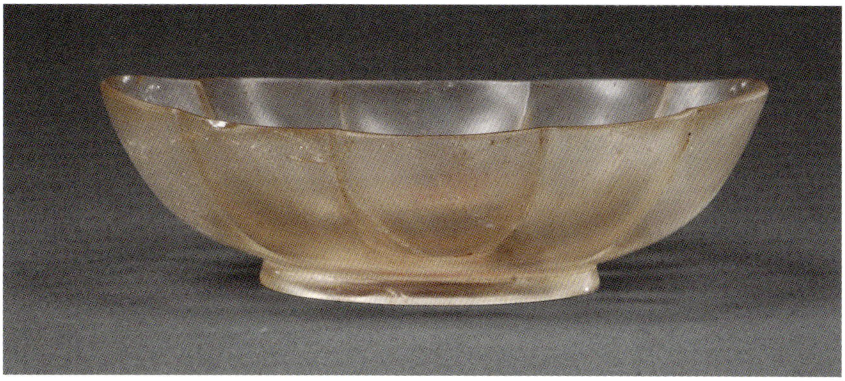

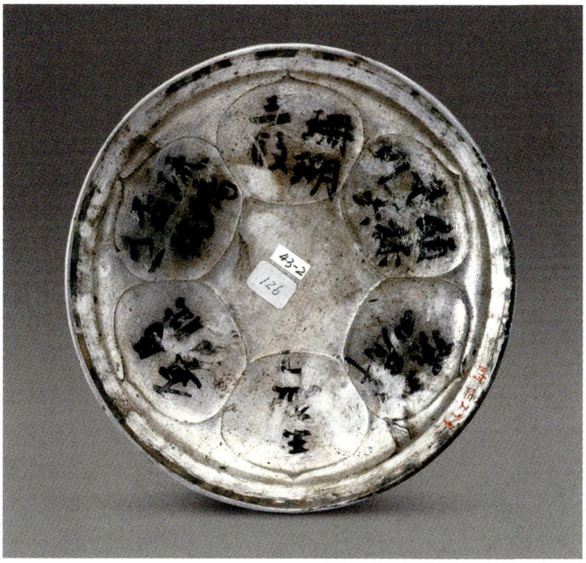

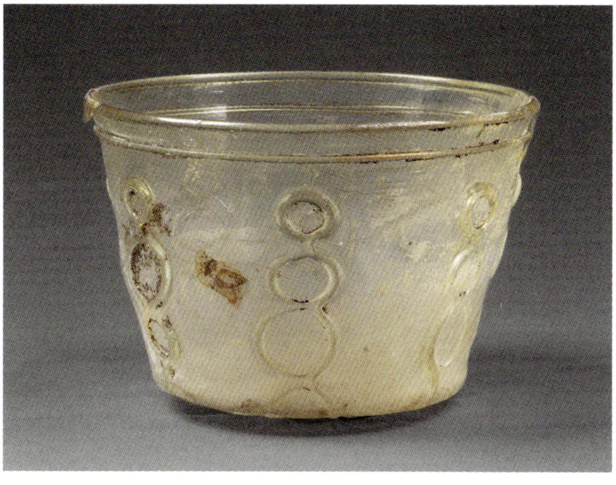

Figure 5 Glass lobed elliptical bowl, Tang dynasty. Found in silver jar, Hejiacun Hoard, Xi'an, Shaanxi province. Glass, height: 2.9 cm, diameter at lip: 5.5–5.9 cm.

Figure 6 Ink inscriptions of contents on the inside of the jar lid, Tang dynasty. Found in silver jar, Hejiacun Hoard, Xi'an, Shaanxi province, China. Silver jar with handle and lotus patterns.

Figure 7 Crystal cup, Tang dynasty. Found in silver jar, Hejiacun Hoard, Xi'an, Shaanxi province, China. Crystal, height: 7.9 cm, diameter at lip: 4.3 cm, diameter at bottom: 10.3 cm.

Both rock crystal and *liuli* belonged to the Seven Jewels of Buddhism and are always mentioned together, causing a semantic convergence between the two materials.[36] Buddhist Pure Lands were suffused with glittering treasures, which included crystal trees full of *liuli* leaves, or jeweled trees with crystal fruits and *liuli* flowers.[37] Tang poets, on the other hand, imagined crystal palaces under the sea for dragons or on the moon, imbuing rock crystal and *liuli* with aquatic and lunar associations.[38] Immortals slept upon glass pillows, while their abodes are furnished with crystal curtains and screens of mica. The eccentric Tang poet Li He (790–816) even goes beyond tactile and optical associations of the material to describe the synesthesia of a "sound of glass" (*bolisheng*) as the deities Xi and He whipped up the sun when driving the solar chariot across the sky.[39] In the Tang imagination, crystal and *liuli*-glass were shimmering, fiery, icy, liquescent, erotic, otherworldly, and unfathomable. When medieval subjects encountered such translucent materials, this endless overlaying of sensations challenged the limits of perception.

When peering into rock crystals and clear glass, viewers are frequently confronted with interpretive difficulties—these transparent objects remind us that we see things differently. At times, the optical quality of transparent vessels can sustain a form of visual trickery in Tang narratives. During the Zhenyuan period (785–805), a certain courtesan in Yangzhou called Hu Meier was well known for her inexplicable glass bottle.[40] The bottle had a thin neck and reflected light "brightly inside and out" (*neiwai yingche*). When objects were inserted into its belly, their sizes vastly diminished. At first coins were shrunk to the size of grains, then horses and donkeys were reduced to the size of flies, and finally ten carts full of cargo were turned into tiny crawling ants. In the end, Meier jumped into the bottle herself and, as the crowd jostled, the glass bottle shattered into pieces and everything disappeared. The name of the courtesan "Hu" (a generic Chinese term for foreigners from the western regions) and "Meier" (the enchanter) invokes a deep suspicion toward foreign bodies and objects, a common trope in Tang tales of the strange, yet the underlying source of deceit remains the glass bottle itself, a contraption that essentially functions as a camera obscura.[41]

Aside from swindlers in the marketplace, the instability of visual perception tied to transparent matter was also a marker of one's religious faith. The eminent Tang monk Daoxuan (596–667) once saw an eight-sided purple crystal that was constantly revealing images.[42] It was called the "Stone Shadow Image" (*shiyingxiang*) and was recorded as a "miraculous image" (*ruixiang*), a type of divine object that provided material and visual proof of the Buddhist dharma.[43] The stone was miraculous because the viewing experience of the crystal was fractured—inside the stone, some could see flying banners, while others saw mountains and forests, even previous lifetimes. Daoxuan himself could only see a nebulous image of a Buddha when he first approached the stone, but after repenting for seven days, he came back and saw a silver pagoda and a silver Buddha.[44] Unlike Hu Meier's deceptive glass bottle—an object of the marketplace—the crystal was sanctioned as a sacred object inside a Buddhist temple. It was rationalized as a "karmic mirror" that was later passed on to the Tang palace.[45] The viewing of this translucent stone quickly became an inspection of the self—an inquiry into one's karmic condition. The experience of transparent objects invites us to gaze inward, for it is our task to discern magic tricks from sacred revelations.

The fracturing of visual experience caused by rock crystal and glass led medieval subjects to see transparency as an inherently volatile state of existence. Translucent things appear unfathomable to us because they seem to encompass a wide range of formal contradictions. Viewers took the two substances to be simultaneously colorless and colorful, and substantial yet void and empty. In the poet Wei Yingwu's (737–792) odes to both materials, he plays with their aquatic associations and their ability to change colors in different environments.

Ode on Crystal
Reflecting things, it takes on their complexion's hue,
Enclosed void, it lacks outside and in.
I hold it up, turned to the luminous moon;
Translumined—I'm anxious lest it turn to water.

Ode on Glass
With form it is like frozen ice,
Without substance it blocks fine dust.
Against an ivory mat, it cannot be seen.
How should one take it towards a jade man?[46]

The odes demonstrate how transparent substances can only be perceived through other things in the environment. Clear glass and crystal are defined through material frames, such as the "fine dust" that settles upon glass, or the colors of objects that crystal reflects (*yingwu*). Though playful in tone, the poems reveal the profound interconnectedness between things—a Mahayana worldview that took force in the Tang period, which embraced the interpenetration of all phenomena.[47] Glass "has form" (*youse*), but is "without substance" (*wuwu*); crystal collapses notions of inside and outside (*wu biaoli*). Fearing how crystal or glass might revert to its original liquified state, Wei Yingwu sets out to show us how transparent matter is ultimately unstable.

TRANSPARENT RELIQUARIES

The phenomenological experience of glass and crystal was generative—visual instability became a prerequisite for divine transformations of matter. Anxieties about the perception of transparent materiality are yoked and translated into the experience of divine manifestations. In Sui-Tang China, transparency was coerced to ensure the religious efficacy of Buddhist relics, while the obtaining and production of glass and crystal objects serviced the display of imperial power. This is most vividly demonstrated by the imperially patronized relic burials of the Sui, in which the innermost container of relics was always small glass bottles, presumably crafted by palace workshops. Throughout the medieval period, there were various attempts to introduce glassblowing technology into China. During the Northern Wei (386–534), a Yuezhi merchant collected stones in the mountains and melted them in the capital to create five-colored *liuli*-glass. He also made a transparent traveling lodge for the emperor that could contain more than one hundred people.[48] A famous craftsman of Sogdian descent called He Chou, who worked for the Sui court, was said to have revived glass manufacturing in China by using "green ceramics" (*lüci*).[49] Archeological evidence shows that glass manufacturing was carried out in China by the Northern dynasties. Although glass vessels such as cups and bowls were still mainly imported, domestically made small glass bottles became the primary container for Buddhist relics by the sixth century.[50] The effect of transparency became an essential vehicle for visualizing sacred power.

Chinese Buddhist reliquaries followed Indic traditions, in which the relic of the Buddha is enclosed in layered containers made of materials from the Seven Jewels.[51] Precious jewels were also donated as devotional objects for the relics. For instance, small pieces of coral, pearls, rock crystal, gold, and silver are often found inside Gandharan reliquaries, and at times the innermost reliquary itself is made of rock crystal (fig. 8).[52] The use of glass bottles for the innermost container for Buddhist relics became widely practiced in East Asia by the eighth century.[53] The design of relic caches is commonly associated with Emperor Wen

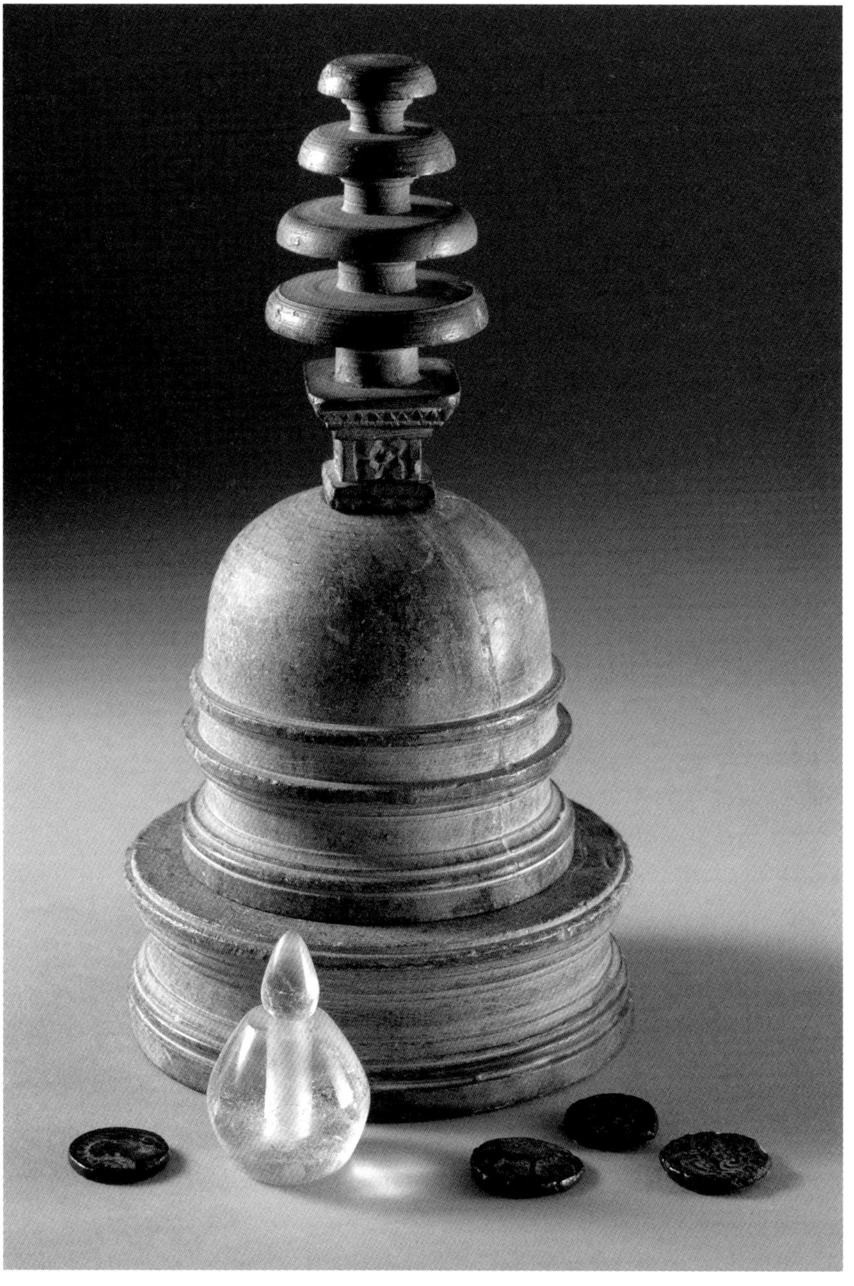

Figure 8 Reliquary set with pear-shaped rock-crystal reliquary with stopper inside, first century. Gandhara, Pakistan. Schist, rock crystal. 1887.0717.34–35 © The Trustees of the British Museum.

(541–604, r. 581–604) of the Sui dynasty (581–618), who distributed relics three times across his empire between 601 and 604.[54] This was a move to imitate the Mauryan ruler King Aśoka (r. 268–232 BCE), who famously distributed relics across his empire as a great patron of Buddhism.[55] Emperor Wen's edict required the preparation of a "seven-treasure box" (*qibaoxiang*). The relic is first placed inside a gold bottle, then a *liuli*-glass bottle, a bronze casket, and finally a stone casket.[56] Archeological findings, however, contradict the edict, revealing that the innermost container of reliquaries was usually a glass bottle instead of a golden one.[57] Miraculous events related to the distribution of relics were meticulously recorded by courtiers to showcase the emperor's support of Buddhism, and many of these events center upon the materiality of the reliquaries.[58]

Buddhist lore concerning light-emitting relics remained ubiquitous in medieval China, and the discovery and reburying of relics were often accompanied by extraordinary light glowing through temples or ancient pagodas or the gathering of multicolored clouds.[59] These divine signs are related to the concept of "spiritual resonance" (*ganying*), in which nature and objects would react to the appearance of a virtuous ruler or the power of the dharma.[60] A principal feature of the Sui miracles is that such optical events took place at the moment when the relic was about to enter the reliquary. These heavenly marvels are visually presented through the outermost container, which is usually a rectangular stone casket.[61]

The Sui took the reliquary materials seriously. Large boulders were all locally sourced, either sent in as tribute or miraculously dug out under the stupa where the relics were meant to be interred. The stones emitted light or glittered with different patterns, as if they were divinely prepared to be turned into containers for relics. Rectangular stone caskets with a truncated-pyramid-shaped lid (*luding fanghan*) were used as reliquary containers in China since the Northern Wei.[62] This type of container differs from Indic or Central Asian reliquaries that took the shape of a cylinder or a round lidded bowl.[63] The ruggedness of these hefty stone caskets directly contrasted with the small and delicate objects they contained. The recently excavated reliquary from the foundations of the Dazhuangyan Monastery in the Northern Qi (550–557) capital Ye epitomizes this juxtaposition between container and content. The sturdy casket was buried under the pagoda and contained a glass bottle, beads of agate, rock crystal, glass, amber, and chalcedony (figs. 9–10).[64] Ceramic jars were placed at the four corners of the stone casket, containing offerings such as jewelry and coins. The unpolished surface of the large stone casket is in direct contrast with the

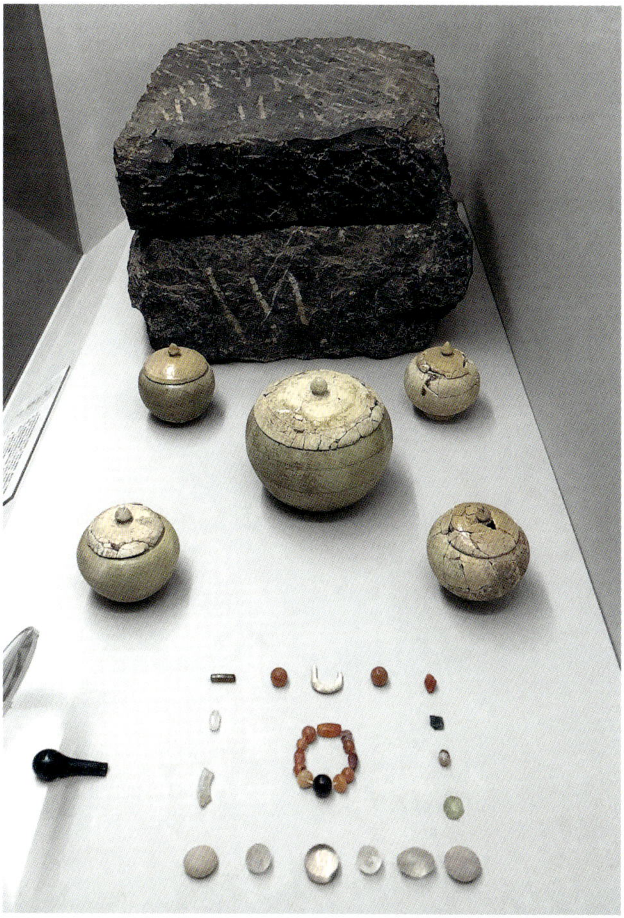

Figure 9 Reliquary set, 550–559. Hetaoyuan Dazhuangyan Monastery Pagoda No. 1, Yecheng, Hebei province, China. Photo: Anne Feng.

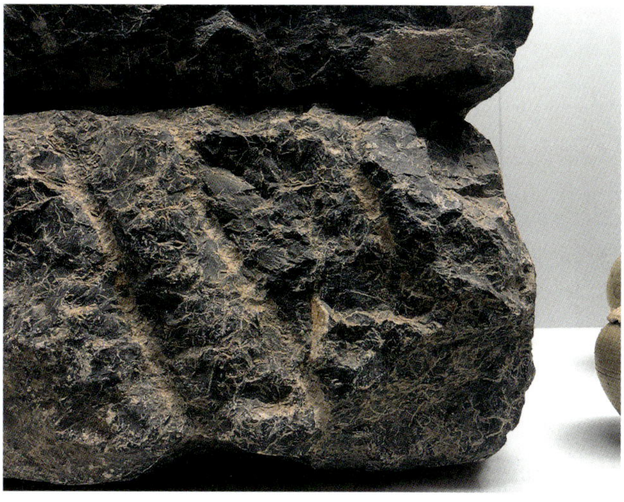

Figure 10 Detail of stone casket of above reliquary set. Photo: Anne Feng.

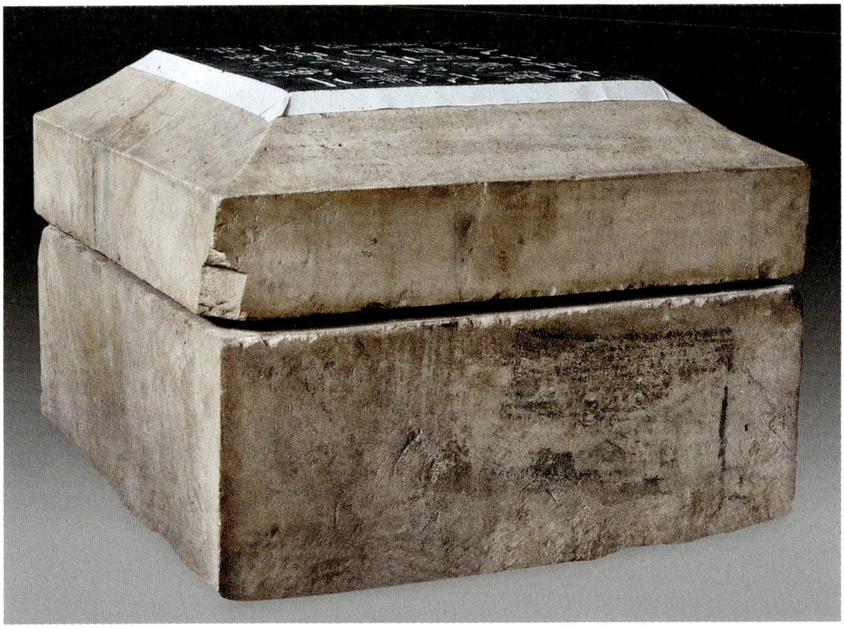

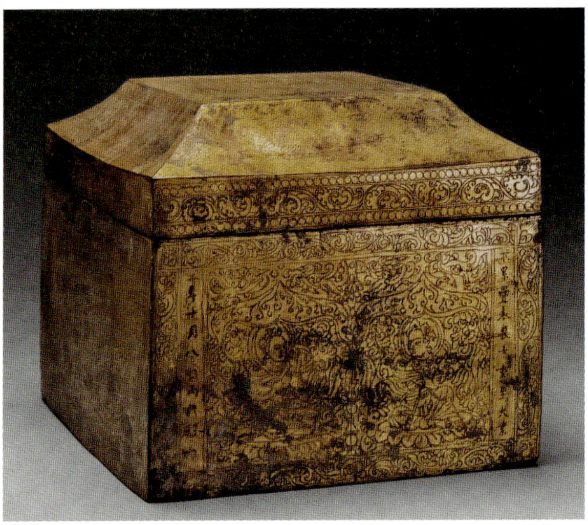

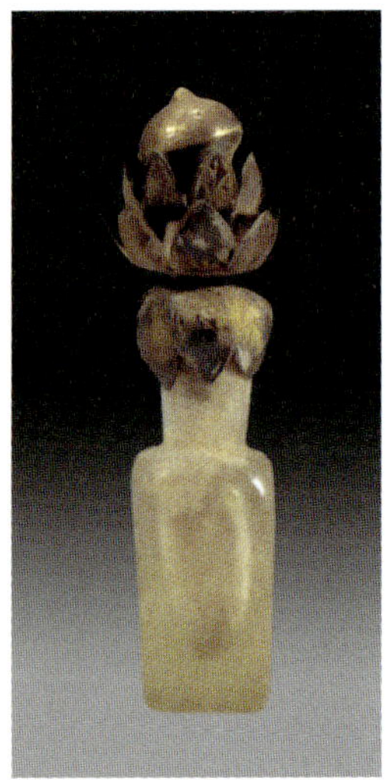

Figures 11–13 Stone casket (top), gilt casket (bottom left), and glass bottle (bottom right) of reliquary set from Jingzhi Monastery, 606. Dingzhou, Hebei province, China. © Dingzhou Museum.

twinkling jewels within it, but as we shall see, divine manifestations are imagined precisely through the collapse of such material distinctions.

The efficacy of the relic is regularly performed through the stone casket. A common trope is the opaque stone container becoming transparent, crystal-like, or turning directly into glass. One record claimed that on the twenty-sixth day of the third month in 604, at the Hongye Monastery in Youzhou, the luminous and transparent state of the casket marked a threshold moment for images to emerge from the stone container:

> When the stone casket was initially polished, its two sides were washed with water, and it was clear like a water mirror, with *its inside and outside interconnected*. Purple light and flames flared up and the stone became speckled like carnelian. It was sleek and shimmering and had *the luster of* liuli-*glass* . . . when the relic entered the casket, patterns appeared on the stone from dawn until dusk. [The patterns] seemed like images of bodhisattvas, which were iridescent and multicolored. [They] also seemed like a multitude of immortals. Between [the immortals] were birds, beasts, trees, and many uncommon beings. This was quite difficult to describe in detail.[65]

As the stone becomes translucent, the stability of its materiality begins to dissolve, simulating carnelian and then glass. Rather than containing substances of the Seven Jewels, the stone casket directly transforms into them. In this process, the interior and exterior of the vessel merge together. Like Wei Yingwu's ode that describes crystal as "without inside and outside," different layers within the casket become meshed within each other. Transparency dislodges the casket from its lithic materiality, preparing the stone to become a surface for images. The images that miraculously emerge from the "transparent" casket are bodhisattvas, immortals, birds, beasts, and paired trees—all of which are common motifs found within Sui reliquaries.

Recent discoveries of Sui-period reliquaries attest to this meticulous choreography of materials. A reliquary set from the year 606 was excavated from the Jingzhi Monastery in Dingzhou (figs. 11–13).[66] An inscription from the year 858 in the relic crypt describes that when the Sui reliquary was later unearthed in 849, the monks found a large stone casket, inside of which was a golden casket. The golden casket was full of the Seven Treasures, and it contained a silver pagoda, which had two glass bottles placed inside the cavity. The smaller bottle was white with a lotus flower-shaped silver cap, while the larger one was blue and crafted in the shape of a *hu*-jar. Both bottles were domestically crafted glassware.[67] The bottles were set within each other, and their color looked like "water turning into ice" (*shuise ningjie*).[68] The relic was first placed in a white glass bottle, a blue glass bottle, a gilded silver pagoda, a gilded bronze casket, and then a stone casket. There are no images on the stone casket, except for inscriptions on the lid (fig. 11), yet the bronze casket is entirely covered with images of flowers, birds, and immortal beings (fig. 12). The figures and patterns are incised onto the vessel, and on each side, there is a seated pair of bodhisattvas or protective deities. The gilded silver pagoda is crafted in a hexagonal shape, with a pair of doors on the front side. The doors are held together with a large lock with keys in place. The remaining five sides of the pagoda are decorated with floral patterns and flying apsaras.[69] This provides us new insight into the optical miracles of the Hongye reliquary—the opaque stone casket is actually described to transform into its inner contents. The inside of the layered casket is put on display upon its outer stone surface, while the material distinctions between the reliquary layers become entangled within each other.

This entanglement or fusion of different materials and layers is understood through the visual qualities of transparent glass. For example, a stone casket in Yanzhou turned into a series of different substances, from carnelian to jade. This transformative state of the casket was described in terms for talking about glass or crystal, for it was seen as an inversion of insides and outsides.

> When [the stone casket] was first polished, the body was of a dark material. When it was finished, it turned into carnelian, with a mixture of five colors. The patterns were iridescent. Inside it, white jade emerged, and its *inside and outside became connected*. It mirrored things like water. The surface and substance were clear and bright, and it reflected humans like a mirror.[70]

Notably, as the opaque stone casket turns transparent or "glass-like," it is in fact embodying the materiality of the innermost container of the relics—the small glass bottle (fig. 13). The distribution of the relics was a public affair that drew large congregations of clergy and laity to witness the event.[71] In the form of ash remains or bone fragments, the dull physicality of relics could only be translated as "divine stuff" through the performance of sensory miracles, such as the diffusion of mysterious fragrance, bright light, or heavenly music. In this process of translation, the containers were a crucial medium for visualizing the efficacy of relics in a highly public manner. Monks officiating the Sui relic interment would raise up the little bottle for the crowd to catch a glimpse of the relic.[72] Vivid descriptions tell of how the relics inside the small *liuli*-glass bottle would emit light and hover inside and outside the vessel.

In this sense, as the hefty stone casket becomes transparent, turning into glass or crystal, this transformation undoes its own opaque materiality as well as the layered nature of the nested containers. Instead of concealing relics, the layered containers are put on display in these optical miracles—a visual testimony of the existence and power of the relics inside. In other words, a container of relics is turned into an optical object. The surface of the Dazhuangyan Monastery reliquary stone casket from the Northern Qi appears to be purposefully jagged (see fig. 10). Compared to rectangular caskets from later periods that are finely polished, the rough surface of the lidded box exaggerates its lithic quality. Northern Qi masons, particularly around the capital Ye, were extremely skilled at stone carving, from the subtle detailing of bodhisattva ornamentation to the excessive use of openwork compositions.[73] The unfinished appearance of the casket must have been left in this state intentionally. Uneven cuts from where the stone has been hewn are still visible on the reliquary, forming an array of textures and crevasses. One cannot help but imagine patterns and images arising from the spontaneous cracks and protrusions of the stone surface. The "seeing-in" of the stone casket is to imagine it becoming "transparent"—to acquire a quality similar to the small rock crystal and glass beads inside it. One's ability to see transparency here transforms the mundane stone vessel into an efficacious Buddhist reliquary. This glass-like phase becomes a necessary procedure in this divine transformation, wherein an object's qualities unravel and new possibilities for transformation are opened up.

TRANSPARENCY AND PICTORIAL SPACE

The stone surface of the reliquary casket is reimagined through these miraculous optical effects. The types of images that arise from stone boxes in these moments of transparency closely correlate with the actual iconography of some stone containers. It is difficult to say if this seeing-in process inspired new iconography, or if new imagery redefined the conceptual surface of stone caskets. There was a system installed by the Sui court to record imagery that emerged during relic miracles; for example, the various bodhisattvas, immortals, and trees that emerged from the Hongye Monastery relic casket were "documented in the form of pictures and sent to the court."[74] New pictorial formulae at that time were

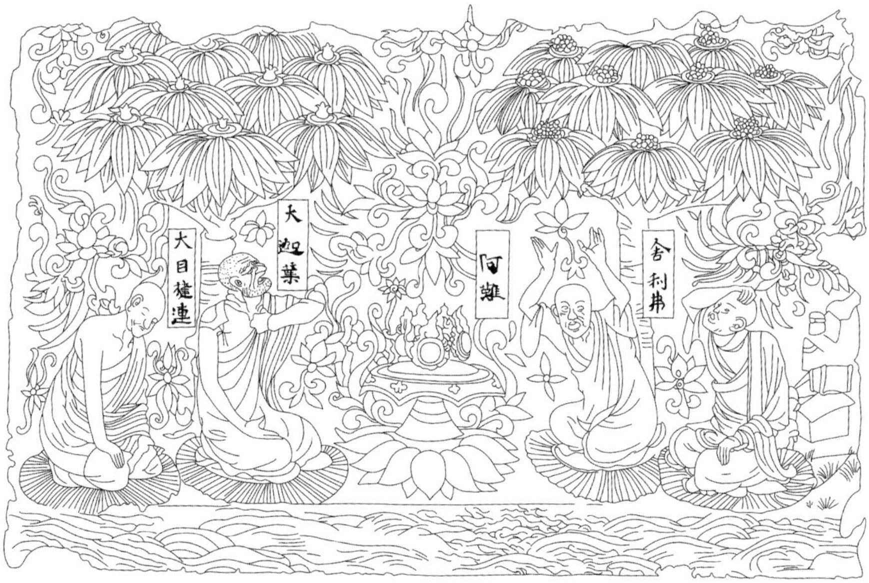

Figure 14 Drawing of casket carvings of the Shende Monastery reliquary stone casket. Line drawings by Li Jiayue, after Yang Xiaojun, Kaogu yu wenwu (Archeology and Cultural Relics), no. 5 (2015): 80–87.

intertwined with these optical events that imagined the putative transparency of stone. Wu Hung has argued that in the sixth century, new pictorial formulae that embraced binary structures and "front-and-back" compositions created a different understanding of pictorial space in Chinese art history, in which pictorial surfaces are imagined to become "transparent." Mausoleum inscriptions that are written in reverse prompt viewers to imagine opaque stone surfaces turning "transparent," thus embodying the viewpoint of the deceased from the netherworld.[75] Imaginations of transparency were ways to fathom the world beyond. By the early seventh century, the influx of transparent materials, such as rock crystal and glass, allowed for a new turn in the development of pictorial space.

A stone casket that was buried in 604 was found at the Shende Monastery in Yaozhou.[76] Inside the casket there was a gilded bronze box that contained three relics, ashes, Sassanian coins, gold and silver bracelets, a round copper box that contained human hair, a rectangular gilded bronze box that contained a green glass bottle, and a bronze bottle that contained ash remains.[77] The outer surface of the large container is entirely covered with incised images (fig. 14). Similar to images that emerged from our previous examples, each side of the casket has a pair of trees, and among the trees are four disciples of the Buddha, four lokapalas, and two deva kings.[78] At the bottom rim of each side, water is depicted by thin, wavy lines. This composition is very similar to a recorded optical miracle performed by a stone casket at Daxingguo Monastery, in which four pairs of sala trees appeared on the four outer sides of the stone casket. There were also water patterns under the trees, and amid the trees there was one Buddha, three bodhisattvas, one nun, one bird, and three flowers.[79] Another casket, from the Fengquan Monastery in Qizhou, also had paired trees and images of birds, beasts, dragons, and elephants emerging within the stone container.[80] Notably, the textual records describe how the foundation stone of the Fengquan casket "gradually turned crystal-like," which may be related to the water patterns at the bottom of the composition.[81]

Four disciples of the Buddha, Śāriputra, Ānanda, Mahākāśyapa, and Maudgalyayana, are shown on the north (frontal) side of the Shende Monastery casket. All the disciples display gestures of grief: Mahākāśyapa is beating his chest with his mouth open, while Ānanda throws his hands in the air. Between the two monks is a lotus stand with five mani-jewels on top of it. The gestures of grief performed by the disciples usually relate to the Buddha's parinirvāṇa, in which disciples respond to the passing of their spiritual master in different forms of anguish. The image program of the reliquary harkens back to the Buddha's nirvana.[82] The flaming jewels in the middle serve as a symbolic image related to the body of the Buddha.[83] On the other three sides of the casket, an incense burner-like object on a lotus pedestal can be found in the middle of the compositions. Yang Xiaojun identifies the central object placed between two pairs of lokapalas and two deva kings as a "relic container" (*sheli rongqi*).[84] If this identification is correct, we may say that the image program of the stone container is designed to be self-reflexive—it is a relic container displaying the images of relic containers. We can also say that the image program is designed to make the stone container appear transparent—similar to the caskets that have turned into glass or crystal. As the "relic container" occupies the central position of each side of the casket, the composition gives the impression that we are *looking through* the "transparent" stone box *into* the core of the reliquary. The visual effect replays the inversion of outside/inside, collapsing the division between surface and content. In short, imagining the stone box becoming transparent and taking the surface as a pictorial space becomes the same process.

This new imagination of pictorial space as "transparent" is taken to a new level by the seventh century, with great advancements in sophisticated perspective and new attention to surface textures in painting. This new awareness can be traced in the transparent bowl gently held in the palm of the Dunhuang bodhisattva (see fig. 1). Through the use of wash and ink outlines, painters of the Western Pure

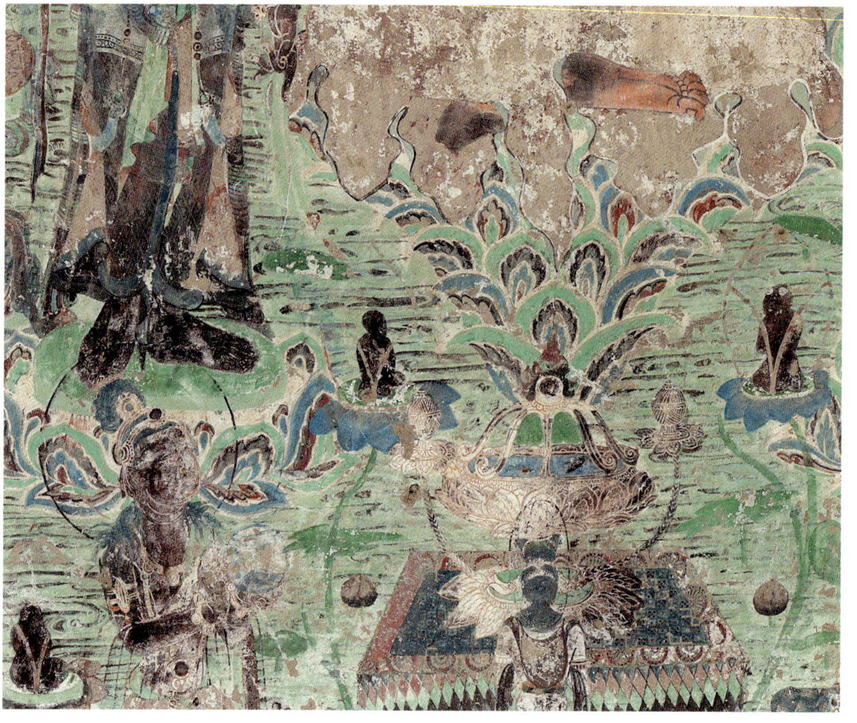

Figure 15 Detail of the Western Pure Land transformation tableau, Tang dynasty. South wall, Cave 220 (642–662), Mogao Grottoes, Dunhuang, Gansu province, China. © Dunhuang Academy.

Land of Amitābha Buddha at Dunhuang suddenly became skilled at depicting transparent things, from halos, vessels, and drapery, to lotus buds that contain newborn souls. Palms and fingers can be seen through glass bowls, while bodies are revealed behind gossamer silks (fig. 15). Halos can maintain integrity without blocking other bodies or interfering with the larger composition. Because of transparency, we now know the lotus bud is pregnant with a newborn soul. At the same time, Tang painters celebrated kaleidoscopic effects, as vividly portrayed by the excessively colorful textile draped over the offering table, patched and woven together by alternating hues and patterns. When viewers imagine painting surfaces as transparent, they embrace the unstable and transformative capacities of pictorial space. In a similar way, painters have the power to dislodge and reassemble materials, textures, and colors. The goal of a good painter is to transform a wall or a stretch of silk into a miraculous surface, summoning immortals and Buddhas, or delineating carnelian or bodies of water.

CONCLUSION

Optical miracles are often related to relics, but the stone caskets discussed here rarely start to emit light and images directly. Solid and heavy, they must first go through a process of becoming transparent. The prerequisite for metamorphosis is the moment of “unravelling.” Transparency here is no longer just an optical quality: to be translucent—to forego stable boundaries and qualities—is to be released from material confinement. It is when matter is dislodged that images, colors, and textures reassemble and transform into something new. The allure of transparency, then, is its power to transform things. New painting modes emerged as pictorial space was understood as being transparent. Exotic glass cups and crystal bowls were deeply intertwined with such imagination in art and representation.

NOTES

1. Dunhuang yanjiuyuan, *Dunhuang shiku neirong zonglu* [Catalogue of Dunhuang cave content] (Beijing: Wenwu chubanshe, 1996), 163–64.
2. Zhao Yong, “Lun Weijin zhi Songyuan shiqi fojiao yicun zhong de boli rongqi” [Glassware in Buddhist remains from the Wei-Jin to the Song-Yuan period], *Gudai shi yu wenwu yanjiu* 135, no. 10 (2014): 44–65.
3. This chapter focuses on the medieval period in China. For the introduction of European glass technology to late-imperial China, see Lihong Liu, “Vitreous Views: Materiality and Mediality of Glass in Qing China through a Transcultural Prism,” *Getty Research Journal* 8 (2016): 17–38.
4. For industrial glassmaking and new urban spaces in the Victorian period, see Isobel Armstrong, *Victorian Glassworlds: Glass Culture and the Imagination, 1830–1880* (Oxford: Oxford University Press, 2008), 37–56, 167–203.
5. Galvez looks at medieval lapidary texts showing how the experience of clear crystal produces heterogeneous experiences, which produce effects of illegibility. Marisa Galvez, “Dark Transparencies: Crystal Poetics in Medieval Texts and Beyond,” *Philological Quarterly* 93, no. 1 (2014): 15–42.
6. Michael Ann Holly, “Notes from the Field,” *The Art Bulletin* 95 (March 2013): 15.
7. Patrick R. Crowley, “Crystalline Aesthetics and the Classical Concept of the Medium,” *West 86th: A Journal of Decorative Arts, Design History, and Material Culture* 23, no. 2 (2016): 220.
8. Bilge Sayim and Patrick Cavanagh, “The Art of Transparency,” *i-Perception (London)* 2, no. 7 (2011): 679–96.
9. Francesca Dell’Acqua Boyvadaoğlu, “Between Nature and Artifice: ‘Transparent Streams of New Liquid,’” *RES: Anthropology and aesthetics*, no. 53/54 (2008): 93–103.
10. Crowley discusses the history of rock crystal in Pliny the Elder’s *Natural History*; see Crowley, “Crystalline Aesthetics,” 221–25. For an overview of glass manufacturing in the ancient world and its transmission to East Asia, see Dedo Von Kerssenbrock-Krosigk, “The Meaning of Glass:

Case Studies from Mesopotamia to Rome," *West 86th: A Journal of Decorative Arts, Design History, and Material Culture* 26, no. 1 (2019): 38–60; William Mierse, "The Significance of the Central Asian Objects in the Shōsōin for Understanding the International Art Trade in the Seventh and Eighth Centuries," *Sino-Platonic Papers* 267 (March 2017): 8–15.

11. Schafer has three entries for "rock-crystal," "glass," and "fire orbs" in his chapter on jewels. Edward H. Schafer, *The Golden Peaches of Samarkand: A Study of T'ang Exotics* (Berkeley: University of California Press, 1985), 227–28, 235–39.

12. See *Taishō shinshū daizōkyō*, ed. Takakusu Junjirō and Watanabe Kaigyoku (Tokyo: Taishō issaikyō kankōkai, 1924–1932) (hereafter *T.*). *Guang hongming ji* [Expanded collection of the propagation and elucidation of Buddhism], Daoxuan (596–667), *T.* 2103, 52: 217c28; *Xu gaoseng zhuan* [Continued biographies of eminent monks], comp. Daoxuan (596–667), *T.* 50, 2060. *T.* 2060, 50: 674a04; *T.* 2103, 52: 214b28.

13. Crowley, "Crystalline Aesthetics," 221.

14. James E. Brady and Keith M. Prufer, "Caves and Crystalmancy: Evidence for the Use of Crystals in Ancient Maya Religion," *Journal of Anthropological Research* 55, no. 1 (1999): 129–44.

15. Carolingian engraved crystals were designed to take advantage of the material's transparency. Generva Kornbluth, "Active Optics: Carolingian Rock Crystal on Medieval Reliquaries," *Different Visions: A Journal of New Perspectives on Medieval Art*, no. 4 (January 2014): 14; Karen Overbey, "Seeing through Stone: Materiality and Place in a Medieval Scottish Pendant Reliquary," *RES: Anthropology and aesthetics*, 65/66 (2014/2015): 232–58.

16. Schafer, *The Golden Peaches of Samarkand*, 227–28.

17. *Hou Han shu* [Book of the later Han], complied by Fan Ye (398–446) (Beijing: Zhonghua shuju, 1965), 2910. Pang Naiming, "Yizhen yihuan Daqinguo: gudai Zhongguo de Luoma diguo xingxiang" [True and imaginary Daqin empire: image of ancient Rome in China], *Shijie lishi*, no. 5 (2017): 141–55. Interestingly, Herodotus (484–425 BCE) and Diodorus Siculus (91–30 BCE) describe how Ethiopians created hollow pillars to encase their dead by gypsum or glass; see Crowley, "Crystalline Aesthetics," 235.

18. Writing on ancient rock crystal in China is usually found in catalogues for precious stones. Most rock crystal are found in elite tombs or Buddhist relic crypts; this information appears in individual archeological reports. Song Haiyang, "Meishi jiazuzhong de shuijing yu manao" [Rock crystal and agate in precious stones], *Shoucangjia*, no. 7 (2010): 73–78. *Zhongguo gudai shuijing manao qi: liushi cangyu (er)* [Rock crystal and agate vessels in ancient China: jade collection of Mr. Liu (II)], ed. Pan Minggao (Shanghai: Shanghai shuhua chubanshe, 2012), 10–18; Shanxi sheng kaogu yanjiusuo, *Famensi kaogu fajue baogao* [Report of archaeological excavation at Famen Temple] (Beijing: Wenwu chubanshe, 2007), 244–52.

19. Berthold Laufer translates rock crystal (*shuijing*) as "water essence," Schafer names rock crystal "germ [or sperm, or essence] of water," Needham mentions that at times rock crystal is called *huojing* or "fire essence" when referring to burning lenses. See Berthold Laufer, "Optical Lenses," *T'oung Pao* 16, no. 2 (1919): 190; Schafer, *Golden Peaches*, 227; Joseph Needham, *Science and Civilization in China*, vol. 4, part 1 (Cambridge: Cambridge University Press, 2004), 100.

20. Lin Meicun, "Tang wude ernian jibinguo gongpin kao—jianlun xian hejiacun tangdai jiaocang yuanwei daminggong qionglinku huangjia baozang" [Research on tribute goods from Jibin in the second year of the Wude reign—with a discussion on how the Hejiacun hoard originally belonged to the royal Qionglin treasury in the Daming palace], *Kaogu yu wenwu*, no. 6 (2017): 98.

21. Burning lenses are called *yangsui*, *huosui*, *huoji*, or *huozhu*. See Chen Cangqi (681–757), *Bencao* *shiyi jishi* [Annotated edition of notes on Materia Medica], ed. Shang Zhijun (Hefei: Anhui kexue jishu chubanshe, 2003), 24; Laufer, "Optical Lenses," 179–81; Needham, *Science and Civilization*, 111–18; Schafer, *Golden Peaches*, 237–39.

22. Wang Pu (922–982), *Tang huiyao* [Institutional history of the Tang dynasty] (Shanghai: shangwu yinshu guan, 1935), 1751; Laufer, "Optical Lenses," 13.

23. The two orbs were first identified as the "Jewel of Suihou" (*Suihou zhi qiu*) by Zhang Enxian based on the term "*suiqiu*" from the unearthed inventory. Recently Huo Wei and Zhu Detao argued that this term refers not to the crystal orbs, but to six gilt-silver esoteric armlets. Zhang Enxian, "Suiqiu yu Suihou zhizhu" [Suiqiu and the jewel of Suihou], *Wenbo*, no. 4 (1993): 49–51; Huo Wei and Zhu Detao, "Famensi digong chutu 'suiqiu' yu sheli yimai zhidu" ["Suiqiu" excavated from the underground crypt of the Famen monastery and relic burial systems], *Wenwu*, no. 2 (2017): 69–76.

24. Anne N. Feng, "Translumined: Rock-Crystal Orbs of the Famen Monastery," in *Chinese Optics: Artful Looking* (Cambridge, MA: Harvard University, forthcoming).

25. In *Bencao shiyi*, Chen Cangqi lists *boli* and *liuli* in two separate entries. *Boli* is described as "thousand-year ice" that grows from the earth and is used as burning lenses, while *liuli* is part of the Seven Jewels of Buddhism and is related to carnelian. For philological discussions on glass and the term *liuli*, see Chen Cangqi, *Bencao shiyi jishi*, 24; Laufer, "Optical Lenses," 179–87; Needham, *Science and Civilization*, 100–111; Schafer, *Golden Peaches*, 227, 235–37. Yu Xin, "Zhonggu Zhongguo fojiao yili yu yishu zhong de liuli" [*Liuli* in Buddhist ritual and art in medieval China], *Fudan Journal* (Social Sciences), no. 6 (2018): 86–87.

26. Cecilia Braghin, "Polychrome and Monochrome Glass of the Warring States and Han Periods," in *Chinese Glass: Archaeological Studies on the Uses and Social Context of Glass Artefacts from the Warring States to the Northern Song Period (Fifth Century B.C. to Twelfth Century A.D.)*, ed. Cecilia Braghin, Orientalia Venetiana, no. 14. (Florence: Leo S. Olschki, 2002), 2–43; Inagaki Hajime, "Ancient Glass in China," in *Kodai garasu* [Ancient glass] ([Shigaraki-cho?]: Miho Museum, 2001), 185–98.

27. See An Jiayao, "*Zhongguo de zaoqi boli qimin*" [Early glass vessels in China], *Kaogu xuebao*, no. 4 (1984): 414–23; An Jiayao, "Glass Vessels and Ornaments of the Wei, Jin and Northern and Southern Dynasties Periods," in *Chinese Glass: Archaeological Studies on the Uses and Social Context of Glass Artefacts from the Warring States to the Northern Song Period (Fifth Century B.C. to Twelfth Century A.D.)*, Orientalia Venetiana, no. 14 (Firenze: Leo S. Olschki, 2002), 45–70; An Jiayao, *Boli qi shihua* [History of glass vessels] (Beijing: shehui kexue wenxian chubanshe, 2011), 69–86; An Jiayao, "The Art of Glass Along the Silk Road," in James C. Y. Watt, Harper Watt, Prudence Oliver Harper, *China: Dawn of a Golden Age, 200–750 AD* (New York: Metropolitan Museum of Art; New Haven: Yale University Press, 2004), 57–66.

28. There are different colors of crystal and glass, which might not seem as "clear" to the modern eye.

29. Yu Xin, "Zhonggu Zhonggu fojiao yili," 87; Lin Meicun, "Tang wude ernian jibinguo gongpin kao," 98.

30. There are also multiple theories concerning the Chinese term for lapis lazuli. In modern Chinese, lapis lazuli is called "*qingjin shi*." Schafer argues that lapis lazuli was called *sese* in medieval China, while Laufer believes that the Chinese term *sese* comes from an unspecified Persian or Sogdian word. Laufer also believes that *liuli*, *boli*, and *biliuli* are different materials, and *liuli* refers to beryl or lapis lazuli. Yu Xin follows Laufer on this issue. Recently, Pu Zhongyuan argues that the word *sese* denotes blue-colored gemstones such as sapphire, and is related to an Arabic term *jaza'*. However, in Arabic "*el jaza'*" is connected to anxiety and restlessness.

In Persian lapis lazuli is called *lajvard*. According to *A Comprehensive Persian-English Dictionary*, the Persian word *jash* denotes a "a kind of blue bead made of glass, in color approaching to that of the turquoise." The origins of the Chinese term *sese* remains unclear, and philologists do not know if it specifically refers to lapis lazuli. It is true that some English translations of Buddhist sutras convert the Chinese "*liuli*" into "lapis lazuli." For example, in the *Princeton Dictionary of Buddhism*, Bhaiṣajyaguru, the Medicine Buddha, is called the *liuli guang rulai*, or "Tathāgata of Lapis-Lazuli Light." İkbal Zeynep Dursunoğlu and Sylvia Wu helped me with the Persian and Arabic terms. Schafer, *Golden Peaches*, 230–34; Pu Zhongyuan, "*Tang wudai sichou zhilu shang de sese yu shuijing*" [Sapphire and crystal on the Silk Road in the Tang and the Five dynasties], *Longdong xueyuan xuebao (shehui kexue ban)* 15, no. 2 (2004): 59–61; Berthold Laufer, *Jade: A Study in Chinese Archaeology and Religion* (Chicago: The Field Museum of Natural History, 1912), 110–12; Yu Xin, "Zhonggu Zhonggu fojiao yili," 87; Berthold Laufer, *Sino-Iranica; Chinese Contributions to the History of Civilization in Ancient Iran, with Special Reference to the History of Cultivated Plants and Products* (New York: Kraus Reprint, 1967), 516; Robert E. Buswell Jr. and Donald S. Lopez Jr., *The Princeton Dictionary of Buddhism* (Princeton: Princeton University Press, 2013), 108–9, F. Steingass, John Richardson, and Francis Johnson, *A Comprehensive Persian-English Dictionary, including the Arabic Words and Phrases to Be Met with in Persian Literature* (London: Routledge & K. Paul, 1892), 363.

31. Ge Hong (283–343), *Baopuzi* [Master who embraces simplicity] (Beijing: Zhonghua shuju, 1980), 22; An Jiayao, "Glass Vessels," *Chinese Glass*, 46.

32. East Asian glass contained a high percentage of barium lead in its chemical composition, while Western glass was soda-lime based. Gan Fuxi, "The Silk Road and Ancient Chinese Glass," in Robert H. Brill and Tian Shouyun, *Ancient Glass Research Along the Silk Road* (Singapore: World Scientific Publishing Company, 2009), 80–86.

33. In a similar fashion, rock crystal (*crystallus*) and glass (*vitreum*) were also used almost interchangeably in ancient Rome; see Crowley, "Crystalline Aesthetics," 230.

34. Shanxi lishi bowuguan, Beijing daxue kaogu wen boxueyuan, Beijing daxue zhendan gudaiwenming yanjiu zhongxin, *Huawu datang chun: hejiacun yibao jingcui* [Flower dances of the great Tang spring: selections from the Hejiacun hoard] (Beijing: Wenwu chubanshe, 2003), 97, 101, 214–15.

35. Ink inscriptions on the lid of a silver jar have "one *liuli* cup and one *liuli* bowl" (*liuli beiwan geyi*) listed among its contents, yet the jar yielded one crystal cup (*shuijing baqu changbei*) and one glass bowl (*tuhuan wen boliwan*). Lin Meicun argues that the vessels are related to a Gandharan emissary to the Tang court in 619; see Lin Meicun, "Tang wude ernian jibinguo gongpin kao," 96–99.

36. The *Amitabha Sutra* lists gold, silver, *liuli* (glass), *boli* (crystal), mother of pearl, red coral, and agate, while the *Lotus Sutra* lists gold, silver, *liuli*, mother-of-pearl, agate, pearls, and *meigui* (powdered crystal). Xuanzang (602–664) provides phonetic translations of Sanskrit terms, listing gold (*jin*), silver (*yin*), beryl (Chi: *feiliuli*, Skt: *vaiḍūrya*), rock crystal (Chi: *podijia*, Skt: *sphaṭka*), rubies/red pearls (Chi: *chizhenzhu*), coral/pearl-shell (Chi: *mousuoluojielapo*, Skt: *musāragalva*), carnelian/agate (Chi: *shimojielapo*, Skt: *aśmagarbha*). *Foshuo amituojing* (Skt. *Sukhāvatīvyūhasūtra*) [Amitabha Sūtra], trans. Kumārajīva (343–413), *T.* 366, 12: 347a3; *Chengzan jingtu fo sheshou jing* [Sūtra on praises of the pure land with Buddhas' protection and reception], Xuanzang (602–664), *T.* 367, 12: 349a2–4; Yu Xin, "Zhonggu Zhonggu fojiao yili," 86–87; Lin Meicun, "Zhubao yizhu Zhong de zhongwai wenhua jiaoliu" [Art of gemstones and cultural exchange between China and foreign regions], *Kaogu yu wenwu*, no. 1 (2014): 80.

37. *Foshuo wuliangshou jing* (Skt. Sukhāvatī-vyūhaḥ-sūtra), trans. Saṃghavarman (active third century), *T.* 360, 12: 270c10–11.

38. Schafer, *Golden Peaches*, 227–28, 235–36; Chen Yiming, "Shuijing ruyi yulian huan—Cong tangshi yushi yuci kan wailai wenming (xu)" [Rock crystal scepters and jade bracelets—a view of foreign culture through the use of precious gemstone vocabulary in Tang poetry], *Yuwen xuekan*, no. 1 (2011): 110–11, 121.

39. From Li He's poem "The King of Qin Drinks Wine." For an English translation of Li He's poem, see Li He, *The Collected Poems of Li He*, trans. J. D. Frodsham (New York: New York Review Books, 2016), 106–7; Li Yongping and Wang Tianjue, "Li He shige yu Tangdai wailai wenming" [Poems by Li He and foreign culture in the Tang dynasty], *Shanxi shifan daxue xuebao (zhexue shehui kexue ban)* 40, no. 2 (March 2011): 64–70.

40. *Taiping guangji xuan* [Selections from the extensive records of the Taiping era], vol. 1, ed. Wang Rushou, Yu Runze, Zhao Jiong, and Qian Qinlai (Jinan: qilu shushe, 1980), 133. Yangzhou was a major port city and trade center for foreign goods by the eighth century; Schafer, *Golden Peaches*, 17–19.

41. For attitudes toward foreigners in Tang literature, see Schafer, *Golden Peaches*, 22–25; Alexei Kamran Ditter, Jessey Choo, and Sarah M. Allen eds., *Tales from Tang Dynasty China* (Indianapolis: Hackett Publishing Company, Inc., 2017), 29.

42. Natural quartz usually forms a six-sided prism instead of being eight-sided. The odd shape of the crystal is probably related to its supernatural quality. Pu Xiaofei helped me identify this feature in quartz. See reference to the monk Daoxuan in *Ji shenzhou sanbao gantong lu* [Collected records of the spiritual resonances and three jewels in China], n42: LC "comp." Daoxuan (596–667), *T.* 2106, 52: 421b4–24.

43. For *ruixiang* in Buddhism in the seventh century, see Koichi Shinohara, "Changing Roles for Miraculous Images in Medieval Chinese Buddhism: A Study of the Miracle Image Section in Daoxuan's 'Collected Records,'" in *Images, Miracles, and Authority in Asian Religious Traditions*, ed. Richard H. Davis (Boulder: Westview Press, 1998), 141–88.

44. *T.* 2106, 52: 421b18–19.

45. A karmic mirror shows the past deeds of a person. Representations of karmic mirrors are often found in images of the Ten Kings of Hell in the Tang period. See Stephen F. Teiser, *The Scripture on the Ten Kings and the Making of Purgatory in Medieval Chinese Buddhism*, Studies in East Asian Buddhism, no. 9 (Honolulu: University of Hawai'i Press, 1994), 33.

46. Wei Yingwu (737–791), *Wei yingwu ji jiaozhu* [Annotated collection of Wei Yingwu's writings], ed. Tao Min and Wang Yousheng (Shanghai: Shanghai guji chubanshe, 2011), 491. Schafer, translated Wei Yingwu's poem on crystal, see Schafer, *Golden Peaches*, 228.

47. This proponent of Mahayana cosmology is central to the *Flower Garland Sutra* (S. *Avataṃsaka sutra*) *T.* 279, 10, which was translated into Chinese by Śikṣānanda (652–710) in 699.

48. Wei Shou (507–572), *Weishu* [Book of the Wei] (Beijing: Zhonghua shuju, 1975), 2275. An Jiayao, "The Art of Glass Along the Silk Road," in *China: Dawn of a Golden Age*, 62; An Jiayao, "Glass Vessels," *Chinese Glass*, 65–66.

49. Some believe this record refers to the making of green tile glazes for buildings, but others believe this is related to glassmaking. Several pieces of Sui glassware were tinted with a green color. Wei Zheng (580–643), *Suishu* [Book of the Sui] (Beijing: Zhonghua shuju, 1973), 1596; An Jiayao, "The Art of Glass Along the Silk Road," in *China: Dawn of a Golden Age*, 65.

50. Shen Hsueh-man, "Luxury or Necessity: Glassware in Sarīra Relic Pagodas of the Tang and Northern Song Periods," in *Chinese Glass*, 75–76.

51. Shen Hsueh-man, "Luxury or Necessity," in *Chinese Glass*, 79.
52. David Jongeward, et al., *Gandharan Buddhist Reliquaries*, Ganharan studies, vol. 1 (Seattle: Early Buddhist Manuscripts Project, 2012), 44–45, 87–90.
53. Akiko Walley, "Instant Bliss: Enactment of the Miraculous Appearance of Relics in the Hōryūji Nested Reliquary Set," *Ars Orientalis* 46 (2016): 150–51.
54. You Ziyong, "Suiwendi Renshou ban tianxia sheli kao" [Notes on Emperor Wen of the Sui's distribution of relics in the Renshou years], *Shijie zongjiao yanjiu*, no. 1 (2003): 24–30. Walley, "Instant Bliss," 153.
55. Yu Wei, *Shengwu zhizao yu zhonggu Zhongguo fojiao sheli gongyang* [The creation of sacred objects and the adoration of Buddhist relics in medieval China] (Beijing: Wenwu chubanshe, 2018), 110.
56. *T.* 2103, 52: 213c2, 18–22.
57. Shen Hsueh-man, "Luxury or Necessity," in *Chinese Glass*, 75–76.
58. Yu Wei, "*Shengwu zhizao*," 111–16; Yan Yaozhong, "Zongshuo Suiwen di guangjian fota de yiyi" [The meaning of pagoda construction by Emperor Wen of the Sui], *Tang yanjiu* 20 (2014): 107–18. Most descriptions of Sui period reliquary caskets in this article are from Wang Shao's *Sheli ganying ji* [Record of numinous responses from relics], in *Guang hongming ji* [Expanded collection of the propagation and elucidation of Buddhism], Daoxuan (596–667). *T.* 2103, 52.
59. Eugene Y. Wang, "Of the True Body: The Famen Monastery Relics and Corporeal Transformation in Tang Imperial Culture," in *Body and Face in Chinese Visual Culture*, ed. Wu Hung and Katherine R. Tsiang, Harvard East Asian Monographs (Cambridge: Harvard University Asia Center, 2005), 83–86.

60. For the theory of *ganying* in medieval Buddhism, see Wu Hung, "Rethinking Liu Sahe: The Creation of a Buddhist Saint and the Invention of a 'Miraculous Image,'" *Orientations* 27, no. 10 (November 1996), 32–43.
61. Rectangular stone caskets with a truncated pyramid-shaped top (*luding fanghan*) were first used in the Northern Wei period in the fifth century, and they became standardized by the Sui dynasty. Yu Wei, "Shengwu zhizao," 59–69, 89–95.
62. Yang Hong, "Zhongguo Suitang shiqi fojiao sheli rongqi" [Relic containers of the Sui and Tang period in China], *Zhongguo lishi wenwu*, no. 4 (2004): 22–35.
63. Yu Wei, "Shengwu zhizao," 17–58.
64. Zhongguo shehui kexue yuan kaogu yanjiusuo, Hebei sheng wenwu yanjiusuo, and Yecheng kaogudui, "Hebei Linzhang yecheng yizhi hetaoyuan yihao jianzhu jizhi fajue baogao" [Excavation report of the foundations of the Hetaoyuan yihao jianzhu in Linzhang, Hebei], *Kaogu xuebao*, no. 4 (2016): 563–91.
65. *T.* 2103, 52: 219b12–19.
66. There are five sets of reliquary deposits at the Jingzhi Monastery, dated to the years 453, 606, 858, 889, and 977. Sonya S. Lee, *Surviving Nirvana: Death of the Buddha in Chinese Visual Culture* (Hong Kong: Hong Kong University Press, 2010), 211–17; Zhejiang sheng bowuguan and Dingzhou shi bowuguan, eds., *Xinfang suwai: Dingzhou jingzhi jingzhong fota digong wenwu* [Mind beyond the mundane world: the Buddhist pagoda and crypt at Jingzhi Jingzhong in Dinzhou], (Beijing: Zhongguo shuju, 2014), 16–17.
67. *Xinfang suwai*, 17.
68. *Xinfang suwai*, 119.
69. *Xinfang suwai*, 69.

70. *T.* 2103, 52: 217c26–29.
71. Yu Wei, "Shengwu zhizao," 109.
72. *T.* 2103, 52: 214b03–05.
73. Zhongguo shehui kexue yuan kaogu yanjiusuo and Hebeisheng wenwu jianjiusuo, eds., *Yecheng Beiwuzhuang chutu fojiao zaoxiang* [Buddhist sculptures excavated from Beiwuzhuang, Yecheng], (Beijing: kexue chubanshe, 2019), 232–42.
74. *T.* 2103, 52: 219b19–20.
75. Wu Hung, "The Transparent Stone: Inverted Vision and Binary Imagery in Medieval Chinese Art," *Representations*, no. 46 (1994): 58–86.
76. Yang Xiaojun, "Suidai jingji diqu Renshou sheli shihan de tuxiang yu fengge – yi shendesi sheli shih an wei zhongxin" [Style and images of the Renshou reign stone caskets in the capital region of the Sui dynasty—a study on the stone caskets from the Shende monastery], *Kaogu yu wenwu*, no. 5 (2015): 80–87.
77. Yang, "Suidai jingji diqu Renshou sheli shihan de tuxiang yu fengge," 80.
78. Yang, "Suidai jingji diqu Renshou sheli shihan de tuxiang yu fengge," 84.
79. *T.* 2103, 52: 220b28–c20.
80. *T.* 2103, 52: 214b23–c2.
81. *T.* 2103, 52: 214b28.
82. In early Nirvana iconography, long-haired figures and disciples are shown displaying extreme grief through exaggerated body gestures. Nirvana imagery became a predominate feature on later Tang period reliquaries. David Jongeward, "The Buddha's Last Days as Portrayed in Gandharan Sculpture," in *Gandharan Buddhist Reliquaries*, 13–15; Sonya Lee, *Surviving Nirvana*, 55–56; Yu Wei, "Shengwu zhizao," 126–41.
83. Yang Xiaojun claims that the Buddha's relics are shown in the form of mani-jewels. Yang, "Suidai jingji diqu Renshou sheli shihan de tuxiang yu fengge," 85.
84. Yang Xiaojun identifies the central objects as relic containers. It is possible that the central objects are actually censers. There is, however, a morphological connection between censers and relic containers. In South Asia, some reliquaries invoked the shape of a censer, while in Gandhara, sometimes round perfume boxes are used as relic containers. In the Northern Qi period the outermost container of relics took the shape of round or cylindrical ceramic urns, which differed from the rectangular stone caskets developed in the Northern Wei period. Akiko Waley believes this practice of using censer-like shapes for relic containers might also have taken place in East Asia. Yu Wei, "Shengwu zhizao," 69–75; Walley, "Instant Bliss," 146–49; Yang, "Suidai jingji diqu Renshou sheli shihan de tuxiang yu fengge," 84; David Jongeward, "Survey of Gandharan Reliquaries," in *Gandharan Buddhist Reliquaries*, 46–47.

Gold-Sprinkled

Chinese Paper and Persian Book Arts during the Fifteenth Century

Yusen Yu

A unique corpus of fifteenth-century Persian manuscripts is known to be made of a special kind of gold-sprinkled paper imported from China (figs. 1–2). Dispersed, small-scale manuscript folios as well as *insha'*, or letters, made of the same type of paper, also randomly appear in the near-contemporaneous albums now in the Topkapi Palace Museum Library in Istanbul. The physical beauty as

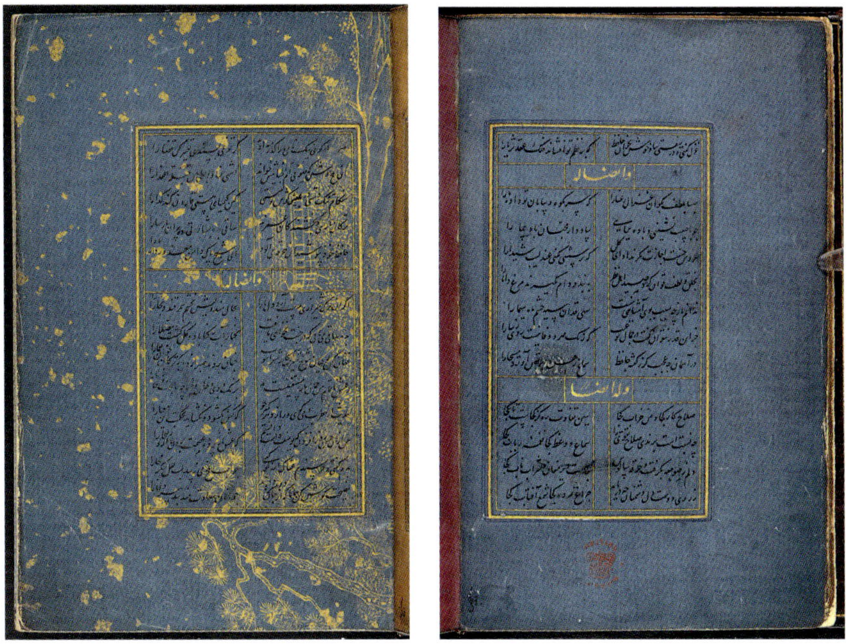

Figure 1 Folios 3a (left) and 3b (right), pages of the *Dīvān* of Hafiz, copied by Sulayman al-Fushanji in 1451. Ink and gold on gold-sprinkled paper. Collection of the British Museum, London. © The British Library Board. Add_MS 7759.

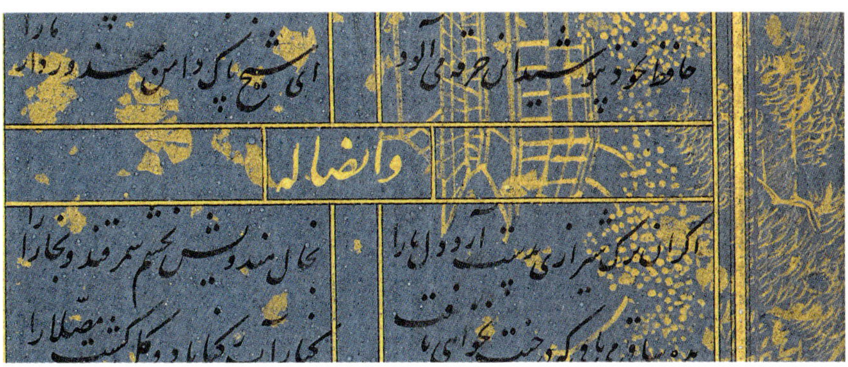

Figure 2 Folio 3a of the *Dīvān* of Hafiz. Detail. Collection of the British Museum, London. © The British Library Board. Add_MS_7759.

well as the exotic provenance of the paper has made it a source of both amazement and puzzlement—then and now. Because of the larger historical circumstances that the gold-sprinkled paper represents, the manuscripts that were made of it have aroused continuing scholarly interests.[1] More recently, the manuscripts have been on show in landmark exhibitions of Asian and Islamic art, including *Ming: 50 Years that Changed China* at the British Museum in 2014–15, which highlighted cross-cultural exchange in the fifteenth century, and the *Art of the Qur'an* exhibition at the Freer and Sackler, Washington, D.C., in 2016–17.

To this author's knowledge, imported paper and local product were used in some, if not all, of the manuscripts at the same time.[2] The latter exceeds the scope of the current study and will only be mentioned briefly in the last part of the chapter. Here, I intend to offer a brief introduction to this mesmerizing material of paper, with a focus on the relationship between its materiality and the physical realization of this corpus of Persian books. Muslim scribes and artists specified provenance, color, and format of paper for different purposes of guiding scribal practices given in practical treatises.[3] The use of the gold-sprinkled paper seems to represent another case of conscious choice in terms of writing material. This chapter argues that the very presence of gold—the glittering yellow metal—on the paper surface played an especially essential role when it came to the experience of the viewer.

TERMINOLOGY AND TECHNOLOGY

The historical background of this chapter is the diplomatic and mercantile contact between the Ming dynasty (1368–1644) and the Islamic world in the fifteenth century, especially the two Timurid (1370–1507) capitals, Herat, now in Afghanistan, and Samarqand, now in Uzbekistan, both seeing a quickening pace of the acquisitions of Chinese objects in the Turco-Persian courts in Central Asia and Iran.[4] According to the Timurid sources, "Chinese paper" (*kaghaz-i khiṭa'i*) was brought as a diplomatic gift by the Ming embassy in 1417 to Herat. Scholars have linked this account to the gold-sprinkled paper used in manuscript production,[5] but this suggestion remains speculative, for the account does not specify whether and how the paper was decorated. Contemporaneous references that I found in the *Translations of the Muslim Office* (*Huihuiguan yiyu*), a compilation of bilingual letters and petitions in Persian and Chinese addressing the Ming emperors, offer more convincing identification. Four petitions are presented to request the gold-sprinkled paper, each respectively from Mecca (*mamlakat ka'ba*), Turfan, Hami (Qamul), and Samarqand. It is notable that, surprisingly enough, none of the letters, twenty-six in total, from the *Translations of the Muslim Office* mentioned any information on Herat, which scholars have tended to consider as being the place where most of the manuscripts made of the Chinese paper were produced. Samarqand, on the other hand, seemed to hold a more prominent status, as evidenced by the following letter:

> The humble servant from Samarqand, Hafiz, being present in front of the Emperor of the Great Ming [Daimin[g] khan]: this time, following the tradition, I kowtowed [*sar zade*] under the Gate of Gold [*dar zarrin*] and presented our tributes that include Arabian horses, Mongol horses, diamonds, and other objects, and I beg for your acceptance. In front of the royal court, I beseech Your Majesty's bestow of the figured brocades woven with gold, gold-sprinkled paper [*sajin jianzhi*; *kaghaz zar-shash*], and so forth.[6]

The petition proves that the paper, as an imperial gift, was indeed gold-sprinkled. It provides both the Chinese term, *sajin jianzhi* (lit., gold-sprinkled paper), as well as its Persian counterpart, *zarshash* (lit., gold-sprinkled paper), that refer to this type of paper. *Zarshash* must have been mistaken by the interpreter-to-be with *zarafshan* (lit., gold-sprinkled paper), for those letters are word-for-word Persian glosses of the Chinese translations of original Persian letters, created to test students who studied Persian language at the Muslim Office during seasonal tests.[7] An interesting question remains: whether the Persian term is a literal translation of the Chinese one, or vice versa. Based on my survey of Persian and Chinese sources, my hypothesis is that both the Chinese and Persian terms were coined in the fifteenth century. No clear trace can be found in Chinese sources of the term *sajin* (gold sprinkling) before the Ming. Likewise, the Persian term *afshan* (sprinkling), or *zarafshan* (gold sprinkling), which refers to the type of paper as well as its technique, only began being used that way in the fifteenth century, when treatises on calligraphic arts randomly mentioned individuals noted for skill in gold sprinkling.[8] The word itself nonetheless existed long before this period, a subject to which I will return in the last part of this chapter.

In all probability, the vogue of fine paper enlivened with flecks of gold was plainly a fifteenth-century phenomenon in the regions under discussion. The origin of the technique in the Ming realm remains a source of speculation. According to paper historian Pan Jixing, the technique of gold sprinkling started in the Tang period (618–907).[9] Nonetheless, no extant Chinese specimens of gold-sprinkled paper predate the fifteenth century. Recent research indicates that the technique has a Japanese origin, especially considering that colored paper decorated with cut or sprinkled gold has survived in considerable numbers from the Heian period (794–1185).[10] In either case, it was the Ming that initiated an overarching interest in the abstract, gilt-splashed decoration of material objects, including bronzes and paper.[11] The gold-sprinkled paper became newly available for Muslim patrons and artists starting from the beginning of the century. The earliest dated example is the calligraphic page compiled in the Topkapi album H. 2153 (fol. 16), which bears the title of Khalil Sulṭan, grandson of Timur, who shortly ruled Transoxania from 1405 to 1409. The gold flecks on the margins of some earlier manuscript folios were most likely added in later periods.[12]

The terminologies, or the naming of, the paper merit further attention because they suggest that the main attraction of this type of paper was the abstract, gilt-splashed decoration. Every sheet of paper must have been sprinkled with gold flecks or powder. According to Pan, the process involves pushing flecks of gold leaf onto a sheet of glued paper, after which a piece of oilpaper covers its surface until the flecks are completely integrated. Once the procedure is finished, polishing is necessary.[13] By varying the shape of the gold dust grains or the density of the sprinkling, different effects can be achieved, as seen in the (larger) "snowy" gold-sprinkled paper (*xuejin xuan*), the (smaller) "rainy" gold-sprinkled paper (*yujin xuan*), and the mixed "snowy and rainy" gold-sprinkled paper (*yuxue xuan*).[14] Indeed, all of those types can be found in the Persian manuscripts. On some sheets, gold powder, rather than flecks, was applied abundantly over the surface, so thinly that it is nearly invisible (as seen in Figure 7, where the painted mountains and pavilion appear as in a mist).

As a result, the smooth, close texture of the highly sized and polished paper has a lesser degree of absorbency. The remarkable "thingness" of the manuscripts strikes one immediately because of its unusual weight, which can only be felt by handling them in person. In describing the copy of *Sitta* (Six Poems) of ʻAttar in the Topkapi Palace Museum Library (A. 3059), Mehmet Aga-Oglu (1896–1949) notes that the manuscript was "written on heavy paper of various colors."[15] Likewise, A. F. L. Beeston (1911–1995) describes the paper used in the 1437 copy of the *Kulliyat* (Anthology) of Sa ʻdi in the Bodleian Library, Oxford, as "unusually heavy, being probably glazed with some sort of clay preparation."[16] Suspicion remains whether the thick leaves were made up of a laminate of more than one sheet of paper, but evidence suggests that the sheet was originally thick. The late-Ming connoisseur Wen Zhenheng (1585–1645) already noted that the gold-sprinkled paper used at the court was "as thick as plank."[17]

Furthermore, many of the paper sheets were decorated with imageries like river and valley landscapes, Chinese pavilions, birds, and blossoming flowers, or melon vines and pomegranate branches. It remains unexplored whether these repetitive unit compositions were hand painted or printed either by stencils or by woodblocks, which had been used widely for the so-called *yahua jianzhi* (pressed paper), a different type of decorated paper. The technique for the pressed paper involves carving a design into the press, yielding a pattern in low hollow relief after use.[18] Some continuous patterns on the gold-sprinkled paper, especially wave compositions, seem likely to have been similarly pressed or printed onto the paper surface. In other cases, however, careful comparison between some extremely similar compositions on different sheets of gold-sprinkled paper reveals that they are not exactly identical. Varying brushstrokes reflect the painter's virtuosity and suggest that they have been executed individually. Such technique, which dates back to the Tang period, is termed as *xiaojin* (lit., dissolved gold) in Chinese, which refers to dissolving gold in order to write (chrysography) and paint with it as ink pigment, most commonly on indigo-dyed paper in Buddhist sutras and their frontispieces in East Asia.[19]

MOBILE MATERIALITY

As with most Chinese objects circulated in the Islamic world, the paper, now the material infrastructure of the manuscripts, is certainly not what it originally looked like. Priscilla Soucek's meticulous examination already reveals that larger sheets of paper were cut into pieces when the books were made. Her reconstruction of the sheet of paper used in the manuscript of *The Treasury of Secrets* (*Makhzan al-asrār*) in the New York Public Library extrapolates on the entire span of the painted imageries (fig. 3), indicating that the original sheet would have been 45 or 46 cm high and the total length would have been at least 324 cm.[20] Such a large sheet was not made in China until the Ming period. One of the mysteries concerning the paper, however, was the virtual lack of identical examples in Chinese collections. In previous studies, scholars could not locate even a single Chinese specimen with which to compare the paper used in the Persian manuscripts. Therefore, before we embark on our line of inquiry into the Persian reception, the domestic consumption of the paper in China merits consideration.

Wen Zhenheng, in his *Treatise on Superfluous Things*, or *Zhangwu zhi*, a text on elite material culture written in the latter half of the Ming dynasty, notices that "the use of gold-sprinkled paper, dyed with five colors, is limited to the

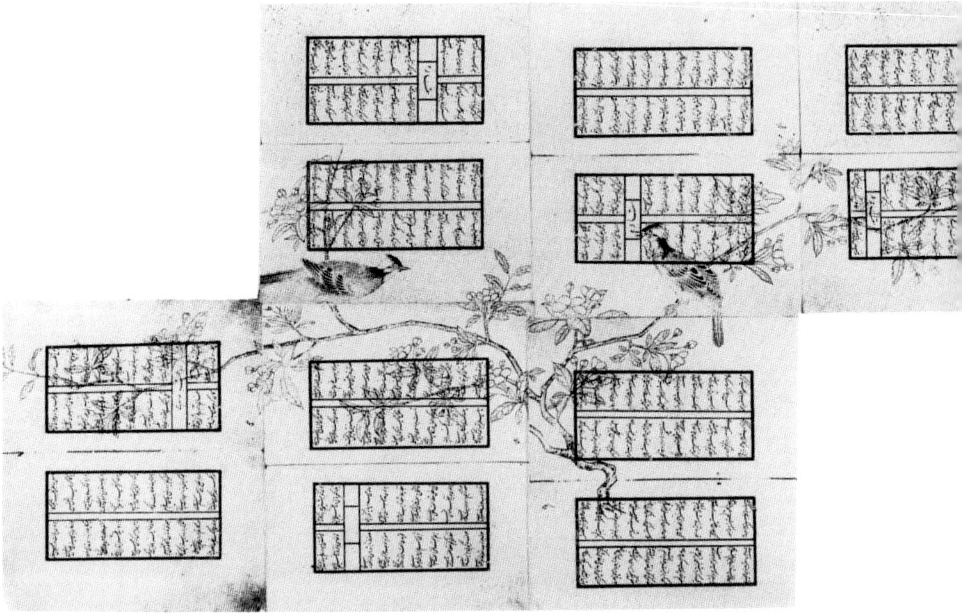

Figure 3 Composite view of fols. 4b, 8b, 9b, 10b–11a, 14b, 16b–17a, copy of *Makhzan al-asrār*. New York Public Library, Persian Ms. 41. From Priscilla Soucek, "The New York Public Library 'Makhzan al-asrār' and Its Importance," *Ars Orientalis* 18 (1988): 31, fig. 15. Courtesy of Priscilla Soucek.

court; it is as thick as plank, and its surface is highly polished thus shiny as white jade."[21] Wen's description accords with the glossiness and density of the paper that is testified to in the Persian manuscripts. Although he does not reveal the place(s) of production of the paper, Wen, an acute commentator on elite taste, further distinguishes it from other, less-prized, gold-sprinkled paper, which seemed more widely available in the Wuzhong region (modern-day Suzhou), as the latter "does not last long."[22] Such paper, rarely dyed or painted but only sprinkled in gold powder rather than flecks, was often employed in calligraphies or paintings in the medium of folding fans.[23]

Instead of being used as a writing surface, the chief function of the gold-sprinkled paper under investigation was to use it as the frontispiece (*yinshou*) of handscrolls (the frontispiece is a piece of silk or decorated paper that is attached to the beginning of a horizontal scroll). Previous scholarship has mostly focused on the central painted image on a scroll; frontispieces instead have remained invisible in exhibitions and rarely published, although they, carefully selected by mounters and collectors, mean to be an integral part of a scroll.[24]

The recent digitalization of a list of important scrolls in the East Asian Scroll Paintings Project by the Center for the Art of East Asia, The University of Chicago, has greatly facilitated my research. Several digitalized works show that they are mounted with a dyed or gold-decorated frontispiece.[25]

According to Wang Yikun, the renowned mounter who worked for the Palace Museum in Beijing, attaching a frontispiece was a new practice in mounting during the Ming period.[26] This supports my hypothesis that while the central calligraphies or paintings in some handscrolls were earlier works, their frontispieces were in fact added later during the fifteenth or sixteenth centuries, though more detailed research is needed to confirm this. One such frontispiece is that of the scroll *Poem on the Hall of Pines and Wind* (*Songfengge shi*) (fig. 4). Its central calligraphic work, done in 1102 by Huang Tingjian (1045–1105), is one of the most esteemed works in the history of Chinese calligraphy, and it is now in the collection of the Palace Museum in Taipei. While frontispieces of other scrolls consist of characters with the name of the painting or a poetic phrase, this one, most likely added during the Ming period, retains the original appearance. Its imagery of two birds interacting with each other on a flowering branch closely resembles that of the reconstructed sheet used in the contemporaneous Chaghatay Turkic manuscript of *The Treasury of Secrets* (see fig. 3), made in western Iran for the Aqqoyulu ruler Sultan Ya ʻqub in 1478, to whom we will return in the last part of this chapter.[27]

In some exceptional cases, Ming artists also painted on the gold-sprinkled surface of the paper. An incredible example of this is the handscroll painting of *Zilu Inquiring about the Ford's Location* (*Wen jin tu*) by Wu Wei (c. 1459–1508) (fig. 5). It was executed on a large sheet of gold-sprinkled paper of the scroll that measures 46.3 cm in height and 110.2 cm in length. The landscape imagery is nearly identical to that of many examples we can find in Persian manuscripts. The painting represents an episode from the *Analects*: Confucius sent his disciple Zilu to ask for directions to the ford, and he was mocked by the recluses Changju and Jieni, who were cultivating the land, for his ambition to change the state of disorder of the world when he did not even know the ford's location.[28] The preexisting landscape of rivers and the hills beyond acts as part of the narrative in the painting, indicating the ford that Confucius inquired about.

The two cases of the domestic consumption show that gold-sprinkled paper was most likely not made with a foreign audience or "export market" in mind; instead, the paper that circulated within China was indistinguishable from

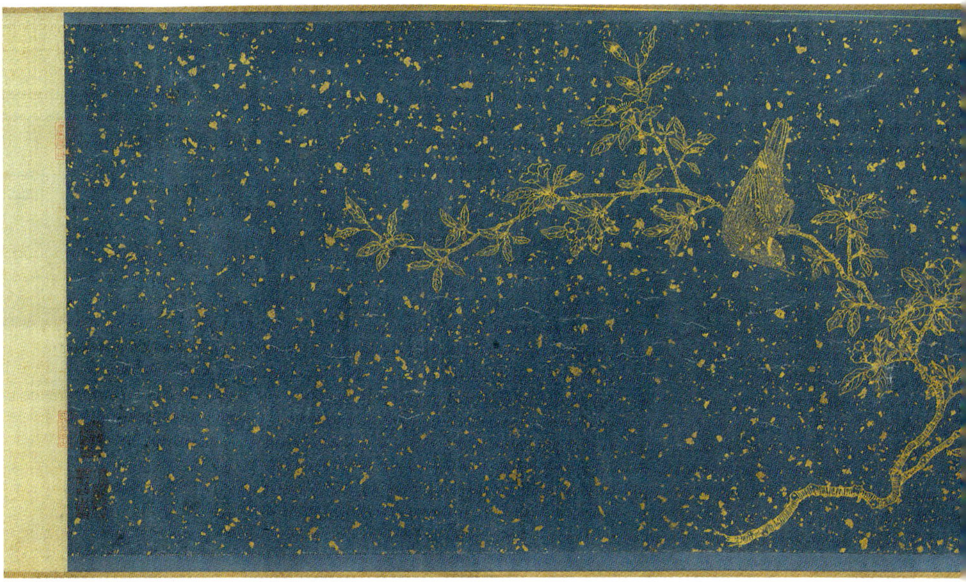

Figure 4 Huang Tingjian, *Poem on the Hall of Pines and Wind*, late eleventh or early twelfth century. 32.8 × 219.2 cm. View of frontispiece, added in late fifteenth or early sixteenth century, gold-sprinkled paper. Collection of the National Palace Museum.

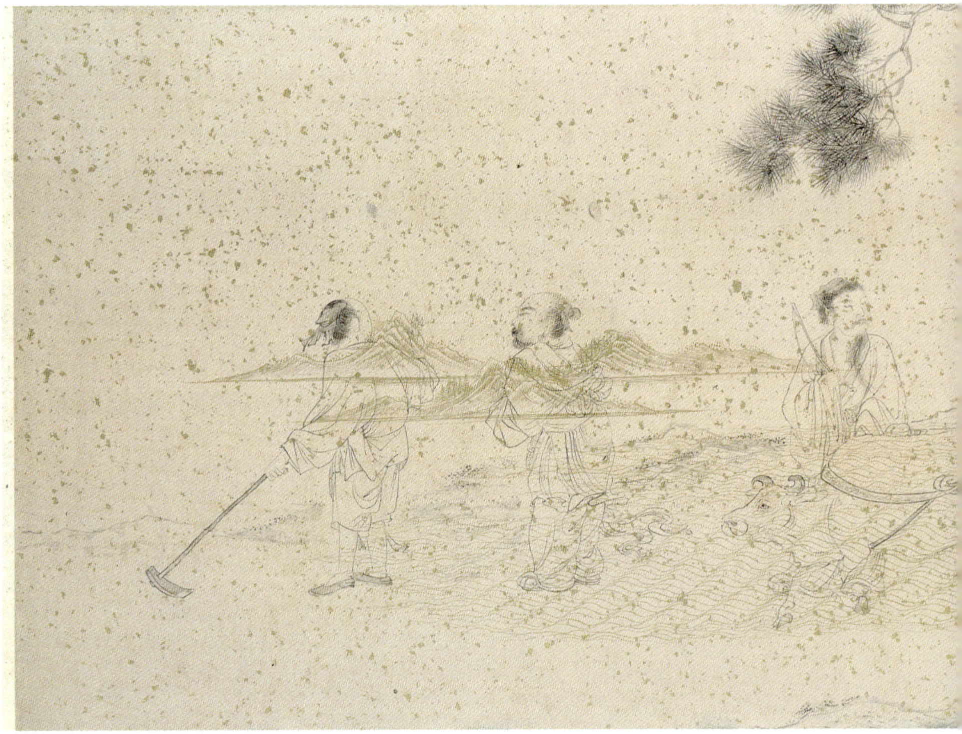

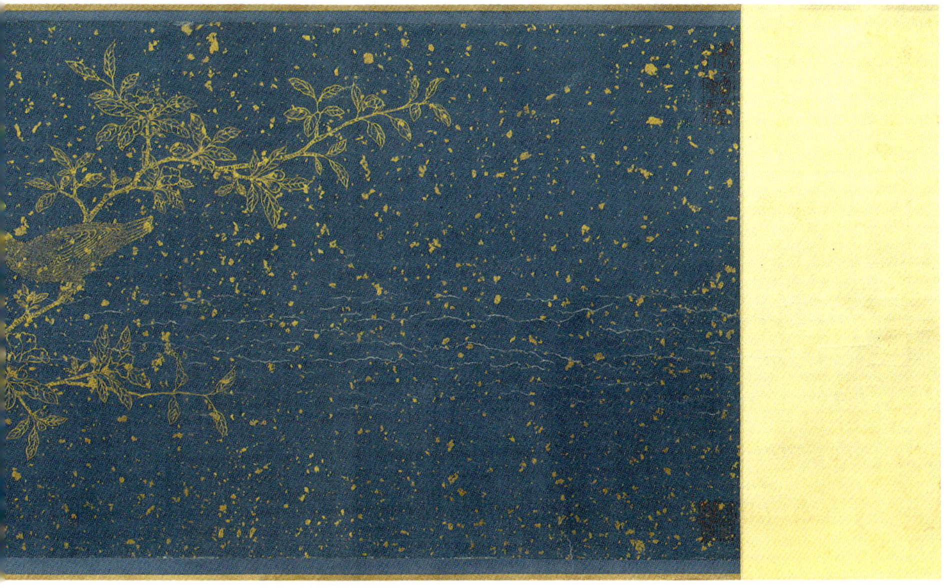

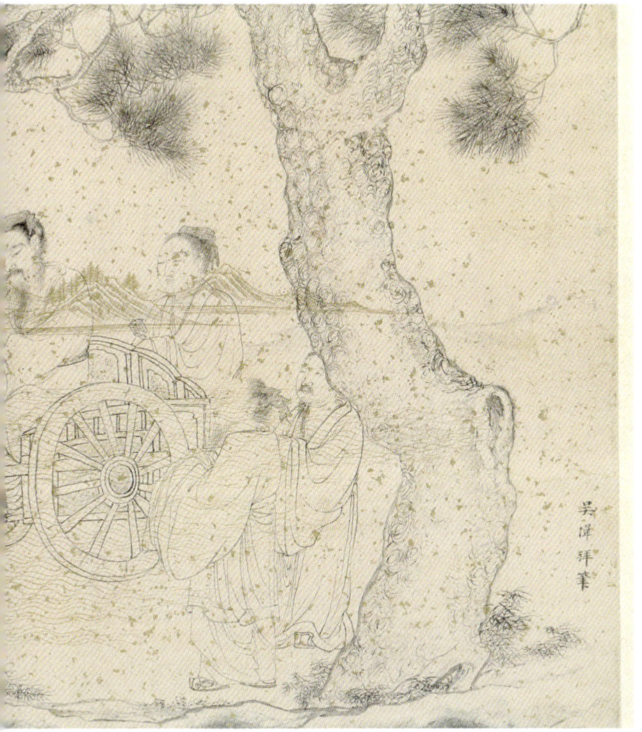

Figure 5 Wu Wei, *Zilu Inquiring about the Ford's Location*, fifteenth century. Section of a handscroll, ink on gold-sprinkled paper. Provided by the Palace Museum.

that which was used in the making of Persian manuscripts. The imageries had followed the popular decorative modules derived from earlier impressed designs, such as the composition of melon vines, and they were used in various mediums of the Ming period, especially in porcelain. They also reveal the reason why only one side of the paper sheet was decorated in gold: in the Ming realm, only a single side was used, while the other side was attached to the sheet of backing paper during the process of mounting and was not intended to be seen.[29]

In contrast, when the paper was brought to the Islamic world, it was mainly used as a writing surface. Priscilla Soucek's precise reconstruction of the original sheet (see fig. 3) clearly suggests a parsimonious use of this precious material. By looking at physical features, it is possible to retrace the steps of how the scribe worked with the material. Take, for instance, the *Divan* (Anthology) of Hafiz, copied by the calligrapher Sulayman al-Fushanji (c. fifteenth century) in 1451. The original sheet of paper was cut into pieces of the required dimensions. Written in the cursive script of Nastaʿliq with black ink, a stable ratio of a thirteen-line text box was then applied throughout the manuscript. Finally, gold frames or rulings were added, which is indicated by the fact that the scripts are underneath the frame lines.

Unlike the transformation of the painted landscape into part of the narrative in Wu Wei's painting, in the Persian manuscripts under investigation in this chapter, the gold decoration, especially the imageries that preexist the written blocks, subverted the traditional relationship between the text and image in Persian book arts. In the latter, especially in narrative genres, image served as illustration to the written text. At first glance, the images appear rather randomly as the background of the text in the Persian manuscripts discussed here, which seems to present an incoordination between the text and the image. Moreover, in contrast to the general trend in Persian manuscripts that emerged in the later centuries, in which decorative vignettes served as frames around the central text blocks of the manuscript surface, the imageries on the Chinese paper are arbitrarily located within the frame of the written area and stretch beyond it. In the following parts of this chapter, I will explore the uneasy interrelationship between the textual genres and the material upon which they are transcribed, especially the sensory potential of manuscripts as material objects beyond the traditional text-image studies.

AESTHETICS OF WONDER

For Persian viewers, some imageries on the paper under investigation, especially birds and flowers, readily resonated with established poetic allusions, which seems to explain the potential rationale for the images on the paper by reference to the text. The most affinitive poetic metaphor is *Gol-o-bolbol*, the rose and the nightingale, more broadly defined as *Gol-o-morgh* (flower and bird), symbolizing the lover who sings endlessly of his longing toward the beloved, a motif that had remained the most common in mystical poetry. However, its textual description predated the visual form. The visualization of the very theme featuring the interacting flower and bird did not seem to have existed before the fifteenth century.[30] In fact, the bird-and-flower compositions on the gold-sprinkled paper may have provided one of the earliest visual representations of the poetic theme that accompanies the text.

Indeed, Persian artists of this period tended to juxtapose Islamic religious texts with birds and flowers in various mediums. One example is an album page with a picture of a Chinese *hwamei* (melodious laughingthrush) standing on peach tree branches (fig. 6), a pairing that is reminiscent of similar images on the gold-sprinkled paper. The juxtaposed calligraphy in Arabic is extracted from a manuscript of the *Qasidat al-Burda* (Ode of the Mantle), a thirteenth-century ode of praise for Prophet Muhammad composed by the eminent Sufi mystic Imam

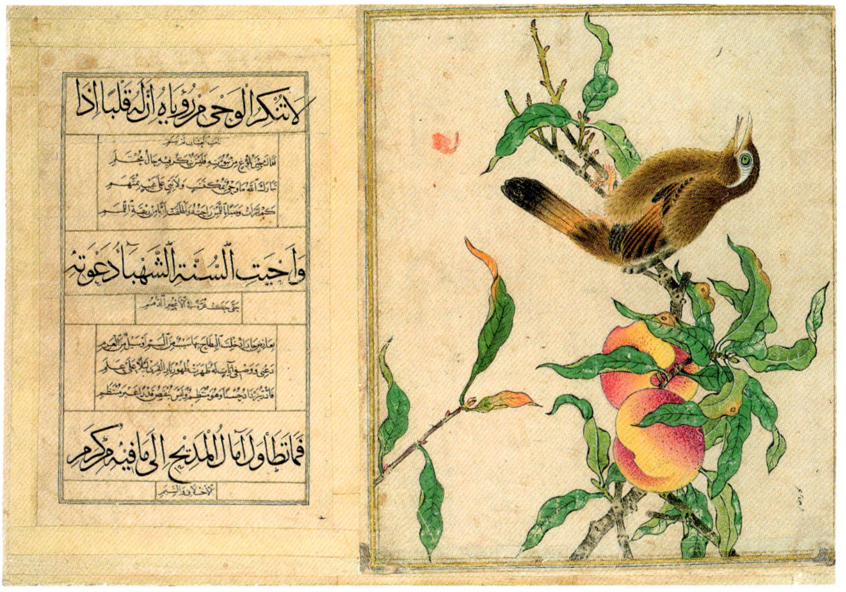

Figure 6 Album H. 2153, fol. 139b, Topkapi Palace Museum Library. Photo: Topkapi Palace Museum, Istanbul.

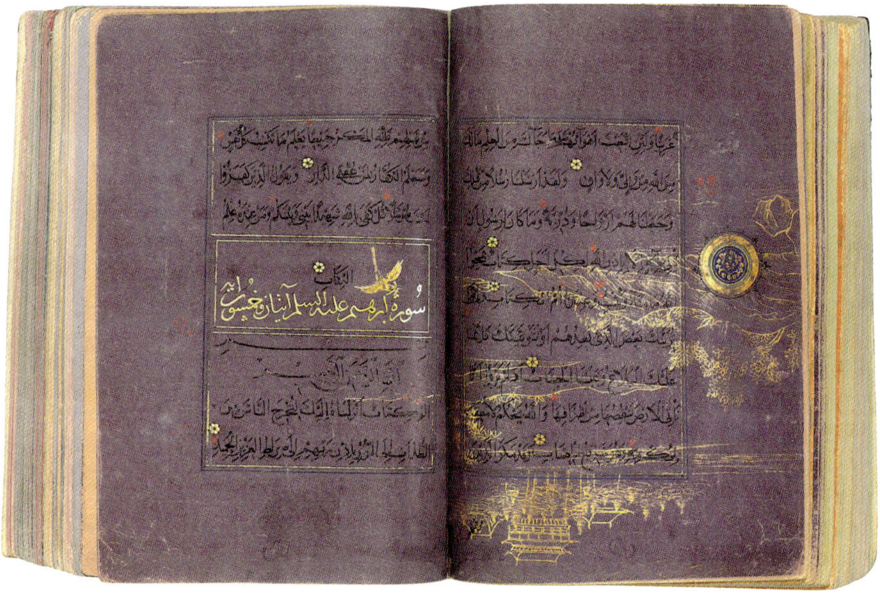

Figure 7 A Timurid or Aqquyunlu Qur'an, fifteenth century. Gold, ink, and colored pigments on Chinese paper. Private Collection. © Christie's Images / Bridgeman Images.

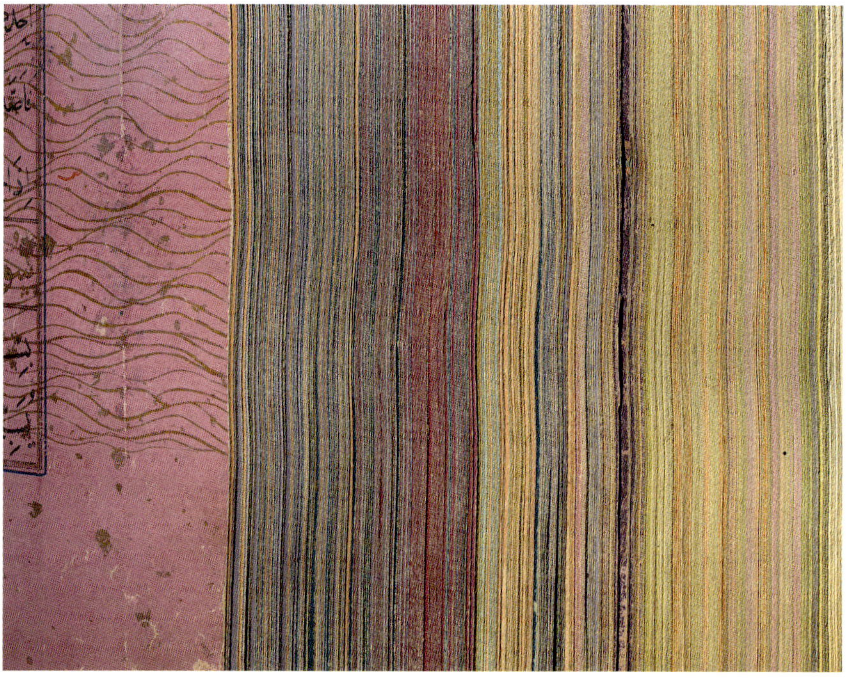

Figure 8 A Timurid or Aqquyunlu Qur'an, fifteenth century. Detail. © Christie's Images / Bridgeman Images.

al-Busiri (1211–1294) of Egypt, which seems to allude to the bird-and-flower image as a visual gloss. The bird symbolizes the afflicted poet who ceaselessly praises the Prophet, to the point that the Prophet appeared in his dream and wrapped him in a mantle. Although my hypothesis here remains only tentative, studies on later Timurid painting do suggest that artists applied enigmatic figures and scenes that did not seem to illustrate the accompanying texts, but were instead intended to convey the mystical teachings of Sufi poets, which were expected to be "deciphered" by elite viewers.[31]

In this regard, the Quranic manuscripts deserve special attention, as traditionally they were predominantly decorated with aniconic repertoire. On a page from the copy recently sold at a Christie's auction (fig. 7), what strikes the viewer is that a bird (a crane?) flies over the heading of the chapter (*sura*) of Ibrahim.[32] The chapter starts with a revelation: "*[This is] a Book which We have revealed unto you in order that you might lead mankind out of darkness into light by their Lord's Leave to the Path of the All-Mighty, the Owner of all Praise.*"[33] Scholars have argued that the glittering substance of gold itself was the one that strikes the deepest resonance with the quest of light (*nur*),[34] as the Qur'an represents a descent of divine light on earth, as asserted in the chapter. The page also contains other preexisting well-realized compositions that could relate to the text. The idyllic scene represents a variation of the Chinese classical "level-distance" landscape, in which the viewer's sight starts with the trees and bamboos that are set against the riverbanks. In recession to a further distance is a Buddhist monastery, half hidden in the woods. The scene would certainly remind the Persian viewer of the two concepts of garden and pavilion in the paradise that appear in the Qur'an.[35]

When shifting imageries like this are included, bound volumes with hundreds of folios therefore appear as repositories of aesthetically pleasing pictures that do not belong to the conventional decorative repertoire in contemporary Persian books.[36] Persian artists paid particular attention to the viewer's experience. The manuscripts were intentionally made from separate sheets of paper brilliantly tinted in different colors, such as orange, pink, dark olive, dark blue, and dark orchid (fig. 8). The Timurid artist Simi Nishapuri explains the impulse to use dyed papers in his time, saying, "people are naturally inclined to grace and elegance," and it is better to give paper a tint because white is hard on the eye.[37] Noteworthily, by the 1400s manuscripts were mainly cream in tone. The luminosity of the page further engages the senses: the dense yellow glare, along with the reflection caused by its highly polished colored surface, in the Timurid master calligrapher Sultan Ali Mashhadi's words, "strikes the eye, like looking at the sun."[38]

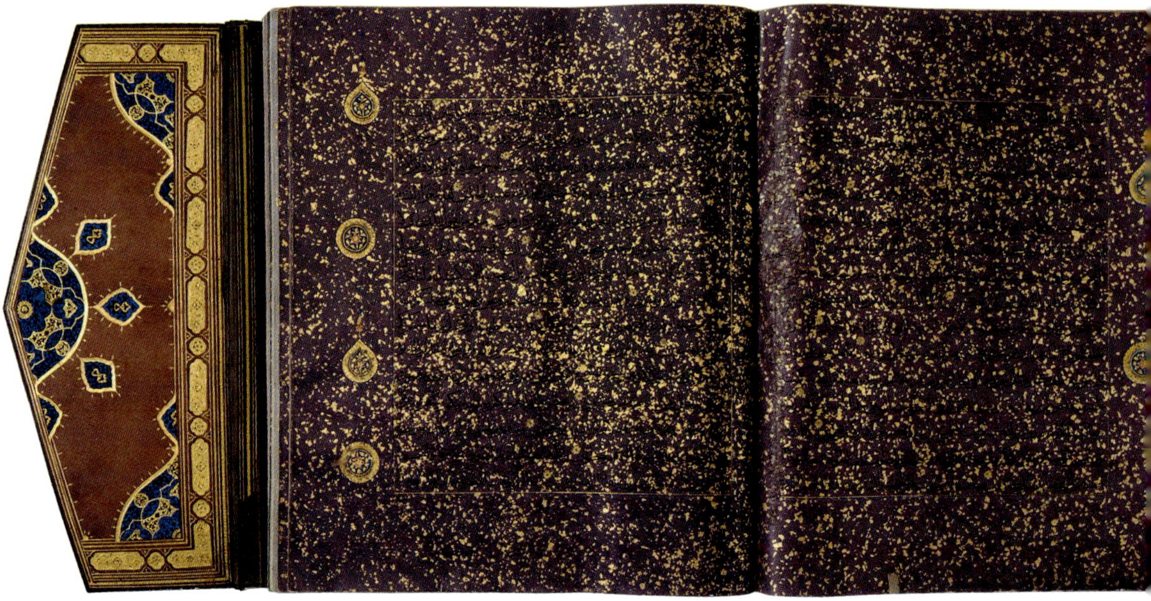

Figure 9 Qur'an, c. 1450–60. Leather and paper with ink and gold. Collection of the Detroit Institute of Arts, USA.

The handwritten text appears to be nearly illegible (fig. 9). Each shining page within the same manuscript therefore does not appear repetitive; compositions change, colors shift, all of which deliberately elicits excitement and pleasurable wonder (*'Adja'ib*), which was defined by the thirteenth-century polymath Qazwini (d. 1283) as "the sense of bewilderment a person feels because of his inability to understand the cause of a thing."[39]

The concept of wonder was not only used to title cosmographical works, such as Qazwini's *'Adja'ib al-makhluqat wa ghara'ib al-mawjudat* (*The Wonders of Creation and the Oddities of Existing Things*), but it also appeared in travel narratives, referring to foreign countries and exotic phenomena, including lands, plants, and animals, as well as built environments. Indeed, the purpose of the famous account of the Timurid embassy to the Ming empire in 1419–22 is to "relate the strange (*gharib*) stories concerning the manners and customs" and present "the description of the country, buildings . . . together with certain wonderful objects (*'Adja'ibi*) which he [the envoy] had observed in that country [the Ming]."[40] Elsewhere I have suggested that the Persian viewers of the fifteenth century showed great interest in visual representations of the Ming land.[41] Leafing through the books made of the gold-sprinkled paper, painted vignettes—elaborate buildings, described in detail in the embassy report, topographies like faraway mountains and waters, as well as flora and fauna that evoke the exotic foreign—would certainly keep the viewer's eye constantly moving around the images while reading the written text.

It is also notable that the orientations of the text and gold image are frequently reversed, which seems to indicate that each page could have been expected to be viewed from individual angles. The discrepancy in orientation between the text and the image therefore made the manuscript more inclusive to accommodate both text and image, and since the text and image are not necessarily related, their orientations do not have to match, and readers can just view them from angles that make sense to either the text or image.

In view of this, the modest size of some of the manuscripts in question deserves special consideration. The folio of the Christie's Qur'an measures about 22.6 by 15.5 cm. Even the copy of *The Treasury of Secrets* in the New York Public Library's collection measures only 10.5 by 18 cm.[42] Similar small-scale dispersed folios have also been dismantled from original manuscripts and pasted in the Topkapi albums. It is thus reasonable to deduce that the "reading" of such manuscripts, including the gold-painted compositions, demands a more intensely immersive engagement on the part of the viewer, for, according to the medieval scholar Ibn al-Haytham (965–1040), the surface of painted pages, especially those of modest size in the current case, can be perceived only by contemplation from close up, and that sight cannot contemplate them unless they are "very near."[43] The close physical contact with the smoothness of the surface further enhanced the tactile intimacy that was navigated by the hands of the viewer.

THE METAPHOR OF GOLD SPRINKLING

As the most prized form of money, gold is the embodiment of wealth. Since the Mongol period, gold had been specially associated with deep and specific cosmological meaning. The most visible form of wearable gold was the famous *nasij* (*tuvur zar-baft*), or "cloth of gold," which was used to cover the tents of the members of the ruling house.[44] The use of gold to establish honor thus effectively marks social status. It is notable that, during this period, "letters . . . were not without ornamental elaboration," some of which were flecked with gold.[45] An *insha'*, addressed to the Aqqoyulu ruler Abu al-Muzaffar Sultan Ya'qub Bahadur Khan, who ruled western Iran between 1478 and 1490, is one such example (figs. 10–11).[46] The surface of the paper is covered in irregular flecks of gold, which were clearly applied locally; the name of the ruler is further highlighted in gold. The addresser, 'Abd al-Hayy bin Hafiz Sheikh Muhammad Bukhari, used the same raw material of gold in both writing and paper decoration, including the gold frame, for the color and grain of the gold script is the same with the gold flecks. This gives the letter a pleasing overall appearance and asserts the authority of the ruler.

It is thus not surprising that, apart from being used as the technical term for gold sprinkling, *zarafshan* is an expression otherwise used to describe the scattering of gold coins as a gesture of largesse on the part of kings and princes in poetic texts.[47] The practice accords with a wealth of corroborative data on charitable practices that distribute gold coinages or dust, especially in ceremonial uses. According to the Timurid court sophisticate Zayn al-Din Wasifi, the painter Bihzad once produced a painting in which Amir 'Ali Shir (1441–1501) is "leaning on his case, with plates full of gold in front of him for distribution as gifts."[48] In classical Persian poetry, the word *zarafshan* is frequently used to praise the generosity of the noble. One such verse is from the the Persian *Book of Kings* (*Shahnama*):

> *Chu bar gah bashad zarafshan bud, chu bar jang bashad sarafshan bud.*
> [On the throne he was generous (*zarafshan*); on the battlefield,
> he was venturous.][49]

The association of *zarafshan* with the charitable distribution of gold offers another dimension to understanding the consumption of the homonymous paper. In embellishment of Quranic manuscripts, the dazzling-ness of substance makes the gold decoration suspect, from certain moral perspectives, especially in critiques of wealth or, more precisely, excess. Islamic polemics warned against accumulation of precious metals in particular, for it would ultimately amount to pagan idolatry. Instead, they specifically emphasize the need for gold to *circulate* in order to fulfill its natural function as instrument for the regulation of value.[50] Due to this subtle association, the gold-sprinkled paper became a suitable choice for making manuscripts objects of devotional interest under princely patronage. The manuscripts of the Qur'an, in particular, were often part of the *waqf*, the inalienable endowment under Islamic law,[51] the voluntary conveyance of private property by the donor-patron to a charitable purpose. It typically involved construction of public religious buildings, but also donation of precious objects, including manuscripts, to the libraries of religious institutions, such as mosques

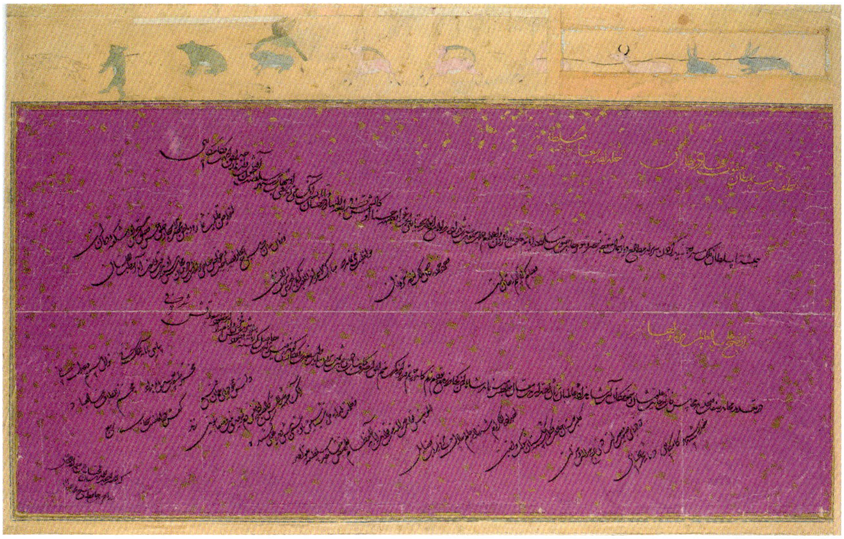

Figure 10 Album H. 2153, fol. 74b, Topkapi Palace Museum Library. Photo: Topkapi Palace Museum, Istanbul. © Presidency of the Republic of Turkey, the Directorate of National Palaces.

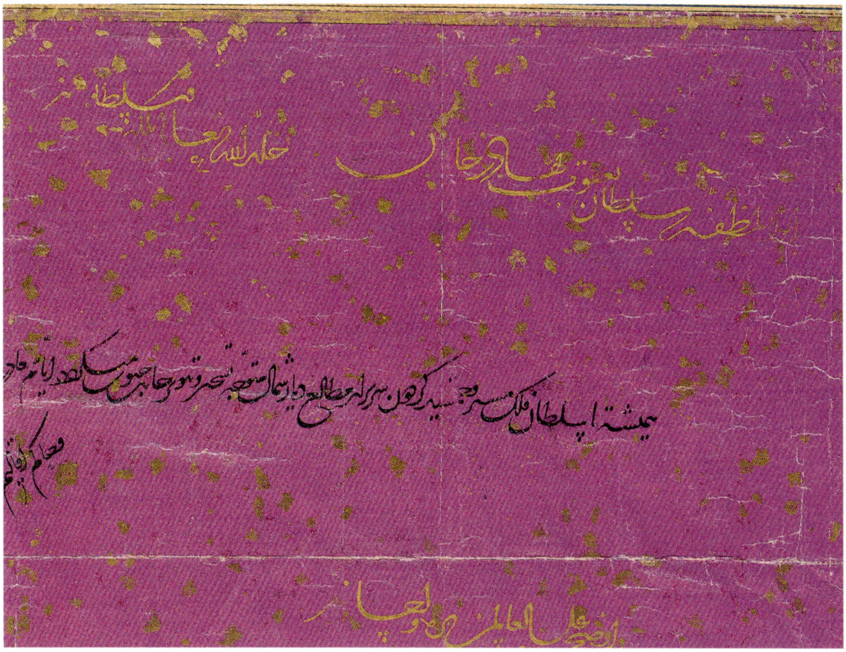

Figure 11 Album H. 2153, fol. 74b, Topkapi Palace Museum Library. Detail showing the name of Abu al-Muzaffar Sultan Yaʿqub Bahadur Khan. Photo: Topkapi Palace Museum, Istanbul. © Presidency of the Republic of Turkey, the Directorate of National Palaces.

and shrines.[52] Indeed, as David J. Roxburgh points out, the gold-sprinkled paper was reserved for fixed genres of texts: the Qur'an, mystical poetry, and treatises on Islamic mysticism.[53] This explains the extreme sensuous beauty of the manuscripts, even as their central purpose is to indicate religious devotion.

The making of such manuscripts with gold-sprinkled paper, employed in order to evoke the distribution of money, thus has both physical and metaphysical dimensions. Once a king or prince patronized a manuscript made of the gold-decorated paper (*zarafshan*), the endowment itself was a gesture of largesse (*zarafshan*). Among the known manuscripts, several can be directly linked with royal patronage. At least two manuscripts made of the gold-sprinkled paper, now in the National Museum of Iran, in Tehran, were given by such a royal patronage to the library of the Shrine of Shaykh Safi in Ardabil, Iran.[54] The materiality of a precious manuscript alludes to the intention of its making, which joins the sacred with the political and thus ensures the patron's representation in the spiritual realm.

As this chapter has suggested, matter itself, such as paper and gold, constituted meaning and had an impact on the viewer's mind. As the most malleable of precious metals, gold is readily hammered into thin sheets or flecks that are used as surface adornment (a one-ounce piece of gold can be hammered into a sheet five-millionths of an inch thick). It embodied monetary value and expressed otherworldly splendor, which invites poetic and metaphysical interpretations. The practice of how the manuscripts were made and experienced also allows us to look at the wider issue of how paper had great potential as a creative material that transformed the sensuous qualities of the book, at a time when artists were exploiting the aesthetic and semantic possibilities of the new substance in a society fully attuned to the subtleties of material culture.

NOTES

1. Priscilla Soucek, “The New York Public Library ‘Makhzan al-asrār’ and Its Importance,” *Ars Orientalis* 18 (1988): 1–37; Sheila S. Blair, “Color and Gold: The Decorated Papers Used in Manuscripts in Later Islamic Times,” *Muqarnas* 17 (2000): 24–36; and David J. Roxburgh, *The Persian Album, 1400–1600: From Dispersal to Collection* (New Haven: Yale University Press, 2005), 159–65.
2. Dr. Cathy Selvius DeRoo, research scientist in the Department of Conservation at the Detroit Institute of Arts, kindly informed me of their technical research with the goal of identifying the inorganic and organic colorants of the paper used in the Qur’an manuscript in their collection (see fig. 9), which hopefully will help to better clarify the exact provenance of the paper.
3. For case studies, see Rémi Dewière, “‘Peace Be upon Those Who Follow the Right Way’: Diplomatic Practices between Mamluk Cairo and the Borno Sultanate at the End of the Eighth/Fourteenth Century,” in *Mamluk Cairo, a Crossroads for Embassies: Studies on Diplomacy and Diplomatics*, ed. Frederic Bauden and Malika Dekkiche (Leiden: Brill, 2019), 658–82; and Annabel Teh Gallop, A. C. S. Peacock, and İsmail Hakkı Kadı, “Introduction: The Language of Letters: Southeast Asian Understandings of Ottoman Diplomatics,” in İsmail Hakkı Kadı and A. C. S. Peacock, *Ottoman-Southeast Asian Relations: Sources from the Ottoman Archives* (Leiden: Brill, 2019), 20–22.
4. On the relationship between the Ming court and Central Asia, see Morris Rossabi, “Ming China’s Relations with Hami and Central Asia, 1404–1513: A Re-examination of Traditional Chinese Foreign Policy” (PhD diss., Columbia University, 1970).
5. *Mujmal-i faṣīhī* by Fasih al-Din Khvafi, and *Maṭla’-i sa’dayn* by ‘Abd al-Razzaq Samarqandi. See Roxburgh, *The Persian Album*, 160.
6. Translated by the author. For the original texts, see Hu Zhenhua and Hu Jun, eds., *Huihui guan yiyu* [Translations of the Muslim office] (Beijing: Zhongyang minzu daxue donggan yanjiusuo, 2005), 244–45.
7. Graeme Ford, “The Uses of Persian in Imperial China: The Translation Practices of the Great Ming,” in *The Persianate World: The Frontiers of a Eurasian Lingua Franca*, ed. Nile Green (Berkeley and Los Angeles: University of California Press, 2019), 113–29.
8. Priscilla P. Soucek, “Afšān,” *Encyclopædia Iranica*, ed. E. Yarshater, I/6: 581–82.
9. Pan Jixing, *Zhongguo zaozhi shihua* [The history of papermaking in China] (Beijing: Commercial Press, 1994), 47–48.
10. Shi Shouqian, *Yidong de taohuayuan: Dongya shijie zhong de shanshuihua* [The moving peach blossom land: Landscape painting in the East Asia world] (Taipei: Yuncheng wenhua, 2012), 231–64.
11. Robert Mowry links gilt-splashed decoration on the so-called Xuande bronzes to gold-sprinkled paper. See Robert Mowry, *China’s Renaissance in Bronze* (Phoenix: Phoenix Art Museum, 1993), 169.
12. One such example is a detached illustrated folio from a *Shahnama* depicting the scene “Yazdegird I Kicked to Death by the Water Horse” in the Metropolitan Museum of Art (Accession Number: 57.51.33). I am grateful to Jake Benson, who kindly shared his insights on the process of (re)mounting this folio.
13. Pan, *Zhongguo zaozhi shihua*, 47–48.
14. Liu Renqing, *Zhongguo shuhuazhi* [Chinese handmade paper for painting and calligraphy] (Beijing: China Water & Power Press, 2007), 79–82.
15. Mehmet Aga-Oglu, *Persian Bookbinding of the Fifteenth Century* (Ann Arbor: University of Michigan Press, 1935), plate 1.

16. A. F. L. Beeston, *Catalogue of the Persian, Turkish, Hindustani and Pushtu Manuscripts in the Bodleian Library: Part III Additional Persian Manuscripts* (Oxford: The Clarendon Press, 1954), 29.
17. Wen Zhenheng, *Zhangwu zhi jiaozhu* [Annotated and collated treatises on superfluous things], annotated by Chen Zhi, ed. Yang Zhaobo (Nanjing: Jiangsu kexue jishu chubanshe, 1984), 307–9.
18. He Yanquan, *Songdai huajian tezhan* [A special exhibition of painting and calligraphy on Song dynasty decorated paper] (Taipei: National Palace Museum, 2017).
19. Chrysography was used to write Qur'ans in the Muslim world; see Alain George, "Calligraphy, Colour and Light in the Blue Qur'an," *Journal of Qur'anic Studies* 11, no. 1 (2009): 75–125.
20. Soucek, "The New York Public Library 'Makhzan al-asrār' and Its Importance," 15–16.
21. Wen, *Zhangwu zhi jiaozhu*, 307–9.
22. Wen, *Zhangwu zhi jiaozhu*, 307–9.
23. Shi, *Yidong de taohuayuan*, 231–64.
24. On artworks as intact objects, see Wu Hung, *The Double Screen: Medium and Representation in Chinese Painting* (London: Reaktion Books, 1996).
25. See the website of the project: https://scrolls.uchicago.edu/.
26. Wang Yikun, *Shuhua zhuanghuang yange kao* [An investigation into the history of the mounting and decorating of painting and calligraphy] (Beijing: Zijincheng chubanshe, 1991), 36–37.
27. Soucek, "The New York Public Library 'Makhzan al-asrār' and Its Importance," 15–16.
28. For an English translation, see James Legge, *The Chinese Classics: With a Translation, Critical and Exegetical Notes, Prolegomena, and Copious Indexes, Vol. 1: Confucian Analects, the Great Learning, and the Doctrine of the Mean* (London: Trübner, 1861), 197–98.
29. On mounting, see Tsien Tsuen-Hsuin, *Science and Civilisation in China Vol. 5: Chemistry and Chemical Technology, Part 1: Paper and Printing*, ed. Joseph Needham (Cambridge: Cambridge University Press, 1985), 79–81.
30. Layla Diba, "The Rose and the Nightingale in Persian Art," *Arts of Asia* 26, no. 6 (1996): 100–112.
31. Chad Kia, *Art, Allegory and the Rise of Shi'ism in Iran, 1487–1565* (Edinburgh: Edinburgh University Press, 2019).
32. Lot 29, Sale 18371, *Art of the Islamic and Indian Worlds Including Oriental Rugs and Carpets*, Christie's, London, June 25, 2020. Christie's, accessed on November 5, 2020, https://www.christies.com/ lotfinder/Lot/a-timurid-or-aqquyunlu-quran-on-chinese-6255702-details.aspx.
33. Translation cited in *Translation of the Meanings of The Noble Qur'an in the English Language*, Dr. Muhammad Muhsin Khan and Dr. Taqi Ud Din Hilali (Madinah, Saudi Arabia: King Fahd Complex for the Printing of the Holy Qur'an, 1998), 328.
34. George, "Calligraphy, Colour and Light in the Blue Qur'an," 75–125. See also Roxburgh, *The Persian Album*, 164–65.
35. On garden and pavilion, see Mohammad Gharipour, *Persian Gardens and Pavilions: Reflections in History, Poetry and the Arts* (London: I. B. Tauris, 2013).
36. On early modern Persian and Ottoman manuscript ornamentation, see Gülru Necipoğlu, "Early Modern Floral: The Agency of Ornament in Ottoman and Safavid Visual Cultures," in *Histories of Ornament: From Global to Local*, ed. Gülru Necipoğlu and Alina Payne (Princeton: Princeton University Press, 2016), 132–55.
37. Wheeler M. Thackston, "Treatise on Calligraphic Arts: A Disquisition on Paper, Colors, Inks, and Pens by Simi of Nishapur," in *Intellectual Studies on Islam: Essays Written in Honour of Martin B. Dickson*, ed. Michel M. Mazzaoui, Vera B. Moreen, and Martin B. Dickson (Salt Lake City: University of Utah Press, 1990), 221–23.

38. The text is inserted in Qādi Ahmad's *Rose Garden of Art*. See *Calligraphers and Painters: A Treatise by Qadi Ahmad, Son of Mir-Munshi (circa A.H. 1015/A.D. 1606)*, translated from Persian by V. Minorsky, translated from Russian by T. Minorsky (Washington, D.C.: Smithsonian Institution, 1959), 113.
39. Cited in Persis Berlekamp, *Wonder, Image, and Cosmos in Medieval Islam* (New Haven: Yale University Press, 2011), 23. See also C. E. Dubler, "'Adja'ib," in *The Encyclopaedia of Islam*, new edition, vol. 1, ed. H. A. R. Gibb, et al. (Leiden: Brill, 1986), 203–4; Marinos Sariyannis, "Ajā'ib ve Gharā'ib: Ottoman Collections of *Mirabilia* and Perceptions of the Supernatural," *Der Islam* 92, no. 2 (2015), 442–67. On the concept of wonder in other mediums of material culture, see Matthew Saba, "Abbasid Lusterware and the Aesthetics of 'Ajab," *Muqarnas* 29 (2012): 187–212; and Orlin Sŭbev, *Waiting for Müteferrika: Glimpses on Ottoman Print Culture* (Boston: Academic Studies Press, 2018), 1–15.
40. Ḥāfiẓ-i Abru, *A Persian Embassy to China: Being an Extract from Zubdatu't Tawarikh of Hafiz Abru*, trans. K. M. Maitra (New York: Paragon Book Reprint Corp, 1970), 6–7. This term also frequently appeared in later-period Persian travel writing to Europe; see Naghmeh Sohrabi, *Taken for Wonder: Nineteenth Century Travel Accounts from Iran to Europe* (Oxford: Oxford University Press, 2012).
41. Yusen Yu, "Representing Ming China in Fifteenth-Century Persianate Painting," *Ming Studies*, no. 78 (2018): 57–73.
42. Soucek, "The New York Public Library 'Makhzan al-asrār' and Its Importance," 15–16.
43. On theories of sight, see Gülru Necipoğlu, "The Scrutinizing Gaze in the Aesthetics of Islamic Visual Cultures: Sight, Insight, and Desire," *Muqarnas* 32 (2015): 23–61.
44. Thomas T. Allsen, *Commodity and Exchange in the Mongol Empire: A Cultural History of Islamic Textiles* (Cambridge: Cambridge University Press, 2002). On the religious and political significance of gold in a Eurasian context, see Michael L. Walter, *Buddhism and Empire: The Political and Religious Culture of Early Tibet* (Leiden: Brill, 2009), 287–91.
45. Thackston, "Treatise on Calligraphic Arts," 219–28. It is worth noting that the Ming diplomatic letters addressed to Muslim rulers were also decorated in gold. For example, see Francis Woodman Cleaves, "The Sino-Mongolian Edict of 1453 in the Topkapi Sarayi Müzesi̧," *Harvard Journal of Asiatic Studies* 13, no. 3/4 (1950): 431–46.
46. Zeren Tanindi, "Some Problems of Two Istanbul Albums, H. 2153 and 2160," *Islamic Art* 1 (1981): 37; Soucek, "The New York Public Library 'Makhzan al-asrār' and Its Importance," 14.
47. See the entry for "zarafshan" in the online edition of the Dehkhoda Dictionary, accessed November 4, 2020, https://dehkhoda.ut.ac.ir/fa/dictionary/172342 زرافشان.
48. Cited in Maria Eva Subtelny, "The Poetic Circle at the Court of the Timurid Sultan Ḥusain. Baiqara and its Political Significance" (PhD diss., Harvard University, 1979), 208. Another famous case is that, according to al-Maqrizi, the Malian ruler Mansa Musa in his pilgrimage to Mecca distributed so much gold dust that he caused a depreciation in the value of the gold dinar.
49. See "zarafshan" in the online edition of the Dehkhoda Dictionary.
50. Finbarr B. Flood, *Objects of Translation: Material Culture and Medieval "Hindu-Muslim" Encounter* (Princeton: Princeton University Press, 2009), 34. See also George, "Calligraphy, Colour and Light in the Blue Qur'an," 98–105.
51. George, "Calligraphy, Colour and Light in the Blue Qur'an," 104.
52. On *waqf* in Timurid period, see Maria E. Subtelny, *Timurids in Transition: Turko-Persian Politics and Acculturation in Medieval Iran* (Leiden: Brill, 2007), 148–91.
53. Roxburgh, *The Persian Album*, 165.
54. On manuscripts as endowed objects, see Sheila R. Canby, *Shah 'Abbas: The Remaking of Iran* (London: British Museum Press, 2009), 116–84.

To Have Temperature

Material and Metamorphosis in Nineteenth-Century China

Catherine Stuer

The expression "to have temperature" is a literal translation of the Chinese *you wendu*, a relatively recent but widely circulating idiom that serves to describe a "warm, human touch" in things and actions. Grounded in figurative reference to the capacity for thermoregulation by living bodies, it is sometimes translated as "warm-bloodedness" but seems to evoke less a fiery passion than a temperate, humane disposition and affect. What is more, this term would appear to refer as much to the affect of things as of human beings, which the warm-blooded/cold-blooded dichotomy does not. I pay some attention to this term here since it figured in conversations I had recently with lacquer carvers in southeast China. In using this term to articulate the attraction lacquer holds as material for making, my interlocutors were tapping into recent discourse about the affectivity of objects and materials, speaking to historically specific conditions of social and material life. I raise these observations to point at an approach to materials in art and craft that seeks to engage the perspective of those who work it and the networks of meaning making of which they are part.

Attending to material from a practitioner's vantage point includes assuming the closeness of touch, not just of the finished product but of the material in the process of its making through transformative manipulation by hands and tools. As it is made, lacquer does not identify with a stable, essential property but instead extends across changing states and sensory qualities. These range from the viscous, liquid form of the lacquer resin and its admixtures to the soft, pliable, almost skin-like stage when it is worked, to its capacity to reach a superbly hard and resilient state after drying. The "warmth" of lacquer the carvers invoked certainly attaches at least in part to the soft tactility of the half-dried surfaces on which they work, especially in the case of thickly layered, monochromatic lacquer. The working of such surfaces is often referred to as *ti*, or "picking," as in the fine clearing of skin or bone, and as such is distinguished from the more general *diao*, or "carving," typically associated with knife-work in harder materials. By the same token, while temperature and atmosphere agreeable to human life are eminently suited to the making of lacquer and its objects—from the zones in which the lacquer tree thrives to the moist and warm environment ideal for its mixing as well as drying and preservation—the sympathetic quality of this material is offset by the effects of the raw sap of the Chinese Lacquer Tree (*Toxicodendron vernicifluum*) on human skin, which when exposed can suffer severe allergic reactions like poison ivy rash. This toxicity is an issue that contemporary practitioners have to contend with, both in their everyday work and in its effects on the public imaginary of their craft.

Early texts on lacquer reference this quality in a number of ways: while singled out for focus in Diderot (1713–1784) and d'Alembert's (1717–1783) *Encyclopédie*, Huang Cheng's (act. late sixteenth c.) *Records of Lacquering* (*Xiushilu*) presents what was once commonly called "to be bitten by lacquer" as a counterpart to the tree's medicinal properties.[1] This juxtaposition of the negative and positive effects of lacquer resin on the human body would be in keeping with the overall interest of this last text, written and annotated by practitioners, to integrate the divergent properties of lacquer and its various applications, exceeding the expertise of a single master or workshop, into a dynamically interrelated whole.

In this chapter, I explore how a maker and a writer in early nineteenth-century China worked and imagined lacquer as material for the crafting of objects and images. Ever since the sixteenth century, lacquer has allured global as well as local audiences as material for making precious objects, acquiring a range of sensory and symbolic associations that might seem at odds with those suggested by its sobriquet as the world's "first plastic."[2] Still, the variety of its mixtures, transformations in tactility, ways in which it is worked, and design of objects and images to which it gives shape, invites thinking about lacquer in relation to wider orders of material marked by plasticity. As a whole, plastic materials such as lacquer offer fertile ground to explore constructions of materiality in art and craft. Georges Didi-Huberman has broached this discussion by taking a closer look at the uses and representations of wax in the European context.[3] He shows that attention to its intrinsic properties raises foundational questions about how art historians have thought the rapport between form and matter. By dint of their materiality alone, such as the propensity to take rather than resist and yield to form, plastic materials in and of themselves challenge dichotomous conceptions of matter-form relations and disrupt their neat alignment with social, gendered, and aesthetic hierarchies. In so doing, Didi-Huberman argues, plastic materials open up new spaces to reflect on histories of creation in art and craft. In that sense, Roland Barthes's negative reading of (industrial) plastic as anti-value that abolishes what he calls the hierarchy of substances may serve as a delightful illustration of the thinking Didi-Huberman interrogates and of its configurations inside industrial modernity.[4] At the same time, attending to the process of making also shows us that the creation of form is always already material, and never a mere matter of dominance and submission. Exploring foundational questions about the ethics of making, Richard Sennett has proposed a few ways to consider such imbrications of thinking with making in craft practice across time.[5] He terms "material consciousness" the way in which materials arouse the mind and suggests that, over time, this thinking has taken shape in three important ways: as metamorphosis, presence, and anthropomorphosis. The first speaks to how we alter materials in craft production, the second to how we mark materials to register human presence, and the third to how we identify materials with ourselves. I have found these perspectives useful when considering engagements with metamorphosis in the lacquer work by Lu Dong (d. 1850) and in contemporary aesthetic writings, especially by the poet and aesthete Chen Wenshu (1771–1843). Together, they invite us to consider historical patterns in craft-based and discursive articulations of material consciousness and reflect on their imbrication in social and material life.

Lu Dong was a lacquer craftsman from Yangzhou known mostly by his style name Kuisheng. As a third-generation practitioner, he followed in the footsteps of his father, Lu Shenzhi (n.d.), and grandfather, Lu Yingzhi (n.d.), active from the late Kangxi (1661–1722) into the Qianlong (1735–1796) eras. While biographical records lodge his identity firmly in this family tradition, Lu Kuisheng is also recorded to have been a National University Student (*jiansheng*), a mark of upward mobility that was the result of a costly process and testifies to the professional success of the family's workshop business.[6] We may thus not be surprised to find that Lu Kuisheng was said to mingle with the scholarly elite, and that extant letters of social and business correspondence attest to a polite, personal rapport in his relations with notable literati of the time.[7] A contemporary account that we will come back to later connects Lu's social affinities with his accomplishments in the art of painting, achievements its author compliments as deserving historical recognition.[8] He is known to have studied with Zhang Cining (1743–1818), a painter from Cangzhou (Hebei) active in Yangzhou who became known for his untrammeled brushwork and was regarded by some as the leader of a so-called Northern School in early nineteenth-century painting.[9] The few landscape paintings carrying Lu's signature and seal that are extant today suggest an interest in late Wu school painting styles that may connect to an early predilection of Zhang's but do not share the energetic expressiveness of his brush.[10] To the extent that contemporary records reference his painting style, they do so in terms closely akin to descriptions of his personality and bearing: just as his person was said to be "honest and careful, modest and respectful, reserved in speech and laughter" (*chunjin qiangong, bugou yanxiao*), his brush was "honest and late in life particularly careful" (*[bi] chun wannian youjin*).[11] For their part, records of his workshop production describe the carved images of mountains and waters, flowers, birds, and ancient engravings on his scholastic objects as being filled with "beauty and ingenuity" (*yanqiao*), and a letter noting the receipt of mirror-boxes praises them for being "ancient and simple, elegant and pure" (*gupu yajie*).[12] The first of these was a significant but standard term of distinction in craft, and the second associates his lacquer objects in a generic sense with well-established literati aesthetic and moral values.[13] In as far as we can tell from extant objects reliably associated with the production of Lu's Old Elm Studio (*Guyu shuwu*) on Yangzhou's Gengzi Street, his brand would mainly have been associated with smaller objects for the gentleman's study, including inkstones and inkstone boxes, writing boxes, wrist rests, snuff bottles, teapots, flower stands, and so on.[14] Written records by and large support this focus, even as an early source and transmitted objects bearing his seal leave open the possibility that he also may have produced larger pieces of household furnishing.[15]

From the early studies by Wang Shixiang (1914–2009) to Chang Bei's recent *History of Yangzhou Lacquerware*, Lu Kuisheng has come to be regarded as maybe the most consummate literati craftsman in the history of lacquering in China.[16] Aspects of his work highlighted in this regard include the types of objects associated with his name and the aesthetic affinities of their design, such as a predilection for subdued tonal and textural values, for modest materials, and for a reserved pictorial and antiquarian décor. In Chang Bei's view, Lu would have been a workshop owner who combined a deep knowledge of his craft with a "more elevated" artistic cultivation and mostly acted in a supervising role to the artisans working for him, picking up the tools of lacquering himself only when inspiration moved him to do so.[17] Exploring the relation between late imperial crafts with literati aesthetics in terms of how it materialized transactions of social power, Craig Clunas has offered another reading of social affinities in Lu's workshop production.[18] Exemplifying his case with a set of carved monochrome panels with Lu's seal featuring scenes of gentlemen in well-appointed gardens (fig. 1), Clunas argues that it shows the effects of how by the Qing dynasty, painting dominated the total field of artistic production, appropriating as it were the pictorial project of the arts and crafts as a whole.[19] Specifically, these objects would serve to illustrate that even a craft with "a separate visual aesthetic" like lacquer turns away and toward the flat surface of the painted image.[20] How should we understand the role of lacquer as material and craft in the transactions or transformations perceived here? Does it "live up to" literati values, as suggested in the first reading, but mainly because of Lu's congenial mindset? Or does it indeed "disappear" into painting, an act of submission to the social power of this medium, as suggested in the second?

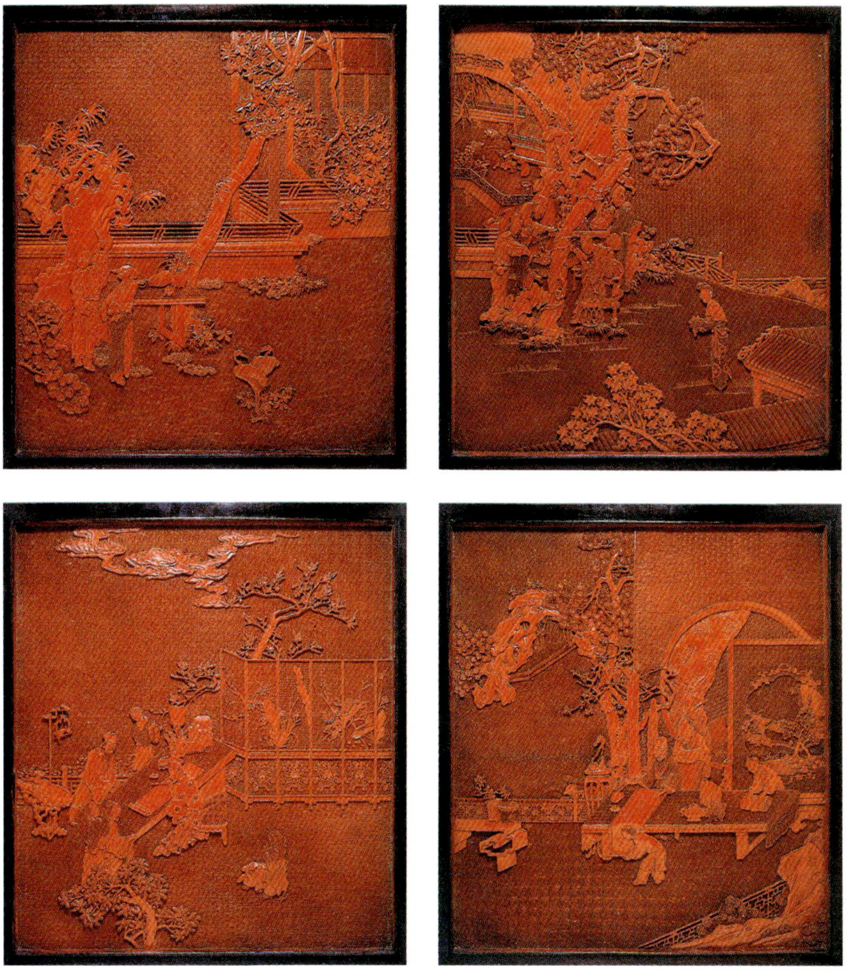

Figure 1 Lu Dong, Set of four panels with scenes of men writing and painting in well-appointed gardens, nineteenth century. Carved red lacquer, each 51 × 56 cm. Incised square seal in the lower right corner of the fourth panel: "*Kuisheng zhiyin*" (seal of Kuisheng). Private Collection. From Paul Moss, *Documentary Chinese Works of Art: In Scholars' Taste* (London: Sydney L. Moss Ltd., 1983), plate 147. Courtesy of Sydney L. Moss, Ltd., London.

Considering that these opposite readings reveal a similar understanding of how material relates to form in Lu's craft, the question becomes if this is indeed how this relation should be understood. Two early nineteenth-century texts dated just one year apart help us approach this question anew. Both anchor Lu's craft to thinking with metamorphosis, but each from a different vantage point: the first presents an object made by Lu as part of the author's vision of an expanded field of the art of painting, and the second mediates

Lu's voice in a self-narrative of craft-based invention. I will first discuss these texts in that sequence, and then reconsider Lu's transmitted work in light of the perspectives they offer.

The catalogue of poems on paintings titled *New Poems on a Forest of Paintings* (*Hualin xinyong*; hereafter *New Poems*) by Chen Wenshu, a onetime celebrated poet from Qiantang and Provincial Graduate of the Jiaqing period (1796–1820), appears at first sight to follow a well-established genre of premodern aesthetic writing.[21] Like any typical poem-on-painting catalogue, artists' names serve as entry titles that are each followed by a short biographical record and a poem. On closer inspection however, this text ends up reimagining the genre from the inside out. In the preface dated mid-autumn day 1827, the author points at what he has in mind:

> In youth I loved cinnabar and azurite, and in old age I am besotted with ink. . . . From my childhood to this day I assembled over 300 people, each with a poem attached, truly a Qilin Pavilion of painters of the last sixty years. Extending to border territories and foreign regions, to patterns on wood and on stone, to the crafts of carving and embroidery: nothing is left out so that its metamorphoses are exhaustively listed [*mobu biju yijin qibian*].[22]

Approaching the age of sixty, Chen reflects back on his engagement with painting (*hua*) and offers a vision that is comprehensive in more than one sense. It captures a lifetime of looking, collecting, and writing about painting, and seeks to embrace the totality of painting's transformations as they unfold across territories, crafts, and materials. The four chapters that follow bear out this promise. For one, the text is deeply personal, representing the author's lifeworld through the artists he has known and the paintings he has collected, seen, or heard of. The 312 artist entries in the first three chapters match the number in the preface, while a fourth, supplemental chapter adds another 117.[23] At a first level, the entries are organized by gender, men occupying the first two chapters and women the third, and the fourth chapter again listing men and then women in the same order and two-to-one distribution. No surprises there. Yet at a second level, this model is disrupted by inserting into these gendered categories entry titles that capture the metamorphoses (*bian*) anticipated in the preface. On closer reading, the content and organization of these peculiar entries point toward a reimagination of the notion of painting as such.

That is, the second chapter ends with four entries that identify not artists but kinds of painting from diverse foreign regions, including "Country of Japan Painting" (*Ribenguo hua*), "Country of Ryukyu Painting" (*Liuqiuguo hua*), "Western Ocean Painting" (*Xiyang hua*), and "Tibet Painting" (*Xizang hua*), while the third chapter concludes with thirty-three entries that distinguish different types of painting by type of materiality. The fourth chapter supplements this last group with seven more of these what we might call "material paintings." By pairing the name of a material or craft with the word "*hua*," Chen Wenshu does not so much coin as cultivate a vocabulary that reconceptualizes what this word means. Structurally parallel to long-existing terms such as "painting on paper" (*zhi hua*) or "painting on silk" (*juan hua*) that identify the surface materials on which painting is executed, and expanding on the principle implied in more recent terms such as "Iron Painting" (*tie hua*), Chen includes cultures, crafts, media, objects, materials, organic matter, and nonhuman creators as part of a new lexicon that reconfigures *hua* as a semantic field.[24] In this interconnected and expanding field, cultural and craft practices, living and atmospheric matter, ancient and ephemeral materials are coextensive with each other in a seemingly limitless realm of transformation. The sequence by which painting's metamorphoses emerge from the categories that stage them tracks this movement of expansion discursively. At the end of the second chapter, an entry named for an ambassador from Korea and another for an unnamed English envoy provide the segue for what one could term "cultural paintings." In their turn, the "material paintings" that follow female artists in the third chapter open with crafts that one way or another occupy an aesthetic space close to that of ink painting, starting with women's crafts such as "Embroidery Painting" (*xiu hua*) and "Woven [Paper] Painting" (*zhi hua*). These provide the segue to images crafted on useful objects, such as "Sprinkled Gold Painting" (*penjin hua*), a Japanese style of lacquer décor (Jap. *maki-e*), and "Carved Lacquer Painting" (*diaoqi hua*), the entry dedicated to Lu Kuisheng's creations. From there, the series expands into the realm of natural images, first made with organic matter, as in "Rice Painting" (*mi hua*) used in Buddhist ritual practice, and then created by nature, as in "Rain Painting" (*yu hua*), a landscape scene created by rain leaking on the worn-out walls of a barn on his grandfather's land. Finally, the author pivots to material evidence of painting's historical transformations, a temporal counterpart to the spatial metamorphoses that conclude the previous chapter, including "Western Territories Han [dynasty] Painting" (*xiyu Han hua*), fragments of wall paintings found in mountain caves in Kashgar, "Stone Carved Han [dynasty] Painting" (*shike Han hua*), or unearthed pictorial reliefs from the Wu Liang shrine, and "Mirror's Back Jin [dynasty] Painting" (*jingbei Jin hua*), a pictorial scene on the reverse side of an ancient mirror. With entries such as "Pinched [Peel] Painting" (*qia hua*) and "[Tobacco] Smoke Painting" (*yan hua*), the fourth chapter extends this sequence yet further into the world of playful and ephemeral image making.

To what extent does this metamorphic unspooling tell us something about how relations between matter and form are thought? For one, the chain of transformations and the author's descriptive and lyric reflections on them progressively dislodge the privileged identification of *hua* as a creative pictorial medium with images brushed in ink on a silk or paper surface.[25] Even if it builds on notions circulating in related discourse, their integration and conceptualization within painting's metamorphoses reveal a dynamic vision of material practices unprecedented in aesthetic writing. The entry "Rain Painting," for example, invokes a well-worn trope about creative inspiration in landscape painting.[26] Here, however, this spontaneous image has become self-sufficient, independent of human mediation but for this record of boyhood fascination with the marvelous landscape, "as if a painting by the Older Mi [Mi Fu, 1051–1107]" (*yanran Da Mi shanshui yifu*) on his grandfather's old barn. The entry "Iron Painting," a term of more recent vintage, in turn highlights the author's attention to the social dimension of aesthetic independence in craft-based material painting. In Chen's telling, the story about the invention of this new craft becomes an explicit act of defiance against the perceived superiority of ink painting. His story goes: in the early days of the dynasty, a blacksmith from Wuhu named Tang Peng (act. seventeenth c.) lives next door to the painter Xiao Yuncong (style name: Chimu, 1596–1673). In his leisure time, he goes to see the man paint but is scolded, to which he responds with indignation: "So you say I can't paint?" Before long Tang creates an ingenious wrought iron screen with landscapes, flowers, and birds that are a marvel to behold, and Xiao the painter is left to gasp in amazement.[27] Chen's version enlivens existing narratives with the craftsman's explicit provocation of the painter, and completes it with the latter's speechless concession.[28] This sense of challenge to established aesthetic and social norms resonates across *New Poems*: the author is clearly interested in creative capacity irrespective of social background and appreciates painting as craft and as trade, whether done in brush and ink or in its other transformations. We see this in the text's self-conscious attention to making and to painting as a means of subsistence, in its inclusion of artists of humble origin such as craftsmen, traders, male and female servants, and by the same token, in its disinterest in privileging the imperial court and officialdom as the center of social power or creativity. In fact, apart from holding with biographical conventions that divide subjects by gender and by secular versus religious identity, there is no discernable social or aesthetic organization in Chen's collection of artists. These are instead clustered by a variety of artistic, social, or family associations, or relation to the author and so on, a meandering sequence that if anything would only reflect the author's wandering memory.[29] Then again, if the allocation of painting's geographical transformations to the domain of men, and its material metamorphoses to that of women reinforces normative hierarchies of patriarchal power and their alignment of male-female with culture-nature binaries, this framework is also disrupted by boundary-crossing content. This happens in two ways: entries on ink painting refer to painting's metamorphoses and vice versa, and women appear unexpectedly inside the chapters on male artists.[30] The inclusion of female religious adepts and performers right after male Daoist and Buddhist artists is certainly related to the author's own spiritual pursuits.[31] At the same time, this boundary crossing resonates with his well-known mentorship of female literary talent, pinpointed by his record of a poetess doing self-portraits in male drag.[32] It would seem that these moves are interconnected and together challenge the symmetries of social and aesthetic hierarchy implied in their textual frame. As such, Chen's text does not completely displace but destabilizes normative constructions of male-female, culture-nature, art-craft, and arguably, form-matter relations. Even if one could argue that *New Poems* draws out an expanding territory of *hua* as totalizing concept, it counteracts a hegemonic, immaterial understanding of this concept by investing its material metamorphoses with creative energies that do not submit to those primarily materialized in the medium of brush and ink. In other words, this text presents less an image of unification and subordination than of progressive untethering and reconnecting to elemental, plural, and novel creative vitalities.[33] The originality of Chen's move is underscored by its impact on an anthology of biographies of painters composed by his younger contemporary, Peng Yuncan (1780–1840). Ostensibly taken with Chen's inventiveness, Peng selectively samples content from Chen's *New Poems*, including from his entries on cultural and material painting, but presents these inside a restored hegemonic order.[34]

Though Lu Kuisheng appears in Chen's text, like Tang Peng as the prime artist associated with one of painting's metamorphoses, he is presented not as its inventor but as an extraordinary practitioner of a hallowed tradition. The entry on "Carved Lacquer Painting" reads:

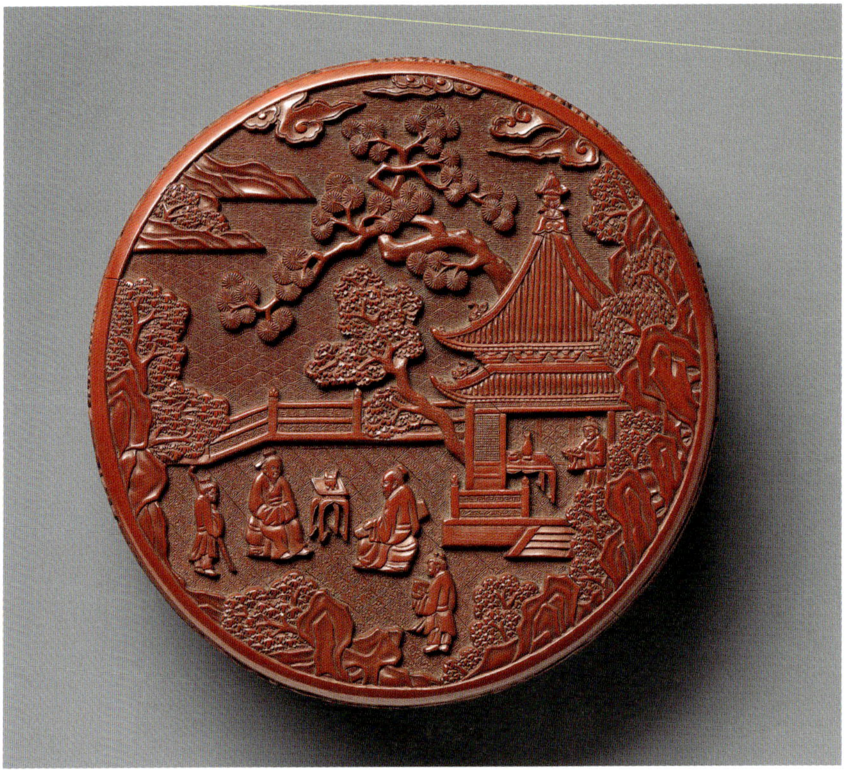

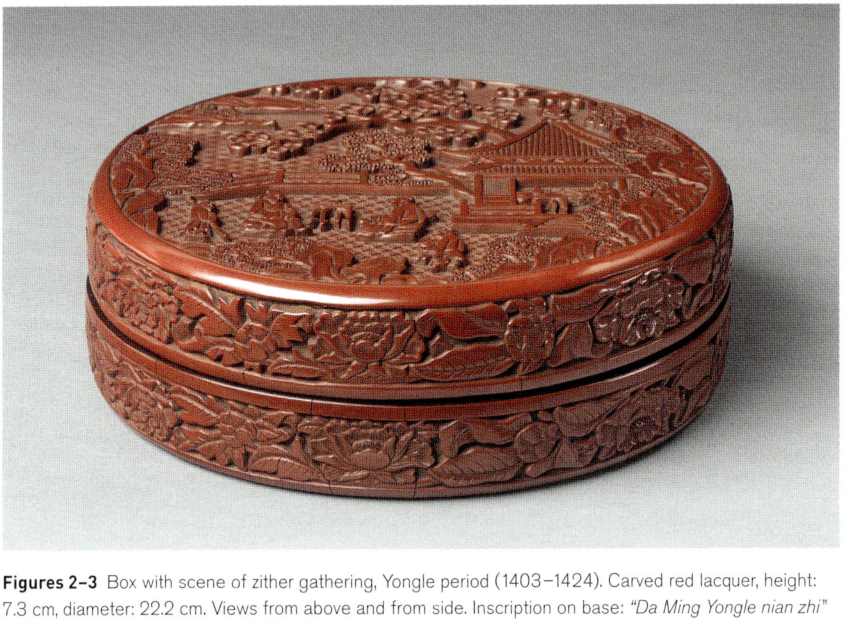

Figures 2–3 Box with scene of zither gathering, Yongle period (1403–1424). Carved red lacquer, height: 7.3 cm, diameter: 22.2 cm. Views from above and from side. Inscription on base: *"Da Ming Yongle nian zhi"* (made in the Yongle era of the great Ming). Collection of the Metropolitan Museum of Art, 2015.500.1.6a, b.

> Carved lacquer is also a tradition dating back to the Song dynasty [960–1279]. Lu Kuisheng of Yangzhou makes fruit boxes that are extremely accomplished, outstanding like Qiu Zhong. Carving flowers inside that reach as deep as the bottom is an especially extraordinary skill.
>
> Crafted as beautiful jade, pure and without blemish
> With a touch of his hand, Spring has given birth to five-colored flowers
> No reason to envy the Orchard Factory of the former dynasty
> Carvers of Yangzhou praise the house of Lu.
> During the Ming dynasty [1368-1644], the Orchard Factory
> in Beijing produced very fine lacquerware.[35]

The kind of object this text evokes would be a box made of tens of layers of lacquer in a single color, its thick surface used to bring out forms that engage the depth of that layering in thought-provoking ways (figs. 2–3).[36] Illustrating the attention to the agency of material and making that runs through *New Poems*, Chen foregrounds the visual and material effects specific to carved monochrome lacquer, identifying the craftsman's hand and the depth of carving as sites of creativity and transformation. Speaking more generally to virtuosity in craft, he compares Lu's work to a legendary bamboo brush holder owned by a brush-based artist *par excellence*, Wang Xianzhi (317–420), so unique it had its own name. Finally, he situates Lu's workshop production both historically and competitively in relation to the carved lacquer made at the Ming dynasty's imperial Orchard Factory. In so doing, Chen holds close to well-established perspectives of famous connoisseurs such as Gao Shiqi (1644–1703), who regarded Ming imperial workshop production as the standard of excellence in this lacquer technique.[37] However, the particular kind of lacquer décor and genealogy invoked here are not representative of Lu Kuisheng's transmitted work, nor of the way in which the craftsman chose to frame his own practice.

That is, a record in the collected writings of the textual scholar Gu Guangqi (style name: Qianli, 1766–1835), dated just one year earlier than Chen's *New Poems*, conveys the craftsman's own account of lineage and transformation. Gu composed this record in appreciation of a sand-lacquer inkstone gifted to him by Lu Kuisheng, recounting the origin story shared with him at that occasion. Quoting Lu directly, Gu writes:

> In the Dingyou Year of the reign of Kangxi [1717], my late grandfather acquired on the market outside the south walls [of Yangzhou] an inkstone inscribed with the six characters: "*Song Xuanhe neifu zhi*" [Manufactured by the Song Imperial Household in the Xuanhe era (1119–1125)]. Its shape and material were like refined clay [*chengni*] but [it was] extremely light and did not sink when placed in water. [My grandfather] was quite puzzled. After a long while, he realized that it was made of sand lacquer [*qisha*]. He instructed [his] artisan to replicate it and only after exhausting the thoughts of his [or: their] heart [*jijie xinsi*] was he [or: were they] finally able to do so successfully. Those who liked to use it all said that they obtained something they never had before. Master Wintry Heart, Jin Nong [1687–1763], wrote an inscription for it. Its method was thereupon passed on to the present.[38]

Gu Guangqi takes it over from there to present his own ranking of the sand lacquer inkstone among the very best, praising Lu's grandfather Yingzhi's "ingenious knowledge and enlightenment" (*jingshi miaowu*) for making the transmission of this ancient but long-lost material possible. He goes on to reference Yuan Mei's (1716–1798) appreciation for Lu Yingzhi's amiable and principled bearing, as well as his "lofty refinement and knowledge of antiquity" (*gaoya tonggu*), and he lauds his grandson Kuisheng for carrying on the family tradition, his accomplishments as a painter, and friendship with gentlemen of letters.

We hear in this text Lu Kuisheng's active promotion of a family and workshop identity centered on the discovery and replication (*fang*) of an ancient craft material and the expert knowledge and creativity required for doing so. Sand lacquer (*qisha*) is a material made by mixing lacquer sap with mineral particles and kaolin clay or ceramic dust.[39] To make an inkstone, this mixture is applied in layers on a wood core. It is key to manage the granularity in such a way as to permit just the right abrasive capacity for grinding the ink—but not too much, otherwise it could damage the brush. As the records note, this kind of inkstone's great advantages over stone and clay are its weight and transportability, and likely related to that, some say that it became associated with success in exams.[40] Quite a few extant inkstones made of sand lacquer carrying Lu's seal share a distinct shape and dimensions that require special attention. Measuring about 14 cm long by 10 cm wide, these unadorned inkstones stand about 4 cm tall, with contours that curve symmetrically outward on the left and right sides, and inward at the front (figs. 4–5). The sides form walls that run straight down, except on the front end, which is left open to form the handle (*chaoshou*).[41]

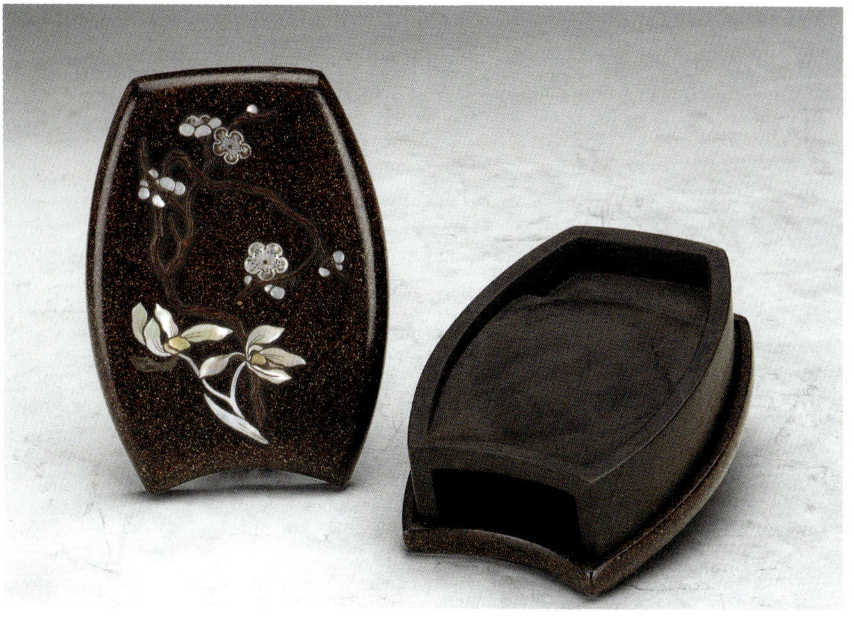

Figure 4 Lu Dong, Copy of Xuanhe-era inkstone with box, first half of nineteenth century. Inkstone: sand lacquer, 3.4 × 9.5 × 13.4 cm, box: *babaohui* lacquer with inlay décor. Courtesy of the Tianjin Museum.

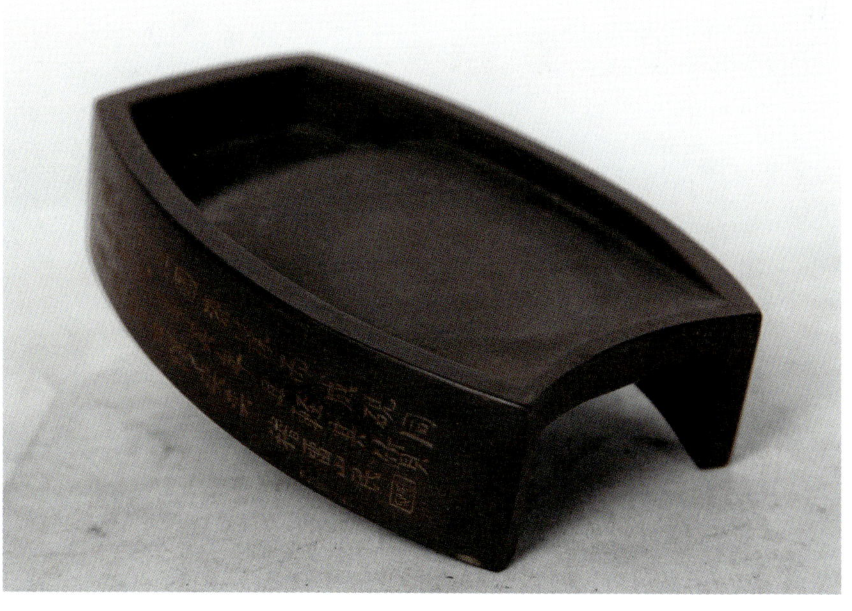

Figure 5 Lu Dong, Copy of Xuanhe-era inkstone. View showing wall with laudatory verse by Jin Nong. Courtesy of the Tianjin Museum.

The hollow base features a round protrusion under the ink pool and slopes down to the water pool on the far end. The right side of the inkstone is engraved in clerical script with the phrase "Replication of Song Xuanhe Imperial Household manufacture" (*fang Song Xuanhe neifu zhi*), matching the inscription noted in Gu's record. In the case illustrated above (see fig. 5), the left side features a laudatory inscription by Jin Nong, the Yangzhou artist of his grandfather's generation mentioned in the same text. In some other cases, the inscription on the left wall may feature a verse by Zhu Yizun (1629–1709) or by Zhou Lianggong (1612–1672), two connoisseurs active earlier in the dynasty.[42] The type-form of these stones is peculiar, consistent, and stands out in Lu's inkstone production as a whole, buffering the idea of a special relation to a unique prototype. The so-called *chaoshou* aspect of its shape, designed to be handy for lifting, was indeed typical for Song dynasty *chengni* inkstones, as exemplified by a large, rectangular one now held in the Tianjin Museum (fig. 6). However, there seems to be no precedent for its curved contours and tall profile, nor a known visual reference or descriptive terminology associated with it. The spare abstraction of this peculiar, symmetrical shape suggests instead kinship with inkstone designs intended to evoke ancient objects or archetypal forms.[43] In fact, to my knowledge there is no other record or material evidence of sand lacquer production in the Song dynasty or thereafter, and all suggestions of its existence in related literature seem to be based on Gu Qianli's "Record on the Sand Lacquer Inkstone" (*Qishayan ji*).[44] Any indications of sand lacquer inkstones seem also absent from Qianlong court collections and archives, in spite of the emperor's keen interest in replicating, imitating, and reimagining ancient inkstones and inkstone materials, leading between 1775 and 1790 to the development of a new formula for making antique-looking *chengni* inkstones by Suzhou craftsmen.[45] One might therefore speculate that this unusual type-form either registers the uniqueness of Lu's connection with a lost craft practice or is made to suggest such a connection and thus cultivate a prehistory for an invention all of his, or of his grandfather's, own. One way or the other, there is no question that the making of this particular inkstone and the telling of the story registered in Gu's record were intimately linked.

While this type-form is clearly unique, it is at the same time connected to other objects in his workshop output. Designed to ensure the visibility of the inscriptions, the fitted base and lid of these inkstones do not meet but instead leave the sides uncovered. Extant objects of this type show that these bases and lids were produced in a variation of ground effects and decorative techniques, including either a monochromatic or mixed ground (*babaohuidi*), featuring inlay

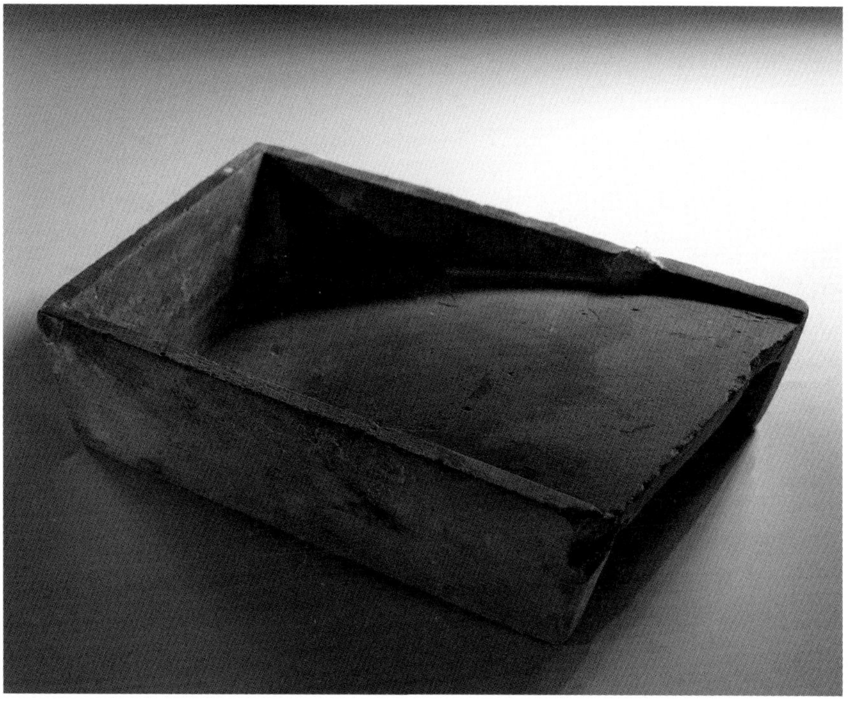

Figure 6 *Chaoshou* shape inkstone, Song dynasty (960–1279). Refined clay (*chengni*), 6.7 × 18.1 × 27.3 cm. Courtesy of the Tianjin Museum.

(*baibaoqian*) or shallow engraved (*qipidiao*) décor.[46] This variation in decorative options, their largely consistent aesthetic effects, the recurrence of the plum blossom as decorative motif, and the sand lacquer material connect this object to the rest of Lu's inkstones and writing boxes, which would together have constituted the bulk of his workshop production.[47] Two documents found inside the original container of an inkstone and fitted box with Lu's seal add another layer to our understanding of these interconnections.[48] The shorter document, written in clerical script on red paper, is a certificate of authenticity of Lu Kuisheng's Old Elm Studio, and the other a copy of Gu Qianli's record printed in standard script on a sheet of ivory-colored paper. Apparently composed around the same time as Gu's record, the certificate attests that the inkstone is made entirely in the sand lacquer method handed down "over 110 years since its creation" by Lu's grandfather. Alerting its readers to the recent and unprecedented appearance of ineffectual fakes on the market, the document recommends checking the presence of the Inkstone Record, workshop seals, and studio address in proof

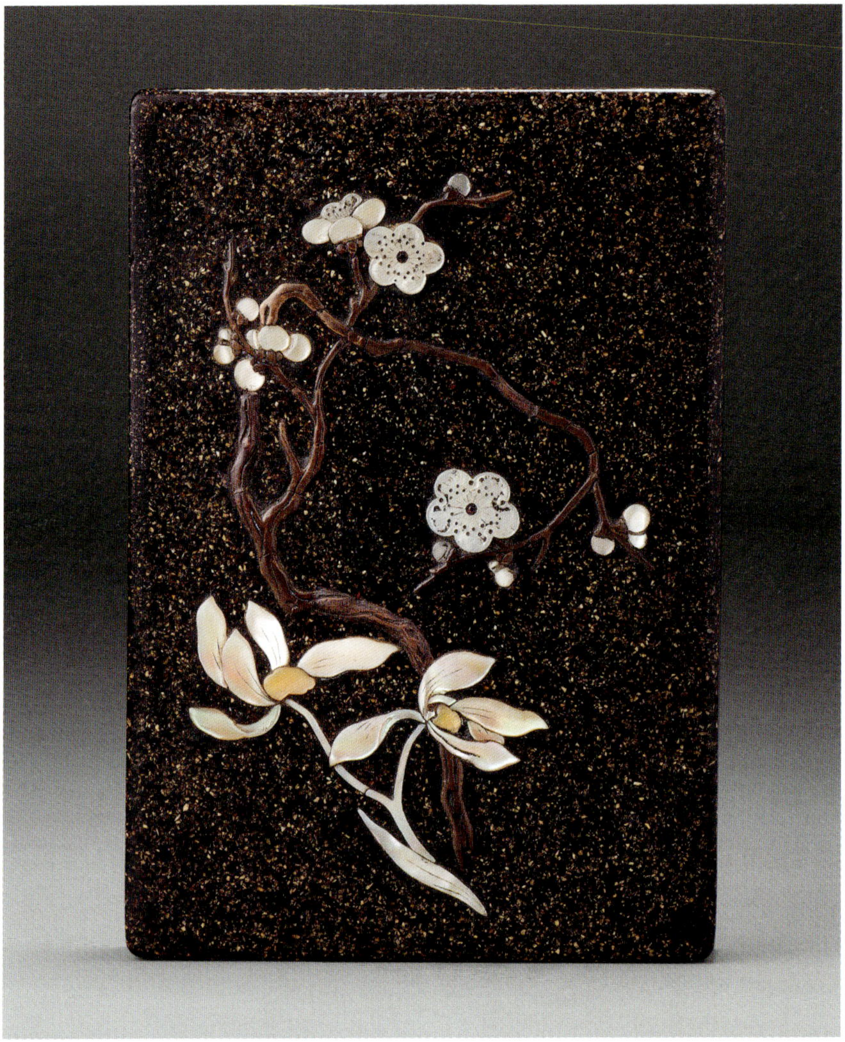

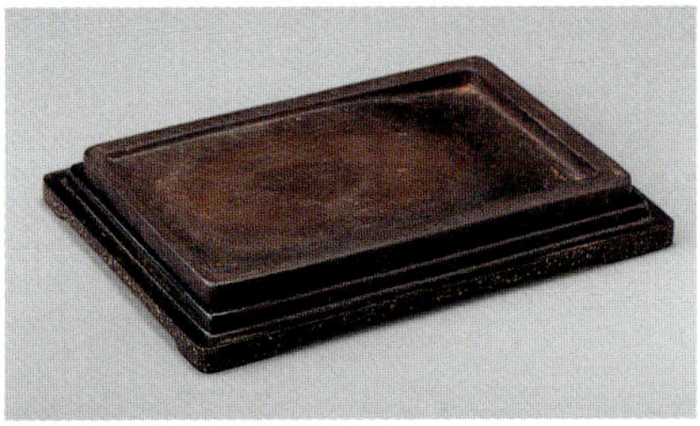

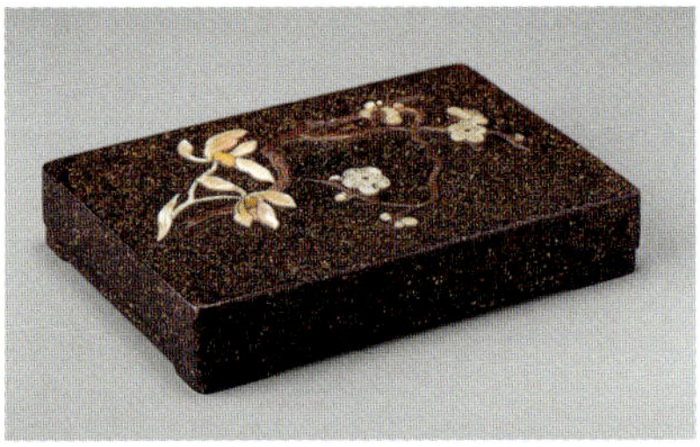

Figures 7–9 Lu Dong, Rectangular tablet-style inkstone and box, first half of nineteenth century. Inkstone: sand lacquer, 1 × 8 × 12.5 cm, box: *babaohui* lacquer with *baibaoqian* prunus and orchid, 2.7 × 10 × 14 cm. Views from above (top), of the interior (bottom left), and from side (bottom right). Red lacquer seal on base: "*Lu Kuisheng zhi*" (made by Lu Kuisheng). Courtesy of the Water, Pine and Stone Retreat Collection.

of authenticity.[49] While Gu's record has here become directly integrated in the marketing of Lu's product, the certificate for its part focuses on the invented material only, and the sand lacquer inkstone it accompanies does not follow the *chaoshou* shape prototype but is instead modeled as a simple, undecorated tablet-style inkstone. Lu Kuisheng's transmitted work includes a fair number of these rectangular-shaped (figs. 7–9), but also round (figs. 10–11) or oval, and gourd-shaped ones, all similarly made of unadorned sand lacquer. While a few carry inscriptions that reference the replication of ancient or historical precedents in broader terms, none of these inscriptions identify with the Song imperial prototype.[50] What is more, while their lids show a similar variation of decorative options seen with the *chaoshou* shape type-form, the inkstones themselves may be separate from but also integrated with their fitted boxes, a new merging of object and container that follows the plasticity of the material of which they are both made. Taken together, these interrelations show that Lu

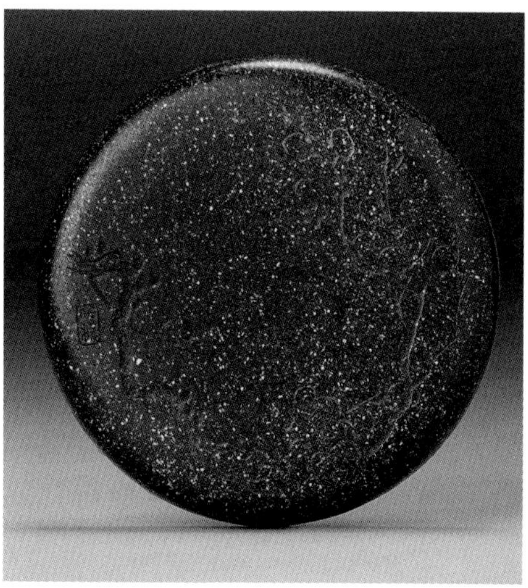

Figures 10–11 Lu Dong, Round tablet-style inkstone and box, 1838. Inkstone: sand lacquer, box: *babaohui* lacquer decorated with shallow engraving of prunus, height: 2.3 cm, diameter: 9.5 cm. Views from above and from side. Incised seal on lid: "Kuisheng." Inscription in seal script on base: "*Daoguang wushu xia liuyue Kuisheng fanggu*" (in the sixth month of summer of the Wushu Year of the reign of Daoguang [1838], by Kuisheng in imitation of antiquity). Courtesy of the Water, Pine and Stone Retreat Collection.

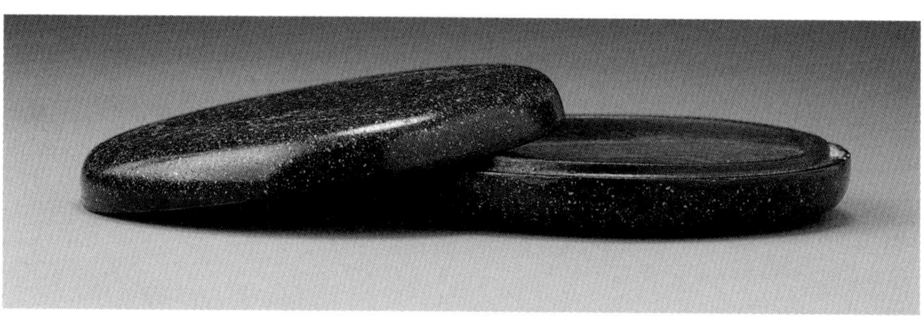

lodges the identity of his grandfather's material invention with a unique type of object, but also transfers this invention to new object shapes, creating a proliferation of distinct but interconnected product lines. Similarly, the variations of décor on the boxes show an interest in translating inlay into engraved imagery or vice versa, as seen with the design of plum blossoms arching their way inside the contours of his inkstone lids.[51] In effect, as Chang Bei points out, Lu Kuisheng appears to have been unique in his use of shallow engraving

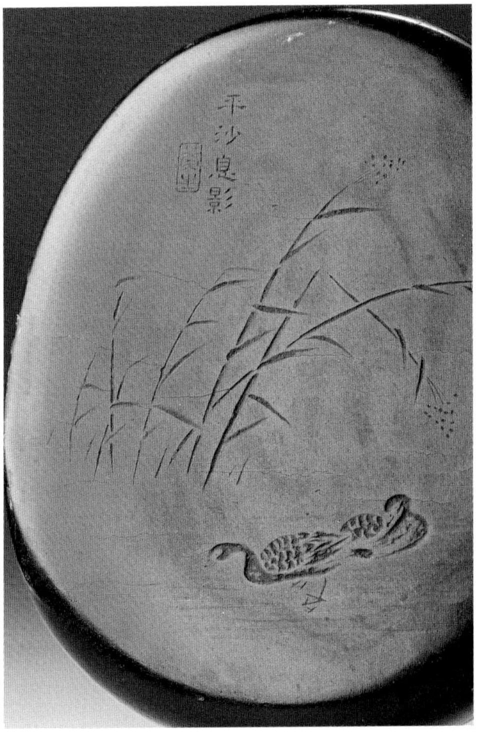

Figures 12–13 Lu Dong, Oval tablet-style inkstone and box, first half of nineteenth century. Inkstone: sand lacquer, 1 × 7.3 × 7 cm, box: monochrome lacquer with shallow engraving (*qipidiao*) of geese among reeds on a monochrome ground, 2 × 8.2 × 9.5 cm. Views from above and from side. Incised inscription in regular script on lid: "*pingsha xiying*" (resting one's shadow on the flat sand). Incised seal on lid: "Kuisheng." Red lacquer seal on base: "Kuisheng." Courtesy of the Water, Pine and Stone Retreat Collection.

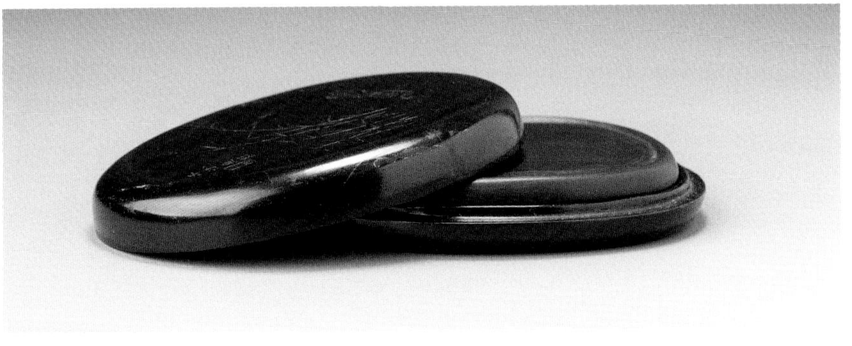

to create pictorial images on lacquer (figs. 12–13), and this technique connects his decoration of inkstone and writing boxes to yet another range of objects made by his workshop, such as teapots, wrist rests, hat stands, and snuff bottles.[52] The first two of these objects share in common that they imitate other craft materials: "purple sand" (*zisha*), i.e., Yixing clay, for the teapots and bamboo for the wrist rests. Since shallow engraving is typically used on both of these materials, it is reasonable to follow Chang Bei's assumption that Lu's imitation of them may have provided inspiration for the adoption of this decorative technique in his other lacquer work.[53] As a notable instance of material transformation, one that Wang Shixiang said was so effective that he could hardly tell the difference even on close observation, Lu's imitation *zisha* teapots connect to a recognizable, contemporary aesthetic that emerged in the artistic circle around Chen Wenshu's cousin Chen Hongshou (style name: Mansheng, 1768–1822).[54] Chen designed small teapots in collaboration with local ceramic craftsmen while stationed in Liyang County, Jiangsu, which is close to Yixing, the heart of *zisha* ware production. Inscribed and decorated by Chen and his friends before the ceramic surface had fully hardened, these objects became famous in their time and were named "Man" or "Mansheng" teapots (*man[sheng] hu*) after this notable designer. Their compact, loveable shapes typically evoke ancient or archetypal objects, to which the inscriptions and, occasionally, pictorial engravings attach witty literary and artistic associations and gestures of sociability. Lu's imitation *zisha* teapots mostly relate generically to this aesthetic, featuring similar shapes engraved with his signature flowering prunus branch and poems or with pictorial scenes and inscriptions after artists and poets of his time.[55] In one case dated to 1848, Lu specifically imitates the "Imitation of a Tang dynasty well ridge" (*fang Tang jinglan*) teapot, made after an old well in Chen's official residence in Liyang and carrying its inscription (fig. 14).[56] This Mansheng teapot appears to have been popular with the artist's circle or with their imitators, and inspired one of Chen's main potter-collaborators, Yang Pengnian (n.d.), to make a waterpot featuring the same shape and inscription.[57] In transforming this prototype into lacquer on a pewter base, Lu Kuisheng participated in this fashionable trend, while updating Chen Hongshou's inscription in fine clerical calligraphy and replacing Chen's signature with his own, and in his own hand. Finally, the perfectly cylindrical imitation hardwood brush holder with Lu's seal now held in the Zhejiang Provincial Museum, designed to replicate the polished, natural surface of organic matter, might serve as a last illustration of Lu's sustained interest in using the plastic qualities of lacquer for material transformation.[58]

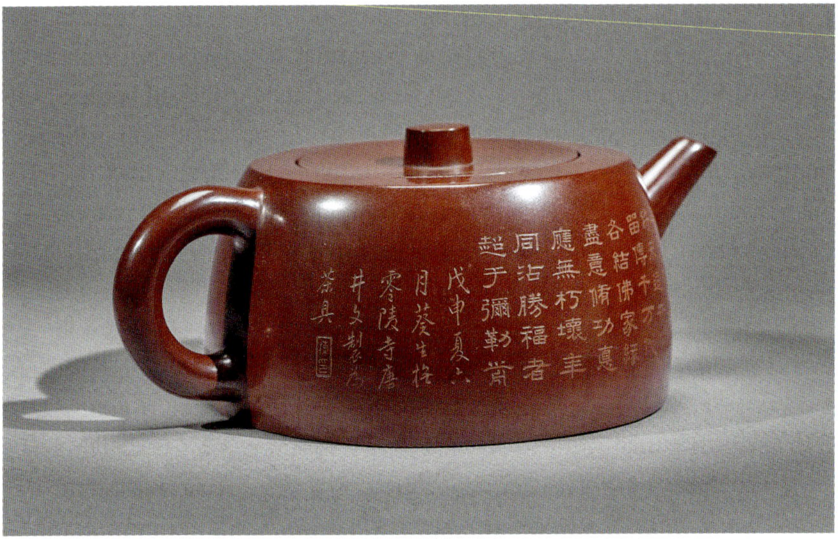

Figure 14 Lu Dong, Imitation *zisha* ware teapot, 1848. Lacquer with a pewter base, height: 8.5 cm, diameter: 14.2 cm. Inscription in clerical script with signature in running script: "*wushen xia liuyue, Kuisheng fu Linglingsi Tang jingwen zhiwei chaju*" (in the sixth month of the summer of the Wushen year [1848], Kuisheng copied the inscription of Lingling Temple's Tang dynasty well and made a teapot). Rectangular seal in seal script: "*Dong yin*" (seal of Dong). Courtesy of the Shanghai Museum.

When looking at these examples of Lu's workshop production, we see the Yangzhou craftsman center his work on his grandfather's (re)invention of sand lacquer as a new synthesis of matter in response to the puzzlement aroused by an unfamiliar material. He expands this metamorphic play across his workshop output by inventing and rearranging this new material across different type-forms, by creating new modes of lacquering to mimic different materials and the objects they shape, and by reinventing decorative possibilities by transferring and translating variations in ground and pictorial décor across their different surfaces. In so doing, we may recognize in Lu's work a number of different modes of metamorphosis described by Richard Sennett, including synthesis (the joining of unlike elements), type-form change (the elaboration of object species), and domain shifts (the application of the principle of one practice to another).[59] In fact, just as the narrative about the encounter with the mysterious Song prototype offers at least a telling metaphor for how materials arouse the mind, the author of this record echoes Sennett's notion of material consciousness in the choice of words used to describe the thinking provoked by that encounter. The phrase "exhausting the thoughts of his [or: their] heart" in Gu's record sources from a classical passage in Mengzi on the highest form of philosophical imagination.[60] This passage emphasizes that the sages not only "exhausted the thoughts of their hearts" to create principles for moral life but were only able to realize these by using benevolent government as their instrument. In referencing this passage, the author, or Lu Kuisheng, whom he quotes, not only assumes for the craftsman a quality of thinking on par with that of philosophers, but also validates, rather than diminishes, its application to the creation of material objects. Building on this legacy, the body of work extant from his grandson's workshop in turn shows how his metamorphic thinking is deliberately oriented toward the creation of a distinctive aesthetic identity. For one, these objects show that, like Chen Wenshu, he too is interested in claiming a history for his craft, albeit not in terms of Ming or Yuan dynasty standards of excellence. Instead, he does so in a number of intersecting ways. Anchored first and foremost in its antiquarian affinity with Song imperial court practice, his lacquerware connects to local Yangzhou craft traditions through the use of *baibaoqian* inlay and *babaohui* ground. Its engraved application of pictorial scenes invokes both Song dynasty ink painting archetypes and the work of celebrated painters active in Yangzhou's recent golden age. The imitation of other material objects in turn echoes with contemporary transformations in the arts and crafts.[61] This network of aesthetic and historical associations certainly identifies with the values of the educated elite of his time but does so by configuring a specific site of intersection made possible only through the affordances of lacquer crafted on his own terms.

This brings us back to the *tihong* panels discussed by Clunas (see fig. 1). In view of the fact that their object type and mode of lacquerware décor are untypical for Lu's extant and recorded work, the question becomes whether they should be taken into account for the study of his craft practice.[62] Some specialists find these panels, regardless of the presence of Lu Kuisheng's seal, hard to integrate with the techniques and styles associated with his hand and suspect them to be the work of brand imitators later in the century. In the framework of the early nineteenth-century metamorphic imagination of *hua* explored above, it is still worth considering these panels, and another monochrome carved panel of the same period carrying the seal of Sun Guoxin (n.d.) (fig. 15), in terms of how they take on the medium of painting itself as object of transformation.[63] Starting with the four panels, the design of the images in the panels with Lu's seal shows an affinity with contemporary compositional sensibilities lodged in the two-dimensionality of that medium. We may observe the dense superimposition of spatial planes played off in contrast against open surface areas, visual play with view-obstructing motifs, such as the tree trunk in the panel in the upper right, and with different perspectives, such as the frontal and bird's-eye view in the one in the lower left of this figure. While forms are finely modeled with delicate linear effects, including in the facial expressions of the figures and the flowing lines of their robes, we should note that they are not lines on a flat surface, and open areas are not really left free, but are defined by a variety of carved patterns. In fact, the pictorial image in these monochrome panels relies on the effects of contrast between the smoothly polished and raised figures and the densely textured, sunken ground. This figure-ground relation was key to *tihong* craft practice from its origins, which may go back to the Tang dynasty, but is first attested by surviving pieces from the Song dynasty.[64] From the earliest extant pieces onward, the fine, so-called diaper patterns defining this ground, termed *jindiwen*, which can be translated as "warp-faced compound tabby ground pattern," were inspired by structures of warp-faced compound tabby or polychrome silk weaves and used to denote environmental matter in the pictorial

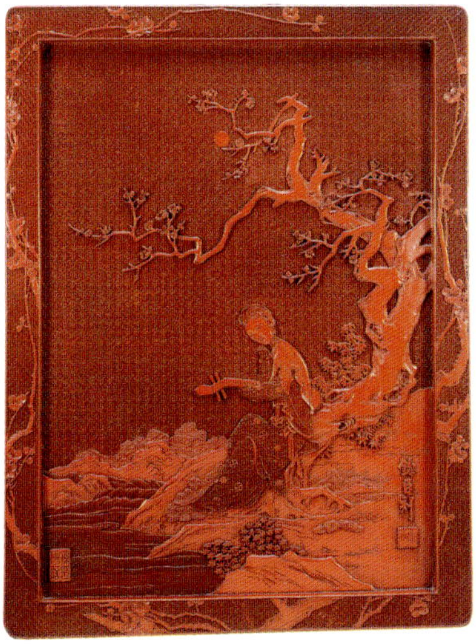

Figure 15 Sun Guoxin, Panel with scene of lutenist in a moonlit landscape, nineteenth century. Carved red lacquer, 60 × 46 cm. Lower right signature in relief: "*Zhuchen ke*" (carved by Zhuchen), engraved relief square seal: "Zhuchen." Lower left engraved relief rectangular seal: "*Sun Guoxin yin*" (seal of Sun Guoxin)." Private Collection. From Paul Moss, *The Literati Mode* (London: Sydney L. Moss, Ltd., 1986), cat. no. 140. Courtesy of Sydney L. Moss Ltd., London.

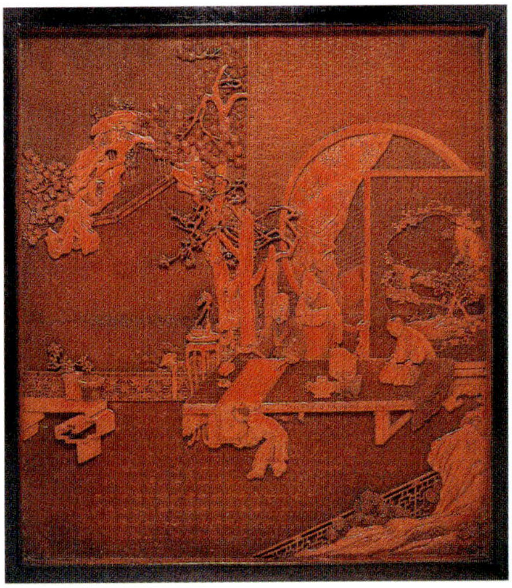

Figure 16 Lu Dong, Panel with scene of men painting in a well-appointed garden. Carved red lacquer, 51 × 56 cm. Incised square seal in lower right: "*Kuisheng zhiyin*" (seal of Kuisheng). Private Collection. From Paul Moss, *Documentary Chinese Works of Art: In Scholars' Taste*, plate 147. Courtesy of Sydney L. Moss, Ltd., London.

image.[65] That is, by differentiating land, water, and air in these images, these ornamental patterns are used to code the materiality of environments represented in the image. At the same time, the regularity of the patterns, suggesting continuity "behind" the figure raised above it, would also invoke the flat surface of painted images. The carved pictorial lacquer was from the get-go a place where representational and decorative, and two and three dimensional modes of image making were brought in dynamic tension with each other by way of more than one trans-medial connection. Late Ming bronze and bamboo imitations of carved lacquer boxes would bear testimony to the fact that the identity of what could be called pictorial carved lacquer was clearly established by at least the late Ming dynasty. A second point to be made with regard to this craft practice is that throughout its history, pictorial carved lacquer entertained a close and playful relation with the painted image, both through carved articulation as well as choices of framing and format. For example, in the carved lines of landscape motifs on a Yuan dynasty box with a scene of Tao Qian picking herbs, in the Shanghai Museum, one recognizes brush idioms associated with Southern Song painting styles.[66] In square and oblong trays, fan-shaped boxes, and desk screens made in the Ming and Qing dynasties, traditional painting formats and their compositions are integrated into three-dimensional objects.[67] Lacquer panels and grand lacquer screens of the Qianlong reign, in which landscape scenes may reflect contemporary painting styles, continue this historical engagement of pictorial carved lacquer with the medium of painting.[68]

Returning to consider the Lu Kuisheng and Sun Guoxin panels in the context of this specific craft history, we may notice not just continuities with but also new interventions in related transmedial practices. As exemplified by the panel illustrated here (fig. 16), Lu's figures are finely modeled and layered, showing three-dimensional modulation that is seemingly less "flat" than in prior examples of pictorial carved lacquer. Gauging the carving depth in Lu's panels, spatial depth seems to be contained in a few recessions into the surface, but at the same time, objects appear to come forward. This is related to the fact that figure-ground distinctions loosen as ground patterns are moving into the figure: the wall of the building in the background, the cloth on the table, some of the vessels standing about, the robe of the main figure, and the surface of the screen behind him, all of these are figurative elements covered with *jindiwen* patterns. And looking closer, the patterns on the wall surface of this panel look like "air diaper" patterns, while the sky in the upper left is covered with hexagonal patterns typically coding land surfaces. In all, there seems to be a complication here of previous distinctions between figure and ground in both their pattern-figure and raised-sunken aspects. In contrast with the interest in pictorial space carved out in deeply layered recession articulated by Chen Wenshu in his entry on "Carved Lacquer Painting," figures here are modeled against a comparatively flat surface. In this panel, which carries the seal and thus concludes the set, visual puns add a sense of self-aware commentary to its display of meta-material consciousness: two sets of vessels are arranged on the two tables, each pair a carved lacquer vessel with a ceramic and bronze one. The curtain hangings over the round entrance combine fine engraving and modeling to create the effect of a compound tabby or polychrome silk. In the screen to the right, a landscape screen profiles a raised figure against a patterned ground, set inside a carved lacquer frame. By contrast, however, the painting of the flowering prunus about to be completed is described in a fine, brush-like, engraved line. These visual statements articulate a self-aware pointing at pictorial carved lacquer and its others, playfully questioning the boundaries between the object and image that it is, and the ones that it represents. The panel of similar format with a Sun Guoxin seal may serve as an ending note to these observations (see fig. 15). In this panel, the earthen riverbank includes areas in textured relief, contrasting with smooth areas carved to evoke both thin, sinuous center-tip and broader side-length movements of brushed ink. On the riverbank, the silhouettes of a lute player and an old prunus tree are sculpturally modeled and set off against the flat surface pattern of the sky. And as if bringing closure to this series of variations in carved depiction, in the lute player's robes, a set of traditional ground patterns slip into the figure and floating surface patterns are added above them in relief, connecting this *jindiwen* representationally back to the material of its origin. What we could call the meta-material play in these panels resonates, if not necessarily directly with Lu's workshop production, still with the material consciousness witnessed by his work.

To retrace the steps of this discussion: the question raised at the outset, how to understand the relation between form and matter in lacquer work by Lu Kuisheng, led us to a text by his contemporary, Chen Wenshu. A box made by Lu appears in this text as part of a reimagination of the field of *hua*, exemplifying its metamorphosis as "Carved Lacquer Painting." If we have since come to understand that Chen's description of Lu's work does not adequately represent this particular craftsman's formal and material project, it should be read in the context of his text as a response aroused by lacquer's capacity for transformative engagement with image making.[69] For his part, Lu Kuisheng's workshop production emerges as a historically specific manipulation of the plasticity of lacquer and its propensity for stimulating material consciousness. Taken as a whole, objects from his Old Elm Studio testify to modes of metamorphic thinking that can usefully be described with the language proposed by Richard Sennett. In so doing, they engage cultural values while self-consciously expressing a series of historical, material, aesthetic, and cultural affinities that do not submit to the hegemonic authority of a single medium or creative principle. Notably, in this body of work, metamorphosis of the image happens as part and parcel of that of material: images in these objects are integral to the material transformations that stage them. By the same token, extant panels by contemporary craftsmen working in carved monochrome lacquer display a similar kind of self-awareness in their play on craft-based relations to painting as material and medium.

When holding these nineteenth-century texts and objects in light of each other, a pattern of interrelations thus emerges, not just of contemporaries tapping directly or indirectly into networks of social and artistic exchange, but between interests centered in engagement with metamorphosis. It is important to underline how these relations invite us to reflect not just on the imbrication of thinking with making in Lu's craft, but also on the impact of work like his on normative conceptions of creativity and materiality in the visual arts. That is, Chen Wenshu's imaginative rethinking represents a shift inside text-based discourse that responds at least in part to the mindfulness articulated in contemporary crafts. *New Poems* connects this challenge to the received boundaries of *hua* and the social power structures in which they were inscribed both to his own literary, artistic, and spiritual pursuits, and to more than one kind of change experienced in the material and visual world around him. The convergence in this text of thinking sparked by craft invention and social nonconformity on the one hand, and art historical perspectives responding to epistemological and geopolitical change on the other, certainly deserves further attention. In the meantime, the objects and texts discussed here bear testimony to the difference between working with words and working with objects, between interventions in practice and in theory, while revealing a moment of shared interest in creative and disruptive meaning making aroused by a provocatively interwoven series of material metamorphoses.

NOTES

The author is grateful to Lin Yi and Jiang He for graciously sharing their insights during the author's visit to their workshops in June 2019, and to Dr. Juliane Noth and Dr. Wei-Cheng Lin for their kind help with source information.

1. Denis Diderot and Jean le Rond d'Alembert, eds., *Encyclopédie, ou dictionnaire raisonné des sciences, des arts et des métiers, etc.* accessed from University of Chicago: ARTFL Encyclopédie Project (Spring 2021 Edition), ed. Robert Morrissey and Glenn Roe, https://artflsrv03.uchicago.edu/philologic4/encyclopedie0521/navigate/17/343/?byte=822570&byte=822577&byte=822580&byte=822583, 17 (1765): 76–77. Yang Ming, preface to *Xiushilu jieshuo* [Records of lacquering with commentary] by Wang Shixiang (Beijing: Sanlian shudian, 2013), 22. My translation of the title follows Craig Clunas, "Luxury Knowledge: The *Xiushilu* ('Records of Lacquering') of 1625," *Techniques & Culture* 29 (1997): 27–40.
2. Joseph Needham quoted in Robert Temple, *The Genius of China: 3,000 Years of Science, Discovery, and Invention* (New York: Simon and Schuster, 1986), 75.
3. Georges Didi-Huberman, "The Order of Material; Plasticities, *Malaises*, Survivals," in *Materiality*, Documents of Contemporary Art, ed. Petra Lange-Berndt (Cambridge, MA: the MIT Press, 2015), 42–53.
4. Roland Barthes, "Plastic," in *Mythologies*, trans. Annette Lavers (New York: Hill and Wang, 1972), 97–99.
5. He does so with the aim to rethink Hannah Arendt's separation of the thinker as *homo faber* from the maker as *animal laborans*. See Richard Sennett, *The Craftsman* (New Haven: Yale University Press, 2008), 119ff.
6. See Yan Duan and Ying Jie, eds., *Xuzuan Yangzhou fuzhi* [Gazetteer of Yangzhou, continued] [1874] (Taipei: Chengwen chubanshe, 1970), *juan* 24, 30a–b; Chang Bei, *Yangzhou qiqishi* [History of Yangzhou lacquerware] (Nanjing: Jiangsu Renmin chubanshe, 2017), 113–14, 125–27; Christine Moll-Murata, *State and Crafts in the Qing Dynasty (1644–1911)* (Amsterdam: Amsterdam University Press, 2018), 38 and 313ff.
7. Fang Chen, "Qingdai zhiqi mingjiang Lu Dong de huihua zuopin ji youguan xinzha" [Paintings and letters by the famous lacquer craftsman of the Qing dynasty, Lu Dong], *Wenwu*, no. 9 (1995): 89–93.
8. See Gu Guangqi, "Qishayan ji" [Record on the sand lacquer inkstone], in *Gu Qianli ji* [Collected writings of Gu Qianli] (Beijing: Zhonghua shuju, 2007), *juan* 6, 99.
9. For an early record that records Zhang Cining's interest in landscape styles of Shen Zhou (1427–1509) and Wen Zhengming (1470–1559), if executed in a "rough and grand brush" (*cuhao zhibi*), see Qian Yong, *Lüyuan huaxue* [Painting studies of the Shoe Garden], in *Huashi congshu* [A collection of painting histories], ed. Yu Anlan (Taipei: Wenshizhe, 1994), 2134. For Zhang's status as leader of the Northern School, see Chen Wenshu, *Hualin xinyong* [New poems on a forest of paintings] (Hangzhou: Xileng yinshe, 1915), *juan* 1, 9a–b.
10. Published information about paintings carrying his signature include a landscape hanging scroll dated 1808 in the Nanjing Museum, a landscape fan dated 1816 in the Yangzhou Museum, a landscape in the handscroll format dated 1823 in the Li Yimang Collection, and a landscape in the hanging scroll format dated 1836 in the Water, Pine and Stone Retreat Collection. See Chang, *Yangzhou*, 127; Fang, "Qingdai zhiqi mingjiang," 89; Li Yimang, "Ba Lu

Kuisheng shanshui huajuan" [Colophon to a landscape scroll by Lu Kuisheng], *Wenwu*, no. 7 (1988): 66, 89; Anita Wong, ed., *Shi Jiu Cha Qing. Qingdai zhihu mingjia yizhen* [Tea, wine and poetry. Qing dynasty literati and their drinking vessels] (Hong Kong: University Museum Art and Gallery, The University of Hong Kong, 2006), 162–63.

11. Wang Yun, *Yangzhou huayuan lu* [A Record of Yangzhou's garden of paintings] [1885] (Yangzhou: Chenshi shulin, 1930–1932), *juan* 2, 22b.

12. For *yanqiao*, see Ye Mingfeng (1812–1859), *Qiaoxi zaji* [Miscellaneous notes west of the bridge] (Taipei: Yiwen yinshuguan, 1967), 9b; for *gupu yajie*, see Fang, "Qingdai zhiqi mingjiang," 92, fig. 8.

13. On *qiao* as both extraordinary skill and (dangerous) cunning and its parallel with the moral ambiguity of "crafty" in the European context, see Moll-Murata, *State and Crafts*, 296.

14. Chang Bei notes in 2017 having seen about forty extant objects in Chinese collections and one in Germany, and more objects carrying Lu's signature that are reliably associated with his workshop are also circulating abroad. See Chang, *Yangzhou*, 114; Paul Moss, *Documentary Works of Chinese Art: In Scholars' Taste* (London: Sydney L. Moss Ltd., 1983), 210–11; Wong ed., *Shi Jiu Cha Qing*, 160ff.

15. Qian Yong (1759–1844) suggests that Lu Dong continued his family's production of both large and small household furnishings in the Yangzhou-style hundred-treasure inlay technique that emerged in the late Ming dynasty. Larger pieces of carved lacquer bearing his seal are extant, but mainly in monochromatic lacquer, as I discuss below in this chapter. See Qian Yong, "Yineng" in *Lüyuan conghua* [Collected sayings from Shoe Garden], ed. Qian Rishou (1870), 14a–15a.

16. From Wang Shixiang and Yuan Quanyu, "Yangzhou mingqigong Lu Kuisheng he tade yixie zuopin" [The renown Yangzhou lacquer artisan Lu Kuisheng and a number of his works], *Wenwu*, no. 7 (1957): 14–17; Chang, *Yangzhou*, 111–31.

17. Chang, *Yangzhou*, 127–31.

18. Craig Clunas, *Art in China* (Oxford: Oxford University Press, 1997), 186.

19. Moss, *In Scholars' Taste*, 210–11.

20. Moss, *In Scholars' Taste*, 210–11.

21. Chen, *Hualin*.

22. Chen, *Hualin*, preface. Author's translation. The Qilin Pavilion was a pavilion in the Han dynasty (206 BCE–220 CE) imperial palace famous for displaying portraits of heroic officials.

23. The supplemental chapter would have been added after the preface was written.

24. To my knowledge, the earliest mention of "iron painting" appears in a mid-eighteenth-century literati poem series on the subject of a work by Tang Peng, "Tie hua ge" [Iron painting song] by Liang Tongshu (1723–1815) and Wei Qianheng (1715–1792); see note 28 below.

25. Space does not allow reviewing the meanings associated with *hua* here: for its primary association in the late imperial era with painted images created by named artists, see Craig Clunas, *Pictures and Visuality in Early Modern China* (Princeton: Princeton University Press, 1997), 184ff. As Francesca Bray points out, printed images that were regarded as aesthetically pleasurable or entertaining could also be classified as *hua*. See Francesca Bray, "Introduction: The Powers of TU," in *Graphics and Text in the Production of Technical Knowledge in China: The Warp and the Weft*, ed. Francesca Bray, Vera Dorofeeva-Lichtmann, and Georges Métailié (Leiden: Brill, 2007), 3ff.

26. As in the story recounted by Shen Kuo (1031–1095), where the painter Song Di advises a novice to derive inspiration for his landscape paintings by suspending a piece of silk over the worn surface of an old wall, and seeing through it, contemplate how over time images of mountains and waters start to emerge from the cracks and crevices on the wall behind. See Shen Kuo, *Mengxi bitan* [Brush talks from dream creek], Yuan dynasty woodblock edition (Taibei: Dingwen Shuju, 1977), 171.

27. Chen, *Hualin*, *juan* 3. Author's translation.

28. The root elements of this story, including that Tang Peng lived next door to a painter who remains unnamed and was scolded when watching his mastery of ink, are present in Wei Qianheng's preface to his poem harmonizing Liang Tongshu's "Tie hua ge." Chen identifies the painter with Xiao Yuncong, as seems to have become the common understanding by his time, and further enlivens this short narrative with direct speech and the painter's reaction. See Yao Wenwang, "Tang Tianchi he Liang Yingda de tiehua" [The iron painting of Tang Tianchi (Peng) and Liang Yingda (Tongshu)], *Wenwu cankao ziliao*, no. 4 (1957): 22–24; Lu Guang, "Wenren bixia de minjian gongjiang xingxiang – yi Tang Peng tiehua weili" [The image of common artisans in literati writing, with Tang Peng's iron painting as example], *Wenhua chanye xunkan*, no. 1 (2020): 30–31. For the "Tie hua ge" poems see Chen Chunhua, Liang Qirang, eds., *Wuhu Xianzhi* (Gazetteer of Wuhu) [twelfth year of Jiaqing (1807)], *juan* 22, 1411–12, 1414–16. Erudition Database of Chinese Local Gazetteers (based on the 1912 reprinted edition), accessed February 1, 2021, server.wenzibase.com.proxy.uchicago.edu/spring/front.read.
29. The chapters on male artists, for example, open with Hua Yan (1682–1756) and other artists active in the early Qianlong era and close with Chen's old servant Tang Zheng (n.d.), and list Buddhists and Daoists after secular artists.
30. However, gendered boundary crossing has its limits: it does not happen the other way around. Chen, *Hualin, juan* 2.
31. Two female practitioners of Daoism and Buddhism and four actresses follow male Daoists and Buddhists in the second chapter; seventy ladies, concubines, and courtesans appear in the third. See Chen, *Hualin, juan* 2, from the entry "Yunxiang" forward. This distinction is in part social in the sense that the former are mostly, but not all, professionals. It would appear that he later regretted the impact of this organization on the ladies in chapter three; see note 32 below. It is worth noting that in the context of his Daoist devotional practice, Chen Wenshu came to regard at least two of his concubines, listed here in the third chapter, as partners in a Daoist brotherhood. See Liu Xun, "An Intoning Immortal at the West Lake: Chen Wenshu and His Daoist Pursuits in Late Qing Jiangnan," *Cahiers d'Extrême-Asie* 25 (2016): 86, 98, 110–11.
32. See Chen, *Hualin, juan* 3, n.p., "Wu Pinxiang" entry. On Chen Wenshu's literary patronage of women and his later notes on their organization in this book, including the intended result of having the third chapter on women precede the men opening the fourth chapter, see Zhong Huiling, "Chen Wenshu yu Bicheng xianguan nudizi de wenxue huodong" [The literary activities of Chen Wenshu and the female disciples of the Azure City Immortals Hall], *Donghai zhongwen xuebao* 13, no. 7 (2001): 175; Zhong Huiling, "'Xiling guiyong' Zhong de nüxing qunxiang" [The image of women in *Poems on Ladies from Xiling*], *Donghai zhongwen xuebao* 17, no. 7 (2005): 61–91.
33. This interlinked movement of untethering and reconnecting is indicated by how his material and cultural paintings lead *hua* back to the primal creative energy of the natural world, to the earliest material remnants of past practices, and to cultural transformations across the globe. If Chen's vision of "Western Ocean Painting" as a development of long-lost practices once held in China's past connection to his mentor Ruan Yuan's expansion of the discourse on the Chinese origins of Western science, it is part of a broader figure of transformation in this context. See Chen, *Hualin, juan* 2, "Xiyang hua" entry.
34. This text, compiled around the same time as *Hualin xinyong*, copies and rearranges, with minor adjustments, entries from Chen Wenshu's "cultural paintings," such as from "English Envoy," "Country of Japan Painting," "Western Ocean Painting," and lists as source instead Peng's own notes. From Chen Wenshu's "material paintings," only the entries from "Iron Painting" seems to be copied for an entry on Tang Peng; the source provided is the Jiaqing era *Wuhu xianzhi*,

which does not include this version of the story. *Hualin xinyong* does not appear in the overview of sources in the opening pages of this anthology but is listed as a source for individual entries on Chen's female protégés. It would appear that the author had access to an early manuscript or imprint of Chen's text. See Peng Yuncan, *Lidai huashi huizhuan* [Collected biographies of painters through the dynasties] (Shanghai: Jinzhang tushuju, 1922), *juan* 63, 1b–2a, *juan* 32, 5a–b.

35. The term "also" refers to a similar point made in the previous entry on "Kesi Painting" (*kesi hua*).

36. Chen uses the generic term *diaoqi* in place of the more specific *tihong* for this kind of carved monochrome red lacquer associated with Orchard Factory lacquer production.

37. Gao Shiqi, *Jin'ao tuishi biji* [Brush notes in retirement from Jin'ao] (Taibei: Yiwen yinshuguan, 1968), *juan xia*, 14b–15a.

38. Gu, "Qishayan ji." Author's translation. The 1826 date does not appear in Gu's collected writings but on the separate imprint of this record found in an extant ink stone and box by Lu Kuisheng; see note 48 below.

39. I have not found any reference to the specific minerals used by Lu Kuisheng, and sand lacquer objects by his grandfather do not seem to be otherwise recorded or extant. Present-day descriptions often reference the use of the rare mineral moissanite or naturally occurring silicon carbide (*jingangsha*), formally discovered in 1893.

40. Wang Qijun and Wang Xieyan, *Zhongguo gongyi meishushi* [Art history of Chinese crafts] (Beijing: Jixie gongye chubanshe, 2008), 407.

41. For the English terms I follow Dorothy Ko, *The Social Life of Inkstones: Artisans and Scholars in Early Qing China* (Seattle: University of Washington Press, 2017).

42. Since these last two died prior to 1717 but their inscriptions praise sand lacquer (in the case of Zhou's) or its properties (in Zhu's), a material purportedly only rediscovered after their death, this raises questions about the authenticity of the inscriptions. Appearing on three out of seven closely related inkstones of this type, this could either illustrate the imitation of Lu's brand-name staples, which, as indicated below, was an issue, or Lu's own creative associations with early Qing connoisseurship. See the discussion that follows.

43. Such as the set of nine *duan* stone inkstones from the Qianlong era in the Beijing Palace Museum, illustrated in Zhao Lihong, "Qingdai gongting wenfang yongju shuyao zhi Qingdai gongting yuyongyan" [Qing dynasty imperial inkstones as key examples of Qing court writing implements], *Shuhua shijie* 180, no. 2 (2017): 9.

44. Some scholars take an inkstone made of lacquered wood excavated from a Han dynasty tomb in Yaozhuang, Yangzhou, now in the National Museum of China, to be the earliest evidence of sand lacquer. Chang Bei does not identify it as such but notes that the ink pool features very fine granules of quartz sand. See Chang, *Yangzhou*, 8.

45. See Zhao Lihong, "Qing Qianlong shiqi fangguyan zhizuo chutan" [A preliminary exploration of archaistic inkstones from the Qianlong Era in the Qing dynasty], *Gugong xuekan* (2017): 167–80. There also seems to be no record of sand lacquer objects received by the court as tribute from Yangzhou workshops. See Chang, *Yangzhou*, 71–92.

46. The mixed ground was representative of Yangzhou lacquer production and is created by mixing granular fragments of materials such as shell, horn, ivory, or minerals into the lacquer to create a textured, and sometimes sparkling, effect. See Chang, *Yangzhou*, 90–92. Of the seven closely related objects of this type, six boxes are preserved. Two in the Beijing Palace Museum have, respectively, an undecorated mixed ground and a chrysanthemum and *lingzhi* motif on mixed ground. Two in the Tianjin Museum carry, respectively, a prunus motif, and another a prunus and orchid motif on a mixed ground. Two in the Water, Pine and Stone

Retreat Collection carry, respectively, a plum blossom motif on a mixed ground, very close to the one in the Tianjin Museum, and a fisherman scene engraved on a monochromatic ground.

47. While deserving further in-person study of individual objects, these observations are made in reference to twenty-nine inkstones in public and private collections, most of which are published, and five writing boxes, some of which hold smaller inkstones and other writing implements. These objects offer a useful body of reference for inkstones that have recently emerged on the market, many of which appear to be fakes.

48. As Wang indicates, both documents appear to be part of the original packaging, as they were stored in a lidded recess inside a movable base, tucked inside a hardwood container custom made for this inkstone and fitted box. Originally in the collection of Zhao Yuanfang, its current whereabouts are unknown to me. Wang Shixiang's description suggests, but does not make explicit, that the certificate was handwritten rather than printed. Wang and Yuan, "Yangzhou mingqigong," 9–10.

49. The fame of Lu's sand lacquer inkstones, and its impact on the production of other lacquer workshops, is noted in Ye, *Qiaoxi zaji*, 9a–b.

50. Such as the round inkstone with engraved prunus décor illustrated in figure 10. Another example is the irregularly shaped inkstone and tall box with prunus inlay in the Shanghai Museum, which has an inscription: "Replicating an inkstone from the Tingyunguan collection," referencing the collection of the Ming dynasty literati painter Wen Zhengming (1470–1559). See Chang, *Yangzhou*, 128.

51. This motif of the arching prunus appears in inlay on the lid of the rectangular stone from the Zhao Yuanfang collection, is engraved on the lid of a rectangular stone in the Water, Pine and Stone Retreat Collection, done in inlay on the lid of a round stone in the Beijing Palace Museum, engraved on the mixedground of lid of a round stone in the Water, Pine and Stone Retreat Collection, and done in inlay on the irregularly shaped lid of the stone in the Shanghai Museum.

52. Chang Bei highlights the distinction between the shallow *qipidiao* in Lu's work and the deeper, so-called *kehuiqi*, used to replicate paintings on lacquer panels in eighteenth-century Yangzhou. See Chang, *Yangzhou*, 94–96 and 121–22.

53. To be noted, a writing box engraved with a scene attributed to Hua Yan and dated 1808 in the Beijing Palace Museum comes quite early and predates at least his imitation of so-called Mansheng teapots, which were designed after Chen Hongshou's stationing in Liyang in 1811. See Chang, *Yangzhou*, 123; Lai Suk Yee, ed., *Shu. Hua. Yin. Hu. Chen Hongshou de yishu* [The art of Chen Hongshou. Painting, calligraphy, seal-carving and teapot design] (Hong Kong: Shanghai Museum, Nanjing Museum, and Art Museum, The Chinese University of Hong Kong, 2005), 164ff.

54. Chang, *Yangzhou*, 123.

55. Such as the teapot in the collection of the National Museum of China with the scene titled after the famous Tang dynasty verse, "Sweeping the rocks, waiting for the tea to brew," signed by Chen Nong (active first half of the nineteenth century) and an inscription by Qian Daxi (1728–1804). Chang, *Yangzhou*, 118.

56. Chang, *Yangzhou*, 117–18.

57. Lai, ed., *Shu. Hua. Yin. Hu*, cat. nos. T3, T10, T11; Cao Qing, "Cong 'Qingdai xuezhe zhuan heji' shang de zaoxiang jiangqi – Cheng Hongshou qiren qishi lun" [From "Portraits and biographies of Qing scholars" to reflections on the life and deeds of Chen Hongshou], in *Shu. Hua. Yin. Hu*, ed. Lai, 191, 198 (fig. 4–5); Lai Suk Yee, "Manhu mingwen gaishuo [An overview of inscriptions on the *manhu* teapots], in Chang, *Yangzhou*," 216. I suspect that the popularity of this form is related to the inscription's attention to the enduring qualities of the well's stone material.

58. See Fan Peiling, ed., *Gaomu qigong* [Wondrous wood craft] (Hangzhou: Zhejiang guji chubanshe, 2009), 9.

59. Sennett, *The Craftsman*, 120–46.
60. The phrase "When they had exerted to the utmost the thoughts of their hearts [*jijie xinsi*]," sources from Mengzi, Li Lou Shang. This translation follows James Legge, *The Chinese Classics* (Taipei: SMC Publishing, 1991), 1:290. Since the translation of this phrase as singular or plural depends on context, the point in Gu's record where this phrase is used leaves open the question if this mental action refers only to Lu Yingzhi, or to both him and the artisan assigned to replicate sand lacquer. The latter reading appears compelling to me since the master craftsman preparing the raw lacquer would then, as they do now, have played a key role in the lacquer workshop, especially when developing new lacquer mixtures.
61. The engraved scenes on his objects include the abovementioned archetypal prunus motif, a scene associated with the famous Song theme of the eight scenes of the Xiao and Xiang rivers, as well as bamboo and landscape scenes carrying the signature of the Yangzhou artists such as Jin Nong, Hua Yan (1682–1756), and Zheng Banqiao (1693–1765). One might also consider the *baibaoqian* inlay scenes on his inkstone and writing boxes, including the prunus and other "cut flower" (*zhezhihua*) motifs and the scenes with ducks, roosters, or horses on a riverbank, to invoke the motifs and reductive compositions in ink and color associated with Song court painting.
62. Apart from Chen Wenshu's association of Lu Kuisheng with what would be *tihong*-carved lacquer, early texts only reference his use of sand lacquer as material for making scholarly objects, inkstones in particular, noting their carved decoration with pictorial scenes and inscriptions (without specifying a carving technique), and one text suggests that his workshop produced larger pieces in *baibaoqian* technique. In addition to the objects discussed above, extant works reliably associated with his name include inkstone boxes, a flower stand, a plate in undecorated monochrome lacquer, snuff bottles, hat stands, wrist rests in *qipidiao* décor, an inkstone box with crackle décor (*duanwen*), writing and other boxes in polychrome lacquer (*kuancai*), and a seated Guanyin statue in purple lacquer. Chang Bei refutes Wang Shixiang's association of an unsigned Chinese lute with *baibaoqian* and crackle décor with Lu's workshop. See Wang and Yuan, "Yangzhou mingqigong," 11. While it is not impossible that Lu produced some objects in *tihong* technique, these four panels stand out.
63. Sun Guoxin is surmised to be a follower of Lu Kuisheng's. See Paul Moss, *The Literati Mode: Chinese Scholar Paintings, Calligraphy and Desk Objects* (London: Sydney L. Moss Ltd., 1986), 282.
64. These include dishes engraved with scenes of the Zuiweng pavilion and of boys playing in a garden, currently in the Engakuji Temple and Tokyo National Museum collections. See Derek Clifford, *Chinese Carved Lacquer* (London: Bamboo Publishing, 1992), plates 12 and 13.
65. For an overview of these patterns, see Sir Harry Garner, "Diaper backgrounds on Chinese Carved Lacquer," *Ars Orientalis* 1966: 6, 165–89.
66. See Clifford, *Chinese Carved Lacquer*, plate 27b.
67. See Clifford, *Chinese Carved Lacquer*, plates 50, 67, 108, and Guoli gugong bowuyuan, *Gogong diaoqiqi xuancui* [Masterpieces of Chinese carved lacquer ware in the National Palace Museum] (Taipei: National Palace Museum, 1971), plates 22 and 33.
68. As in the three-panel screen made for the occasion of the Qianlong Emperor's seventieth birthday, now in the Beijing Palace Museum. See Museum Boymans-van Beuningen, *The Forbidden City* (Rotterdam: Museum Boymans-van Beuningen, 1990), plate 64.
69. His familiarity with Lu's name but less with the specifics of his work is notable: Chen Wenshu was magistrate in Yangzhou from 1821 to 1823 and would have returned to the city from 1827 to 1830, thus possibly composing the preface to this text there. For Chen's biographical trajectory, see Liu, "An Intoning Immortal," 83.

Burning Big Dharma Boats

Paper as an Efficacious Medium

Yuhang Li

INTRODUCTION

The burning of vibrant paper boats in ceremonies to commemorate the dead or to expel pestilences was a common public spectacle from the end of the eighteenth century into the first half of the twentieth century. These boats belong to a larger category of items identified by contemporary scholars as "pasted-paper objects" in English and as *zhizha* (tied-together paper) and *zhihu* (pasted paper) in pre-modern and modern Chinese sources.[1] Both terms explain their techniques: paper is worked over an armature. Fire is implied in the very conception of using this material—the items are so constructed in order to be delivered to the spirits by burning. Most such paper objects were created for funeral and memorial practices; hence, *zhizha* often stood in as a synonym for *mingqi* (spirit vessel or spirit object).[2] A range of other terms, such as *zhima* (paper horse), *zhi mingqi* (paper spirit object), and *zhiren zhima* (paper figure and paper horse) have been associated with this practice since the Song period (960–1279).[3]

Due to the ephemeral nature of *zhizha* objects, scholars have had to resort to accounts of them in historical documents and interviews with contemporary artisans from different regions.[4] These investigations provide critical evidence on the historical development of the objects, the techniques of their making, choices in artistic design, regional styles, and local patronage customs. Most of these discussions have focused on funerary items, mainly commissions by individual families. Consequently, they have overlooked the important role of objects burned in public commemorations or for collective sanitization. At the imperial court, in cities, and in the countryside, right across the year—from the Beginning Spring Rite (Lichun), the Lantern Festival (Shangyuan jie), the Tomb Sweeping Festival (Qingming jie), the Dragon Boat Festival (Duanwu jie), the Hungry Ghost Festival (Zhongyuan jie), to the Double Ninth Festival (Chongyang jie)—paper artifacts were burned as sacrificial objects. In this chapter, I concentrate on an item used in the Hungry Ghost Festival known as a "paper dharma boat"—a relatively independent *zhizha* object and also a universal vehicle for salvation. The dharma boat lets me consider how the transformative nature of paper as a medium, the mimetic power of artisanal labor, rituals around "enacting" a paper boat, and public spectatorship came together in a new type of ritualized spectacle from mid to late Qing China.[5]

The rise of spectacles featuring paper objects is not unique to China. The use of enormous papier-mâché sculptures in public celebrations was observed since the emergence of the early modern world.[6] From this perspective, we can de-provincialize China and underscore the simultaneity of Chinese spectacles with their Western counterparts. Still, mid and late Qing Chinese spectacles were different from their Western counterparts.[7] Rather than emerging from the disenchanted world of modern industrialism, Chinese paper boat spectacles were mediated by Buddhist notions of transcendence to paradise. The relationship to hierarchy was different, too. The mid-Qing period experienced a certain degree of marketization, which entailed the idea of an infinite, qualitatively similar series. In the *zhizha* context, paper can substitute for various qualitatively different goods, and therefore it turns them into a series of formally equal entities. In early modern and modern Europe, equality among human beings was premised on the universalization of the equality among commodities. In other words, from the standpoint of money, the qualitative differences between commodities vanish, and they become numbers or expressions of value; that is, some commodities are priced higher than others.

Equality is a fundamental concept of Buddhism that was assimilated into Daoism and other indigenous religions. Thus, paper boats ritually transported everyone, without exception, to the other shore. However, Qing rulers and religious institutions integrated that equality with hierarchy. For instance, dharma boats commissioned by the imperial family and those made for common people were distinct, since certain symbols and materials were reserved solely for those with royal status. European spectacle, in contrast, was connected to a new type of commodity-based domination associated with the destabilizing of earlier hierarchies. In Qing China, paper-boat-burning spectacles were ambivalent, since they reproduced existing hierarchies but also contained a religious equalizing tendency that predated commodity domination. This ambivalence does not merely lie in the use of paper, but also in its symbolic function, which goes beyond simple materiality. Hierarchy is produced by the manner in which that materiality is sublimated within the world of meaning. For instance, the imperial palace custom built its own dharma boats, and the spectacle they provided was distinguished from those of commoners by the imperial workshop's artisanal skill level, the court style, and the freedom to augment the boat with a host of other material media. From this perspective, the boat's materiality is incorporated into a world of meaning that is itself hierarchically structured while simultaneously containing elements that challenge existing hierarchies.

PASTED-PAPER OBJECTS
A DIFFERENT VALUE SYSTEM

Paper, according to Xu Shen's (58–148) definition in the *Analytical Dictionary of Characters* (*Shuowen jiezi*), is *xu yi shan ye*, meaning "a mat of refuse fibers."[8] This points to two essential aspects of paper: it was 1) made of fibers and 2) appeared as a thin sheet.[9] Paper is commonly recognized as a medium that can carry text and image; however, starting from at least the fourth century, paper was also used to replace or to represent other media, such as metal, fabric, and wood, to form a wide range of burial objects, including coins, shoes, hats, clothes, belts, and bedcovers, like those excavated from the tombs in Astana, Xinjiang.[10] Two types of substitution are indicated in these early paper objects. In the first category, the paper is clearly visible. In paper coins, it signifies the value of another medium (metal) and the physical form of the coin itself. This type eventually developed into the spirit objects that are burned in above-ground funerary ceremonies.[11] In the second category, the materiality of paper is concealed. Paper or recycled paper carrying written texts was used as a foundation to support the structure of an object and was then covered by other materials such as hemp.[12] Although the paper is hidden, its durability and ability to retain warmth inspired the later practice of living people who used paper as padding in cloth, quilts, and even armor.[13] Both ways of replacing other media indicate one important notion about paper: it can be easily shaped to supplement or represent other objects, whether practically or symbolically.[14] Through various techniques and a wide range of decorating methods, paper can be made into various configurations.[15]

A value system for paper and paper objects for spirits was gradually established in the seventh century. For instance, the method of using tin-coated paper and plain paper to replicate gold and silk for spirits is explained as a form of knowledge in *Record of Miraculous Retribution* (*Mingbao ji*). Sui Renqian, originally an agnostic scholar who was curious about the existence of phantoms, became an expert on ghosts after establishing a friendship with the ghost official Cheng Jingben from the Western Jin period (266–422). When Sui shared his expertise on how to offer a gift to his ghost friend, he explained to his student: "All ghosts' things are different from those of human beings. The only exceptions are gold and silk, which can be used universally by both humans and ghosts. However, [real gold and silk] are not as good as the unreal ones. It is most valued and preferred to use yellow color painted over tin-coated paper to imitate gold, and use paper to substitute for silk."[16] The student followed Sui's instructions and made a paper object for Cheng, who was very pleased with the gift.

This account is repeated in the contemporaneous popular Buddhist encyclopedia *Forest of Gems in the Garden of Law* (*Fayuan zhulin*), in which burning spirit money was recorded as a way to comfort ghosts.[17] The use of paper objects for spirits also comes up in other miraculous stories. In *Great Book of Marvels* (*Guangyi ji*), a Tang dynasty (618–907) collection of short tales about laypeople's experience of the other world, one episode describes how a young boy named Wang Qi asks his family to burn a paper garment for a hungry ghost who was chasing him.[18]

The above anecdotes indicate that, already in the early Tang, the value of a thing or the thingness of a thing can be separate from the actual qualities of the thing. Gold and silk may represent a value that transcends the human and spirit realms. However, paper as a spirit medium gives the lie to that, which underscores both its mimetic power and its power as "other." Human beings might consider things made of paper as fake, but in the ghostly realm, this valuation becomes inverted, and copies become more valuable than the originals. Through this new value system, paper becomes a universal equivalent, one that can not only substitute for gold and silk but can also surpass their value in the other world. Appearance becomes more useful and fungible than reality. The substitution of paper for gold and silk anticipates the later function of paper money as a measure of value, rather than gold. In fact, such a distinctive value system established for ghosts started with making spirit money.[19] Here the idea is that the living owe a debt to those who have passed away, and this debt can be paid in paper money.[20] This implies the partial quantification of Confucian values such as filial piety, especially when dealing with the deceased. We must understand this as only a partial quantification because a specific number is not given; however, paper money, which is inherently numerical, can serve as a means of payment. Yet in this value system, the qualitative dimension is not completely negated; it remains in a sublated form. One cannot just burn plain paper and substitute it for things. The making process of the imitation is crucial, and so one must make the paper into a particular thing before it takes on value. Paper, then, is a universal equivalent, but not in and of itself. It gains equivalency through artisanal labor that makes it into qualitatively different things. In other words, the efficacy of paper lies not merely in its materiality, but in the transformation of its shape, color, and texture by the intervention of human skill and labor.[21]

By the early Qing period, this mimetic power materialized through the artisans' ability to create in paper life-sized houses, boats, and any other object attached to human beings.[22] As the text on the *Dianshizhai Pictorial* illustration titled *Grand Opening of a Spirit House* (*Mingzhai hongkai*) (fig. 1) explains, a spectacular paper house about one *zhang*, four *chi* tall (about 4.6 meters) and four or five *zhang* wide (about 12 or 15 meters) was dedicated to an ill-fated young man, Mr. Long. The artificial house was staged on open ground close to the Long family ancestral shrine in the Daliang Village, Shunde, Guangdong province, in the 1890s.[23] Inside the house, realistic furniture and domestic household items—including a full-length mirror, a mechanical clock, and hanging scrolls of painting and calligraphy on the walls—were all made of paper. Life-size servants were garbed in real clothes. Given the labor and time committed to mimicking real items, such paper objects became luxury commodities.

The power of paper as a ghostly medium or *lingmei* (efficacious medium) is widely observed by artisans in contemporary practice. Paper is believed to connect this world to the spirit realm. If any part of *zhizha* objects does not count as part of the offering, such as the stalks used to stabilize the four legs of an ox (fig. 2), such parts are not concealed by paper. This means that when this ox is burned, the parts lacking paper will not be visible in the other world.[24]

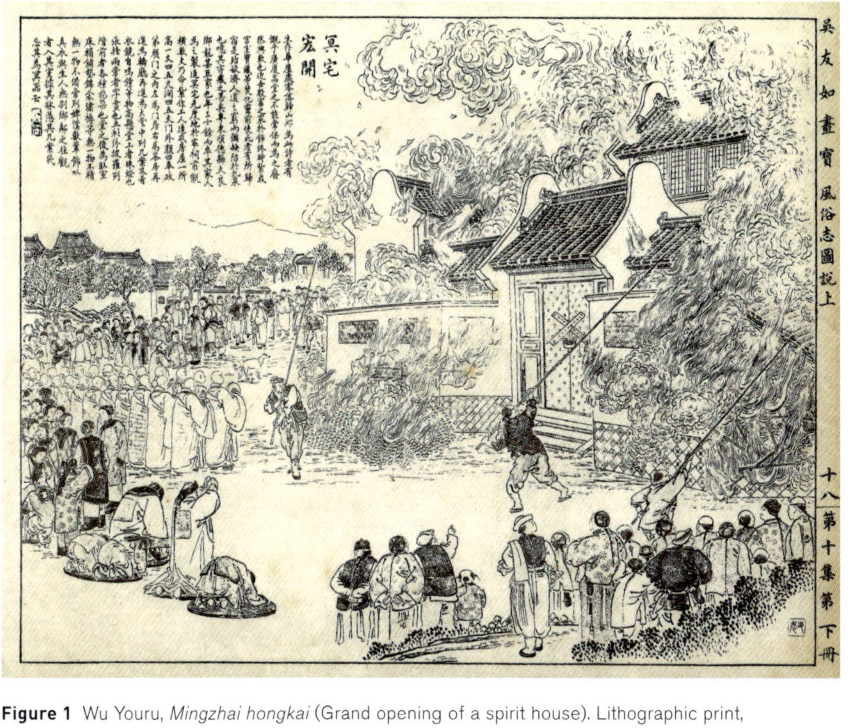

Figure 1 Wu Youru, *Mingzhai hongkai* (Grand opening of a spirit house). Lithographic print, 27 × 20 cm. From *Fengsuzhi tushuo* (Illustrated record of customs), vol. 10, *Wu Youru huabao* (Treasures of Wu Youru's paintings) (Shanghai: Biyuan huishe, 1909), 18b. University of Wisconsin-Madison, Kohler Art Library collection.

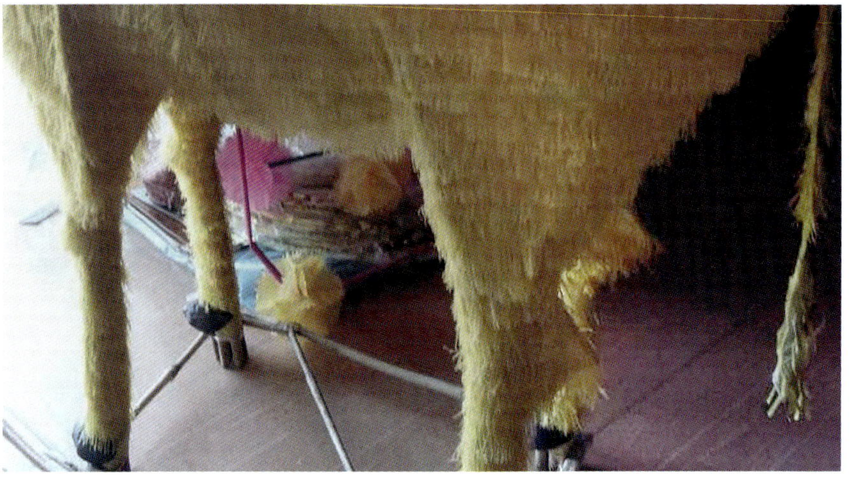

Figure 2 Tian Xilai, White ox base with paper and sorghum stalk, 2016. Qinglongxian, Qinhuangdao, Hebei. Courtesy of Zhang Weisheng.

Paper used for venerating spirits, such as *shenzhi* (deific paper), *shaozhi* (burning paper), and *Guanyin zhi* (Guanyin paper), were distinct from stationery papers during Ming times (1368–1644).[25] Paper objects were defined not only by their medium, but also by the unique color-coded papers that separate them from paper used by the living. *Wuse zhi* (five-color papers) is often mentioned in late imperial textual sources about *zhizha* objects.[26] An advertisement for the Chen Quan Ji Paper Shop in Chaozhou, Guangdong province, from the early twentieth century highlights *mingliao* (spirit pigments) or *shenliao* (deific pigments) that were applied to five-color papers.[27] Anthropological research on regional *zhizha* practices tells us that different areas use a different palette in their spirit color-coding system. It seems that blue, green, pink, white, and red are often seen on items from the nineteenth century onward.[28] The illustration of the funeral for Grandmother Jia in Sun Wen's (fl. 1862–1908) illustrated *Dream of the Red Chamber* (*Hongloumeng*) shows a paper building staged in the middle of a temporary ritual space in the courtyard (fig. 3).[29] Although Sun Wen used similar coloring and shading techniques to portray both real architecture and this paper house, by adding more saturated colors of red, white, blue, green, and black on the paper stand, beams, roof, and balustrades, the distinct materiality of the paper house is subtly represented.

Moreover, the tale of Sui Renqian from the Tang period and later stories of paper objects reveal that a ghost's satisfaction with an object announces the completeness of *zhizha* as a product and an offering. For instance, a story recorded by Hong Mai (1123–1202) in *Record of a Listener* (*Yijian zhi*) tells of an unsuccessful delivery caused by the incomplete burning of a paper garment. A local official from Haimen near today's Nantong, Jiangsu, encountered a female ghost as he carried out his patrol on the sea. The ghost told him that she needed a *beizi* (long jacket). So the official's wife stitched a jacket out of red paper and sent it to the ghost by burning it. The next day, the female ghost appeared in the official's dream and first expressed her gratitude, then complained that one side of the jacket was missing. The wife immediately checked the ashes and found that it was only halfway incinerated. Hence she made another one and sent it to the ghost, making sure it burned completely.[30]

Such anecdotes remind us that it is essential to conceive of *zhizha* objects in space and time, namely in their coming into being and then ceasing to be. As a transitory art form, *zhizha* combines material and action, the paper medium and the ritual of burning. The speed of ignition and the color of the flames are crucial with respect to the transformative process.[31] The plant materials, such as sorghum stalk, reeds, or bamboo strips used for building an object's framework, are also essential to generating the speed and redness of the flame during the burning. The physical forming of *zhizha* is only the first stage of the object's purpose; its "deconstruction" by fire—or, more precisely, its disappearance from this world—and its appearance in the other world is its second stage. These stages together determine the completeness of the *zhizha*.

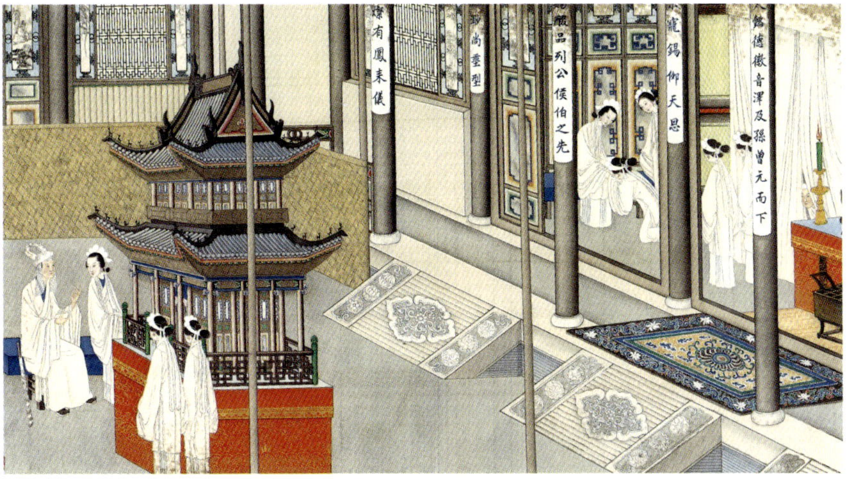

Figure 3 Sun Wen, *Grandmother Jia's Funeral*, illustration of a scene from chapter 110 of *Dream of the Red Chamber*, nineteenth century. Color on silk, 76.6 × 43.3 cm. From *A Dream of Red Mansions: As Portrayed through the Brush of Sun Wen* (New York: Better Link Press, 2010), 211. Courtesy of Lüshun Museum.

A proper delivery to the other world includes the rituals to carefully transport the objects in a funeral procession and a complete burning. These rituals include priests chanting scriptures and *dharani*, musicians performing ritual music, and professional grievers reading aloud the names of each pasted paper object prepared for the dead.[32] The belief in *zhizha* items as valuable commodities is further revealed by such itemizations. These processes along with the artisanal labor of production together reveal the mimetic power of paper.[33] As the grand ceremony at the paper house in the *Dianshizhai Pictorial* demonstrates, the labor involved in *zhizha* is not only artisanal labor, but also that of religious services and the funeral professionals who transport and ignite the object to complete its transformation.

THE DHARMA BOAT AND THE PLAGUE-EXPELLING BOAT

The dharma boat first appears in *Scriptures of Great Treasure Storehouse* (*Da baoji jing*), one of the central Mahayana Buddhist texts that teaches the idea of the Great Vehicle. In volume 43, the Buddha uses a boat allegory to explain to the Bodhisattva Puming the importance of determination to cultivating one's compassion to help all sentient beings. If a bodhisattva were affected by destructive emotions and stopped persistent cultivation, it would be like a broken boat sucked into the water in the middle of a voyage. As a result, they would have failed in their mission to transport the suffering to the other shore.[34] Hence, the bodhisattvas needed to use a dharma boat as a device to perfect their way of being a bodhisattva; namely, by "practicing dharma boat" (*xi fachuan*).[35] The boat represents the compassion of a bodhisattva who can travel between the living and the dead, no matter how much turmoil they might encounter. Hence, the indestructibleness of the dharma boat is created by a bodhisattva's willpower and is described as manifesting Buddha's and a bodhisattva's wisdom, compassion, mind of equality, and calm temper, as well as the physical form of a boat—for instance, "a pure mind in the way of the Buddha is a wooden material for building a boat,"[36] or "tolerance, malleability of consciousness, and persisting mindfulness are like nails."[37] Hence, an indestructible dharma boat becomes reliable transportation by which all sentient beings with karmic affinities can reach the other shore. From the Song to the Ming periods, the term "big dharma boat" (*da fachuan*) was constantly employed by the monks and Buddhist literati scholars as an abstract expression in discussing the path to the Pure Land.[38] The immense size of the big dharma boat refers to its infinite capacity to transport all sentient beings to cross the sea between living and dead and is used to explain the idea of universal transcendence.[39] Such texts directly express faith in the dharma boat. However, in late imperial China this rhetoric was materialized in huge paper dharma boats. This inflated boat form not only served as a vehicle for all sentient beings and a means to send off all ghosts (good or evil, named individual ghosts or anonymous wandering ghosts) and demons, but by its material turn it also became intertwined with hierarchy.

The early history of the dharma boat in ritual remains unsettled. The use of *zhizha* techniques to produce dharma boats only seems to have appeared in late imperial times and become fully popularized in the nineteenth century and early twentieth century. Another type of boat, the plague-expelling boat (*songwen chuan*), was originally associated with the Daoist exorcist tradition and healing practice, and it might have influenced the invention of the paper dharma boat. According to Jiang Shoucheng, a scholar of the rite of plague exorcism during the Northern Song dynasty (960–1127), people set up altar tables next to rivers from the middle of the fourth lunar month to the Dragon Boat Festival, usually held on the fifth day of the fifth month, when wines and food were offered to Wenshen, the God of Pestilence. The boat competition began as part of a ceremony to dispel evil spirits. Straw boats were pushed into the water to "send off" the disease.[40] In the Southern Song (1127–1279), in the lower Yangzi delta, plague-expelling boat rituals underwent a rapid material transformation. People started to construct enormous boats of light wood and decorate them in *wucai* (the five colors); they wrote down individual names, birth dates, and wishes on pieces of paper and stored these inside the boats. Then the boats would be pushed into water to the accompaniment of loud ritual music. They began their journey, following the river's flow.[41] The idea that a larger boat could carry collective wishes was clearly already a factor in this time period.

The ritual manuals on plague-expelling boats describe individual portable boats used in healing practice during the Yuan period (1279–1368). In *Collection of Principal Methods of the Dao* (*Daofa huiyuan*), two manuals, "The Divine Empyrean's Exegesis and Rites to Dispel Epidemics and Cure Illness" and "The Divine Empyrean's Rites to Send off a Boat," provide detailed instructions on how a Daoist priest would activate the function of a boat, from inviting various deities and demons onboard to sending it off through fire and smoke.[42] When a boat was to be used for healing practice, a ritual master would bring it to the patient's home and load all the evil spirits onto it. According to both manuals, the boat is to be made of clean thatch, a medium that traditionally served as an efficacious substitution. Two terms—*huachuan* (luxurious boat) and *huachuan* (painted boat)—are also used in the text to refer to the thatch boat. It is unclear at this point whether these references indicate the physical materials used to make a boat (like the painted wood boats developed in the Southern Song), or whether these two terms are primarily used as appealing ways to point to the transformative status of the boat as a ritual transport after the calling in of the deities and ghosts.

Starting from the Ming period (1368–1644), burning a plague-expelling boat gradually developed for both public festival and private recovery. Records of thatch boats filled with paper *zhima* used in the Lantern Festival or a *zhihu chuan* (pasted-paper boat) appear in a Ming gazetteer.[43] A custom from Fujian reveals that a healing paper boat was not used as a curing method at the beginning of an epidemic, but rather toward the end when someone had gone through all the possible treatments and finally survived. Then the family invited a priest, who brought a boat to the residence, to perform a rite in the evening. This information is crucial, since it indicates that the plague-expelling boat functioned as the final sanitization of the place and the patient.[44]

During the Qing dynasty (1644–1911), paper plague-expelling boats and dharma boats coexisted: the former were used for personal and public health threats and the latter assisted with individual and universal salvation. A dharma boat's sanitizing purpose would have been similar to that of a plague expeller, because all lonely souls, rancorous spirits, and devils causing individual sickness or epidemics were called to get onboard, leave the place, and no longer disturb the living. However, the destinations of the two were different: whereas a dharma boat carried its passengers to the Pure Land, the plague-expelling boat induced devils and diseases to leave the polluted dwelling or town for an open and undetermined destination.[45]

Following the increased use of paper dharma boats in various religious rituals, the rhetoric around them shifted from representing Buddhist willpower in the practice of the bodhisattva's path, as recounted in Buddhist doctrinal texts, to being a luxury vehicle that can transport everyone to the other shore, as described in expository literature. One scripture titled *Fachuan jing* (*Scripture of Dharma Boat*) circulated in different editions and was often added as an appendix in precious scrolls (*baojuan*) at the end of the nineteenth century. The scripture explains that the boat was made by the Amitabha Buddha using lavish materials that are specified as Agarwood (on the bow and stern), jade (railings), coral and agate (deck), maṇi jewels (along both sides of the boat), an osmanthus tree trunk from the moon (mast), an embroidered red damask (sail), and colorful lanterns.[46] Some of these materials, such as coral and agate, are associated with treasures in Buddhist paradise.[47] Other substances may have had certain efficacious power related to transcendence. In particular, the maṇi jewels that decorate the sides of a dharma boat are believed to have the power to manipulate water.[48] The boat is operated by various Buddhist deities such as the Old Mother (Laomu, a sectarian form of Guanyin), who sits in the middle of the boat; Bodhisattvas Puxian (Samantabhadra) and Guanyin (Avalokiteśvara) as boatmen; Wenshu (Mañjuśrī) as a weatherman; and Weituo as punter. Five hundred Arhats and four heavenly kings safeguard the passengers' journey to the blissful Buddhist land.[49] Paper, as the actual medium of the dharma boat, is certainly not mentioned in the scriptures, but the cherished materials can be visualized through painted paper and paper cutouts pasted onto a paper dharma boat.

Dharma boats were commissioned for a wide range of needs, from funerals to individual self-cultivation and merit-making, to collective use for occasions such as the Hungry Ghost Festival. During the festival, a dharma boat is often burned in conjunction with a *yulan* rite. A *yulan* rite is usually categorized as a Buddhist and Daoist mortuary ritual to venerate one's deceased relatives and all sentient beings. It includes offering food to hungry ghosts and burning various paper objects for the dead, in the hope that they can be released from suffering and transported to paradise.[50] A surviving image titled *Salvation from Suffering Dharma Boat* (*Jiuku fachuan*) represents the Amitabha Buddha holding an alms bowl and standing to the front of the boat (fig. 4). The Earth Official, who can release

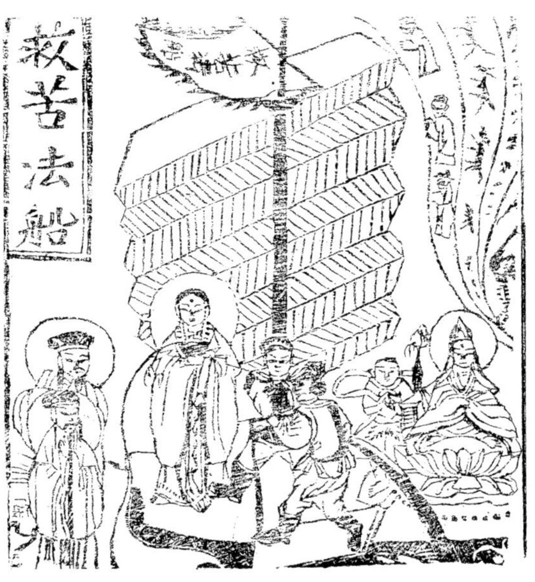

Figure 4 *Jiuku fachuan* (Salvation from suffering dharma boat), Qing dynasty (1644–1911). Woodblock print, 22 × 20 cm. From Wang Shucun, *Guanyin baitu* (A hundred pictures of Guanyin) (Guangzhou: Lingnan meishu chubanshe, 1997), plate 93.

all sinful human beings and the dead, is stationed to the Amitabha Buddha's immediate right. Guanyin sits at the back, accompanied by Sudhana (Shancai). Behind her figure, ghosts and animals are rendered in different ways, which indicate they are getting on board. This print was likely to be burned during the Hungry Ghost Festival. Indeed, many temples would conduct the *yulan* rite and burn a three-dimensional paper dharma boat as an annual event during late Qing China.[51] A photograph taken by Sidney Gamble (1890–1968) in Dingzhou, Hebei, between 1931 and 1932 shows a paper dharma boat displayed on a commercial street during the Hungry Ghost Festival (fig. 5). Unlike the print, here the demonic manifestation of Guanyin—often called Mianran gui (Burning-face Ghost), Mianran dashi (Burning-face Great Being), Dashi ye (Father Great Being), or Daju gui (Big Ghostly King)—replaces both Amitabha Buddha and Guanyin, and precedes other ghosts such as Heibai wuchang gui (Black and White Ghosts of Impermanence) on the boat.[52] The boat represents a standardized form: a water-absorbing beast with a widely open mouth decorates the boat's bow, and waves with various sea creatures are painted along the surface of the hull. Human figurines, likely representing ghosts, sit inside the pavilion. Boatmen facing outward are arranged on the edge of the deck. Although it is hard to imagine the bright colors of the boat through a black and white photograph, the fully decorated surface still conveys that this boat is a blissful vehicle on its voyage to paradise.

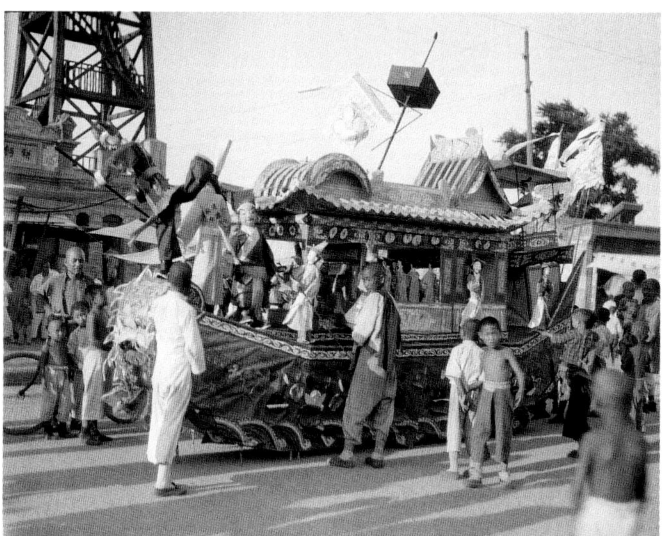

Figure 5
Sidney D. Gamble, A paper Dharma boat, 1931–1932. Photograph, taken in Dingzhou, Hebei. Courtesy of Duke University Libraries, Sidney D. Gamble Photograph Collection.

The patronage behind dharma boats was very much linked to ideas of merit-making and merit-transfer. On the doctrinal level, for instance, as Wendi Adamek's research reminds us, in the Mahayana Buddhist context generosity is understood to be one of the excellences performed by bodhisattvas on their path to Buddhahood, and both lay and monastic devotees can achieve this path.[53] The exercise of merit-making and merit-transfer is also another form of filial piety. Paper boats became a vehicle to demonstrate one's generosity by loading them with paper goods for one's deceased relatives.

In addition to being part of the Hungry Ghost Festival, one Republican-period gazetteer of Jiading (near Shanghai) records a tradition whereby elder laywomen offered collectively a paper boat called a *hua lianchuan* (transforming lotus boat) on Guanyin's birthday, the Buddha's birthday, and the day of Guanyin's attainment of Buddhahood. These boats were burned in front of temples.[54] The merit accrued by burning these paper boats has presumably increased the laywomen's chances to safely reach the other shore via the lotus boat.

By the Qing period, both the dharma boat and the plague-expelling boat were assimilated into various popular beliefs and, in some regions, even gave rise to the names of esoteric sects such as the Fachuan pai (Dharma Boat sect) and Wenchuan pai (Plague Boat sect). Universal salvation and sanitization were mobilized as political ideologies against the Qing during the White Lotus Rebellion (1796–1804) and other uprisings.[55] The relationship between the material practices of dharma and plague-expelling boats and contemporaneous political movements requires further scrutiny. Needless to say, the widespread practice of making paper boats in China during the nineteenth and early twentieth centuries was not simply rooted in various religious and social historical backgrounds: it also represented the most visible enchantments of Buddhist, Daoist, and other popular religious notions of transcendence.

DHARMA BOAT AT THE QING COURT

The Qing imperial documents reveal that dharma boats began to be used by the court from the first year of Jiaqing reign (1796–1820). That first instance took place in a *yulan daochang* (*yulan* enclosure of *dao*, another term for the *yulan* rite) held in Jehol, and might have been sanctified by Tibetan lamas.[56] Since that instance, a paper dharma boat was subsequently operated in four different courtly contexts. First, after being deceased for two months, an emperor, empress dowager, empress, or high-ranking imperial consort was granted a dharma boat for the second full-month ritual (*er manyue li fachuan*).[57] The boat was likely decorated with gendered symbols. For instance, a large paper phoenix boat and a paper dragon boat were dedicated to Empress Dowager Cixi (1835–1908) and Emperor Guangxu (1871–1908), respectively.[58] Second, a dharma boat was placed in front of the coffin during the Rite of Offering Food (*zigong qian shishi yingyong fachuan*) to honor the deceased emperor or imperial woman during their first posthumous Hungry Ghost Festival.[59] A set of spirit objects representing furniture and clothes such as table screens, robes, jewelry, and accessories, as well as silver and gold ingots were all loaded onto the boat. Third, a Double Seventh dharma boat (*qixi fachuan*) was ordered for imperial consorts during the Double Seventh Festival.[60] Fourth, a fireworks dharma boat (*yanhuo fachuan*), also called a fireworks dharma boat for the yulan enclosure of *dao* rite (*yulan daochang yanhuo fachuan*), was created for universal deliverance.[61] These rites were conducted in both Jehol and Beijing. In Beijing, the boat was staged in the middle of Lake of Happiness (Fuhai) in the Garden of Perfect Brightness (Yuanmingyuan) or on Kunming Lake (Kunming hu) at the Summer Palace (Yiheyuan) after the old summer palace was destroyed. Such aquatic ritual performance is likely another manifestation of the imperial waterborne amusements of various performances supported by the Qing rulers as a way to exercise imperial authority from the High Qing era.[62]

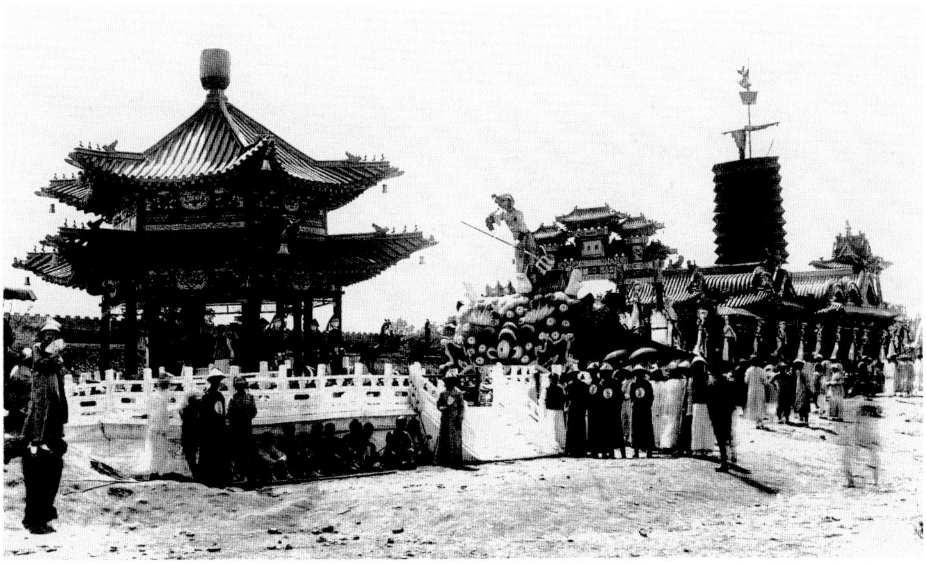

Figure 6 Empress Dowager Cixi's dharma boat, a pavilion, and a lotus pond, August 30, 1909 (originally dated the fifteenth day of the seventh month in the lunar calendar).

Empress Dowager Cixi, the de facto ruler of late Qing China, passed away on November 15, 1908, a day after Emperor Guangxu's death. The Office of Palace Construction (Yingzao si) submitted one memorial concerning Cixi on lunar May 29 and another one for Guangxu on June 1 to the new emperor in 1909. The officials proposed to arrange a Daoist Ritual of Offering Food (*shishi yitan*) on the fifteenth day of the seventh lunar month, and to burn a dharma boat, a "cool pavilion" (*liangting*), a lotus pond, and other items for the Empress Dowager Cixi and Emperor Guangxu separately (fig. 6). Since the Emperor Xuantong (1906–1967) was only three years old, it is likely the reply was issued by his father, the prince regent, Prince Chun Zaifeng (1883–1951), or perhaps by Empress Dowager Longyu (1868–1913). The edicts thus sent down provide precise and identical descriptions and instructions regarding the subjects and architectural space of these two sets of items. The two edicts may appear indistinguishable as imperial documents; nonetheless, the actual making and use, as well as the styles of the two pavilions, were not same, and the locations and burning procedures for the two sets of mortuary goods were completely distinct. Emperor Guangxu's funeral took place on the twelfth day of the third lunar month in 1909, while his tomb was still under construction.[63] His dharma boat was constructed on open ground close to the village Lianggezhuang in Hebei where his body was temporarily housed in an imperial earthen structure.[64] Hence, the burning of his boat would be silent and invisible from the public except for one formal photograph taken by the Imperial Household Department. That being the case, Empress Dowager Cixi's dharma boat is our best resource simply because visual evidence and textual accounts enable us to understand how an imperial dharma boat was made and burned as spectacle.

In the corresponding imperial edicts, the boat's size, form, pattern, color, and material are each meticulously described and certainly provided practical guidance for the artisans. Technical terms that are elsewhere used to describe architectural models (*tangyang*, ironed paper model) suggest that the knowledge behind certain construction methods of the two boats might be similar to that of architectural modeling. Both *tangyang* and *zhizha* require a number of identical materials such as paper, sorghum stalk, reed, and bamboo strips, as well as the skills for making an armature and for mounting and painting papers. It is unclear whether a miniature model of a paper dharma boat was made prior to the boat's full-scale construction, but this could have been the case because it was common to make ship models at the Qing court. As noted by Dagmar Schäfer, the architectural model served as a communication device between the Qing emperor, officials, and craftsmen and functioned as a conclusive design as well.[65] The precision of the descriptions of Cixi's and Guangxu's dharma boats may reflect the practice of circulation and standardization of designs within the Qing bureaucratic system. Instructions for the front part of Cixi's dharma boat run as follows:

> One dharma boat, its length is eighteen *zhang* [about 56 meters], its width is two *zhang* and six *chi* [about 6.7 meters], its height is six *chi* and four *cun* [about 2 meters]. The front of the boat is mounted with the face of a water-absorbing beast, the body of the boat is fully painted with ocean animals in five colors; lotus leaves and flowers with eight treasures are arranged around the boat. On the front deck is a gigantic ghost. His height is one *zhang* and six *chi* [about 3.6 meters]. He wears a gold helmet, patterned satin armor, and a pair of tiger skin shoes and holds a trident. On the deck, an archway is erected. The roof is mounted with tube-shaped green tiles. Walking animals are placed along the main roof ridges.[66]

A photograph published in the *Illustrated London News* on October 2, 1909, reveals that the boat's embellishment and its gigantic ghost were each faithfully produced in accordance with these guidelines (fig. 7). The edict goes on to provide specific instructions about how the arched roof, beams, and columns were to be mounted with painted paper to imitate wooden brackets, and that the red-lacquered and polychrome-painted surfaces were to be further enhanced with gold foil leaves (*caihua tiejin*).

Details about the decoration on the arch, as well as a female deity and her setting, are specified as follows:

> Under the archway, a Holy Mother of Yulan [Yulan Shengmu] is installed. Her height is five *chi* and five *cun* [about 1.65 meters]. She wears a Guanyin hood, a long blue satin robe, and shoes decorated with clouds. One hand holds a bejeweled flywhisk. A small palanquin is arranged near the archway and is made of yellow satin with cloud patterns and a golden rooftop. Two porters follow the palanquin.[67]

The outfit and attributes of the Holy Mother of Yulan together signal that she is another form of Guanyin.[68] On Cixi's dharma boat, however, the precise description of the Holy Mother or Guanyin also points to a connection with

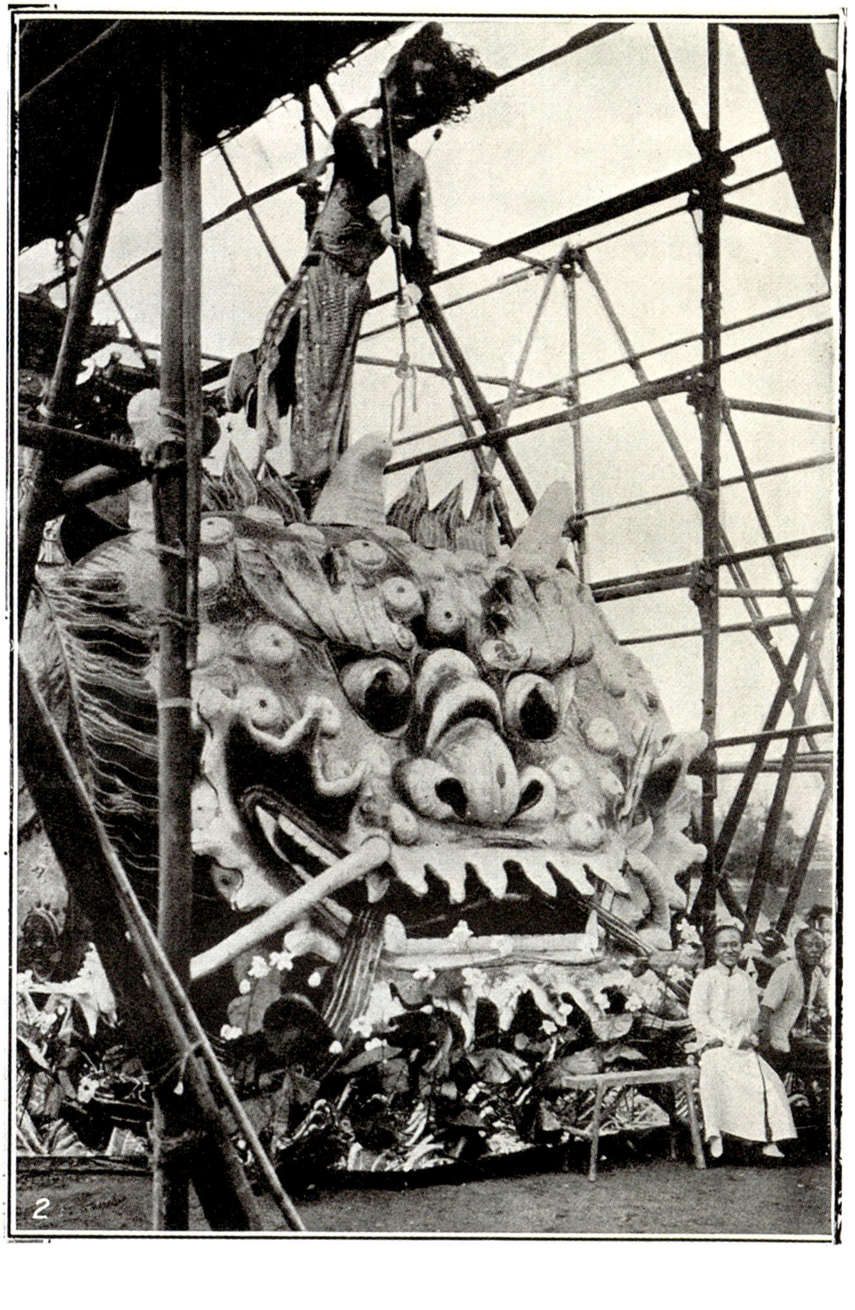

Figure 7 "Built to be burnt: a £7500 boat for a Chinese funeral" (1), Oct. 2, 1909, *Illustrated London News*. Picture No. 13156675 © Illustrated London News, Ltd./Mary Evans.

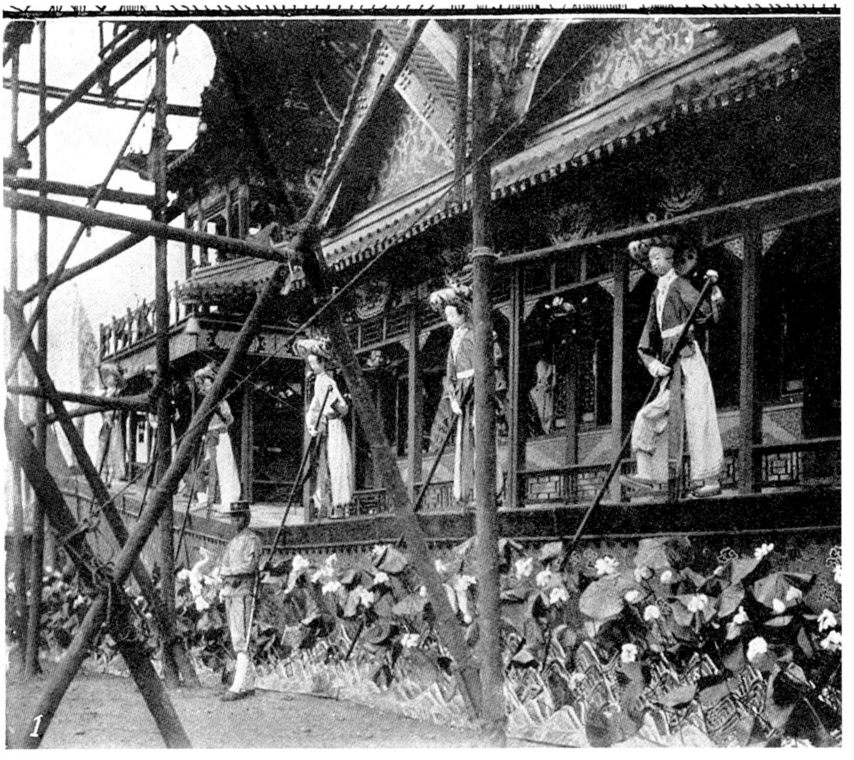

Figure 8 "Built to be burnt: a £7500 boat for a Chinese funeral" (2), Oct. 2, 1909, *Illustrated London News*. Picture No. 13156675 © Illustrated London News, Ltd./Mary Evans.

Cixi herself: Guanyin's height is also five *chi* and five *cun* (about 1.65 meters), which is a life-sized figure, and the deity's hood and blue robe offer obvious analogy with Cixi's headdress and costume when she was depicted as Guanyin.[69] Moreover, the palanquin and canopy—perhaps a real canopy in the photograph of the dharma boat—belonged to Cixi, thereby suggesting the dual identity of Guanyin and the female monarch. During Cixi's lifetime, she was very cautious about using typical items identified with the authority of a monarch, such as the screen and canopy, and consistently staged herself in front of, rather than proximate to, such furniture.[70]

Such a dual identity is further conveyed by the architectural space of a composite imperial residential area and temple behind the archway. There appears a palace courtyard, with two golden lions placed in front of the palace gate. Once entering the gate, one finds two corridors attached to the walls of the palace, followed by a hall with three rooms, all adorned with yellow tiles.

Inside the main hall, a table painted in the color of sandalwood, a throne, and a screen are arranged. A Suzhou-style clock, along with plates full of fruits and jade objects, presumably made of paper, are arranged on the table. The throne is covered with a satin mat of yellow clouds. The floor plan, yellow tiles, and throne confirm the setting as an imperial palace, where ten servants are positioned, both inside and out. A Buddha hall with a green tile roof hosts deities such as the Bodhisattva Dizang (Kṣitigarbha), the Sixteen Arhats, and the Ten Kings of Hell. About thirty boatmen are lined up along the side of the building (fig. 8).

Cixi's mortuary dharma boat amalgamates all the possible venues to the other shore, securing her transcendence. Although dharma boats were widely used in the funerary practices of the late Qing, we should recognize the special relationship of Cixi's dharma boat with her lifetime religious practices, particularly that of dressing up as Guanyin in her later years. Notably, Cixi's longstanding patronage of dharma boats in the Hungry Ghost Festival and her self-empowerment through merit-making surely signaled how her own dharma boat was designed. While Guangxu received a duplicate boat, at least according to the textual record, the connection between Cixi and the Holy Mother of Yulan demonstrates how Cixi continues to overshadow Guangxu in the afterlife: by Guangxu's boat featuring the Holy Mother, another Cixi avatar, we see that she has shifted to safeguarding or overseeing Guangxu's transcendence to the Pure Land.

The extravagance of Cixi's dharma boat lies in its monumental size and magnifies the mimetic power of paper. This blissful dharma cruise, costing about 14,700 silver taels, was made of paper, various plant materials, wood, silk, glass, and expensive artisanal labors.[71] To fully grasp how this spectacle functioned, we need to return to the media. Paper can be substituted for all things and consequently plays the role of the commodity, value, or money. Just like money or the abstract side of a commodity—namely, its exchange value—paper becomes a universal equivalent that can potentially stand in for other concrete objects. As explained earlier, this has to do with the additional labor required to make paper into the concrete shape of various things with meticulous surface treatments. All things are identical insofar as they can be replicated in paper. But paper gets its power only because of its connection to the other world. Paper's mimetic power as a medium to substitute for all things is confirmed by the remarkable structure and opulence of the paper objects, but in the case of Cixi's dharma boat, the addition of real garments onto the figurines and real damasks to furnish the space does not negate the power of paper so much as reinforce a lay hierarchy.

BURNING A DHARMA BOAT AS A SPECTACLE

The spectacle of the dharma boat was created through the fusion of different religious traditions within Buddhist, Daoist, and various local beliefs. In the late Qing period, three sets of distinct rituals could be performed simultaneously at the court to venerate the same dharma boat. For instance, during the Hungry Ghost Festival in about 1898, three large tents were constructed on the north shore of Kunming Lake to host priests from three religious institutions: one hundred Buddhist monks from the Fayuan Temple (Fayuansi), one hundred Daoist priests from the White Cloud Temple (Baiyunguan), and one hundred Tibetan lamas from the Harmony and Peace Palace Lamasery (Yonghegong). Each of these three religious groups built a temporary altar. The primary icon for the Buddhist altar is Dizang, and the monks performed the ritual related to transcended souls. The Daoist ritual masters used exorcism and enacted the power of the Face-flaming King of Ghosts (Mianran guiwang) or the Flaming-mouth King of Ghosts (Yankou guiwang). These rituals usually started on the thirteenth of the seventh lunar month and lasted for three days. The evening of the fifteenth was the climax of the observances when the dharma boat was burned. Inside the dharma boat, various paper objects offered by designated temples in Beijing, imperial family members, and sometimes even palace girls, had been piled up in advance. All the Buddhist and Daoist ritual masters would chant sutras and magic spells together. The deafening sounds of chanting, ceremonial music, the conflagration, and the fire flame reflected in water all converged to create a spectacular farewell to the ghosts. After the burning, fireworks began to extend a wish for a good journey to all the ghosts. With this collective effort, the ghosts were happily sent away.[72]

The combination of a dharma boat burning and pyrotechnic displays was likely a court invention of waterscape combined with religious spectacle instituted sometime in the nineteenth century.[73] The symbolic meaning of water as the sea between living and dead is staged as a sublime site through a series of spectacles. The fireworks presented a second climax by which human beings could confirm the success of the first climax, the burning of the boat, in the ghostly world. According to the memoir of Empress Dowager Cixi's serving girl Ronger (fl. 1898–1950), Cixi often sat on the terrace of the Hall for Listening to Orioles (Tingli guan) to watch the ceremonies. When the ghosts were fed and sent on their way, she would pray with palms pressed together and experience a deep joy.[74] Ronger's recollection of Cixi's response to the ritual reveals the shared sense of satisfaction and merit-making.

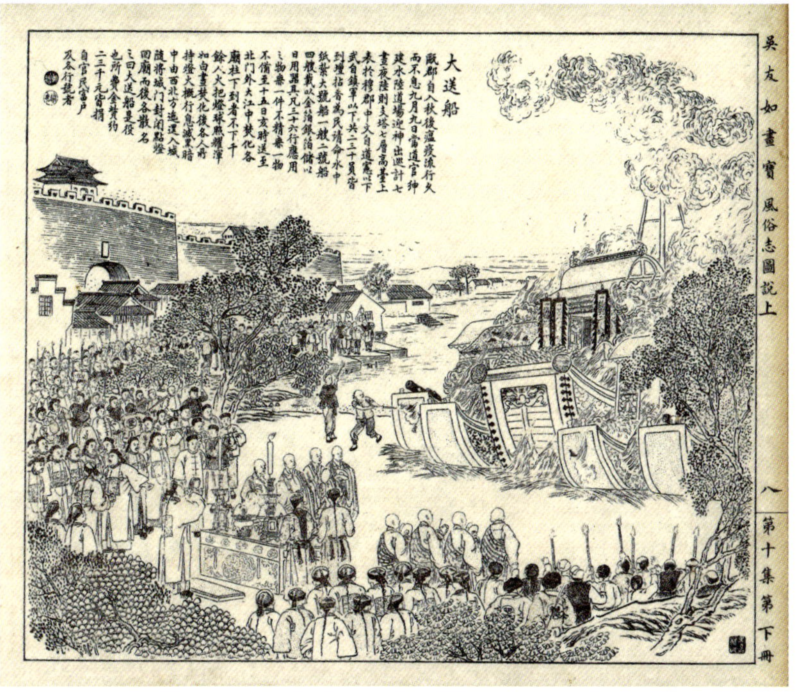

Figure 9 Wu Youru, *Da song chuan* (Grandly Sending Off the Boat). Lithographic print, 27 × 20 cm. From *Fengsuzhi tushuo* (Illustrated record of customs), vol. 10, *Wu Youru huabao* (Treasures of Wu Youru's paintings), 8b. University of Wisconsin-Madison, Kohler Art Library collection.

Cixi's first posthumous dharma boat prepared for the Hungry Ghost Festival, together with a pavilion and lotus pond, was staged outside Donghua Gate (Donghuamen), the eastern gate of the Forbidden City. The Donghua Gate is commonly referred to as the ghost gate, through which dead bodies were removed from the Forbidden City. The burning of this boat functioned as the first public display to send off her spirit.[75] Sadly, no picture preserves the precise moment when this ritual was enacted. An illustration titled *Grandly Sending off the Boat* (*Da song chuan*) can be considered in comparison with Cixi's dharma boat (fig. 9). The illustration was published in the *Dianshizhai Pictorial* as recent news. The caption states that a six-day-long Water and Land rite had been conducted between September 9 and 15, 1894, in Wenzhou, Zhejiang province, during an epidemic. Local officials, gentry elites, and shop owners together commissioned one large boat and four small boats that were set up by the water outside Wenzhou's north gate. The illustration depicts the moment when the boats are set ablaze and are about to be pushed into the water. About 1,000 people came to witness this sanitizing event.

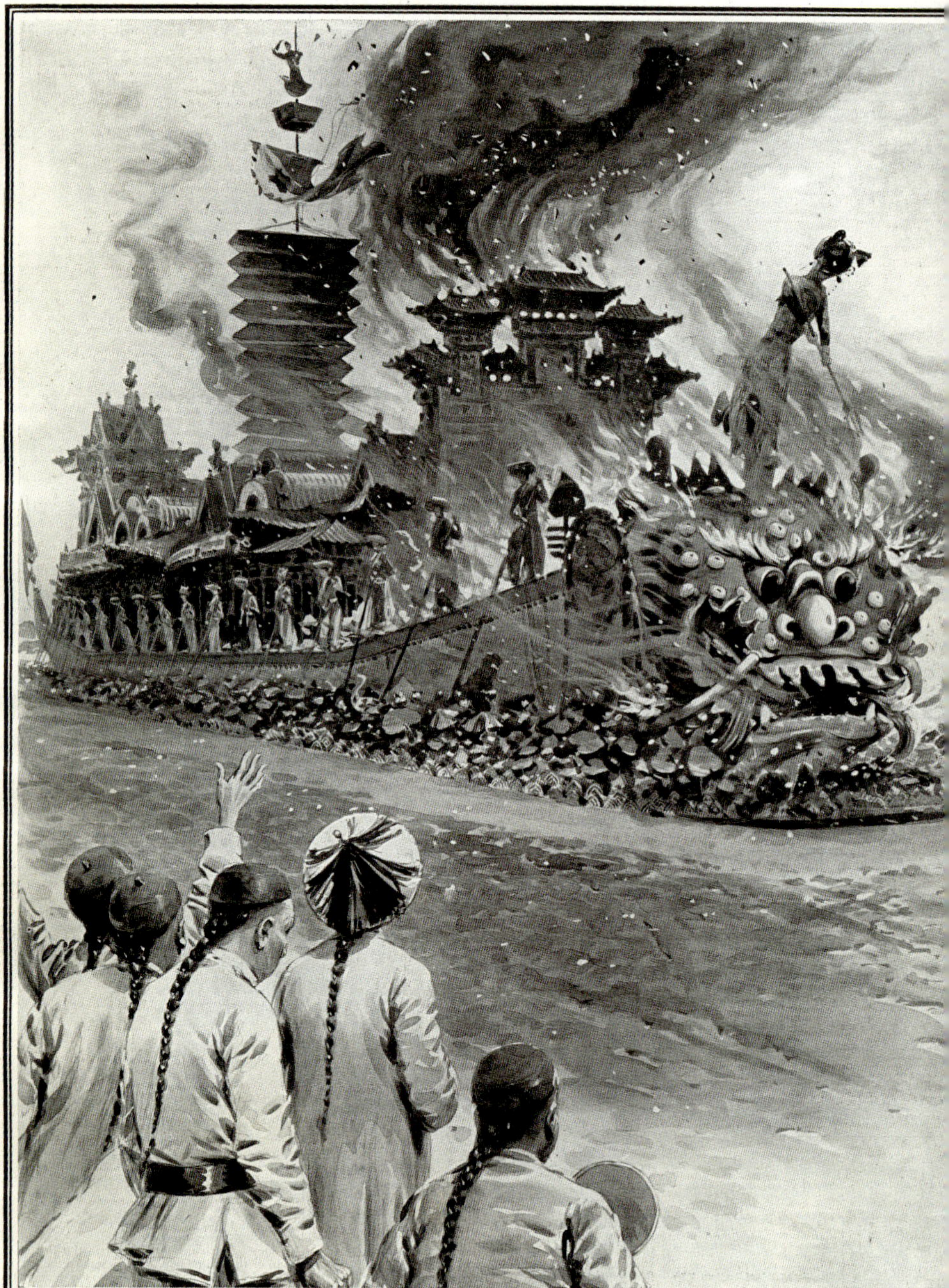

MAKING A VESSEL OF SMOKE FOR A DEAD EMPRESS: BURNING THE BOAT DESIGNED TO CARRY THE SPIRIT OF LATE EMPRESS DOWAGER OF CHINA ACROSS THE RIVER SEPARATING IT FROM THE HEAVENLY NIRVANA.

Figure 10 Samuel Begg, "Burning boat for spirit of Dowager Empress of China," Oct. 9, 1909, *Illustrated London News*. Picture No. 1315667 6 © Illustrated London News, Ltd./Mary Evans.

Unlike the visual conventions of a ceremony shown in *Grandly Sending off the Boat*, foreign photographers captured the process of constructing Cixi's boat as an engineering feat and its burning as a visual feast. The imperial foreman, architectural builders, painting artisans (*huajiang*), and scaffolding are all visible through the camera's lens. Qing court officials, project managers, and artisans stand for the camera in front of the dharma boat to preserve the collective memory of creating such a monumental piece.[76] The *Illustrated London News* reported on Cixi's boat on October 2 and 10, 1909. The magnificent "burning moment" was recreated by illustrator Samuel Begg (1854–1936) based on a photograph (fig. 10). One court official and four other men are featured in the lower left corner to represent onlookers. Although the caption introduces substantial information—including the religious meaning of burning a boat, as well as the location and the cost of this boat—paper, as the boat's primary medium, was not mentioned at all. Instead, the caption misinterprets the creative technique as one of carving. Paper successfully stood in for other mediums and even fooled the eyes of foreigners observing the spectacle.

Jonathan Crary makes an important point when regarding the historical conditions for spectacle in a Western context; he asks how it is connected to industrial society. The spectacle of the burning of a paper boat allows us to see the logic of visuality specific to nineteenth- and early twentieth-century China. In nineteenth-century Europe, signs were destabilized, which undermined hierarchy.[77] Mimesis, reflecting power, played a key role in destabilizing society. This paradigm allowed "newly empowered classes to overcome 'this exclusiveness of signs' and to initiate a 'proliferation of signs' on demand."[78] In short, the sign became dislocated from hierarchy. In the Chinese case, the mobility of signs that destabilizes hierarchy only partially takes place. In the late Qing, there was a conjuncture of structures. Buddhist ideology of universal transcendence, the idea of paper as a universal equivalent, and the spectacle associated with burning paper boats formed a relatively stable configuration, in which each moment cannot be reduced to the other. Because they cannot be reduced to one another, they might form different relationships. For example, the Qing court only assimilated the boat-burning spectacle as a means of reinforcing its status at the end of the eighteenth century. On the other hand, there is also an equalizing tendency that allows all people in a given district to be liberated by the burning of a paper boat. The amalgam of these different practices and beliefs underpins the historical specificity of the spectacle in nineteenth- and early twentieth-century China.

NOTES

1. For the first comprehensive discussion of this practice and term in English, see Ellen Johnston Laing and Helen Hui-Ling Liu, *Up in Flames: The Ephemeral Art of Pasted-Paper Sculpture in Taiwan* (Palo Alto: Stanford University Press, 2004). I will use the term "pasted-paper objects" instead of "pasted-paper sculpture" to stress their function as substitutes for daily-use items. In the Yuan and Ming periods, the characters for *zhizha* might have been pronounced the same as *zhiza* (a bundle of paper), which refers to the kind of paper associated with office supplies. See Chen Gaohua, Zhang Fan, Liu Xiao, Dang Baohai, *Yuan dianzhang* [Statutes and precedents of the Yuan dynasty], vol. 2 (Beijing: Zhonghua shuju and Tianjin: Tianjin guji chubanshe, 2011), 798. For a discussion of various terms referring to pasted-paper objects, see Pan Lusheng and Huang Yongjian, *Zhiren zhima* [Paper figurines and paper horses] (Shijiazhuang: Hebei meishu chubanshe, 2003), 1–5. For the crucial techniques of zha, see Pan and Huang, *Zhiren zhima*, 24–27.

2. See entry "*zangli*," in Yu Jiaji and Xu Jianguan, eds., Yu Tingliang comp., *Linjin xianzhi* [The gazetteer of Linjin], 1923 edition, *juan* 4, 14a. Diaolong: Zhongri guji quanwen ziliao ku [Diaolong: A full-text database of Chinese & Japanese ancient books] (hereafter Diaolong database). For the discussion of spirit vessel, see Wu Hung, "'Mingqi' de lilun he shijian: Zhan'guo shiqi liyi meishu zhong de guannianhua qingxiang" [The theory and practice of "Spirit Vessels"—a conceptual tendency in Warring States ritual art], *Wenwu*, no. 6 (2006): 72–81.

3. In the Song period, *zhima* usually referred to two-dimensional prints with the image of a messenger on horseback. However, its connotation has changed over time. *Zhima* became the common term for ephemeral prints that were burned in various rituals. See Laing and Liu, *Up in Flames*, 2. Shih-shan Susan Huang, *Picture the True Form: Daoist Visual Culture in Traditional China* (Cambridge, MA: Harvard University Asia Center, 2012), 240–41. In the phrase "*zhiren zhima*," zhima refers to a three-dimensional paper horse and other animals; see the entry "*zao mingqi*" in "Zhang Huang zhuan fu Zhang Menjin xiansheng xingzhuang" [Zhang Huang composed, appending Mr. Zhang Menjin's biography], in Zhang Huang, *Tushu bian* [The collections of books], *juan* 110, 7a, Diaolong database. *Zhimingqi* is associated with sangyi or funerals. Lü Kun, *Quweizhai wenji* [Collected writings from the studio of expelling falsehood], *juan* 8, 29a, Diaolong database. For another term, *mingqi zhizha* (spirit objects made of paper), see Lanling xiaoxiaosheng, *Jinpingmei* [The plum in the golden vase] (Beijing: Zhonghua shuju, 1998), 896. There is also a wide range of colloquial terms in different regions. See Rong Xin, "Luxinan cangzang zhizha yanjiu" [Study of funerary pasted paper objects in the southwest regions of Shandong province] (PhD diss., Shandong University, 2014), 10.

4. For the two representative studies on this subject, see Laing and Liu, *Up in Flames*; Rong Xin, "Luxinan cangzang zhizha yanjiu."

5. In this chapter, I concentrate on the practice of dharma boats in the late Qing period, but it continued in the first half of the twentieth century. For instance, after the imperial garden Beihai (North Sea), next to the Forbidden City, became a public park in 1925, pasted-paper dharma boats were sometimes displayed and burned on the north shore of the lake for public memorial services. For instance, during the Northern Warlords era, the dharma boats were dedicated to the soldiers who sacrificed their lives in the battles. See *Shibao* [Daily events], August 31, 1936, and September 7, 1941.

6. Pamela Smith, et al., "The Matter of Ephemeral Art: Craft, Spectacle, and Power in Early Modern Europe," *Renaissance Quarterly*, 73, no. 1 (2020): 78–131. For the representation of temporary paper-made large sculptures and pop-up buildings installed on the street for imperial celebrations of empress dowagers' and emperors' birthday celebrations in eighteenth-century China, see Lin Shu, "Chongqing huangtaihou de wanshou qingdiantu" [The picture of celebrating Empress Dowager Chongqing's birthday], *Zijincheng*, no. 10 (2015): 45–55. See also the entry on this painting in Daisy Yiyou Wang and Jan Stuart, eds., *Empresses of China's Forbidden City 1644–1912* (Salem: Peabody Essex Museum, 2018), 156–59. I want to thank Gil Raz for alerting me about the connotation of "ephemeral art" in the Western context, which is different from the religious context in which the *zhizha* objects are used.

7. Jonathan Crary, "Spectacle, Attention, Counter-Memory," *October* 50 (1989): 96–107. See also *Guy Debord, Society of the Spectacle* (Detroit: Black & Red, 1983).

8. Here I use Tsien Tsuen-Hsuin's translation. Tsien Tsuen-Hsuin, *Science and Civilisation in China* Vol. 5: *Chemistry and Chemical Technology*, Part 1: *Paper and Printing*, ed. Joseph Needham (Cambridge: Cambridge University Press, 1985), 35.

9. For an in-depth discussion on the nature of paper, see Tsien Tsuen-Hsuin, *Paper and Printing*.

10. Lu Xixing, "Tulufan gumu zhi mingqi yanjiu" [The study of the spirit objects excavated from ancient tombs in Turpan], *Xiyu yanjiu* 3 (2006): 50–55. Paper decorations were also widely used in religious practice during the Tang period. For examples of paper cut flowers that were found in cave 17 in Dunhuang, see Roderick Whitfield, *Caves of the Thousand Buddhas: Chinese Art from the Silk Route* (New York: G. Braziller, 1990), cat. no. 148.

11. The earliest example of burned paper ash in a funerary setting was found in the tomb of the sixth daughter of the Tang Emperor Gaozu (566–635). That tomb has been dated to 673–674. An Jingdi, "Tang Fangling dazhang gongzhu mu qingli jianbao" [A brief excavation report of Princess Fangling's tomb from Tang period], *Wenbo*, no. 1 (1990): 6.

12. Yu Ziyong and Xu Jianhua, "Astana gumu chutu de zhixie de xiufu" [The conservation of paper shoes excavated from a tomb in Astana], *Yishu shichang*, no. 7 (2007): 72–73. In general, scholars have agreed that early paper objects were substitutions for silk and other media. Franciscus Verellen, *Imperiled Destinies: The Daoist Quest for Deliverance in Medieval China* (Cambridge, MA: Harvard University Asia Center, 2019), 266–72.

13. Tsien Tsuen-Hsuin, *Paper and Printing*, 109–16.

14. Wang Juhua, *Zhongguo gudai zaozhi gongcheng jishushi* [The history of the technology of papermaking in ancient China] (Taiyuan: Shanxi jiaoyu chubanshe, 2006).

15. As Laing and Liu's study on modern *zhizha* craftsmanship in Taiwan demonstrates, sculptural techniques include "cutting, folding, punching, crashing, shaping and 'pulling.'" Laing and Liu, *Up in Flames*, 132.

16. Tang Lin, *Mingbao ji* [Record of miraculous retribution], *zhong juan*, 7a. This story is also included in *Fayuan zhulin*. See Shi Daoshi, *Fayuan zhulin* [Forest of gems in the garden of law], *juan* 10, 7a–12a, in *Wenyuange siku quanshu* [The complete library of four treasuries], vol. 1049 (Taiwan: Shangwu yinshuguan, 1982–1986).

17. Daoshi, *Fayuan zhulin, juan* 48, 8–19, *Sibu congkan* (Shanghai: Shangwu yinshuguan, 1929). Also see Tsien Tsuen-Hsuin, *Zaozhi ji yinshua* [Paper and printing] (Taipei: Taiwan shangwu yishuguan gufen youxian gongsi, 1995), 134.

18. Dai Fu, *Guangyi ji* [Extensive records of the marvelous] (Beijing: Zhonghua shuju, 1992), 28. See also Glen Dudbridge, *Religious Experience and Lay Society in T'ang China—A Reading of Tai Fu's*

Kuang-I chi (Cambridge: Cambridge University Press, 1995), 5.

19. Tsien Tsuen-Hsuin, *Paper and Printing*, 102–4.

20. Verellen, *Imperiled Destinies*, 269.

21. I am grateful for Dorothy Ko's comments about human labor in relation to the efficacy of paper.

22. The story of "Monk Jin" (*jin heshang*), written by Pu Songling (1640–1715), vividly describes the gigantic figurines of the ghost exorcists Fangbi and Fangxiang, life-sized servants and beauties, and a splendid spirit paper house occupied with various paper-made spirit objects. These literary descriptions might be informed by actual practices. Pu Songling, *Liaozhai zhiyi* [Liaozhai's records of the strange] (Beijing: Renmin wenxue chubanshe, 1989), 1007.

23. "Mingzhai hongkai," *Wu Youru huabao* [Treasures of Wu Youru's paintings], *Fengsuzhi tushuo* [Illustrated account of manners and customs], vol. 10 (Shanghai: Biyuan huishe, 1909), 18b.

24. Zhang Weisheng, "Jidong sangzang zhizha de shenmei tezheng" [The characteristic of aesthetics of the pasted-paper objects used in funeral practice in Jidong] (master's thesis, Central Academy of Fine Arts, 2015), 40.

25. Wang Juhua, *Zhongguo gudai zaozhi*, 317.

26. This term might just indicate multicolored papers.

27. The text reads: "Qinzi duzao ruya mingliao shenliao wucai zhipin fashou." (We personally inspect the production of the elegant spirit pigment, deific pigment and we sell five-color papers.) Haks Collection, mid-twentieth century, National Museum of World Cultures, the Netherlands.

28. For the customs in Beijing from the late Qing to the Republication period, see Chang Renchun, *Hongbai xishi: jiujing hunsang lisu* [Red and white joyous ceremonies: wedding and funeral customs in old Beijing] (Beijing: Beijing yanshan chubanshe), 262–63. Zhang Weisheng also points out that the white-colored paper is often used to make objects that are used to lead souls. This practice is mainly found in the eastern part of Hebei province. See Zhang Weisheng, "Jidong sangzang zhizha," 39–40. Niuli or Artocarpus is the plant for making the green color used only for *zhima*. Zhang Sanxi, *Yixue liuyao, shijiu juan* [The six principles of medicine, nineteen volumes], *juan* 3, 48a, Diaolong database.

29. Sun Wen (fl. 1862–1908), *A Dream of Red Mansions as Portrayed through the Brush of Sun Wen* (New York: Better Link Press, 2010), 211.

30. Hong Mai, *Yijian zhi* [Record of the listener], vol. 7 (Beijing: Zhonghua shuju, 1985), 23.

31. I thank Zhang Weisheng for explaining to me the significance of the speed of the firing process and the color of the flame.

32. See *Kusang ge* [Songs for crying in funerals], early twentieth century, private collection.

33. For a comprehensive discussion of rituals for sending off pasted-paper objects to the dead in Beijing, see Chang Renchun, *Hongbai xishi*, 357–61. For an example of a pasted-paper object that was damaged before burning, see the anecdote of a crippled horse received by the dead in Ji Yun, *Yuewei caotang biji* [Jottings from the grass hut for examining minutiae], *juan* 5, 2a–b, 1800 edition, Diaolong database.

34. *Da bao ji jing* [Scriptures of great treasure storehouse], *Taishō shinshū daizōkyō*, ed. Takakusu Junjirō and Watanabe Kaigyoku (Tokyo: Taishō issaikyō kankōkai, 1924–1932) (hereafter *T.*), 11–310: 638a28.

35. *Da bao ji jing*, 11–310: 638a28.

36. "Jingxin fodao yiwei zhu mucai," *Da bao ji jing*, 11–310: 638a28.

37. "Renru rouruan yinian wei ding," *Da bao ji jing*, 11–310: 638a28.

38. For instance, see Qu Ruji, comp., *Zhiyue lu* [The record of pointing to the moon], *juan* 4,

39a–b, Mingshantang 1743 edition, Diaolong database.

39. See *Dafang guangfo huayanjing* [Great righteous vast Buddha ornamented with flowers scriptures], *T.* 10–293, 35: 84b10.

40. Jiang Shoucheng, *Zhongguo jinshi daojiao songwen yishi yanjiu* [The Daoist rites of plague exorcism: from Song dynasty to contemporary China] (Beijing: Renmin chubanshe, 2017), 29.

41. Jiang Shoucheng, *Zhongguo jinshi daojiao*, 31–32.

42. "Shenxiao qianwen songchuan yi" in *Daofa huiyuan* [Collection of principal methods of the Dao], *juan* 220. "Shenxiao qianwen zhibing juefa," in *Daofa huiyuan*, *juan* 221. I thank Tao Jin for providing the citation information.

43. Jiang Shoucheng, *Zhongguo jinshi daojiao*, 35. A paper boat and the waterscape as part of religious ceremonies cannot be separated from the development of other types of boats during the Ming period. For a discussion of a boat that was used by scholars as a space to conduct artistic activities in the Jiangnan area during the Ming period, see Einor K. Cervone, "Art Adrift: Curating Selves aboard Ming-Dynasty Painting and Calligraphy Boats," *Archives of Asian Art* 69, no. 2 (2019): 155–79.

44. Jiang Shoucheng, *Zhongguo jinshi daojiao*, 36. This is still widely practiced in lower Yangzi River delta in contemporary China.

45. I also want to express gratitude to Shih-shan Susan Huang for calling my attention to the major differences in destination for these two boat types. For the possible destinations of a plague-expelling boat, see also Jiang Shoucheng, *Zhongguo jinshi daojiao*, 59.

46. *Fachuan jing* [Scripture of the dharma boat], *yijuan*, in *Jiangnan songjiangfu huating xian baishacun xiaoxiu huilang baojuan* [The precious scroll of filial Huilang in Baisha village in Huating County, Songjiang District, Jiangnan], 1900 ed. (Shanghai: Yihua tang, Guangxu gengzi, 1900), 43a. Harvard Yenching Library collection.

47. *Foshuo wu liang shou jing* [Sutra on the Buddha of immeasurable life], trans. Saṃghavarman (active 3rd century), *T.* 12–360,1: 270a–6.

48. Anne Ning Feng, "*Water, Ice, Lapis Lazuli: The Metamorphosis of Pure Land Art in Tang China*" (PhD diss., University of Chicago, 2018), 174–75.

49. *Fachuan jing*, 43a.

50. For a comprehensive introduction of this rite, see Chün-fang Yü, *Kuan-yin: the Chinese Transformation of Avalokiteśvara* (New York: Columbia University Press, 2001), 320–31.

51. For instance, in late Qing Beijing, every temple near Fuchengmen burned a paper boat. Xu Ke, *Qingbai leichao* [Categorized anthology of petty matters from the Qing period], *shiling lei*, 22, Diaolong database. Also, for a brief discussion of Buddhist temples burning pasted-paper objects during the Hungry Ghost Festival, see Susan Naquin, *Peking: Temples and City Life, 1400–1900* (Berkeley: University of California Press, 2000), 440.

52. Mark Meulenbeld correctly alerts us to the demonic aspect of the ill-fated Princess Miaoshan, who might have had a relationship with this demonic figure. Mark Meulenbeld, "Death and Demonization of a Bodhisattva: Guanyin's Reformulation within Chinese Religion," *Journal of the American Academy of Religion* 84, no. 3 (September 2016): 11–12 and 690–726.

53. Wendi Adamek, "The Impossibility of the Given: Representations of Merit and Emptiness in Medieval Chinese Buddhism," *History of Religions* 45, no. 2 (2005): 135–80.

54. Huang Shizuo, *Jiading xian xuzhi* [Supplementary gazetteer of Jiading County], ed. Fan Zhongxiang, *juan* 5, 3b, Diaolong database.

55. Yu Songqing, "*Fachuan jing* yanjiu" [Study of the scripture of the dharma boat], *Hebei daxue xuebao*, no. 3 (1993): 1–8.
56. Zhongguo diyi lishi dangan guan, No. 05-08-006-000004-0013. The exact location of this dharma boat needs to be further researched.
57. The ritual began immediately after death and lasted for twelve months. A different set of rituals were conducted each month. For instance, to have a full picture of Empress Dowager Cixi's year-long death rites, see Margareta T. J. Griessler, "The Last Dynastic Funeral: Ritual Sequence at the Demise of the Empress Dowager Cixi," *Oriens Extremus* 34, no. 1/2 (1991): 7–35.
58. Zhongguo diyi lishi dangan guan, Yingzao si, No. 05-08-030-00606-0013, No. 05-08-030-00606-0014. These two boats were also made with precious real materials such as sandalwood for the structure. See Zhongguo diyi lishi dangan guan, Yingzao si, No. 05-08-030-00606-0034. The size of Guangxu's dragon boat is about thirteen *zhang* (40 meters) long, which is slightly scaled down from the dharma boat dedicated to him at the Hungry Ghost Festival.
59. Mid-July Day Ritual is another name for the rite conducted during the Hungry Ghost Festival. Sometimes, this type of boat is recorded as "the Mid-July Day Ritual Dharma Boat" (*zhongyuan li fachuan*). Zhongguo diyi lishi dangan guan, Yingzao si, No. 05-08-006-000590-0021.
60. There is only one week between the Double Seventh Festival and the Hungry Ghost Festival. During the Qianlong period, there was a tradition in Fujian in which women made paper silver and gold ingots during the Double Seventh Festival and had them burned on the day of the Hungry Ghost Festival. Shen Chengguo, *Shanghang xianzhi* [The gazetteer of Shanghang], *juan* 11, 629, Diaolong database. The relationship between a Double Seventh dharma boat and Qing court women's artisanal skill needs to be further researched. Sometimes a Double Seventh dharma boat could be ordered for an individual deceased imperial woman during her posthumous Double Seventh Festival if her body was not entombed. For instance, Xiaoshen Empress (1792–1833), the second empress of Daoguang Emperor (1782–1850), was entombed two and half years after she passed away, and she continued to receive dharma boats during three consecutive Double Seventh Festivals and Hungry Ghost Festivals before she was officially buried in the imperial Muling mausoleum. See Zhongguo diyi lishi dangan guan, Yingzao si, No. 05-08-006-000590-0021, No. 05-08-006-000599-0010, No. 05-08-006-000599-0013.
61. Another term, *feihuo fachuan* (flying fire dharma boat), was also used to refer to the fireworks dharma boat.
62. For a comprehensive discussion of this subject, see Einor K. Cervone, "Waterscapes: Aquatic Theater and Other Floating Pleasures in Late Imperial Jiangnan" (PhD diss., Harvard University, 2017), 217–99.
63. Emperor Guangxu's body was entombed in November 1913, five years after his death.
64. Zhongguo diyi lishi dangan guan, see a memorial submitted by the Ministry of Rites on lunar May 23, 1909, No. 06-01-001-000680-0146.
65. Dagmar Schäfer, "Knowledge by Design—Architecture and Jade Models during the Qianlong Reign (1735–1796)," in *The Structures of Practical Knowledge*, ed. Matteo Valleriani (Cham, Switzerland: Springer, 2017), 271–86.
66. Zhongguo diyi lishi dangan guan, Yingzao si, No. 05-08-030-00606-0034.
67. Zhongguo diyi lishi dangan guan, Yingzao si, No. 05-08-030-00606-0034.
68. In the early twentieth century, the Big Ghostly King, as a wrathful manifestation of Guanyin, was not so frequently grouped together with Guanyin on a dharma boat. The Big Ghostly King often carries a sign of Guanyin on his head. See Meulenbeld, "Death and Demonization

of a Bodhisattva," 12.
69. Yuhang Li, "Oneself as a Female Deity: Representations of Cixi Posing as Guanyin," *Nan Nü: Men, Women, and Gender in China* 14, no. 1 (2012): 75–118. A blue robe identifies every main religious figure in this boat.
70. Ying-chen Peng, "Lingering between Tradition and Innovation: Photographic Portraits of Empress Dowager Cixi," *Ars Orientalis* 43 (2013): 157–70.
71. The Office of Palace Construction asked for this amount of money for both materials and artisans. Zhongguo diyi lishi dangan guan, Yingzao si, No. 05-08-030-00606-0034.
72. Jin Yi and Shen Yiling, *Gongnü tanwang lu* [Memoir of a palace maid] (Beijing: Zijincheng chubanshe, 1992), 193. The imperial document of this event needs to be further verified. For more information on Cixi's relationship to Baiyun guan, see Xun Liu, "Visualizing Perfection: Daoist Paintings of Our Lady, Court Patronage, and Elite Female Piety in the Late Qing," *Harvard Journal of Asiatic Studies* 64, no. 1 (2004): 57–115.
73. Lihong Liu has recently shown that fireworks at the Qing court in the eighteenth century constituted an innovation in exercising art and power. Lihong Liu, "Pyrotechnic Profusion: Fireworks, Spectacles, and Automata in Time," *Journal 18*, no. 3, *Lifelike* (Spring 2017), https://www.journal18.org/1550.
74. Jin Yi and Shen Yiling, *Gongnü tanwang lu*, 195.
75. The public viewing is briefly mentioned under the entry of "Da fachuan" (Big dharma boat) in *Xiaoheng xiangshi zhuren, comp., Qingchao yeshi daguan* [Overview of the unofficial histories of the Qing dynasty], *diyiji, Qinggong yiwen* [Lost tales of the Qing palace] (Shanghai: Zhonghua shuju, Shangwu yinshu guan, 1936), 117–18.
76. For the group photo of artisans, please see illustration 3 under the title "Built to be burnt: a £7500 boat for a Chinese funeral." *Illustrated London News*, October 2, 1909.
77. Jean Baudrilliard, *The Consumer Society: Myths and Structures* (London: Sage Publications, 2016).
78. Crary, "Spectacle, Attention, Counter-Memory," 98.

PART II
CONTEMPORARY CHINESE ART

To Attack and Abandon Representation

Huang Yong Ping's Redefinition of Materials and Modern Art

Orianna Cacchione

In 1986, Huang Yong Ping (1954–2019) and the other members of Xiamen Dada, an artist group in the eponymous city, moved construction materials and garbage into the Exhibition Hall of the Fujian Museum of Art (Fujiansheng meishu zhanlanguan) in Xiamen, China. Boards, sections of iron fence, bamboo scaffolding, and a ladder were stacked against the walls. Old beams, paving stones, wood, and dirt were piled on the floor, circled by white chalk powder (fig. 1). Pots were collected and displayed in deliberate configurations. Sections of iron fence were constructed into a cage-like installation, surrounding a chair stacked with stuffed bags. Piles of sand were adorned with found objects. Photographs of these objects in their original locations outside the museum were hung on the wall. On another wall, newspaper broadsheets from the group's previous exhibition were pasted in a scattered installation stretching from the floor to the ceiling. Arrows were painted in red on the walls and drawn in white chalk powder on the floor. Big, thick, black characters explained to those entering: "As a place for the exchange of art ideas, the art exhibition hall introduces the activities of a small group of the Art New Wave. The audience will make their own judgment."

The *Events Exhibition That Happened at the Fujian Museum of Art* (*Fasheng zai Fujiansheng meishu zhanlanguan nei de shijian zhanlan*), also known as the *Events Exhibition* (*Shijian zhanlan*), went far beyond merely introducing the activities of an artist group that was part of the larger national avant-garde artistic

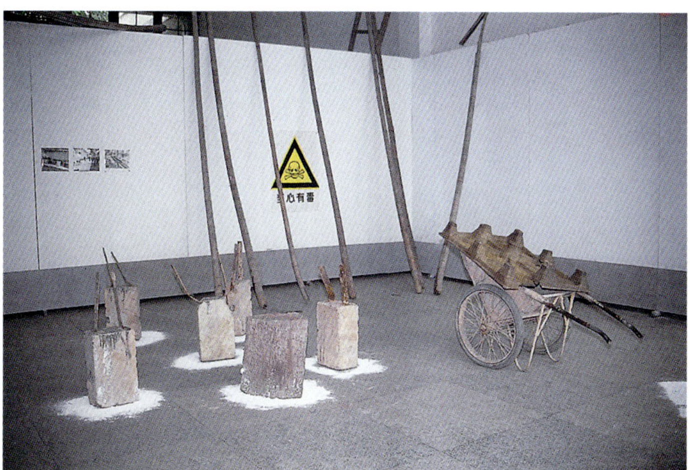

Figure 1 Installation view of the *Events Exhibition*, Fujian Museum of Art, Xiamen, China, 1986. Courtesy of Gladstone Gallery, New York and Brussels. © Huang Yong Ping.

experiments known as the '85 Art New Wave ('85 Meishu xinchao) or '85 Art Movement. The *Events Exhibition* was a radical intervention and a claim for new theorizations of art making in China, a claim however that was staked through the *materials* the artists put on view. Huang Yong Ping, the main protagonist of the group, declared: "That these materials suddenly were rushed into the exhibition hall generates a sense of assault. This assault, however, is not aimed at the visitors but their views of 'art.' Similarly, the target of the attack is the exhibition hall as a model of the art system, not the exhibition hall itself."[1] What led to this attack? Or rather, what led to this "sneak attack" (*xiji*), as Huang calls out in the original Chinese text? And why are these materials—wood beams, boards, ceramic jars, trash, and other detritus—in particular so assaulting?

Throughout the 1980s, unconventional materials and found objects—or as Huang Yong Ping would call them, "nontraditional materials" (*fei chuangtong cailiao*)—transformed into artistic materials became a hallmark of Huang's individual practice and the activities of the artist group Xiamen Dada, of which he was a founding member.[2] These materials would be used to attack representational painting, assault the institutional expectations for art at the time that had been defined by the Chinese Artists Association (Zhongguo meishu xiehui) and art museums and exhibition halls throughout the country, and eventually to assail the symbolic chain of the materials themselves. Yet despite the primacy of these materials, few scholars who have studied Huang or Xiamen Dada more broadly focus on the materials themselves, favoring instead Huang's conceptual strategies and/or the ways in which he complexly critiqued hierarches of cultural production and the interaction between Chinese and "Western" art. For scholar and curator Hou Hanru, the attack in Huang's practice is directed at the "legitimacy of the West-centric monopoly in intellectual and everyday life" through Huang's use of indigenous cultural practices, including the *Book of Changes* (*Yijing*), an ancient divination system.[3] Other scholars, including art historians Britta Erickson and Paul Gladston, emphasize the conceptual dimensions of Huang's practice, discounting and often concealing the primacy of materials and the varying and various ways in which they are deployed and transformed.[4] I argue that these materials, specifically nontraditional materials, were as assaulting if not more assaulting than Huang's conceptual strategies.

Expanding beyond this, I reconsider Huang Yong Ping's and, by extension, Xiamen Dada's practices through the lens of materiality, analyzing how "nontraditional materials," as Huang himself named them, operated in and were operative of their practices. By focusing on artworks exhibited at four seminal exhibitions in the 1980s, I locate three loosely bound stages in the development of his practice and the ways in which Huang radically questioned the definitions of art, its role in society, and the potential of its materials. First, unconventional, nontraditional materials in his early works, made roughly between 1983 and 1986, provided one way to question the terms of realism and representational art in China, confronting the recent history and uses of socialist realism to project (government) ideology in order to develop new art forms. Second, and perhaps more importantly, the insistent and often aggressive use of these materials in Huang's work with Xiamen Dada helped redefine the relationship between the artist, artwork, and viewer. Unconventional materials and found objects disrupted standard practices of viewing, questioned conventional artforms, and challenged the ways art institutions, including the art academies, museums, exhibition halls, and the Chinese Artists Association, defined art. Ultimately, through these experiments with materials, Huang and his fellow members of Xiamen Dada radically questioned the meaning of art and its role in society. Finally, these nontraditional materials take on a new ontology within Huang's individual practice in the late 1980s—no longer employed to deconstruct or attack but for the ways in which the materials themselves become empty signifiers in his work. Here, the material itself breaks away from its traditional significance, taking on various and variable meanings and playfully evading static definitions. Moving beyond an assault and abandonment of representation, materials allowed Huang to redefine modern art as it was being experimented with in China in the 1980s.

THE FIVE-PERSON MODERN ART EXHIBITION
INTRODUCING MATERIAL OBJECT COLLAGE RELIEFS AND READYMADE OBJECT COLLAGES

In 1983, Huang Yong Ping, Lin Jiahua (b. 1953), Xu Zhandou, Jiao Yaoming (b. 1957), and Yu Xiaogang (b. 1958) organized the *Five-Person Modern Art Exhibition* (*Wu ren xiandai yishu zuopin zhanlan*) at the Xiamen People's Art Museum (Xiamenshi qunzhong yishuguan). The artists displayed both purely abstract paintings and sculptures and other works that had been amended with strange, "non-traditional" materials—animal bones, straw, and plaster molds. Writing two years after the exhibition, Huang named these works made with nontraditional materials "material object collage reliefs" (*shiwu pintie fudiao*) and "readymade object collages" (*xianchangpin pintie*), staking a claim for their novelty and also the importance of their debut. Representative of these were Huang's *Haymakers*

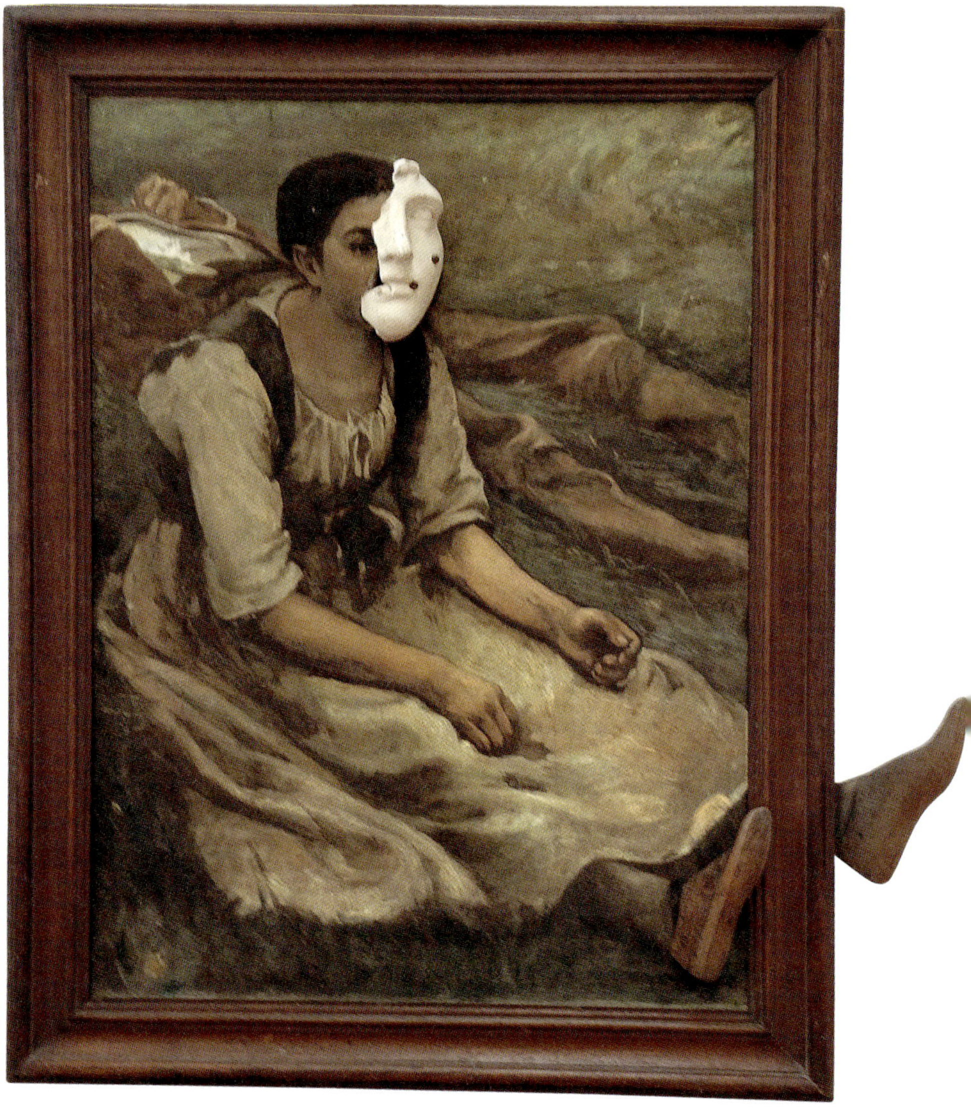

Figure 2 Huang Yong Ping, *Haymakers (Les Foins) by Jules Bastien-Lepage Was Exhibited in Shanghai in April 1978,* 1983. Oil on canvas and collage on wood, 120 × 110 cm. Courtesy of Gladstone Gallery, New York and Brussels. © Huang Yong Ping.

(Les Foins) by Jules Bastien-Lepage Was Exhibited in Shanghai in April 1978 (1983) (fig. 2), a meticulous copy of the French artist's iconic painting *Haymakers* (*Les Foins*) (1877) amended with a plaster cast and two shoe molds; and Jiao Yaoming's *Ecological Balance* (*Shengtai pingheng*), a sculpture composed of an animal skull wrapped repeatedly with loose wire. Local officials in the Xiamen Artists Association (Xiamen meixie) who were charged with the bureaucratic management of art at the time did not allow the exhibition to be seen by the public, effectively censoring the exhibition. Instead, only members of the Association were able to view the exhibition during its short four-day run. In the early years of Deng Xiaoping's reform and opening (*gaige kaifang*) policy, the government resisted dictating strict guidelines for what types of art were acceptable to be shown to the public, leaving local officials to make their own decisions. Accustomed to seeing realist paintings, sculptures, and prints on view, these officials often erred on the side of caution, permitting the display of only types of art that had been previously considered acceptable. Critics, too, denounced the exhibition, writing in local papers that the highly trained artists were merely "hobbyists" and arguing that the works on view weren't really art at all.[6]

Defending the exhibition two years later, Huang Yong Ping responded to the criticism it received in the newly established art journal *The Trend of Art Thought* (*Meishu sichao*), asserting that works on view demonstrated the ways in which the artists were attempting to innovate new, modern styles in their works. Huang explained the intentions of the artists who organized the *Five-Person Modern Art Exhibition*:

> The artists daringly opened themselves to question the value of the concept of customary representational art, including the law of so-called beauty (*mei*), as well as artworks that are exhibited should have some type of fixed view: in reality modern art advances by a synthesis of trying, exploring many manifesting methods of the reflection of the modern spirit.[7]

For Huang, the abstract paintings and sculptures on view tested the limits of the language of "pure" (*chun*) or autonomous art; while those made with so-called nontraditional materials—including plaster casts, animal bones, electric wire, straw cloth, hard foam, wood, metal, straw mats, and clothing—surpassed these limits.[8] Huang argued, if the works on view, all either abstract or made with nontraditional materials, could not be considered art (by the Xiamen Artists Association and local critics), then art had become synonymous with representation and representational art was concretely tied to realism.[9] Ultimately, for Huang, the works exhibited in the *Five-Person Exhibition* questioned the conventions of representational art and attempted to redefine modern art in China.[10]

Haymakers (Les Foins) by Jules Bastien-Lepage Was Exhibited in Shanghai in April 1978 provides an elegant example of Huang Yong Ping's critique of representational painting through the use of nontraditional materials. To make the work, Huang affixed a cast of a face and two shoe molds onto an expertly painted copy of *Haymakers* (*Les Foins*) by Jules Bastien-Lapage (1848–1884). Oversized and rendered in a classical style, the cast coyly covers the face of a plainly dressed woman sitting in a field and obscures Huang's advanced skill and academic training in painting. It is attached by two prominent nails that appear as if exaggerated birthmarks. The figure is so tightly cropped by the frame that her left foot is cut off by it. In order to make the woman whole, Huang amends the painting with two shoe molds. One is attached to the frame, the other onto the canvas, extending the figure's feet off the picture plane and into its surrounding space. Representative of Huang's earliest experiments with unconventional materials, *Haymakers* evades the standard conventions of realism and representational painting through his application of the shoe molds and plaster cast. The heavily modified copy of an outmoded naturalist painting calls into question the international histories that informed representational painting at the time in China, especially those taught at the Chinese art academies, including nineteenth-century French realism and naturalism, Mexican Muralism, Soviet and Sino socialist realism, and the newer realist styles of Rustic Realism and Scar Art. For Huang, these nontraditional materials resisted the possibility that the works would be ascribed to a single representational style, and especially to the institutionalized dominance of realism, or a language of "pure" art. Furthermore, the addition of the plaster cast and shoe molds emphasizes the contradiction between the supposedly "real" scene painted on the canvas and the real (*actual*) cast and molds.

These real-life objects allowed Huang Yong Ping to more directly access the world around him, yet their conceptual precedent was informed in the graduation paintings he completed for the Zhejiang Academy of Fine Arts (Zhejiang meishu xueyuan). For the assignment, Huang and his classmates were sent to a factory to observe the workers and paint from daily life. Instead of merely painting the workers, Huang appropriated their tools, using industrial spray guns to make his graduation works in order to access and harness the modern spirit of the factory. The resulting paintings verged on abstraction. In *Molten Steel Container in Motion* (*Yunxingzhong de gangbao*, 1981) and *Winding Steel Plates* (*Ji kuai wanqu de gangban*,

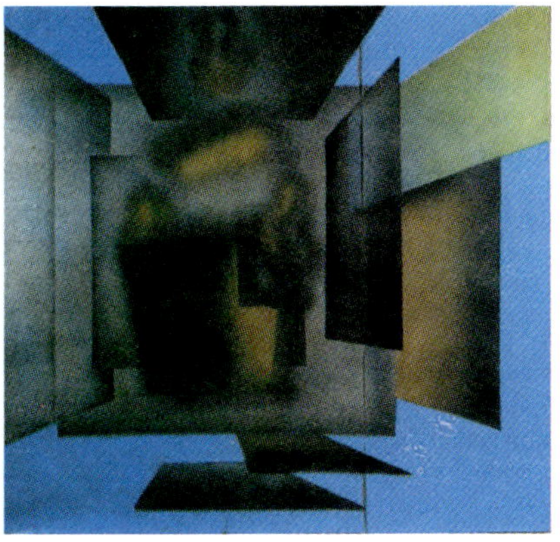

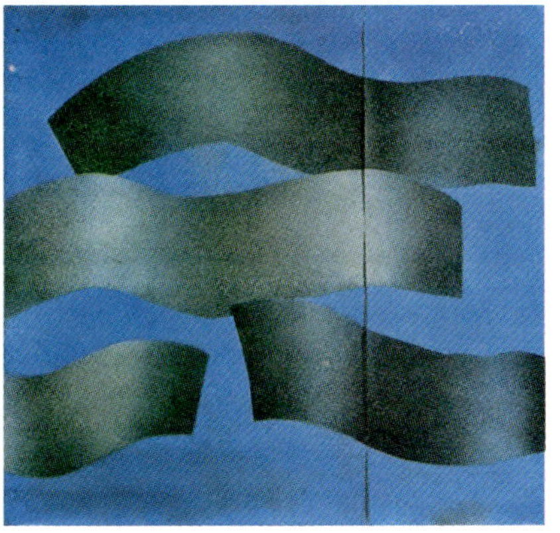

Figure 3 Huang Yong Ping, *Molten Steel Container in Motion,* 1981. Acrylic spray paint on paperboard, 108 × 116 cm. From Huang Yong Ping, "Tan wo de jizhang hua" (On a few of my paintings), *Meishu* (Art), no. 1 (1983). Courtesy of Estate of Huang Yong Ping and *Meishu* magazine, 1983, issue 1.

Figure 4 Huang Yong Ping, *Winding Steel Plates,* 1981. Acrylic spray paint on paperboard, 108 × 116 cm. From Huang Yong Ping, "Tan wo de jizhang hua." Courtesy of Estate of Huang Yong Ping and *Meishu* magazine, 1983, issue 1.

1981) (figs. 3–4), the containers and plates become almost fully abstract shapes moving in space. The context of the factory dissolved into the blue backgrounds that Huang "unconsciously" sprayed onto the paperboard. It was in the factory that Huang's conceptualization of the represented object shifted as he observed the autonomy of objects: "In a spray worker's eyes, a steel plate is nothing but itself."[11] Seeking to replicate a similar experience of representing a thing as itself, Huang reconsidered how representation functions on the surface of the canvas. Huang mused, "It is not to represent a square using different ways of painting, but to represent a square using a square, to represent an object using an object, to represent a man using a man, and to represent meaninglessness using meaninglessness. That is, to abandon representation itself."[12] Huang began to question the ways in which meaning is produced or constructed, separating it from representation and connecting it to objects themselves. From industrial tools used in real life by factory workers, Huang shifted to incorporating real-life objects into his paintings. In *Haymakers*, Huang consciously doubled the represented image with the real object—the painted face is covered over by the plaster cast, the painted foot amputated and replaced by the shoe mold. The painted images could no longer be seen as stand-ins for the objects they depict; instead, the sheer presence of the real objects interrupts the possibility of representation in painting at all by foregrounding the material as itself. For the next three years, nontraditional materials proliferated in Huang's practice as his work increasingly abandoned all forms of representational art.

THE BURNING EVENT AND THE EVENTS EXHIBITION
TESTING THE LIMITS OF THE INSTITUTION

The 1983 *Five-Person Modern Art Exhibition* was followed in 1986 by the *Xiamen Dada—Modern Art Exhibition* (*Xiamen Dada—Xiandai yishuzhan*) that similarly showcased abstract paintings and other artworks that used nontraditional materials. The exhibition included works such as Huang Yong Ping's *Pistol* (*Huixiang de shouqiang*, 1984) (see fig. 6), a handgun made from an assemblage of pipes, a padlock, and a bicycle bell, and Huang's *The Remaking of Ingres's Painting* (*Ange'er hua de gaizhuang*, 1986), a copy of a European painting combined with found objects that was similar to *Haymakers*. The canvas depicted the back of a naked figure—an imprecise copy of *The Valpinçon Bather* (1808) by Jean-Auguste-Dominique Ingres (1780–1867)—with a thermometer playfully affixed next to the figure's turbaned head. Jiao Yaoming provided *Folded White* (*Zhecheng de baise*, 1986) (see fig. 5), an abstract sculpture made from white fabric pulled over a wire frame. Yu Xiaogang's abstract paintings (see fig. 6) of exaggerated brush-strokes were included. Wooden sculptures by Lin Chun (b. 1960) and Lin Jiahua were also displayed. The exhibition provided a snapshot of the practices of the artists in the newly formed art group Xiamen Dada, but fundamentally the works on view were a continuum of those displayed three years earlier at the *Five-Person Exhibition*. And yet, a curious sign was hung on one of the walls announcing that after the exhibition the artists would burn all of the works on view. The *Xiamen Dada—Modern Art Exhibition* wasn't necessarily a showcase of their recent artworks but rather a referendum on them.

Two months later, on November 23, 1986, the artists staged the "Burning the Previously Exhibited Xiamen Dada Works Art Event" (Fenshao Xiamen dada zhanchu zuopin yishu huodong), known as the Burning Event, in which they refitted (*gaizhuang*), destroyed (*huihuai*), and burned (*fenshao*) their artworks in the empty yard in front of the museum. They collected their paintings, sculptures, and material object collages and broke them apart, cutting a small square from some of the works to keep as a record of the original. Next, they randomly scattered the mutilated works across the yard, writing slogans on the ground in chalk. Eventually, the now destroyed artworks were thrown into a pile and set on fire, and Huang declared the "end of painting." While not actually a literal death

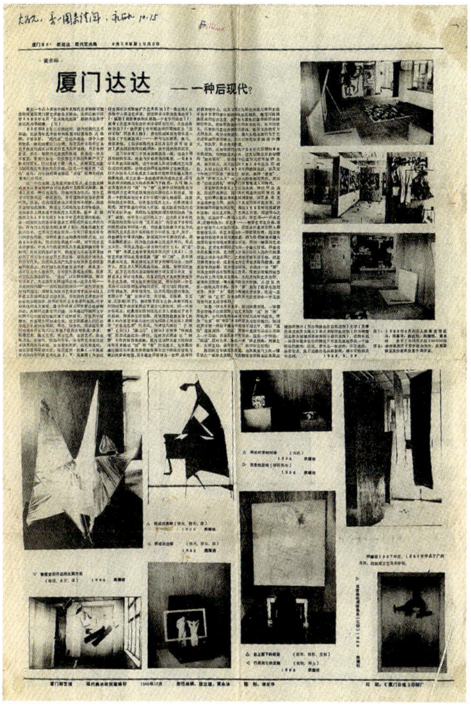

厦门达达 ——一种后现代?

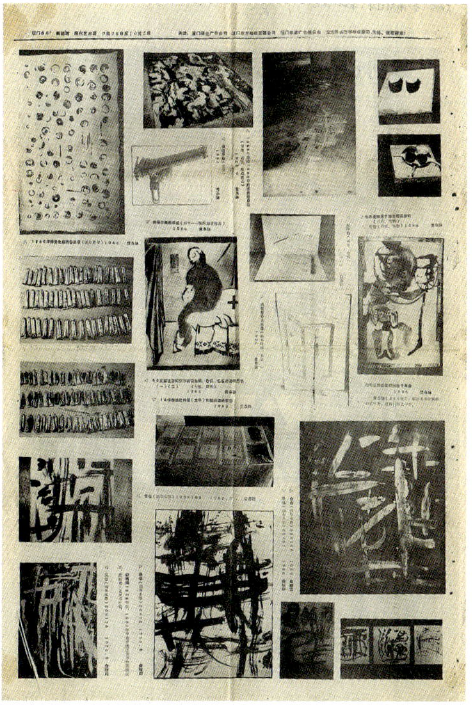

Figures 5–6 Huang Yong Ping, "Xiamen Dada–yi zhong houxiandai?" (Xiamen Dada–a kind of postmodernism?) in "Xianmen '86 xin dada xiandai yishu zhan, 9.28–10.5" (Xiamen '86 new Dada modern art exhibition, September 28–October 5), special issue, *Xiamen Daily,* October 15, 1986. Fei Dawei Archive. Courtesy of Huang Yong Ping, Xiamen Dada, and Asia Art Archive.

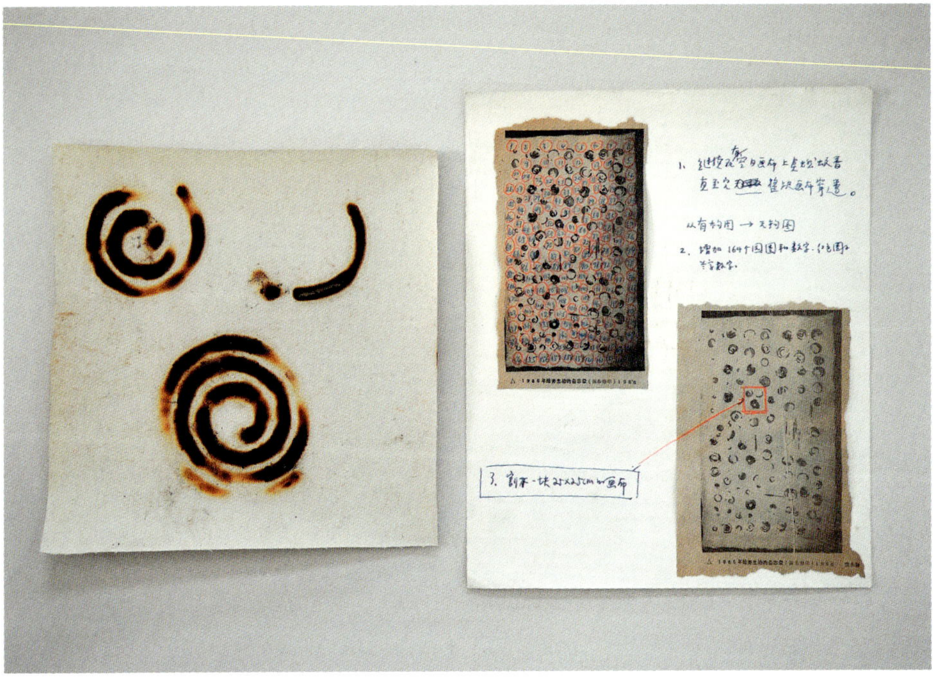

Figure 7 Huang Yong Ping, *Alteration and Breakage of Artworks Before Burning*, 1986. Left: mosquito coils' burn marks on canvas, 25 × 25 cm, right: newspaper and handwritten notes, 25.5 × 30.8 cm. Courtesy of Gladstone Gallery, New York and Brussels.

of painting (Huang Yong Ping and other Xiamen Dada members would in fact continue painting as appropriate), the Burning Event was a definitive break in the activities of Xiamen Dada and Huang Yong Ping's individual practice, precisely around their conceptualizations of the object as material. They began to conceptualize the capacity of nontraditional materials to move beyond their previous critique of representation to focus instead on the ways in which materials themselves could attack or assault the art system in China.

This break could have been necessitated by the recent "Rauschenberg Fever" (*Luoshengbai re*) that followed the first exhibition in China of work by American artist Robert Rauschenberg (1925–2008), organized in 1985 at the National Art Museum of China (Zhongguo meishu guan).[13] After the exhibition, unconventional materials were increasingly affixed, attached, and included in contemporary artworks throughout the country supposedly in response to or inspired by Robert Rauschenberg's "combines"—his signature type of artwork that combined unconventional materials and found objects with painting and sculpture.

However, artists throughout the country—not just Huang Yong Ping and the other members of Xiamen Dada—had experimented with nontraditional materials, making "combine"-like paintings and sculptures for years.[14] Even before the Rauschenberg exhibition opened, Huang published his treatise on the *Five-Person Modern Art Exhibition* in *The Trend of Art Thought* magazine, naming "material object collage reliefs" and "readymade object collages" for the first time.[15] Huang's retrospective review of the exhibition points to the importance of claiming the existence of these types of artworks in China before the Rauschenberg exhibition but also suggests a need to reject the comparisons to Rauschenberg all together. One of the artworks that was destroyed and documented by removing a small square from the canvas before it was set on fire in 1986 was Huang's *A Memorandum of Rauschenberg in 1986* (*1986 Nian gei Luoshengbai de beiwanglu*) (see fig. 7), a loose canvas branded by the rings of mosquito coils burned onto its surface. The mosquito coils anticipate the eventual burning of the work itself, further suggesting a renunciation of the ways in which Rauschenberg used materials in his combines and indicating that Huang had begun to conceptualize a new theorization of material in his work.

Moving beyond the ways in which nontraditional materials operated on the surface of a canvas or affixed onto a sculpture, Huang Yong Ping and the members Xiamen Dada began to more profoundly question the ways in which artworks were substantiated and valued as art. Huang himself suggested burning is "a kind of extreme form of handling. . . . This clearly signifies the elimination of the work of art as idol."[16] For Huang, burning represented a process to eliminate the physical, material artwork that "corresponds to a conscious renouncing" of the value artists and critics alike place on artworks.[17] This could have been necessitated by the acrimonious reception that the *Five-Person Modern Art Exhibition* received compared to the generally laudatory albeit conflicted responses to the Rauschenberg exhibition. Writing in the text published with the *Xiamen Dada—Modern Art Exhibition*, Huang evokes Rauschenberg's use of diverse objects:

> A work by Robert Rauschenberg can exist over a long or short time period, be made of any material, in any place, for any purpose, and have any outcome. This corresponds closely to the ubiquity of Tao [Dao], which is found "in an ant, in weeds, in a potsherd, and in urine" (Zhuangzi). Rauschenberg's use of whatever elements he came across and his juxtaposing of diverse objects in his paintings are very much in tune with Taoism's [Daoism's] ideas of the equality, sameness, and coexistence of everything.[18]

Instead of dwelling on the ways in which objects operate within Rauschenberg's practice, Huang emphasizes the ubiquity of Dao that can be found in any object, which for Huang can be extended to art that could likewise be found in any object. Here a Rauschenberg artwork, just like Dao, can be anything, made from "any material"—from urine to the umbrellas, tires, and stuffed animals often found in Rauschenberg's work. Following Zhuangzi (369–c. 301 BCE), Huang rejects the notion of the intrinsic value of the artwork residing in the work itself or the materials used to make it, suggesting instead that all objects—artworks or not—coexist and therefore have the capacity to be art.

Freed of the burden of their physical artworks and the weight of influence, the members of Xiamen Dada began to focus on context and "events" or actions to create and subsequently destroy, eliminate, or relinquish new artworks in the *Events Exhibition* that was held just a month after the Burning Event. As discussed in this chapter's introduction, the members of Xiamen Dada collected construction debris, boards, trash, and other found objects outside of the museum, carried them inside the museum, and put them on display in varied arrangements. In Huang Yong Ping's descriptions of the event, he asserts the ways in which the materials functioned beyond conventional art mediums:

> All works on display must come from the various materials stocked in the open air around the museum. These materials are not used as "art mediums" to be decorated or constructed from, but are simply displaced to the exhibition hall. . . . The difference is that these materials are now treated in the same way as works of art found in previous exhibitions—furnished with labels, visited by an audience, supported by art theories, and completed by artists.[19]

These nontraditional materials—wooden boards, clay pots, stones, and fence sections, to name a few—could simultaneously signify different things based on where they were placed and how they were perceived. When treated as artworks through their contextualization by labels, being placed in the museum, "completed" by artists, and visited by people in the museum, these objects signified artwork. But when they were outside, they were called trash. For Huang, this becomes similar to how "Chan Buddhism sees a wooden statue of Sakyamuni: both as Buddha and as a piece of firewood. As 'Buddha,' so as to connect to the living world; as 'wood,' so as to go beyond it."[20] These materials allowed Huang and the other members of Xiamen Dada to provocatively question what was art and, perhaps more precisely, what the contemporaneous art system would sanction as or allow to be called art. Ultimately, the exhibition was closed two hours after it opened, demonstrating that in fact these objects would not be considered art. By shifting the context of the objects, from piles of trash outside the museum to artworks selected by artists, described by labels, and seen by visitors to the exhibition hall, the members of Xiamen Dada assaulted not only conventional definitions of the art object and systems of representation, but also the system that designated and validated them as art in the first place by demanding viewers question why exactly these objects are art. Ultimately, attacking the visitor's views on art and the art system presented one of the few ways to change how art signified in society. Depending on the context in which an artwork was placed, displayed, or even discarded, it could take on or, as I will discuss in the next section, be "filled up" with different meanings. In one place, a nontraditional material might signify an artwork, whereas in another, the same material could be emptied of this significance as artwork, and instead signify trash, convention, or even sameness.

MAGICIANS OF THE EARTH
EMPTYING THE MATERIAL

In 1989, Huang Yong Ping joined two other artists from China to make work at the Centre Pompidou for the French museum's pioneering exhibition of contemporary art from around the world, titled *Magicians of the Earth* (*Magiciens de la terre*). Debuting his art abroad for the first time, Huang worked in situ, washing hundreds of books in three washing machines that were stationed in the gallery. He used the pulpy remains of the books to sculpt a turtleback tomb (*guikemu*) commonly found in Fujian province. Beside the tomb were sloppy piles of the pulped pages. On the wall, Huang pasted the pulp from the floor to the ceiling. The work, *Reptiles* (1989) (fig. 8), was made using the "wet method" (*chaoshi de shouduan*) originally developed in 1987 from a prompt on the *Large Turntable* (*Da zhuanpan*, 1987), a device Huang created to remove "aesthetic consciousness" from his artmaking while imbuing it with chance.[21] Based on the *Book of Changes*, the *Large Turntable* consisted of a big and small disk, divided into 384 and 64 entries, respectively. Each entry acted as an instruction, point of departure, or material for Huang to use to make an artwork. The instructions ranged from the mundane ("monthly reading of the electricity meter") to the perplexing ("enter or supervise corner fresh"), the obvious ("paper crumbled in balls") to the obscure ("stimulus"), direct actions ("break a bowl") to materials ("sand, earth, water").[22]

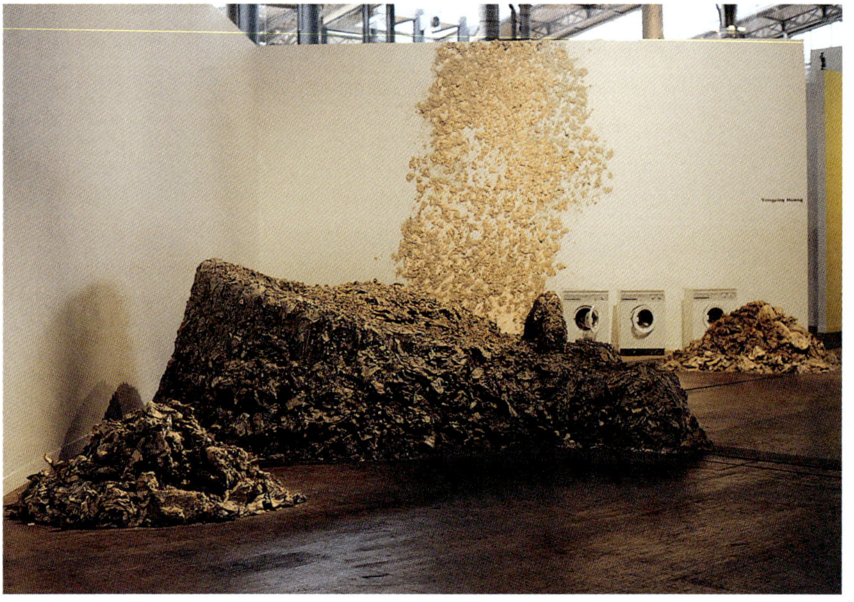

Figure 8 Huang Yong Ping, *Reptiles*, 1989. Paper pulp, iron, and washing machines, 495 × 1300 × 900 cm. Installation view, *Magiciens de la terre*, Centre Pompidou, Paris, 1989. Courtesy of Gladstone Gallery, New York and Brussels. © Huang Yong Ping.

Huang Yong Ping first used the wet method in 1987 for *The History of Chinese Art and A Concise History of Modern Painting Washed in a Washing Machine for Two Minutes* (《*Zhongguo huihuashi*》 *he* 《*Xiandai huihua jianshi*》 *zai xiyiji li jiaoban le liang fenzhong*) (fig. 9). To make the work, as the title suggests, Huang washed the Chinese translation of Herbert Read's *A Concise History of Modern Painting* with Wang Bomin's *History of Chinese Painting* (*Zhongguo huihuashi*) in a washing machine for two minutes. The resulting pulp was displayed on top of a broken piece of glass placed on a wooden box. This work is consistently interpreted through the lens of the relationship between "Eastern" and "Western" art.[23] This response has been incited by Huang's own commentary that asserts the work was a response to the question, "What should an amalgamation of modern Western and native Chinese culture look like?"[24] However, I want to shift away from interpretations that foreground cultural duality and instead focus on the work Huang does to the books as nontraditional materials because it is distinct from his previous uses of nontraditional materials in material object collage reliefs, readymade object collages, and also his work with Xiamen Dada. In these earlier artworks, nontraditional materials remain largely unchanged by the

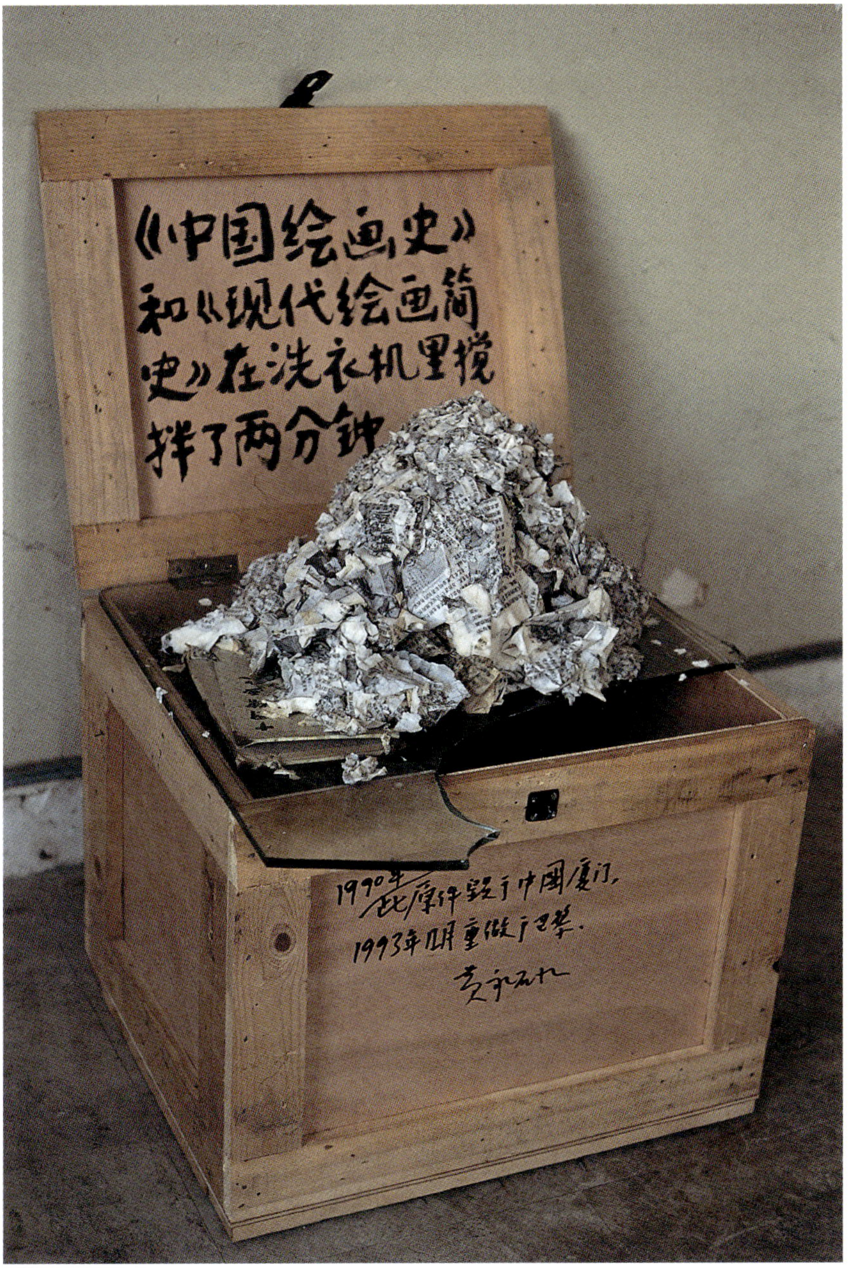

Figure 9 Huang Yong Ping, *The History of Chinese Art and A Concise History of Modern Painting Washed in a Washing Machine for Two Minutes*, 1987, remade 1993. Chinese tea box, paper pulp, and glass, 76 × 48 × 70 cm. Courtesy of Gladstone Gallery, New York and Brussels. © Huang Yong Ping.

artist; these objects are moved from one place to another, affixed to flat surfaces, or combined together into new constructions or formations. However, works made by the wet method involve the irreversible transformation of the nontraditional material itself—its form is altered beyond recognition or usefulness. Huang originally described book washing through a reversal of the proposition by philosopher Ludwig Wittgenstein (1889–1951) that words could be removed from language, washed, and then returned into communication; but for Huang, communication was a "dirty form" and thus words could not "be brought back into communication after having been washed."[25] In *Two Minutes*, the books are not just dirtied when they are washed; they are destroyed, eradicated of their expected form and their standard communicative function. In effect, Huang empties the books of their sensible meaning by destroying the ability to actually read the texts themselves. The pulp no longer signifies the specific books or meanings contained within *A Concise History of Modern Painting* and *History of Chinese Painting*, hence the books are emptied of their original meanings. Ultimately, Huang recast the nontraditional material as a "completely empty signifier" (*wanquan kong de nengzhi*) or a signifier that is disconnected from what it originally signifies, waiting to be "filled up" with various and changing meaning depending on the context in which it is placed and the interpretations of multiple viewers.

As seen in both Huang Yong Ping's individual practice and participation in Xiamen Dada, the teleological shift from nontraditional material to completely empty signifier corresponded to his disavowal or moving away from Wittgenstein's theorization of language and semiotics in favor of Chan Buddhist and Dadaist practices. Writing in the broadsheet that was published as a makeshift catalogue for the *Xiamen Dada—Modern Art Exhibition*, Huang began to theorize Xiamen Dada as both an art group and a form of postmodernism by calling into question what modern art was at the time. Ultimately, he connected the philosophical and often absurdist underpinnings of Chan Buddhism and Dada, respectively, and rejected the perceived dualism between "Eastern" thought and "Western" art when he declared "Chan is Dada, Dada is Chan."[26] Yet later writings in 1988 demonstrate significant advances in the way Huang connected the two—particularly around what he would call the "completely empty signifier" as he pushed further away from semiotics. For Huang, both the terms "Dada" (the European art movement) and "Chan Buddhism" are examples of "completely empty signifiers." Huang explained:

> The term *dada* for the Dada idea is a completely empty signifier because the Dada idea means neither "rocking horse" nor "yes, yes," but symbolizes destruction, nihilism, mockery, anti-art, and so on, as is described in art history books. So is Chan Buddhism. Although it too is a completely empty signifier, in the history of thought, it symbolized mysticism, transcendence, nonego and nonsubstantiality, enlightenment, and so on.[27]

For Huang, both the terms "Dada" and "Chan Buddhism" radically transformed and expanded beyond the original meanings they signified once each term was unmoored from the signifier-signified chain. Completely empty signifiers are produced by an "ever-growing inflation and an overstretched time space, or people paying too much attention or discussing too much" that allows a term to be "filled up" with various and varying significances.[28] This yielded an original indeterminacy between words and their meaning that could extend to found objects and nontraditional materials, as well as to the ways they signify not only within artworks but in relation to the viewer and the art system.

Like the books Huang washed, materials across his works were emptied of their original meaning and began to take on different significances, i.e., broke the normal signifying chain, as they moved between contexts and physical transformations. In 1987, Huang declared, "we must oppose all kinds of forms," and called for their destruction.[29] "To destroy form, you must first break the necessary bond between the name and the things the name refers to."[30] For Huang, stereotyped form negated or occluded the "necessary logic of interrelationship," whereas the ability to connect a name to its form is determined through relationality between people, things, and chance. In this sense, by extending his theorization of the completely empty signifier to nontraditional materials at large, Huang surpassed purely linguistic forms, shifting instead to focus on the ways in which meaning is constructed and impressed upon objects as well. In *Two Minutes* and *Reptiles*, washing destroyed the form of the books, thus breaking the connection between external appearance with intrinsic meaning and the book's ability to signify. As the wet method developed in Huang's practice, the onus of the washing was pushed away from making dirty or illegible to the ways in which the materials themselves are transformed and emptied. In this empty state, or completely empty signifier, they propel new juxtapositions and interpretations in Huang's artwork, which are dependent on relationality. In future works, Huang would playfully dismember nontraditional materials from the original contexts in which they acted as stable signifiers, and allow them instead to be filled up through the new ways in which Huang would employ them. This handling of nontraditional materials would become a signature aspect of his practice.

CONCLUSION

Nontraditional materials played an important role in the development of Huang Yong Ping's early practice throughout the 1980s. Huang's earliest experiments with nontraditional materials interrupted the continuity of the picture plane and rules guiding representational painting and sculpture in China. Here, nontraditional material doubled or mirrored representational images to break their signifying chains. This was followed by Huang's work with Xiamen Dada, where nontraditional materials—often trash—could become and unbecome artworks through the context in which they were placed. Huang, importantly, selected these materials because they conventionally signified trash, garbage, or discarded detritus and as such tested the limits of Chinese art institutions through their radical rejection of how art was defined at the time. At the same time, in his own practice, Huang began to theorize the completely empty signifier, a concept that entangled both his collective and individual practices as he pushed away from static definitions of words and materials. Freed from the restraints of words or, by extension, objects being tied to a singular or stable, signified meaning, Huang was able to radically reassert the ways nontraditional materials could become operative in his own practice. From trash to art or art to trash, Huang was liberated from rote definitions of art making and art objects declared by the art system and the Chinese Artists Association and the conventions of viewers that he and the members of Xiamen Dada had attacked, contested, and contradicted for years. By extension, he was also liberated from definitions of modern art and comparisons to other historical canons to which his art might be compared. In his theorization of the completely empty signifier, Huang asserted:

> We are left with a big pile of garbage, where we might find culture, philosophy, religion, and art at the disposal of the people. If you remain silent with this pile, it means that you don't exist; if you don't rise up out of the garbage of texts (our history, thoughts, and culture), you'll be crushed by all sorts of theories, values, and preaching. The only thing we can do is to make old and new myths become completely empty signifiers. Even if you constantly take the floor to speak, constantly copy and paste, constantly "fill," and constantly "consume," however, this is still only a temporary existence.[31]

Here, Huang materializes culture through the nontraditional materials he empties. The completely empty signifier had a profound impact on the ways in which Huang employed and transformed everyday objects, opening new modes of artistic production. Importantly, this emphasis on materials generates new understandings of the conceptual trajectory of Huang's art practice that move beyond staid readings of his interrogation of the differences between "Eastern" and "Western" art, demonstrating instead the contribution his work has made to materiality studies globally.

NOTES

The author expresses her sincere gratitude to Mariola V. Alvarez and Birgit Hopfener for their close reading of this text and the insightful discussion and suggestions that they provided.

1. Huang Yong Ping, "Introduction to *The Events Exhibition That Took Place at the Exhibition Hall of the Fujian Art Museum*," originally written in December 1986, translated and reprinted in Wu Hung and Peggy Wang, eds., *Contemporary Chinese Art: Primary Documents* (New York: Museum of Modern Art, 2010), 96. Please note, this English version translates *xiji* (sneak attack) as "assault."
2. At its largest, the Xiamen Dada artist group included Huang Yong Ping, Lin Jiahua, Yu Xiaogang, Jiao Yaoming, Ji Nai Jin, Chen Lixiong, Chen Chengzong, Li Xiang, Li Yaonian, Huang Yong, Wu Yanping, Liu Yiling, and Lin Chun.
3. Hou Hanru and Hsiao-hwei Yu, *On the Mid-Ground* (Hong Kong: Timezone 8, 2002), 62.
4. See Martina Köppel-Yang, *Semiotic Warfare: A Semiotic Analysis, the Chinese Avant-Garde, 1979–1989* (Hong Kong: Timezone 8, 2003). Also see Paul Gladston, *Contemporary Chinese Art: A Critical History* (London: Reaktion Books, 2014).
5. Huang Yong Ping, "Yi ci weineng gongkai de huazhan" [The exhibition that was not made public], *Meishu Sichao (The Trend of Art Thought)*, no. 6 (1985): 24.
6. Huang, "Yi ci weineng gongkai de huazhan," 24.
7. Huang, "Yi ci weineng gongkai de huazhan," 23.
8. Huang, "Yi ci weineng gongkai de huazhan," 23.
9. Huang, "Yi ci weineng gongkai de huazhan," 24.
10. Huang, "Yi ci weineng gongkai de huazhan," 23.
11. Huang Yong Ping, "Painting with Industrial Technology: Looking for New Substitutions," trans. Lin Xiaoping, *Leonardo* 18, no. 2 (April 1985): 92.
12. Huang Yong Ping, "80–86 nian yishu huodong zishu" [The artist's statement on his activities from 1980 to 1986], translated and reprinted in Philippe Vergne, Huang Yong Ping, and Fei Dawei, eds., *House of Oracles: A Huang Yong Ping Retrospective* (Minneapolis: Walker Art Center, 2005), 36.
13. For more context on the national reaction to the Rauschenberg exhibition, please see "Beijing bufen lilunjia dui Laoshengbo zuopin de fanyin" [Beijing theorists' reactions to the art of Robert Rauschenberg], *Zhongguo meishu bao* [*Fine Arts in China*], no. 22 (December 21, 1985), translated and reprinted in Wu and Wang, eds., *Contemporary Chinese Art*, 42–45.
14. Collage appeared in the early 1980s across China and informed artistic practice throughout the decade. Perhaps one of the earliest instances of collage were those made by Huang Rui, who affixed newspaper, pages from magazines, and found sheets of paper onto his canvases, often painting over them in thick, abstract brush strokes. The *Five-Person Modern Art Exhibition* marked the first known exhibition expressly dedicated to showcasing works that incorporated nontraditional materials. By 1985, artists throughout the country increasingly combined, attached, appropriated, and affixed found objects, newspapers, magazine pages, and other unconventional materials onto and into their artworks. Examples of the vibrancy and extent of the practice throughout the country include Wu Pingren's *History: Series of Conflicts* (1985), a wall-mounted installation that combined painting, reproductions of iconic paintings, plaster casts, and busts with swirling metal strips and other industrial objects; and Luo Mingjun's *I* (1985), a white monochrome painting attached with two girls' shoes and a cloth belt.

15. While the exact publication date of this issue of *The Trend of Art Thought* magazine is not recorded in the publication, the essay was published in the sixth issue (*ji*) of 1985. In 1985, eight issues in total were published, indicating that the sixth issue would have been published before the Rauschenberg exhibition opened November 1985.

16. Huang Yong Ping, "Reflections, Creation and Events of 1987," translated and reprinted in Köppel-Yang, *Semiotic Warfare*, 201–2.

17. Huang, "Reflections, Creation and Events of 1987," 202. The importance of Huang Yong Ping's renunciation of his past artworks was underscored almost a year later when he and the other artists threw almost all of the artworks originally exhibited at the *Five-Person Modern Art Exhibition* onto a trash pile on a street in Xiamen. The artists observed and documented the confused reactions of people passing by the unexpected trash, taking photos of people as they took entire paintings or broke them apart. When the passersby noticed that they were being photographed, many immediately got upset, "attacking" the artists and eventually calling the police.

18. Huang Yong Ping, "Xiamen Dada—Postmodern?," translated and reprinted in Vergne, Huang, and Fei, eds., *House of Oracles*, 76.

19. Huang, "Introduction to *The Events Exhibition*," 96.

20. Huang, "Xiamen Dada—Postmodern?," 77.

21. Despite the *Large Turntable* providing instructions and designating multiple objects for varied artworks, only the wet method was used by Huang repeatedly and after he immigrated to France. Other works made this way include *A Humid "Critique of Pure Reason"* (1988), a bookshelf in his house in Xiamen filled with washed books; *Reptiles* (1989) in Paris, as previously discussed; *Unreadable Humidity* (1991) at the Carnegie Library in Pittsburgh, where he washed books in the historic library; washed books appeared in sections of *The House of Oracles* (1989–1992); *The First Phone Call to Joseph Beuys after his Death* (1991), which combined a telephone with washed books about Beuys; *Should We Build Another Cathedral?* (1991); *Library Canteen* (1992), a long table adorned with plates of washed books at the Bibliothèque Forney in Paris; *9 Pillars for China Avantgarde* (1993), in which pulped books and newspaper were affixed around columns throughout the exhibition space; *Kiosk* (1994), a German newspaper kiosk whose contents were removed, washed, and displayed as pulp; and *Floating Kiosk* (2000).

22. Huang Yong Ping, "The Sixty-Four Entries on the Small Disk of the Big Roulette Wheel," in Vergne, Huang, and Fei, eds., *House of Oracles*, 67–74.

23. See Fei Dawei, "Two-Minute Wash Cycle: Huang Yong Ping's Chinese Period" and Hou Hanru, "Change Is the Rule," in Vergne, Huang, and Fei, eds., *House of Oracles*. See also Köppel-Yang, *Semiotic Warfare*.

24. Köppel-Yang, *Semiotic Warfare*, 140.

25. Hou Hanru, "Change Is the Rule," 14.

26. Huang, "Xiamen Dada—Postmodern?," 77.

27. Huang Yong Ping, "The Completely Empty Signifier," translated and reprinted in Vergne, Huang, and Fei, eds., *House of Oracles*, 79.

28. Huang, "The Completely Empty Signifier," 79.

29. Huang Yong Ping, "An Essay on Starting from Emptiness," excerpted, translated, and reprinted in Vergne, Huang, and Fei, eds., *House of Oracles*, 66.

30. Huang, "An Essay on Starting from Emptiness," 66.

31. Huang, "The Completely Empty Signifier," 79.

The Fleeting Eternity of Chaos

Materials and Process in the Art of Cai Guo-Qiang

Rachel Rivenc

INTRODUCTION

Cai Guo-Qiang (b. 1957) has a remarkably far-ranging artistic practice, in terms of genres, media, and subject matter. He is equally comfortable with large-scale installations, daytime fireworks, participative events, and time-based media, but he is probably best known for his signature use of gunpowder as an artistic medium (fig. 1). Cai's personal cosmology freely and broadly blends Asian and Western cultures (both North American and European) in an attempt to transcend the truism of this dichotomy. His work is infused with a strong sense of spirituality and symbolism, and it integrates Chinese traditions such as Daoism and Fengshui. Having left China in 1986, Cai spent a very formative decade in Japan, where he started developing *Project for Extraterrestrials*, a series in which Cai metaphorically and literally imagines looking at the earth from an extraterrestrial point of view. In 1995, he moved to the U.S. and has had a studio in Manhattan since then. In the first two decades of his arrival in the U.S., his work increasingly responded to international social and political events. In recent years, however, Cai's work has turned toward more personal and intimate subject matter, such as love, lust, longing, and loss, alongside social, political, and philosophical issues. Cai retains very strong ties with Asia in general and China in particular, but has become a truly international and itinerant artist, who travels the world to realize his many projects and aims to establish bridges between different cultures.

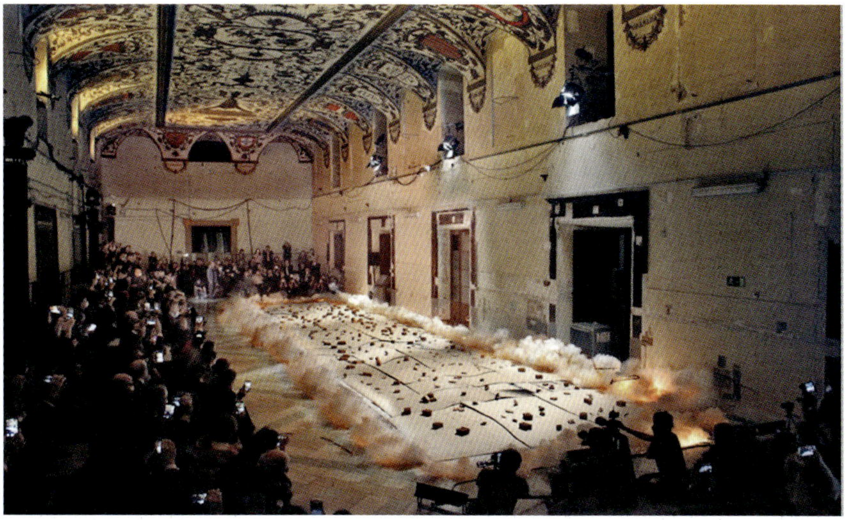

Figure 1 Ignition of Cai Guo-Qiang's gunpowder painting *The Spirit of Painting* at the Salón de Reinos (Hall of Realms), Madrid, 2017. Courtesy of Cai Studio. © Museo Nacional del Prado.

Material experimentation has been essential to Cai's work throughout the arc of his career. Initially adopted out of necessity, it became the instrument of his artistic liberation and paved the path to his individual expression—as well as a reliable, yet unpredictable, source of inspiration. In every material, but especially in Cai's chosen media, gunpowder and fireworks, the symbolic, aesthetic, and handling properties converge to give materials the ability to create meaning. After practically three decades dedicated to exploring the expressive potential of black gunpowder in his gunpowder drawings, Cai returned to using colored pyrotechnic powders, starting in 2015 (fig. 2). This went way beyond simply adding color to his work, and represented an important reconnection of his practice to painting. Although the materials that he uses are far removed from traditional painting materials, Cai's current artistic practice is very much a quest for the essence or spirit of painting.[1] It is a quest that involves a thorough questioning of traditional aesthetic tenets and a relinquishing of preconceived ideas in favor of material experimentation and complete aesthetic ingenuity. At the same time, it is also a quest for continuity and what might unite the practice of painting throughout different time periods, cultures, and geographies.

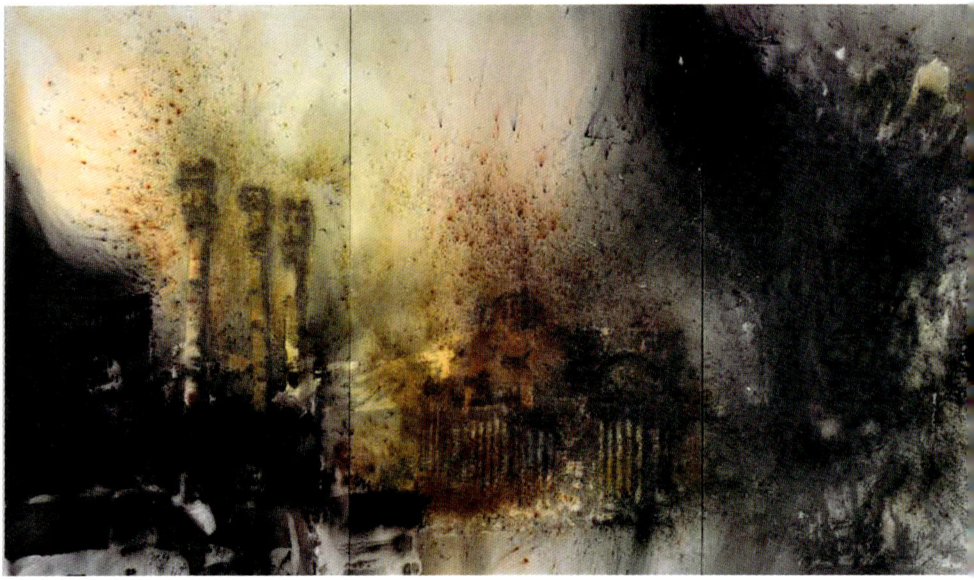

Figure 2 Cai Guo-Qiang, *Palmyra*, 2017. Gunpowder on canvas, 240 × 450 cm. Photo: Wen-You Cai. Courtesy of Cai Studio.

This chapter examines the materials and processes used by Cai Guo-Qiang to create his gunpowder drawings and paintings, as well as their role in his artistic practice and its evolution. It presents the results of a four-year research project carried out at the Getty Conservation Institute (GCI),[2] drawing on scientific analyses aimed at identifying the media, pigments, and various components of gunpowder and pyrotechnic powders, as well as on numerous lengthy interviews with the artist and his collaborators. It starts by offering some elements of explication for why Cai turned to the use of gunpowder, and how the material opened up extraordinary new artistic avenues for him. It then describes essential properties of gunpowder and colored pyrotechnics, as well as the processes that Cai has perfected over the course of decades of experimentation. It ends with a look toward the future and considers how the aging of material might impact the perception of Cai's work.

WHY GUNPOWDER?

Originally a painter, Cai started experimenting with burning his paint layers and combining them with gunpowder in the early 1980s in China. After moving to Japan, he soon dispensed with paint altogether to explore the sole use of gunpowder as a drawing medium. For years, he worked with black gunpowder, perfecting his techniques to create drawings that were at once strikingly beautiful and strongly conceptual.

When asked why he started using gunpowder, Cai often gives circumstantial explanations. Fireworks and firecrackers were everywhere in his hometown of Quanzhou in the 1960s of his youth—at festivals, weddings, and funerals, children were constantly playing with them. Cai even remembers how one of his cousins was maimed, and another killed, while playing with firecrackers. The danger was not a deterrent; on the contrary, it was all the more attractive to a young man looking to embolden himself. Indeed, Cai has repeatedly explained his choice of using gunpowder as related to his desire to liberate himself from what he perceived as a timid, cautious, and overly controlling personality.[3]

Cai's early drawings and paintings show clearly his talent as a draftsman and great appetite for learning. For years, Cai experimented with a wide range of European styles, including fauvism, impressionism, and pointillism, and made other works inspired by Cézanne and El Greco. Starting in 1981, he attended classes taught by Zhou Benyi (1931–2021) in the Department of Stage Design at the Shanghai Theatre Academy (Shanghai xiju xueyuan, or STA). Zhou had studied in Leningrad at the Repin Institute of Arts and had visited the United States.

According to Zhou, the teachings at the STA placed emphasis on self-expression and experimentation. These years were critical to Cai's artistic training on a number of counts. At the STA, he cemented his habit of painting outdoors, perfected his technique, and was encouraged to experiment. Perhaps more importantly, the stage design techniques that Cai learned at the STA profoundly influenced his practice of installation art, informing his sense of space, infusing it with theatricality and an acute understanding of how to impact viewers. At the conclusion of his years in Shanghai, however, Cai felt lost and frustrated. While his facility with painting enabled him to rapidly emulate and absorb external influences, it might have also, in a way, prevented him from carving out a truly unique and individual path. It was in this moment of creative crisis that he sought to dramatically alter his painting style and liberate his creativity. He wanted to find the way to manipulate the paint while relinquishing control over the results, and to unleash natural forces for bolder results than what he was able to achieve with traditional materials and processes. So, he turned toward what he saw in his everyday life—gunpowder.[4]

Once Cai embarked on his long journey with gunpowder, everything he learned about it only deepened his attraction to the material. He became enamored not just with the physical potential of the gunpowder, but also with its history and symbolic associations. Discovered by Chinese alchemists in search of the elixir of life, gunpowder is for Cai closely linked to Asian philosophies such as Daoism and Fengshui. The main appeal of gunpowder to Cai remains its unpredictability and uncontrollability, and through this, the sensation that forces greater than himself are at work and contributing to the creation of his artwork. Gunpowder became the vessel for Cai's dialogue with a source of invisible energy, and therefore an indispensable instrument of his attempts to bridge what he calls the seen and the unseen world. Gunpowder is essentially an agent of chaos: symbolically, but also literally. In order for a particular mixture to be a viable and useful pyrotechnic mixture, the entropy of the system, i.e., the randomness or disorder of the system, must increase as a result of the reaction. The greater the entropy, the greater the stability of the system, paradoxically.

For Cai, the uncontrollable nature of gunpowder and its propensity to chaos relate to the climate of the Communist China he grew up in. Superficially, as rebellion: "It was also a way for me to fight against the oppressive social climate and relatively closed environment of China at the time."[5] But perhaps more profoundly, embracing gunpowder and its uncontrollable nature might be a continuation of the Maoist spirit rather than a rebellion against it. Cai has explained that the essential creed of Mao's Cultural Revolution was one of chaos and disruption, of questioning rules and upsetting the established order. For Cai, Mao Zedong (1893–1976) himself was the incarnation of "the rebellious spirit, being disrespectful to authority and to the great people . . . such a skeptical and rebellious spirit."[6] Eventually this very spirit of doubt and questioning preached by Mao is precisely what made Cai question and turn away from Mao's teachings.

Gunpowder is also for Cai a way to reconcile with the violence of his upbringing, by using violence for creation:

> I have totally lived in this earth-shaking age. Therefore, the times have left me with many things. Of course, [given] the poverty of this age, there were also armed fights and conflicts and class struggle[s]. During the Cultural Revolution, this was an age of violence with many different Red Guards, which has had an impact on me. Of course, the misfortune and sadness of this era, or the pains, poverty and lack of education of the people, many schools were shut down [reordered]. This has something to do with my use of gunpowder, to create culture from such violence or using destruction to build.[7]

Gunpowder's ability to reconcile destruction and creation, to embrace paradoxes, and to create beauty and meaning out of chaos and violence, is probably for Cai what embodies his artistic pursuit the most.

FROM PAINT TO GUNPOWDER

Before gunpowder, the materials that Cai used for his early paintings were in themselves unremarkable. Cai had access to only a very limited range of painting materials, but he demonstrated great resourcefulness in their deployment. Once he started to paint stage sets for the Chairman Mao Thought Propaganda Team (Mao Zedong sixiang xuanchuan dui) in his teens,[8] Cai was able to buy cheap gouache paints and sometimes more expensive paints for small renderings made for the director of the troupe—occasionally smuggling more material than needed to use on his own paintings. Cai used all kinds of expedients to imitate expensive canvas; for example, gluing the gauze from facial masks or old pieces of clothing onto cardboard that he procured from a shoe box factory. Cai also made his own white oil paint using lithopone, a white pigment made of zinc sulfide and barium sulfate, mixed with linseed. The process was lengthy and labor intensive. He mostly prepared white paint, reckoning that's what he'd need in largest quantities. For colors, he'd purchased very parsimoniously

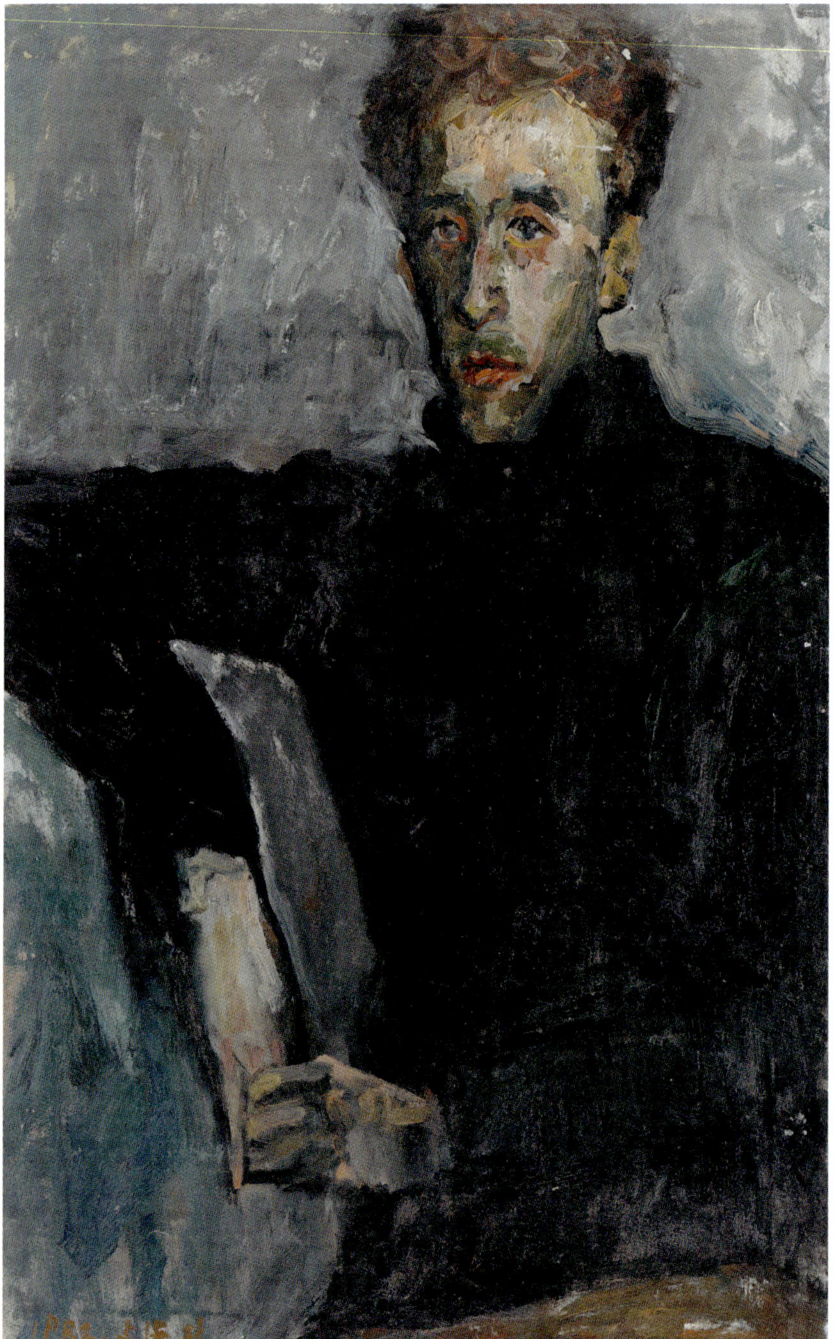

Figure 3 Cai Guo-Qiang, *Classmate*, 1982. Oil on canvas, 78.5 × 49.5 cm. Photo: Ron Amstutz. Courtesy of Cai Studio.

tubes from the Shanghai Fine Arts Supply Company (Shanghai meishu yongping chang)—often sharing them with friends: "If someone has a great paint, for example violet, everyone borrows some from the tube."[9]

Analyses of Cai's early paintings by and large confirm the artist's accounts and reveal a very restricted palette, predominantly white paint and very few colors.[10] *Classmate* (*Tongxue*, 1982) (fig. 3), for example, contains large amounts of barium sulfate and zinc oxide, probably the lithopone that Cai described using. Besides the white, the only colors are blue (imparted by the pigment Prussian blue; i.e., ferric ferrocyanide) and a few earth tones for the flesh. The medium is a drying oil, possibly linseed, with one sample containing fruit tree gum—perhaps an indication that Cai mixed gouache with the oil paint. Cai was so reluctant to apply too much expensive oil paint that when he wanted to achieve a thicker, more impastoed texture, he would mix all sorts of substances into the paint, including the debris from burned firewood and the soil from the yard.[11]

The creative crisis that Cai went through led him to look for new sources of inspiration. He started making ink rubbings of ancient carvings from the Han dynasty and of abstract natural patterns he would encounter in his surroundings, such as rocks, reefs, and tree roots. Cai then selected individual motifs from the ink rubbings and transformed them into paintings that looked more and more abstract. He did not pursue abstraction for itself, but as part of a personal search for new artistic horizons and individual expression. Cai was not only looking at different subject matter or sources of inspiration; he also got more and more experimental with materials around 1984–85. He looked for different ways to manipulate paint while relinquishing control of the artist's hand. For example, he tried using a fan or a blow dryer to liquefy the paint and move it around the canvas, and he even attempted to burn the paint directly—but these efforts all led to dead ends. He still had too much control.[12] This is when Cai first thought of using gunpowder. In retrospect, this creative crisis was a momentous one, as it opened up possibilities that Cai had only dreamed of before.

Initially, Cai used firecrackers and toy rockets,[13] attempting to throw them on his paintings while they hung on the wall. To his dissatisfaction, however, the paint just ended up getting burnt, so he resorted to breaking open the firecrackers and toy rockets to get at and use the gunpowder that was inside them. This was expensive and time consuming, so eventually Cai just went to the firecracker factory to purchase bags of gunpowder. There, Cai remembers that he could simply purchase a whole bag of gunpowder that would weigh a couple of kilograms. Cai then started mixing the gunpowder into the paint or sprinkling

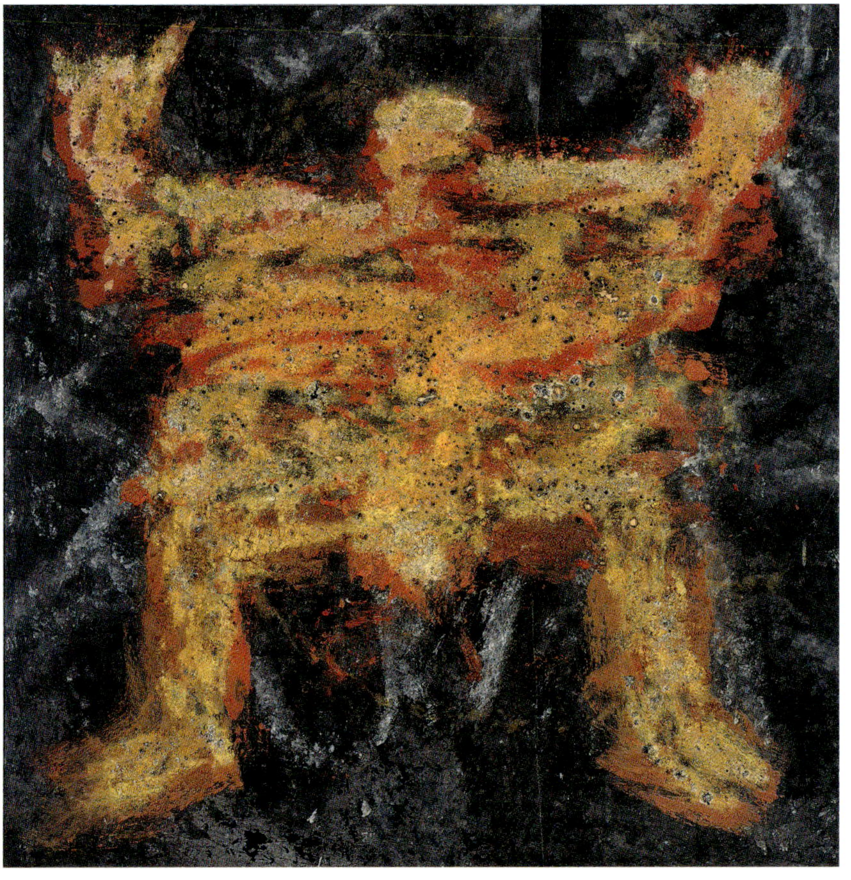

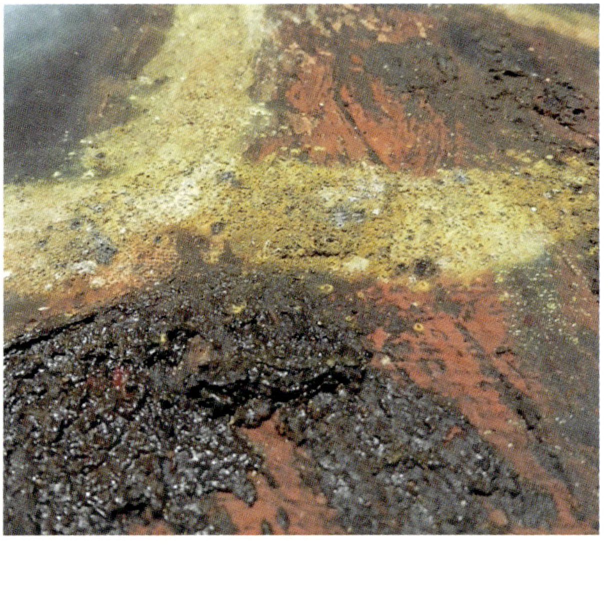

Figure 4 Cai Guo-Qiang, *Chu Ba Wang*, 1985. Gunpowder, oil, and ink on canvas, 155 × 150 cm. Photo: Hiro Ihara. Courtesy of Cai Studio.

Figure 5 Cai Guo-Qiang, *Chu Ba Wang*. Detail of burnt texture of the paint. Photo: Rachel Rivenc.

it on top of the paint and then attempting to detonate it with a lit-up incense stick.[14] In the first paintings that Cai made with gunpowder, the gunpowder plays little more than a supporting role. It was mixed with the paint and therefore would not detonate properly. Still, Cai feverishly pursued the relinquishing of control he was after, and this altered his paintings drastically.

Cai stressed that the gunpowder made for firecrackers—including the kind he bought directly from the firecracker factory—is different from the gunpowder used in fireworks. The gunpowder used for firecrackers contains a lot of added sulfur, which gives it a much yellower hue. In addition, when the firecracker is assembled, the bottom is sealed with reddish earth and the top is folded in to create the pressure needed for the explosion. According to Cai, the gunpowder used in firecrackers is much less powerful than in fireworks. Its color is diluted by sulfur and red earth, and it created additional patterns in his paintings. The gunpowder used in fireworks is much purer and more powerful, but also more expensive, so Cai did not use it until later, when he moved to Japan.[15]

It is clear when looking at Cai's paintings of the time that he was still working with limited resources. However, instead of trying to disguise this fact and emulate the look of expensive art supplies, Cai started to embrace this DIY approach to making art; born out of necessity, it was now serving his new aesthetic. The paintings of 1984–86 look rough and unpolished, earthy, fleshy, and burnt (figs. 4–5). Cai made his own strainers, and then he stretched coarse canvases over them. In several paintings of the time, the seam is visible and in fact quite prominently located on the front of the painting, suggesting that this was on purpose.

In two paintings of the time, *Pillar for the Sky* (*Tian zhi zhu*, 1985) (fig. 6) and *Chu Ba Wang* (1985) (see fig. 4), analyses reveal that Cai used gunpowder with an oil-based paint. Both paintings feature abstracted characters inspired by his ink rubbings of ancient carvings from the Han dynasty. In *Pillar for the Sky*, Cai felt that the paint was too bright, so he sprinkled ashes from burned charcoal and wood on top of the paint when it was still wet. Analyses of the painting show the presence of large amounts of potassium throughout the painting, which is consistent with ashes being added to the paint, and this presumably explains the overall grayish color of the paint. Analyses also reveal that the yellow color of the contour lines is imparted by realgar, an arsenic sulfide compound (fig. 7).[16] The paints that Cai used were still cheap ones, as indicated by the large quantities of barium sulfate, a common paint filler/extender, and his palette was still very limited. In *Pillar for the Sky*, the red and dark brown colors are imparted by iron oxide pigments. The dark paint appears waxy and glossy, probably as a result of the intense heat it has been

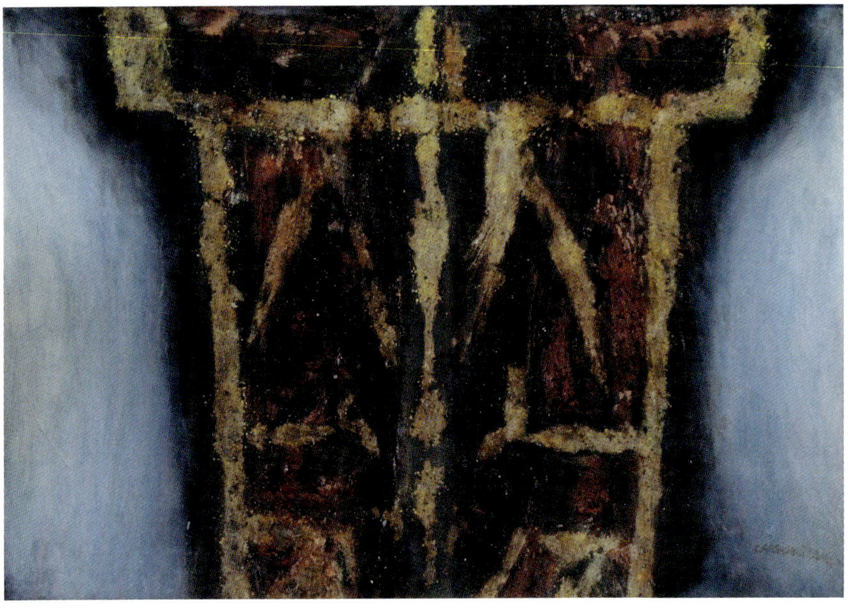

Figure 6 Cai Guo-Qiang, *Pillar for the Sky*, 1985. Gunpowder and oil on canvas, 80.1 × 116.8 cm. Photo: Tatsumi Masatoshi. Courtesy of Cai Studio.

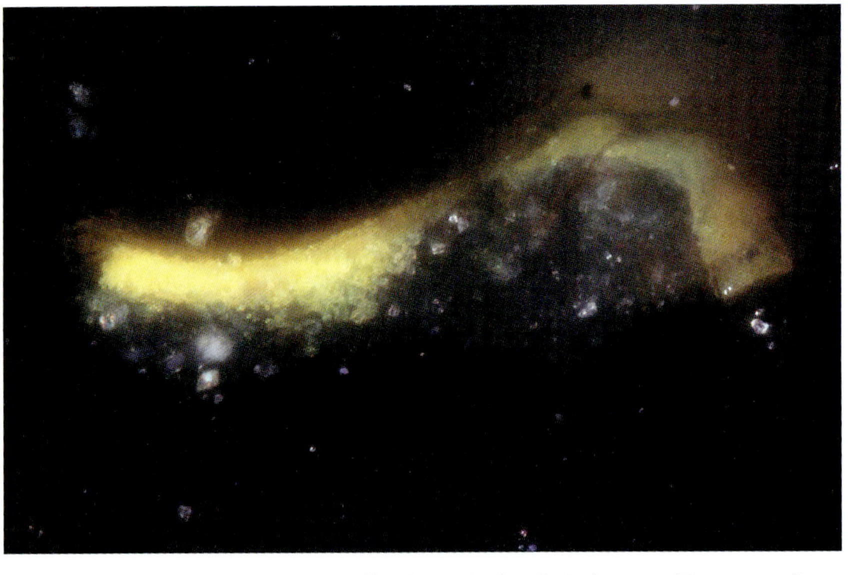

Figure 7 A cross section from *Pillar for the Sky*, observed with optical microscopy. The cross section reveals the presence of a layer of realgar on top (yellow layer). Cross section and photo: Michael Doutre. Courtesy of Getty Conservation Institute. © J. Paul Getty Trust.

exposed to. Another painting from 1985, *The Brand of Archean Era* (*Taigu de laoyin*), suggests that Cai was also experimenting with different binding media. As in *Chu Ba Wang* and *Pillar for the Sky*, realgar was used as a source of yellow color, but in *The Brand of Archean Era* it is mixed with a collagen-based glue to paint the characters, while the background is a PVA-bound paint containing Prussian blue—one of the few bright and perhaps more expensive pigments to appear in Cai's early works, as in the painting *Classmate* discussed earlier.

DRAWING VERSUS PAINTING

In 1986, Cai moved to Japan, and remained there for almost a decade, mostly in Tokyo and its surroundings, except for a year spent in Iwaki in 1993–94. While in Japan, Cai was able to gain easier access to better quality gunpowder, and in 1987–88, he started exploring the use of pure black gunpowder as the sole medium for his drawings. He also briefly experimented with colored pyrotechnic powders around that time, but then felt that there was so much to explore with the black gunpowder, both technically and conceptually, that using paint or color could be distracting.[17] Cai's exploration continued for the following three decades. During this time, Cai's process of drawing with gunpowder has essentially remained the same, but with increased refinement, mastery, and sophistication, as well as a spectacular increase in scale (fig. 8).

In 2015, however, Cai returned to the use of colored pyrotechnic powders, sparingly at first, but eventually lavishly and exuberantly. Although the term is not technically accurate, the colorful paintings created by Cai after that date are colloquially referred to as "colored gunpowder paintings," and this terminology will be used here. Significantly, Cai considers this new development in his work to be a reawakening of his painting practice, and through this renewed use of

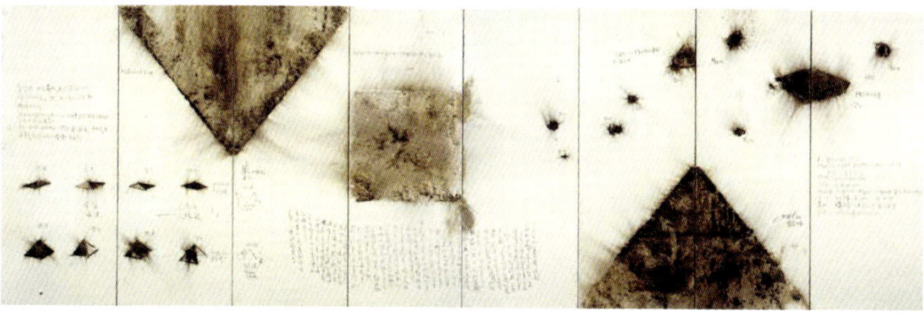

Figure 8 Cai Guo-Qiang, *Inverted Pyramid on the Moon: Project for Humankind No. 3*, 1991. Gunpowder and ink on paper, mounted on wood as eight-panel folding screen, 200 × 680 cm. Photo: André Morin. Courtesy of Fondation Cartier pour l'art contemporain.

color he has engaged in a fervent dialogue with European art history the past few years. For Cai, this return to painting started with a shift in subject matter, which he attributes to the nostalgia and longing he felt during his long absence from home while working on the Beijing Olympics ceremony:

> Before 2008 I was intrigued by the sense of the larger cosmos, the relationship between human and the universe, the earth and land, and the society. During the two years of Olympics preparation time, I started to think a lot about the Chinese culture. For the opening I was seeking the essence of Chinese culture and its significance to the world. . . . The other reality is, during the two years preparing for the Olympics, I was mainly residing in Beijing. On my birthday I received a big poster written by the studio staff and hand carried by Hong Hong from New York. . . . This suggests that I have left my family, my studio for a year now. So I had more emotions towards my children; without even realizing [it], my eldest has graduated from high school and entered college. That's why after the Olympics I had experienced this huge change, which is focusing on florals and nature [fig. 9] . . . this change has continuously evolved to this day, from florals and slowly evolving to colors. . . . Installations and large outdoor explosion events are like social activities and revolutions. But paintings are similar to making love on the bed, it's about intimacy and materiality.[18]

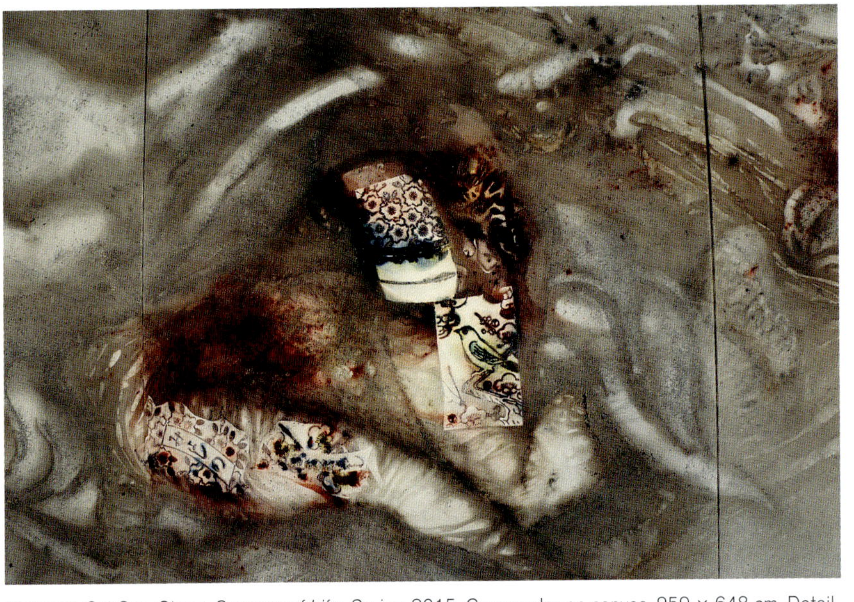

Figure 9 Cai Guo-Qiang, *Seasons of Life: Spring*, 2015. Gunpowder on canvas, 259 × 648 cm. Detail. Photo: Rachel Rivenc.

Painting for Cai is not only about the subject, but also about the purpose. For decades, most of his gunpowder drawings were related to ideas that he had for explosion events: they were sketches, or preparatory drawings meant to convey the ideas he had for particular projects and events. Part of Cai's renewed and feverish dialogue with paintings includes a thorough deconstruction and questioning of the tenets of painting:

> Right now I'm not rushing into mixing and pairing colors. I'm trying to avoid what I had learned when I studied art, the good color palettes and bad palettes, how colors should be paired together to achieve harmony and beauty. I'm also trying to avoid my impressions of good paintings and paintings of the old masters. I'm intentionally trying to put that away. Of course, it's impossible to completely let go, but I don't want to use these as references. I want to use gunpowder colors in ways that are more spontaneous, improvised, discordant, and unrationed. There are several potential objectives for this. The first is the wild and not so rational. The second is to expose the core energy of this material, including its problems. The third is the encounter with the unknown. Since now I'm returning to painting, I'm faced with the history of painting and my own art, so there is this stage where we start from the beginning to historicize. Sometimes it may be difficult to appreciate and it may not feel harmonized, but isn't that what you're looking forward to see[ing]?[19]

MATERIALS AND PROCESS

BLACK GUNPOWDER

Gunpowder is mainly composed of black powder, i.e., a mixture of an oxidizer, a source of sulfur, and fuels. As with other combustion processes, the ignition and combustion of gunpowder require oxygen. The oxidizer is a compound that releases oxygen as it burns, thus feeding the reaction. Saltpeter (potassium nitrate) has historically been the most commonly used oxidizer, but various other nitrates, chlorates, and perchlorates can also be found in black powder formulations. Sulfur is found as elemental sulfur, or as sulfide minerals such as realgar, and it serves as fuel for the ignition reaction.

The first firecrackers are widely believed to have appeared in China sometime in the second century BCE. They were simply bamboo stalks that, when thrown into the fire, exploded with a bang because of the overheating of the compressed air. Actual gunpowder was likely discovered fortuitously in the first half of the ninth century by Chinese alchemists in search of the elixir of life. Having prepared a concoction of honey, sulfur, and saltpeter, they saw it abruptly erupt in flames, as the sulfur and honey acted as fuels and were subsequently oxidized by the saltpeter.[20]

Traditional black gunpowder has had a very set composition for centuries: seventy-five percent potassium nitrate; fifteen percent charcoal; and ten percent sulfur. To be reactive and properly ignite and detonate, ingredients must be brought together into intimate contact, which is done by milling them with water then pressing them into a cake that then needs to be broken. Overall, the methods of preparation and conditions of use are crucial to the resulting properties and behavior. Depending on the intended use, fuels can be provided by different forms of carbon in addition to charcoal, such as resins, gums, or carbohydrates.

By the eleventh century, Chinese court records include texts outlining recipes for "fire drug" (*huoyao*) to be used in incendiary bombs for warfare. Military applications continued to develop in the twelfth and thirteenth centuries to respond to the military threats posed first by the Jurchens, then the Mongols. While it is not clear exactly when gunpowder appeared in Europe, it is known that chemists and alchemists were experimenting with different proportions of saltpeter/sulfur/charcoal by the thirteenth century. They realized that "a loose, open tray of powder was all that was needed to produce a flash, but in order to produce the bang the powder needed to be confined."[21] The use of black powder as a propellant for cannons was widespread in Europe by the fourteenth century and has been essential to military advances in modern Europe ever since.

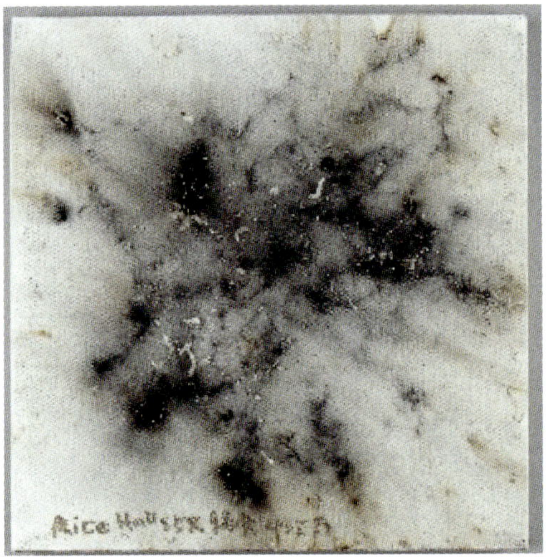

Figure 10 Cai Guo-Qiang, Test of gunpowder: rice hulls covered with gunpowder four times, 2017. Photo: Michael Doutre. Courtesy of Getty Conservation Institute. © J. Paul Getty Trust.

Over the years, Cai has explored the use of many different types of black gunpowder, and he has expanded his "palette" to include gunpowder of several different sizes and granulometries, as well as smokeless powders that create a grayer trace, and a few custom-made gunpowders developed specifically for him. In the United States, Cai has been working for many years with Fireworks by Grucci, Inc., whose owner and CEO, Phil Grucci, took a personal interest in the collaboration. Products developed specifically for Cai include gunpowder-coated rice puffs and rice hulls, which are coated one to three times. These coated materials contribute to producing different effects: the air pockets in the rice puffs and hulls make them move very quickly on the substrate, creating a very distinctive scatter pattern (fig. 10). The organic material burns and only leaves the gunpowder behind, along with some carbon residue.[22]

When Cai creates projects abroad, he also likes to use locally sourced gunpowder, as part of his overall philosophy of exploring and creating dialogues between different cultures and incorporating them in his work. He has observed that gunpowders sourced from different locations often behave differently, and he in fact always incorporates a period of experimentation in the lead-up to a major exhibition or drawing production to allow him to get accustomed to the properties of the new products. He has observed in particular that some mixtures burn faster and release more heat than others, leading to increased risks of creating burns and holes in the paper. This may relate more to differences in preparation—how intimately the components are mixed and pressed together, for example—and their morphology than differences in chemistry. Depending on the preparation method used, analyses of samples show mostly variations in the quantity of organic residues present: rice hulls tend to leave more residues than rice puffs.

DAYTIME FIREWORKS

The colored powders that Cai Guo-Qiang started using again in 2015 to create his paintings are pyrotechnic mixtures designed for daytime fireworks. The compounds used are very different than the compounds used to create color in nighttime fireworks. In daytime fireworks, a colored smoke is produced by volatilizing an organic dye that then condenses in air to form small solid particles. The dyes are strong absorbers of visible light. The light reflected off the vaporized particles is missing the absorbed wavelengths, so that the complementary hue is perceived by observers. This is the opposite of nighttime fireworks, which produce a colored flame. In this case the emitted wavelengths are perceived as color by viewers.

To be visible during the daytime, these types of fireworks have a number of very specific requirements. The mixture needs to produce sufficient heat to vaporize the dye and a sufficient volume and density of gas to disperse the dye into the surrounding space—to produce a substantial enough cloud of colored smoke. At the same time, the mixture must ignite and burn smoothly at a low enough temperature to avoid decomposition of the dye. The dyes must be volatile enough to convert to the vapor state upon heating without substantial decomposition. For this reason, fairly low molecular weight dyes are generally used. A crucial requirement is also that the smokes produced be non-toxic, since they are released into the atmosphere in close proximity to the audience.

Because of these requirements, potassium chlorate ($KClO_3$) is often used as an oxidizer: it provides a low ignition temperature with reliable burning at low temperatures. Coolants such as sodium bicarbonate or magnesium carbonate are often added to the mixture, in the proportions required to obtain the desired rate of burning and correct reaction temperature. Carbohydrates (i.e., sugars such as lactose or sucrose) are often used as a fuel in combination with the potassium chlorate. The amount of heat can also be controlled by adjusting the potassium chlorate to fuel ratio.

In terms of color, the range is limited by the number of heat-resistant dyestuff that are commercially available. Anthraquinones are commonly used and can provide colors from orange to green depending on the level of conjugation—increased conjugation will cause a shift to longer wavelengths. Cai Guo-Qiang works mostly with six colors sourced from Japan and six colors sourced from China, as well as with locally sourced colors when needed. Besides its volatility, the quantity of dye present in the mixture will also affect the burning rate. The dye acts as a diluent, so the greater the quantity of dye used, the slower the burning rate. At the same time, the dye needs to be present in sufficient amounts to account for the partial decomposition that inevitably occurs because of the heat. A typical colored smoke composition often contains forty to sixty percent dye by weight. Cai Guo-Qiang generally adds black gunpowder to the daytime fireworks he uses for his paintings, to offset their slower burning rate and produce a more spectacular deflagration.

Cai prepared tests, made by detonating both the Japanese and the Chinese colored powders that he has been using, and these tests were analyzed with a range of analytical techniques to better understand their composition. The analyses confirmed that potassium chlorate or perchlorate was used as the oxidizer, and that potassium sulfate was present, presumably as a result of the addition of black gunpowder to the colored fireworks by Cai to promote a more explosive reaction. A range of additives and reaction byproducts were also identified. The blue colorant was identified as phthalocyanine blue pigment PB:15, a copper-containing pigment very commonly used in paint formulations. Analyses also revealed that the red and yellow colorants were respectively an anthraquinone dye, probably Solvent Red III, and an azo dye, probably Solvent Yellow 56. The green and purple powders both contain PB:15, and for both colors, the color appears to be produced by mixing the PB:15 pigment with another dye. Solvent Green 3, an anthraquinone dye, was also identified in the green color. PV1 (Rhodamine B), a dye, was identified in the very bright pink-purple Chinese powder.

SUBSTRATES

For his gunpowder drawings, Cai has mostly been using Japanese paper, preferring when possible handmade raw hemp fiber paper ordered from a traditional paper mill, Ozaki Seishijo, in the Kochi prefecture of Japan. Since 2015, Cai has used predominantly commercially prepared canvases on stretchers for his colored paintings. Cai also uses rigid substrates, notably porcelain, in the form of tiles bearing intricate flowery reliefs of fully three-dimensional sculptures (figs. 11–12). These are handmade by a factory in Dehua, a small town about an hour's drive from Quanzhou specializing in the craft of porcelain. The porcelain used is an unglazed, hard paste made of high-purity kaolin extracted from local deposits.[23] Cai has also used silk and glass, exploring the aesthetic possibilities opened by the latter's transparency, and he has also on occasion experimented with other hard substrates including metal.

APPLICATION PROCESS

Cai's drawings with gunpowder were often part of larger projects and concepts. While working toward a project, a small constellation of artworks is often created, from the actual realized projects to large-scale drawings (sometimes several of them), as well as smaller sketches, drawings, and albums. Some projects are never realized, so the drawings are the only actualization of Cai's ideas. Cai always sketched extensively and kept sketchbooks, in which he jotted down ideas for projects, as well as figurative sketches and drawings. Cai continues to sketch today, but the preparatory process is now also often accompanied by lengthy iconographic research and the use of computer-assisted drawings.

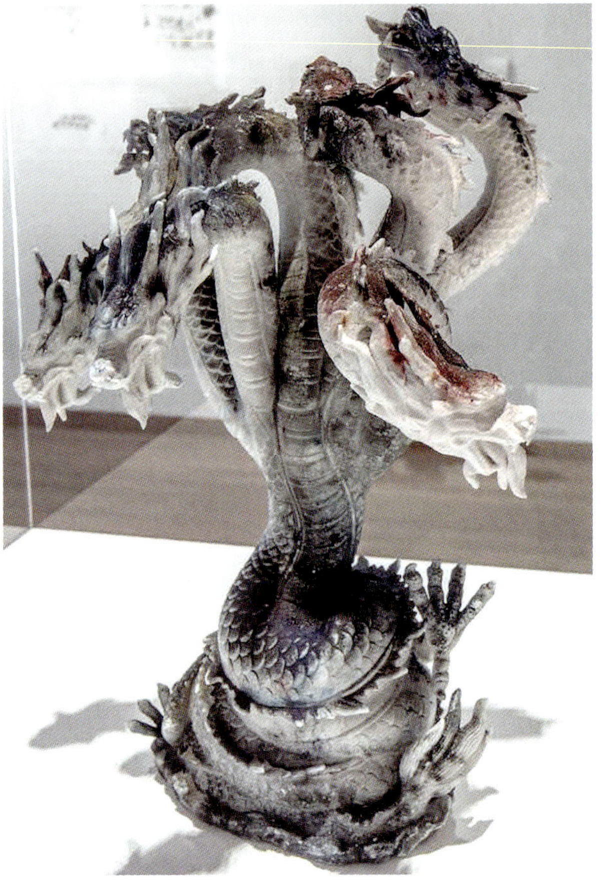

Figure 11 Cai Guo-Qiang, *Study for Seven-Headed Dragon*, 2016. Gunpowder on porcelain, approx. 37 × 26 × 17 cm. Photo: Harry Heuts. Courtesy of Bonnefantenmuseum.

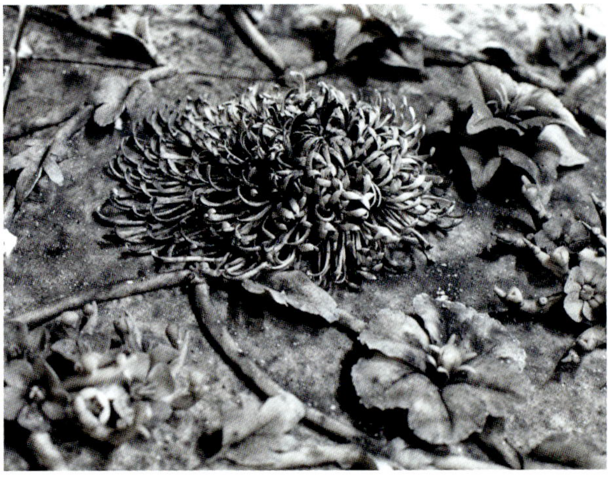

Figure 12 Cai Guo-Qiang, *Fragile*, 2011. Gunpowder on porcelain, 318 × 1800 cm. Detail. Collection of Mathaf: Arab Museum of Modern Art. Photo: Hiro Ihara. Courtesy of Cai Studio.

DRAWING AND STENCIL

For a relatively simple or abstract drawing, Cai lays the gunpowder directly onto the paper. He also frequently uses black Sumi ink and calligraphy brushes to write or draw. For more complex drawings, Cai draws a stencil first. His studio assistants, with additional help from teams of local volunteers for very large drawings, then cut the stencils.

APPLICATION OF THE GUNPOWDER

Preparing the actual drawing can take up to several days, depending on the size of the painting. The floor is protected with butcher paper and the substrate is laid flat over it. The stencil is laid over the substrate, and the process of applying the gunpowder starts. Cai sprinkles and rubs the different powders slowly, deliberately, almost meditatively. That process looks deceptively simple, but it relies on Cai's consummate knowledge of the properties, reactivity, and appearance of the different powders. If the drawing is very large, Cai walks on it, using white socks or slippers to protect the surface of the drawing, or he builds small wooden bridges over it, and he might use a small plastic broom to spread the gunpowder. Sometimes, instead of, or in addition to, the stencils, Cai uses foliage, branches, flowers, or other actual objects and garments. He sprinkles the gunpowder around them, and after ignition, most of the material is burnt off while the outline remains. The organic matter that these objects are made of burns and gets mostly consumed during the deflagration, leaving behind their charred residues, as well as their outlines in gunpowder.

IGNITION

Once Cai is satisfied with the drawing, it is prepared for the moment of ignition. The method depends on the result that Cai wants to achieve. Sometimes, the whole drawing or painting is covered with glassine; the glassine traps the smoke resulting from the ignition and creates drapery effects. The drawing is covered with cardboard and weights are placed on top of it to contain the deflagration—projected matter could injure Cai, his team, or the audience—and prevent the displacement of matter that would disturb the drawing. The moment of ignition is always a surprise: Will the fuse behave as expected? Will the gunpowder combust fully? Even though the technique is perfected, and every precaution is taken, there is always an element of danger. The studio team always has fire extinguishers on hand, and as soon as the ignition is over, they rush to extinguish any small flames remaining with a studio-made device called "pom-poms," which are round balls made of white cotton painter's rags.

The process for black gunpowder drawings and colored paintings is fundamentally the same, i.e., laying the gunpowder and colored powders down on the paper, canvas, or other substrate to create the drawing, then igniting it (figs. 13–14). However, the process for colored paintings has become increasingly varied and complex as Cai's appetite for experimentation was re-ignited by the expansion of his color palette. Recently, Cai has experimented with a whole range of additional effects, such as covering the canvas with a second, blank canvas of equal shape and size, creating a mirror painting; igniting a painting twice, with additional black gunpowder, creating a darker, often more ominous version; or using incense sticks or fuse lines dipped into colored powders to create the drawing (fig. 15).

AGING AND CONSERVATION

When it comes to conservation, Cai's work poses concerns similar to drawings made with other friable media, such as charcoal or pastel; namely, because of the absence of a binder, the surface is very delicate. After ignition, when the drawing or painting is stood up, some loose matter might fall off. This is a part of the process, and Cai accepts it. Of course, the works still need to be handled with great care; conservators in some institutions have experimented with a variety of fixatives to consolidate the charred matter. The difficulty resides in not altering the appearance or modifying the matt surface by adding gloss, but treatments of traditional powdery drawing media can be adapted.

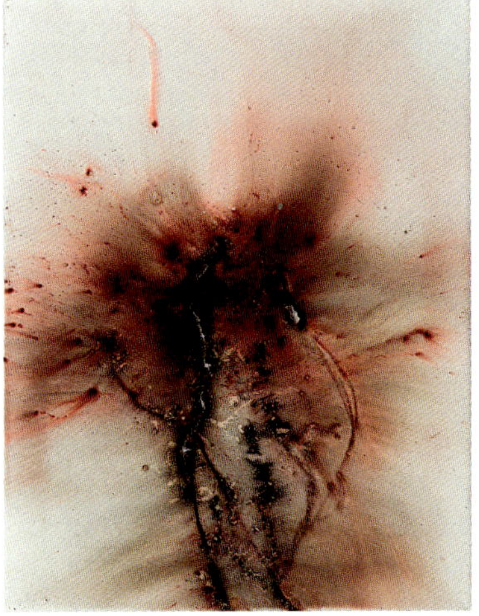

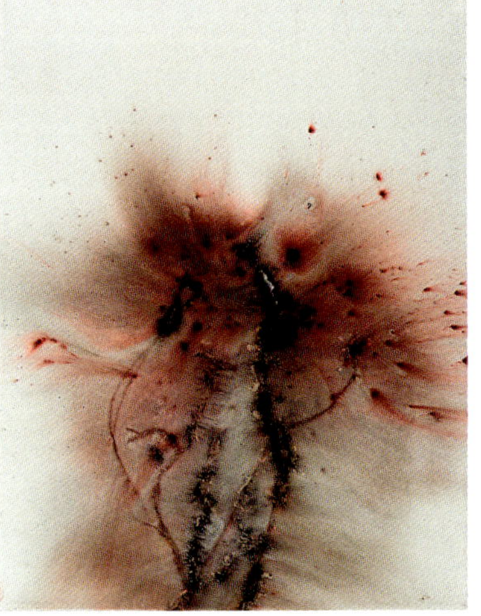

Figures 13–14 Cai Guo-Qiang, *Study for Cosmos No. 1* and *Study for Cosmos No. 2*, 2018. Gunpowder on canvas, each 35.4 × 28 cm. Collection of the artist. Photos: Yvonne Zhao. Courtesy of Cai Studio.

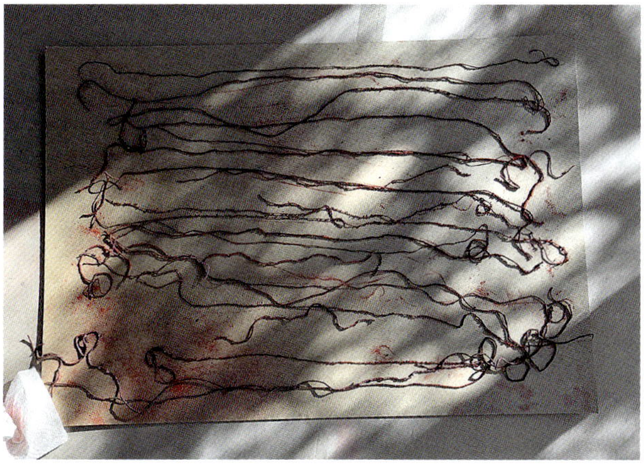

Figure 15 Cai Guo-Qiang, Fuses covered in gunpowder dyed with red powder for *Study for Cosmos No. 3*, 2018. Photo: Ting Ting Chen. Courtesy of Cai Studio.

The dyes and pigments in the colored pyrotechnic powders used to make paintings are also sensitive to light and require adequate lighting policies—also not unlike sensitive colored drawing media. A study of the lightfastness of the main colors used by Cai has been performed by the Getty Conservation Institute with two main techniques, microfadeometry and artificial aging in a weathering chamber,[24] using tests prepared by the artist. The sensitivity of the colors varied widely depending on the dye; for example, the PB:15 pigment used on both Chinese and Japanese blue powders proved to be extremely stable, while the Rhodamine B used in the bright pink powder quickly lost the intensity of its color as it settled on a rather beautifully muted salmon shade of pink.[25]

Overall, it is important to stress that these studies are not predictors of what will happen, but rather what can happen if these delicate works are not lit with the care they deserve or according to museum standards. Cai has been very interested in the study and understanding of the aging properties of his material; but while he wants his work to endure, he also does not want this knowledge to shackle his creativity. Ultimately, change is inevitable and can also bring beauty.

> Even when something is eternal, you can't own it forever. Eternity and permanence are different in Chinese. Eternity transcends the existence of time whereas permanence remains in the realm of time. So when we have dialogues with and associate with eternity through art, we don't attempt to tackle it from the permanence point of view; rather, we use the instantaneous way to grasp it. It feels like the myth of eternity, you could only taste it at the fleeting moment of chaos.[26]

NOTES

The author wishes to thank Cai Guo-Qiang, Cai Studio, especially Silin Chow, Sang Luo, and Lydia Ohl, and Cai's wife, Hong Wu, for their generosity in supporting this study. The author also acknowledges with gratitude that Michael Doutre, Vincent Dion, Alan Phenix, Joy Mazurek, Vincent Beltran, Lynn Lee, and Douglas MacLennan carried out most of the analyses described in this chapter and contributed their extensive professional expertise to the interpretation of the results. At the Getty, Tom Learner, Tim Whalen, Mary Miller, and Jim Cuno also greatly supported and contributed to this project.

1. *The Spirit of Painting* was the title of Cai's solo show at the Museo Nacional del Prado, Madrid, October 25, 2017–March 4, 2018.
2. Before her current position at the Getty Research Institute, the author worked as associate scientist and project specialist at the Getty Conservation Institute (GCI).
3. Cai Guo-Qiang, interview with the author, with translation by Cai Studio, November 17, 2016, Cai Studio, New York.
4. Cai, interview with the author, July 22, 2016.
5. Cai, interview with the author, July 22, 2016.
6. Cai Guo-Qiang, interview with the author, April 14, 2019, Cai Studio, New York; transcript and translation arranged by author.
7. Cai, interview with the author, April 14, 2019.
8. Later the Quanzhou Gaojia Opera Theater Troupe (Quanzhou Gaojia Xijutuan).

9. Cai, interview with the author, July 22, 2016.
10. All the analyses described in this chapter were carried out by the Science Department of the Getty Conservation Institute (GCI). Analyses included Fourier Transform Infrared Spectroscopy (FTIR), pyrolysis-Gas Chromatography coupled with Mass Spectrometry (py-GCMS), Raman spectroscopy, X-ray fluorescence elemental analyses (XRF), and Environmental Scanning Electron Microscopy coupled with Energy-dispersive X-ray spectroscopy (ESEM-EDX). For more on the analytical aspects of this study, see Rachel Rivenc, Vincent Dion, Michael Doutre, and Tim Learner, "Explosive Beauty: The Art of Cai Guo-Qiang," in *Science and Art: The Contemporary Painted Surface*, ed. Antonio Sgamellotti, Brunetto Giovanni Brunetti, and Costanza Miliani (Cambridge: Royal Society of Chemistry, 2020).
11. Cai, interview with the author, July 22, 2016.
12. Cai, interview with the author, July 22, 2016.
13. Firecrackers are small explosive devices containing gunpowder and are primarily designed to produce loud noises. Fireworks are also a form of low-explosion devices designed to produce visual effects such as light, color, sparks, and movement, as well as sound. All firecrackers are rockets as they contain a lifting charge that will propel them in the air, but Cai probably refers to the variety that is cylindrical in shape with a conical top—very similar to a space rocket—and that comes on a long stick. Rockets using gunpowder are also used to launch fireworks into the sky and are more powerful than simple firecrackers, as they need to go much higher.
14. Cai, interview with the author, July 22, 2016.
15. Cai, interview with the author, July 22, 2016.
16. Realgar is an arsenic sulfide mineral (alpha-As_4S_4). It is not only found as an ingredient in gunpowder as a source of sulfur, but it also has a long history of use in Chinese medicine.

It has also been used in European painting as a pigment.
17. Cai, interview with the author, July 22, 2016.
18. Cai, interview with the author, July 22, 2016.
19. Cai, interview with the author, July 22, 2016.
20. Jack Kelly, *Gunpowder Alchemy, Bombards, and Pyrotechnics: The History of the Explosive that Changed the World* (New York: Basic Books, 2004); J. A. Conkling, *Chemistry of Pyrotechnics: Basic Principles and Theory* (New York: M. Dekker, 1985); and Michael S. Russell, *The Chemistry of Fireworks*, 2nd ed. (Cambridge: Royal Society of Chemistry, 2009).
21. Phil Grucci, interview with the author, November 11, 2017, Long Island, NY.
22. The composition of the porcelain was confirmed by ESEM-EDX analyses.
23. Fading refers to the loss of color that happens as a result of light exposure. The microfadeometer (MFT) sends an enormous amount of light through an optic fiber on a microscopic spot—the spot is too small to be visible to the naked eye, but the instrument measures the color changes that happen as a result of light exposure. In addition, the instrument is so sensitive that the fading can be stopped before it gets visible. As a result, this technique can be used on actual works of art to determine their sensitivity to light.
24. The chamber produces extremely bright light. The tests were aged for four, 144-hour segments, for a total of 576 hours in an Atlas xenon arc Weatherometer chamber. These aging conditions equated to up to 300 years of exposure in a museum-like, controlled lighting environment, or up to thirty years of display in a home or office environment with bright lighting.
25. Rivenc, Dion, Doutre, and Learner, "Explosive Beauty" in *Science and Art: The Contemporary Painted Surface*.
26. Cai, interview with the author, November 17, 2016.

The Contingent Life of the Artwork

Conserving the Works of Gu Dexin

Sara A. Moy

The works of Gu Dexin (b. 1962) arrest the viewer and assault the senses. Rooms and walls are covered in burned plastic forms, and glass containers filled with putrefying meat or viscera ooze decay onto the floor. One of the most important and enigmatic figures in Chinese contemporary art, Gu was one of the first artists in China to work with nontraditional materials prone to decompose, rot, and dematerialize. Working with plastic, flesh, and viscera, and later with fruit, Gu created works that explore transformation and decay—processes that frustrate the efforts of the conservator. Indeed, many of Gu's larger works were destroyed or discarded at the end of an exhibition. Characterized by their instability, impermanence, and ephemerality, the works that remain challenge perpetuation, a defining principle of heritage stewardship and preservation. Known for his adamant critiques of the commercialization of art and his rejection of exhibitions and retrospectives as vehicles of the art market,[1] he was ambivalent about preservation as a practice because it supports the system of art sales, collection, and display. Gu was famed for his lack of participation with a work once it was staged, a stance that he took to its extreme conclusion when he departed the art world in 2009.

Gu's refusal to take part in decision-making processes regarding his work is atypical. In general, determinations in the conservation, care, and display of artworks involve discussion and negotiation between multiple stakeholders that include the artist along with conservators, collectors, and museums, among others.[2] Together, these stakeholders assess an artwork's current state or condition, research its meaning and desired state, and identify the discrepancy between current and desired state. This research and negotiation typically leads to a proposal that provides options for conservation, their considerations, and eventually to a strategy. In the case of Gu's works, the artist's resistance to engage in these conversations leaves conservators and other stakeholders with the responsibility of making the primary decisions about the works' care and preservation, without any further instructions from the artist in this regard.

Numerous studies have explored various dimensions of contemporary art conservation that are relevant to Gu's works: the definition of performance or participatory art and how it can be historicized and preserved for the future; the implementation of visual documentation as a form of materialized memory; models or concepts developed from social science, namely ethnology, providing a framework for gathering and analyzing documents that facilitate interaction with the artist; and autoethnography as an approach for understanding cultural experience by describing and systematically analyzing how participants perceive their own and others' personal experiences.[3] These existing frameworks or systematic conservation approaches do not, however, offer clear answers. Each may have some relevance to Gu's work, but the complex and unclassifiable nature of Gu's works makes it difficult to apply a single approach. Furthermore, following conventional conservation decision-making processes would entail an approach that is highly structured and normative—qualities that run counter to the tenets of Gu's practice.

Given all of these complicated factors, how should the care and oversight of Gu's works proceed, and what considerations should inform conservation decision making? Rather than drawing on the tools, rules, guidelines, models, and methodologies currently offered by conservation and humanities fields, I propose instead an approach guided by the principles that characterized Gu's artistic practice and rooted specifically in Gu's belief that each artwork has a life of its own that is the outcome of specific contingencies. In short, I suggest stakeholders base their decisions on a thorough understanding of his practice and creative process, accepting the transformations that may arise in an individual work through the inherent (physical) behavior—expected or unexpected—of its materials and the participation of viewers and caretakers in his works. I base this proposed approach on extensive examination of Gu's body of work and my participation in the conservation of two artworks, *Untitled* (1989) and *2004-6-16* (2004). In the absence of Gu's explicit direction regarding the exhibition and preservation of his work and resistance to participate in these discussions, I instead rely on Gu's statements in manifestos, interviews, and archival documents to gain insight into Gu's views on his art and its perpetuation in order to make specific recommendations for its continued care.

In this chapter, I first present an overview of Gu's practice and work to foreground the ideas, artistic concerns, and characteristics of Gu's work: performativity; the participation and equal importance of the artist, materials, and viewer in the creative process; the inevitable transformation of both materials and artworks; and the consequently contingent and unique life of each artwork. I argue that these should form the basis for any stakeholder negotiations related to the preservation and display of his work. I then present two case studies of the artworks, *Untitled* (1989) and *2004-6-16* (2004), that illustrate how an approach informed by Gu's artistic principles can lead to different decisions for different artworks.

AN ARTISTIC AND INTELLECTUAL NONCONFORMIST

A significant figure in the '85 Art New Wave ('85 Meishu xinchao), Gu Dexin was one of the first artists in China to work with nontraditional or nonconventional materials, and he is considered one of the most important and influential artists of his generation. Unlike many of his peers, Gu was self-taught, eschewing formal study after failing to gain admission to Beijing's Central Academy of Fine Arts (Zhongyang meishu xueyuan). This rejection led Gu to likewise reject prescribed conventions of art making, furthering a tendency toward nonconformity that had been evident since childhood and would characterize his entire career. It also strongly influenced his skepticism of institutions and institutional value systems, from Chinese bureaucracies to the standards governing art.[4] By the 1980s, Gu abandoned his early medium—painting—because he felt it constrained the expression of his personal ideals.

Gu's departure from painting marked the beginning of a vigorously experimental period, during which he explored materials in and of themselves as well as the viewer's corporeal engagement with his works and their material. Observing that many artworks tended to push viewers away rather than engage them, Gu and fellow artist Wang Luyan (b. 1956) formed the two-person Tactile Sensation Group (Chujue yishu) in 1987. The group stemmed from an exhibition concept: the audience, led into a dark room, would be left to touch and feel their way around in silence. The artists' mission was to present an occasion for viewers to experience touch; they sought to activate viewers' consciousness of their bodies and surroundings and awareness of their own sensory functions.[5] Their manifesto explained their view of the parity between artist and viewer:

> The artist and the public participate together. The relationship between them is not active or passive, but is, without precedent, equal. Apart from naming some common objects of touch, the artist is exactly the same as the public. The artist does not impose a subjective and personal view to provoke the public. No explanation is needed, nor understanding. No discussion is wanted, nor is communication. No domineering artist making indiscriminate decisions or any "manmade" inequalities. There are no meaningless questions about misunderstanding, likes or dislikes.[6]

Gu and Wang's artworks involved artists and viewers equally involved in constituting the work. The artists created the circumstances for viewers to experience a direct, physical encounter, and participation on both sides of this reciprocal relationship was integral to the work.

After the short-lived Tactile Sensation Group ended in 1988, Gu, Wang, and several other artists founded the New Measurement Group (Xin kedu xiaozu; initially named the New Analyst Group, Xin jiexin xiaozu) in 1989. Adopting an inward focus, the group's members took as their subject the process of making an artwork, rather than the work's reception. Not only did they abstain from conventional exhibition formats, but they also attempted to suppress each artist's individuality from informing either the concept or the process of the work. Before making an artwork, the members collectively set rules for its execution that would ensure each member would contribute equally to the creative process. By agreeing to follow these rules, the artists were able to "transcend the constraints imposed by ideology and sentimentality."[7] There was commonality and continuity between these groups; most notably, both challenged the individual artist's role and the constraints imposed on the artist's subjectivity within the confines of larger governing systems.[8] In 1995, six years after its inception, the New Measurement Group disbanded. Their work had become subject to increased demand, and success threatened to draw them into the systems and structures of the global art market that they adamantly opposed.[9]

At the same time, Gu continued to produce works independently, challenging the fundamental doctrines of traditional or conventional art with each successive project. As he did so, he carried with him the tenets of the groups to which he previously or contemporaneously belonged, particularly a rejection of the hierarchies of conventional art practices, a focus on process, the suppression of the artist's individuality and subjectivity, and the viewer's direct engagement with the work. Gu produced works characterized by staging, transformation, and alteration in which both the artist and the audience are equally necessary to the creative process.

MATERIAL TRANSFORMATIONS

After transitioning from the picture plane, Gu Dexin began experimenting with nontraditional materials, most notably plastic and, later, organic matter. In both cases, Gu was drawn to the material's tendency to decay and the effects created by that deterioration. He mobilized the transformative qualities of his materials, intentionally selecting them because of the ways they changed through his manipulations and during the course of an exhibition or over an artwork's life. Gu transmutes his materials in creating his artworks, and once he is done, he cedes control, giving the work and its materials over to the varied transformations that they might undergo. In their transformations, these works are both performative and participatory. The process of mutation is the material's participation and performance, drawing viewers and caretakers into that process. In all cases, the works were shaped by how Gu understood his own role in his artwork, not only equal to that of viewers but also ending after he had finished his material manipulations and staged the work.

PERFORMANCE AND PARTICIPATION

PLASTIC

Gu Dexin's experiments with plastic began in the early 1980s. For Gu, plastic was more than just a new art material; in contrast to tradition-bound paintings, plastic represented and allowed an uninhibited level of experimentation. Plastic's inherent properties fascinated Gu, and he was drawn to its tactility, colors, and textures, as well as its ability to be rigid yet pliable and easily shaped.[10] To learn more about its properties and behavior, he even took a part-time job at a small plastics factory. In his artworks, he began fusing plastic waste into organic

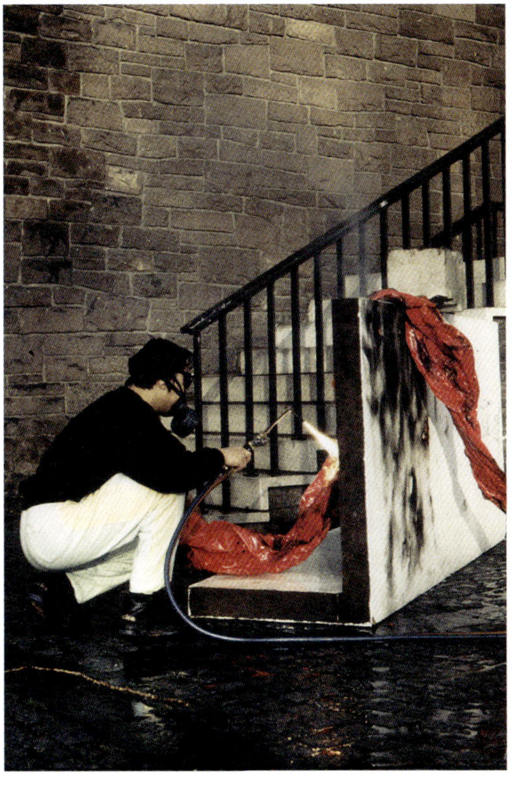

Figure 1 Gu Dexin using a blowtorch to distort plastic pieces. Hans van Dijk Archive. Courtesy of Gu Dexin and Asia Art Archive.

structures and distorting familiar objects with a blowtorch, reconstituting them into unrecognizable textured masses or abstract compositions (fig. 1). Gu was also fascinated by plastic's instability and susceptibility to degrade, an interest in material transformation that later extended to organic material. Like the fruit and animal products in Gu's later work, plastic is also perishable. Some synthetic polymers deteriorate in ways that are nothing short of catastrophic for an artwork. Over time, environmental factors, such as light, heat, moisture, chemical conditions, or biological activity, can lead to embrittlement, distortion, tearing, and cracking; there can also be changes in the material's haptic and tactile properties, color, transparency, and odor.

Plastic Pieces–287 (1983–85) (fig. 2) is an early plastic work, first shown in the landmark *China/Avant-Garde* exhibition (*Zhongguo xiandai yishuzhan*) at Beijing's National Art Gallery (Zhongguo meishuguan) in 1989. Consisting of 287 pieces of melted and charred plastic, the work provokes a physical reaction in the viewer and evokes a sense of tenuousness, mortality, and decay. In the same year, Gu's *Untitled* (see fig. 9) debuted at the Grande Halle de la Villette in Paris, as part of the exhibition *Magiciens de la terre*. Organized by the Centre

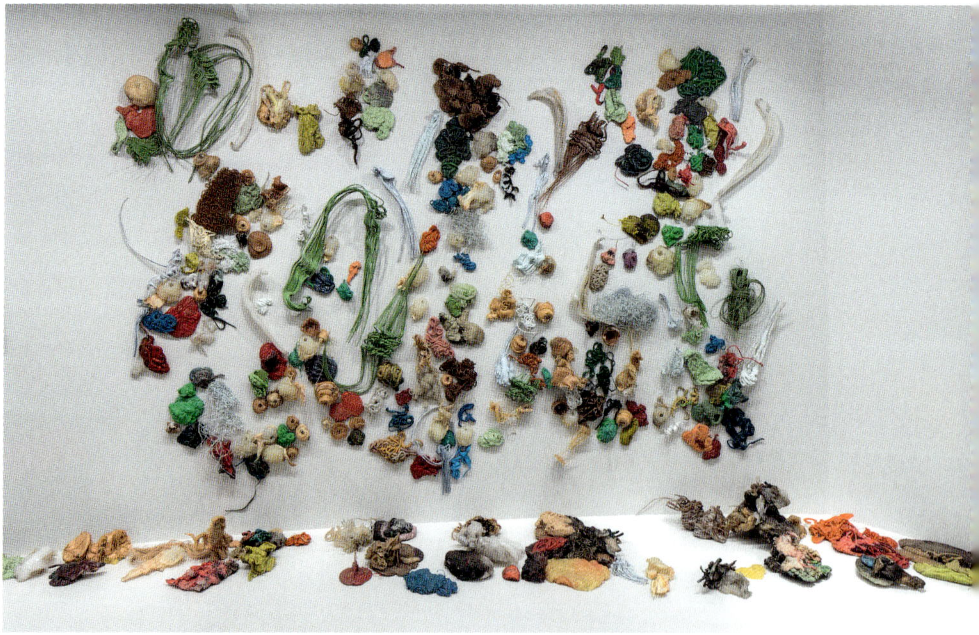

Figure 2 Gu Dexin, *Plastic Pieces–287*, 1983–85. Installation view, *Art and China after 1989: Theater of the World*, Solomon R. Guggenheim Museum, New York, 2017–2018. Photo: David Heald. © SRGF.

Pompidou, it was one of the first exhibitions of contemporary art to showcase artists from around the world, including those from mainland China. It was this installation that brought Gu into the international spotlight. Installed in an enclosed space, 600 cm by 420 cm with a ceiling height of 320 cm and entered through a single doorway, *Untitled* is composed of hundreds of industrial plastic pieces and sheets, all formed and altered with a blowtorch. Gu created the work on site, charring and melting the plastic and allowing it to solidify in ways that responded to the exhibition space. The plastic pieces were attached to the white walls, which were scorched and marked with soot from the torch flames. These were embellished with other plastic pieces vaguely resembling entrails or parts in *Plastic Pieces-287*. The plastic extended from the walls into coagulated mounds on the ground; scorched plastic sheets hung from nails; distorted and charred U-Channels with colorful blown attachments leaned and balanced precariously; and clusters of modified plastic elements coalesced into sculptural forms. When completed, the installation had a distinct odor that permeated the space, affecting the viewers' senses beyond sight.

This work's performative and participatory dimensions inhere in the artist, the work's materials, and its viewers. The direct heating and scorching of the unaltered plastic and the evidence of soot suggest the artist as performer. Gu is the performer not in the traditional sense (physically present to perform to an audience), but rather in the preparatory process: the process of assembly and manipulation implies the staging of the event and constitutes Gu's performance. As the work's material and viewers share the space, material and sensory interactions take place. The charred plastic and its odor evoke nearly imperceptible somatic responses, such as a furrowed brow or change in breath. Such subtle shifts in the viewer are similar to the minute but dynamic changes occurring with the work's plastic pieces, as natural forces shape the materials. Some transformations are not immediately perceptible, such as the development of a crease or withering. Others call attention to the constant shifts in the material. The force of gravity causes the plastic sheets to tear away from the nails on which they are hung, as evinced by numerous torn holes. Pieces precariously balanced or unsteadily placed crack and shatter as they fall into each other or hit the ground. Such material shifts can in turn necessitate the organizer, curator, installer, or even conservator to participate by remedying the fallen or torn pieces. Through its transformations performed in the gallery space, the materials participate in the work, occasioning responsive actions on the part of certain viewers. This reciprocity between material and viewer is an idea that Gu extended in his works using organic matter.

THE FETOR OF DECAY

INTERVENTIONS AND ANIMAL PARTS

As Gu Dexin continued to experiment with materials, he made a radical shift in the mid-1990s: introducing organic materials, especially animal products. The works he produced during this time involved flesh, fat, and viscera, all of which he left to decompose.[11] He first used vast quantities of raw animal matter in *1995-6-8* (1995) (fig. 3), exhibited in *Asiana: Contemporary Art from the Far East*, a satellite show at the 1995 Venice Biennale. He staged three transparent coffins filled with bloody meat in the Venetian Palace, where the summer heat accelerated decay. A later installation, *2004-6-16* (2004) (see fig. 7), featured five tons of visceral pork fat in an iron-and-glass structure that was commissioned by Chinese art collector Guan Yi (b. 1966) and built into an enclosed space in his residence in Beijing's Songzhuang art district (Songzhuang yishuqu). The structure stretched beyond the height of the building and pierced through the roof. Its top was left open, exposing the pork fat, placed within the structure on clear perforated panels about two meters from the ground, to a range of outdoor conditions, including Beijing's intense summer heat. Not long after the work's installation, the fat dripped through the panels onto the bottom of the vitrine.

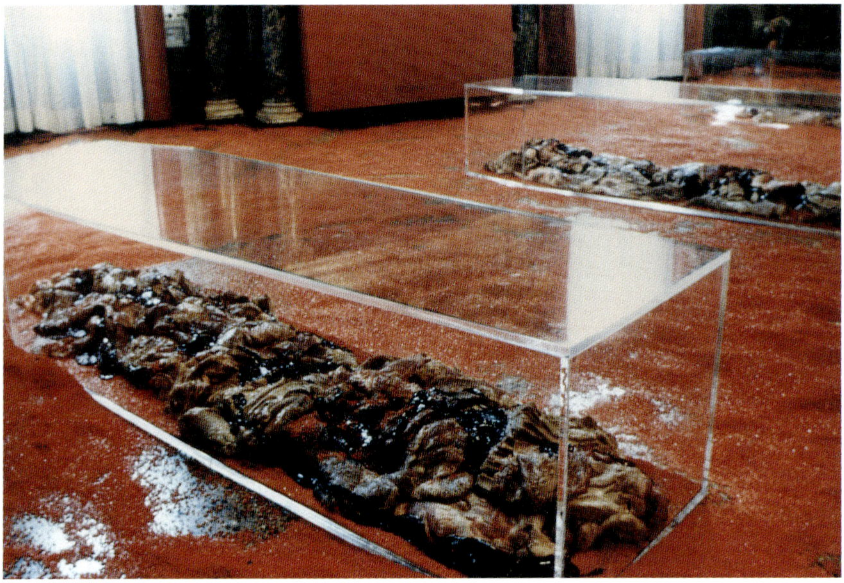

Figure 3 Gu Dexin, *1995-6-8*, 1995. 100 kg of raw beef, plexiglass. Installation view, *Asiana: Contemporary Art from the Far East*, Venice, 1995. Hans van Dijk Archive. Courtesy of Gu Dexin and Asia Art Archive.

Organic materials will inevitably decay, giving way to a fetid smell and maggots if conditions are right. In *1995-6-8*, exhibited at *Asiana*, the gas emitted by the rotting meat created misty patterns that denied visitors clear views of the coffins' contents. The room filled with miasma, and when it became intolerable after only three days, the exhibition organizers removed the work's contents and displayed the empty, blood-encrusted containers. With *2004-6-16*, the work's open top began attracting numerous pests, including maggots, and the fat liquefied and seeped out from the bottom of the structure and threatened to flow into the collector's office space located on the same floor. As with the coffins in the *Asiana* exhibition, the effects of this decay impelled intervention. A year after the work's installation, the collector implemented physical changes that altered the course of the work. The top was sealed to prevent further infestation. A trough was fabricated in the concrete floor to collect the seeping fat; a pipe penetrating the building's wall drained the fat into a bucket (see fig. 8), which had to be repeatedly emptied as the work continued to ooze.

Gu is cognizant of the materials he selects, especially with regard to decay, and the response such materials might elicit after a work is staged. With each succeeding project using organic matter, Gu intensified not only viewers' engagement with the work's material but also the materials' transformative contribution to the work, which in turn invited deeper viewer participation, while he refrained from participating himself. In an interview in 2004, he stated:

> I'm conscious of the changes that it [the material] will go through. The process of choosing the materials (and, in turn, the nature of the materials) is all conceptually part of creating the work. They all manifest something or express something, but after the materials are put together and become the work, I leave it to the viewer to make what they will of it. Once the work is exhibited, it's only the viewer's feeling that matters. When the exhibit opens, my work is over.[12]

Once Gu relinquishes control over his work, the viewers, collectors, conservators, curators, caretakers, and the material itself become the main participants. As the material transforms, the work activates the intervention of others—making way for further change and a dynamic interplay of various participants' creative exchanges with the work. In the case of *1995-6-8* and *2004-6-16*, as these two works underwent degenerative transformation, the exhibition organizers and the collector took up the role Gu had given up, making decisions about the work's trajectory. Their participation subsequently elicited the engagement of additional participants who moved, removed, and implemented physical changes to the work. In this form of participation, decision-making stakeholders, entrusted with a work surrendered to them by Gu, act more like collaborators, much like those of the earlier groups to which he belonged. Collaboration is "the act of working together with . . . [others] to create or achieve something,"[13] often with the intent to create greater meaning or substance. Gu's decaying works, rather than keeping to Gu's singular voice or vision, activate "users" to take part in a nonhierarchical collaboration to contribute to the life course of a work. The natural trajectory of decay and the consequent contributions of others are the very content of the work. Considered in this way, Gu's works are frameworks for participation, the outcome of which is always contingent.

THE CONTINGENT LIFE OF THE ARTWORK

Many of Gu Dexin's installations created in the late 1980s through the 1990s were conceived for a particular place and time and for a single occasion. Although a small handful unexpectedly survive, these site-specific works were not conceived with re-presentation in mind, and most were eventually destroyed, obliterated, or lost. However, in approximately the last decade of his career, Gu created works that expanded beyond strict conceptualization of site specificity, becoming less focused on Gu's intervention to a specific site than they were about a concept that could be recreated or re-produced in different venues. They may not have been necessarily bound to a specific time and place and were, in some cases, purchased by collectors. They thus presumed a certain longevity. The shift seems to represent the differing life courses Gu set in motion for his artworks and suggests different possibilities for the stakeholders who must make decisions about the future of Gu's work.

ONE SITE, ONE VIEWING

Many of Gu Dexin's works were not intended to be re-exhibited but were rather conceived for a specific exhibition, at a particular site, and for a set duration. Responding to a particular location, its physical elements and qualities, and the site's history, meaning, or association, Gu used elements of the site as part of his media to create an interplay with his materials that commented on the site itself. For *1990-09-06* (fig. 4), a 1990 plastic work created for the exhibition *Next Phase*, Gu adorned the unoccupied Victorian-era Wapping Hydraulic Power Station, which housed its original hydraulic equipment and machinery. Gu suspended undulating torch-manipulated and charred plastic from the ceiling.

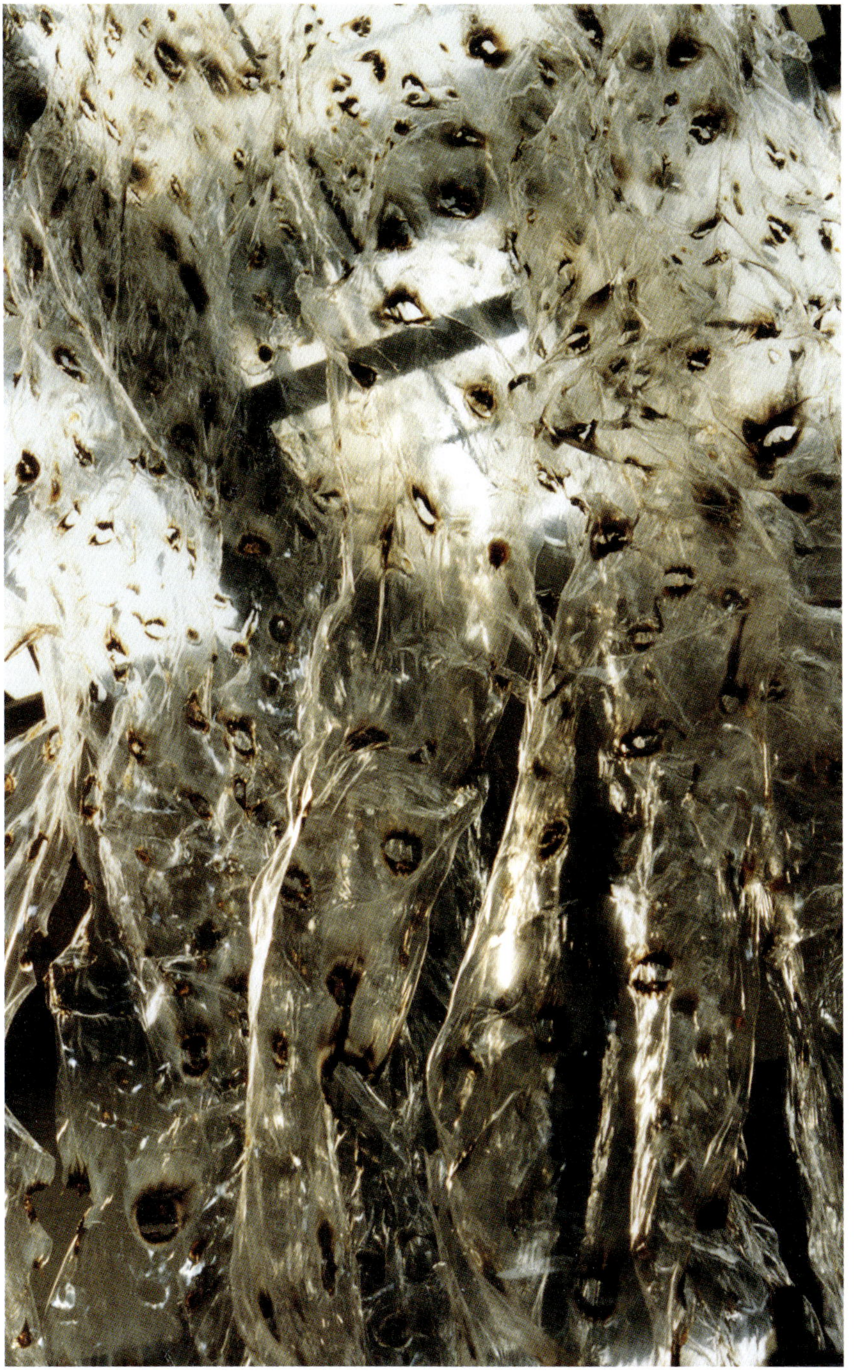

Figure 4 Gu Dexin, *1990-09-06*, 1990. Burned plastic. Installation view, *Next Phase*, Wapping Hydraulic Power Station, London, 1990. Hans van Dijk Archive. Courtesy of Gu Dexin and Asia Art Archive.

The plastic pieces stretched across the room, covering the original hydraulic equipment and machinery and terminating gracefully onto the ground. Gu's view on the artwork's life and its potential for re-exhibition can be guessed using this odd fact: when the exhibition came to a close, the work was collected not by Gu, but by the custodians who mistook it as trash. In 1996, as part of the *Shelter* exhibition in the Dutch city of Breda, Gu created a work on a private estate with a later nineteenth-century villa (fig. 5). Gu placed six mirrors on the lawn in front of the villa horizontally, to create a reflection of the edifice. Hidden below each mirror was more than twenty kilograms of raw meat, while five thousand plastic flowers infused with Dior Poison perfume surrounded the mirrors. Together, the meat and perfume gave off a powerful aroma. While the installation remained on view for two months, the fresh meat prematurely disappeared. The parkland where the villa was located was home to abundant wildlife, which quickly pilfered the meat.

With installations as exemplified by Gu's works, place and space are selected relative to the specific character of the work, and they are then considered integral elements of it. A kind of attachment occurs. The host environment is referred to by the work, which the work then reconfigures. Space becomes a material, emerges as the center of the work, and provides the means through which the work is physically entered. Exhibited elsewhere, the same work may have a different meaning. Occasions for re-exhibition thus raise questions about and require negotiation of whether and how to display a work outside of its original context.

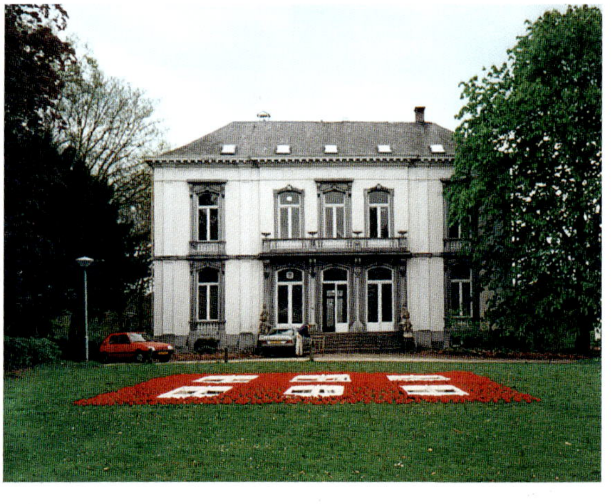

Figure 5 Gu Dexin, *1996-05-05*, 1996. Artificial flowers, wood, mirror, meat. Installation view, Chassé Kazerne, Breda, 1996. Courtesy of David Spalding.

BEYOND A SINGLE SITE

Gu Dexin did not limit his work to large installations and produced a body of smaller-scale works. In many cases, these involved similar materials to his site-specific installations, but these works were (or had the potential to be) exhibited multiple times.

In 1997, Gu created *1997-5-20* for *Another Long March: Chinese Conceptual and Installation Art in the Nineties*. This work contained pieces of raw meat held within a transparent container that sat atop a tall, mirrored column installed in the courtyard of Chassé Kazerne, the main building of an expansive former military complex east of Breda. Comparable to the *Shelter* exhibition, but on a significantly smaller scale, *2000-4-11* (2000) (one of the purchased works) involved a chair with a cushion stuffed with raw meat (fig. 6). Displayed at Shanghai's Eastlink Gallery, a long vermillion-red carpet runner stretched from the chair along the floor to the wall. Across from the chair, set at eye level, the same vermillion-red carpet is showcased in a gold frame. The viewer was invited to sit in the chair and experience the feeling and smell of the spongy, rotting flesh while contemplating the framed flat red plane.

Gu was known for rejecting the commercialization of art throughout his career, yet smaller-scale works such as *1997-5-20* and *2000-4-11* might indicate that he began to consider the market. According to Karen Smith, this was caused by not only his shifting interests but also the difficulties caused by the expanding scale of his works and the subconscious influence of collectors' desire to preserve his work.[14] His experience of the pressures of the art market may thus have impacted how he practiced.[15] In creating works that were (or could be) acquired, Gu also created new possibilities for the lifespan of a work, as acquired works may imply a longer timeline of deterioration. Acquisition can also imply the work's preservation for an even longer period and hence the intervention required for such preservation. Finally, by implicating a broader range of viewers—such as conservators, collectors, and gallerists—these works suggest the possibility that Gu was exploring different kinds of viewer participation. As Gu himself stated, in explaining his use of dates as titles: "From my personal perspective, the inscription of a date also signifies the opening or closing of an event. For me, this date is a closing. But for others, it is the beginning."[16] These date titles mark the precise moment that Gu relinquishes his active role; the work's material transformations and viewer participations are set into motion, and the life of the work has begun.[17]

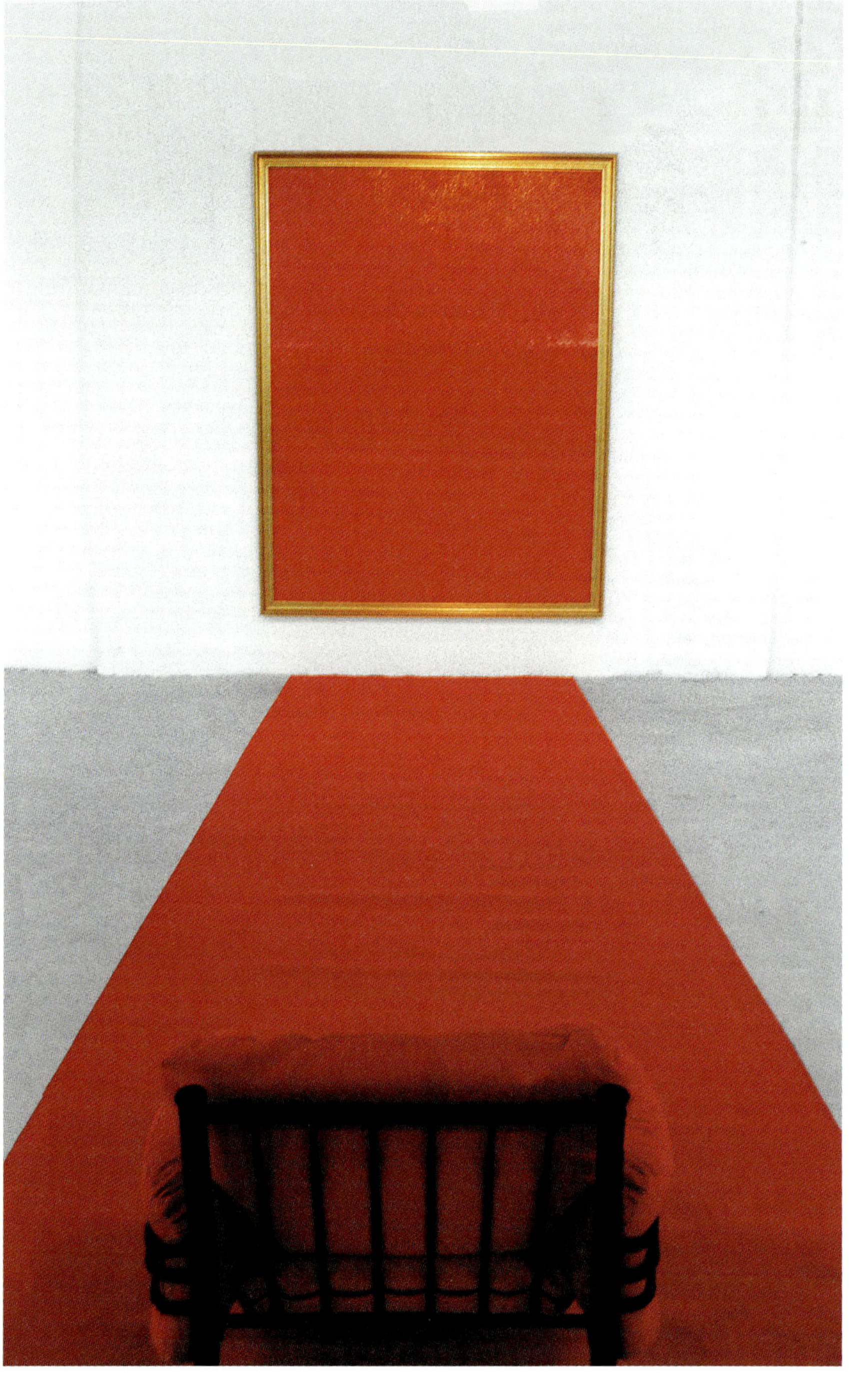

Figure 6 Gu Dexin, *2000-4-11*, 2000. Red carpet, upholstered chair, meat, and gilded frame, dimensions variable. M+ Sigg Collection, Hong Kong. © Gu Dexin.

CONSERVING GU'S WORK
CASE STUDIES IN A PRINCIPLE-DRIVEN APPROACH

In this section, I present two cases demonstrating how a conservation decision-making process informed by the tenets of Gu Dexin's work can lead to different outcomes depending on the artwork being considered. The first describes the challenges posed by the preservation efforts associated with *2004-6-16*, the Chinese collector-commissioned installation completed in 2004 in Beijing that was later acquired by a museum. Those efforts challenged traditional professional ethics and conservation standards, namely by considering the option to surrender the life of the work, the option chosen in the end. The second describes the deliberations involved in the re-exhibition of *Untitled*, the 1989 installation from *Magiciens de la terre*. The instability of the ephemeral materials used in the work raises questions about its perpetuity and best practices for the work's care and exhibition that also respect the artist's beliefs regarding adaptation to contingencies throughout the life of the work. The outcome of each case study evolved through the collaborative participation and decision making of the work's stakeholders.

2004-6-16

The fat-filled iron-and-glass installation *2004-6-16* (figs. 7–8) was originally commissioned by Guan Yi, one of China's most important contemporary art collectors, for an industrial building in Songzhuang, a Beijing arts district. The vast space served as both the collector's new residence and the site of the Guan Yi Contemporary Art Archive (Guan Yi dangdai yishu wenxianguan), which housed his collection. In 2013, Guan Yi donated the work to the Hong Kong museum M+. Shortly after, Guan Yi informed the museum that the Chinese government, which held the building's lease, planned to demolish the building and that its contents, including *2004-6-16*, had to be removed. The prospect of removing Gu Dexin's work presented obvious problems: its massive scale and its attachment to the structure of the building, to say nothing of the five tons of pork fat that had been liquefying, solidifying, and decomposing for a decade. In addition to the work's size, weight, organic content, and overall condition, the logistics involved in removing and transporting it through Beijing and exporting it to Hong Kong also proved complicated. It soon became clear to the curatorial/conservation team (on which I was the project lead and conservator) that Gu's work could not be removed from the building, neither whole nor in pieces. The other option was to allow the work to be demolished with the building.

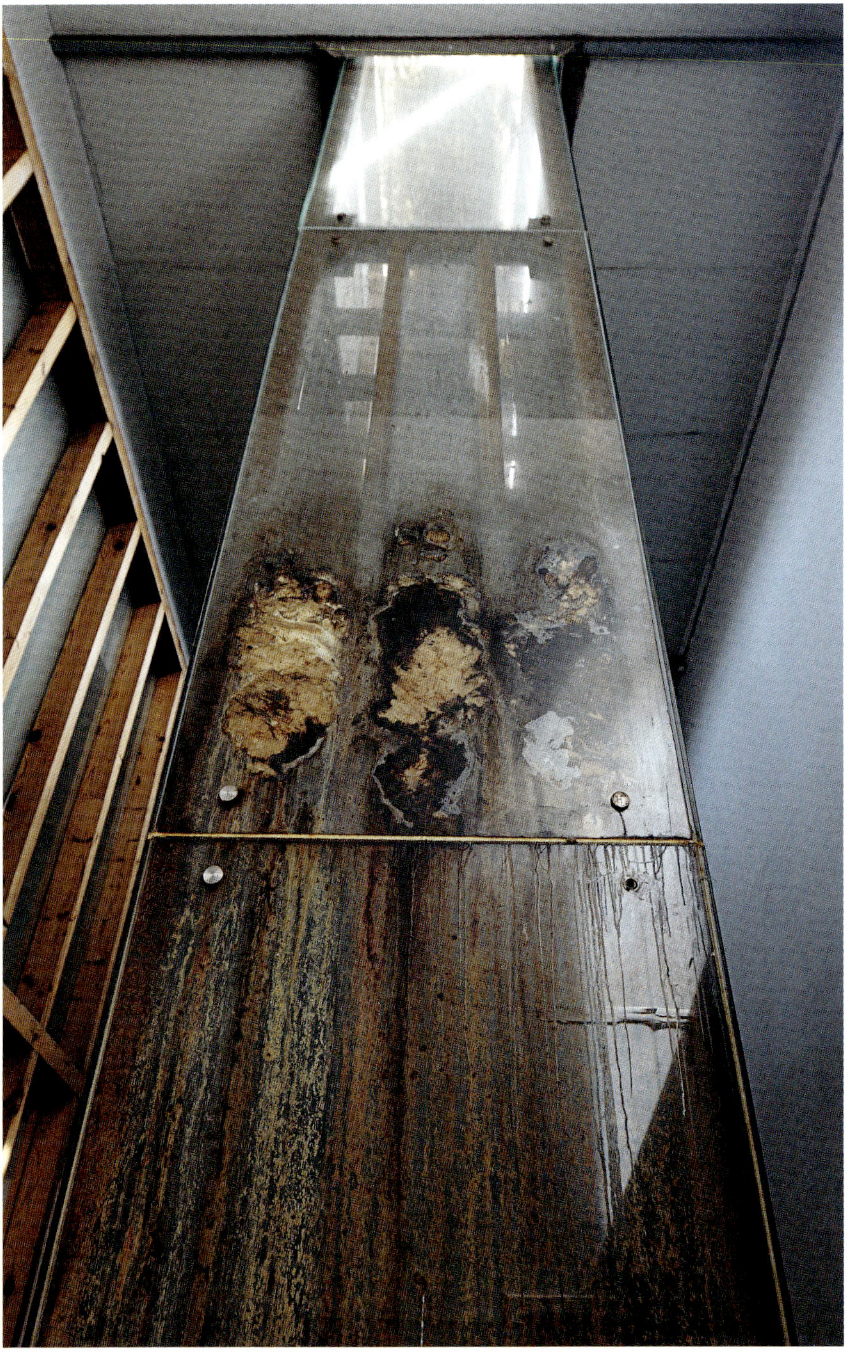

Figure 7 Gu Dexin, *2004-6-16*, 2004. Animal visceral fat, iron, and glass, overall: 372 × 663 × 88 cm. M+, Hong Kong. Gift of Guan Yi, 2013. © Gu Dexin.

At the same time, both options—allowing the work's destruction and removing it from its original context—would violate the classic conservation doctrine.[18]

In the case of *2004-6-16*, our decision of how to proceed was informed by the artist's sanction. Philosopher Sherri Irvin has proposed that an artist's actions and communications that convey the artist's effective intentions for a work (which she calls "artist sanction") give us better information about a work than what is more standardly termed "artist intention."[19] In 2014, Gu hesitantly accepted the M+ curatorial and conservation teams' request to discuss the work's fate. Anticipating Gu's recalcitrance, multiple members of the team took part in the phone call with Gu, which leveraged various members' expertise to coax answers from the artist. As expected, Gu largely refused to answer any detailed questions regarding his work. He was also adamant about not becoming involved with any aspect of its reconstruction or destruction. He expressed clearly, although laconically, his view that *2004-6-16* is inextricably linked to the site. Removing any component of the work, such as the fat, he noted, would be inconsequential, because the work's life span was ending. Gu's statement implies his belief that the specific place, time, and environment were all essential

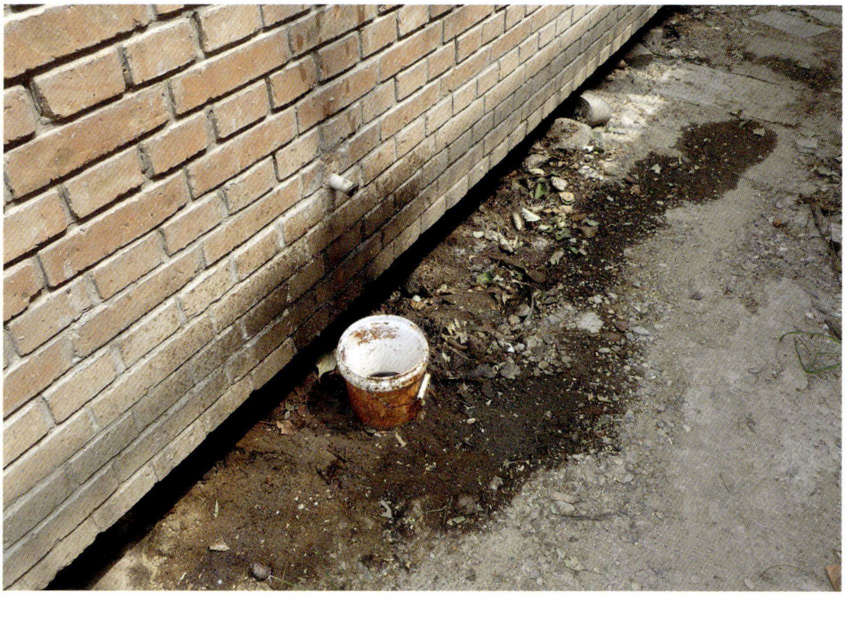

Figure 8 Bucket located outside of the Guan Yi Art Archive, collecting fat that dripped from *2004-06-16*. © Gu Dexin.

to the work's existence: he had created *2004-6-16* as a site-specific work and never intended it to be mobile. The character of installation art forces us to preserve not only the object itself but also the meanings deriving from its original location and the experiences the work provokes in that site. In the case of *2004-6-16*, the loss of its original location—a compact space shared by the collector's office, which the installation overwhelmed with its immense scale and sensory assaults—were essential to the work. Any reconstruction with one but not the other would likely not be authentic or complete, and would only offer a glimpse of the original.[20] Its intent and impact on viewers would be changed, thus rendering the work meaningless. The life of *2004-6-16* therefore ended in 2014, when the building where the installation resided for nearly a decade was demolished.

UNTITLED

Gu's plastic installation for *Magiciens de la terre* (fig. 9) offers a case for examining the repeated exhibition of one of his works. Although the work was thought to

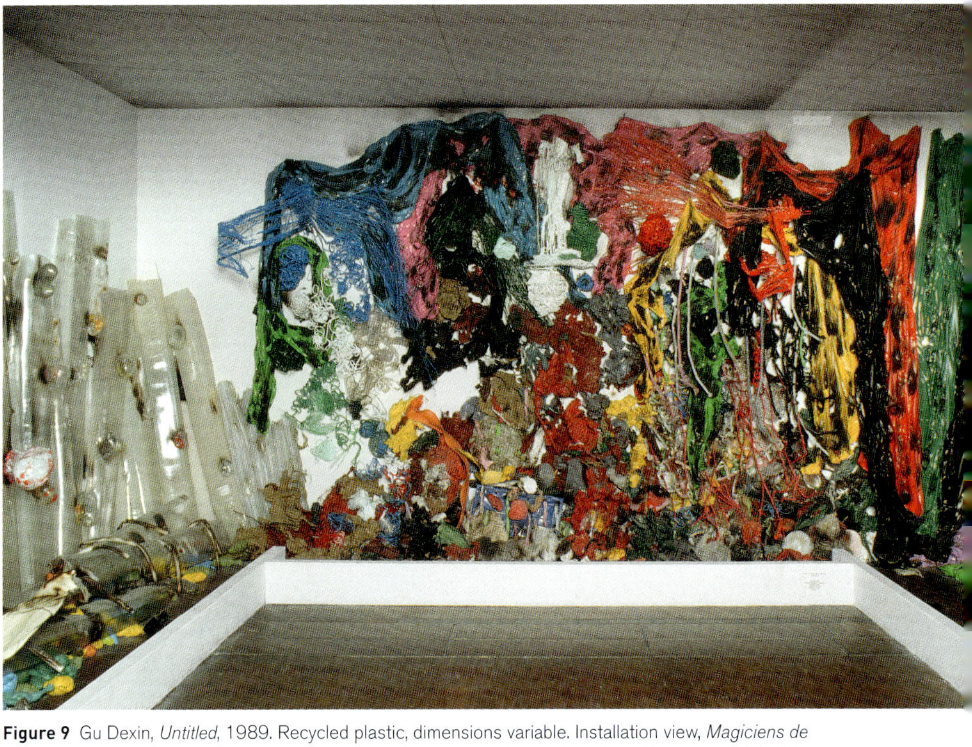

Figure 9 Gu Dexin, *Untitled*, 1989. Recycled plastic, dimensions variable. Installation view, *Magiciens de la terre*, Centre Pompidou, Grande galerie, La Grande Halle de la Villette, Paris, May 18–August 28, 1989. Photo: Béatrice Hatala / Konstantinos Ignatiadis. © CNAC / MNAM / Dist. RMN-Grand Palais / Art Resource, NY.

have been destroyed after the Centre Pompidou exhibition, *Untitled* is actually held in the collection of Musée d'art contemporain de Lyon.[21] Since its first showing, the work has been exhibited on four occasions: at the Musée d'art contemporain de Lyon in the 1990s; the UCCA Center for Contemporary Art (Beijing) in 2007; *The Allure of Matter: Material Art from China* exhibition at Los Angeles County Museum of Art in 2019; and *The Allure of Matter* exhibition at the University of Chicago's Smart Museum of Art in 2020 (fig. 10). Because Gu repeatedly declined to take part in the decision-making process regarding the re-installation of this work, it fell in each case to the exhibiting institution or the various stakeholders involved to decide how to display the work. The Lyon and UCCA shows were installed while Gu was still active; however, it is unknown whether he participated in the decision-making process or if he rejected or endorsed the work's installation. Gu did not contribute to or advise on the Los Angeles County Museum of Art or the Smart Museum installations; instead, both organizations consulted with the Lyon representative and attempted to replicate the assembly of the 1989 Paris showing.

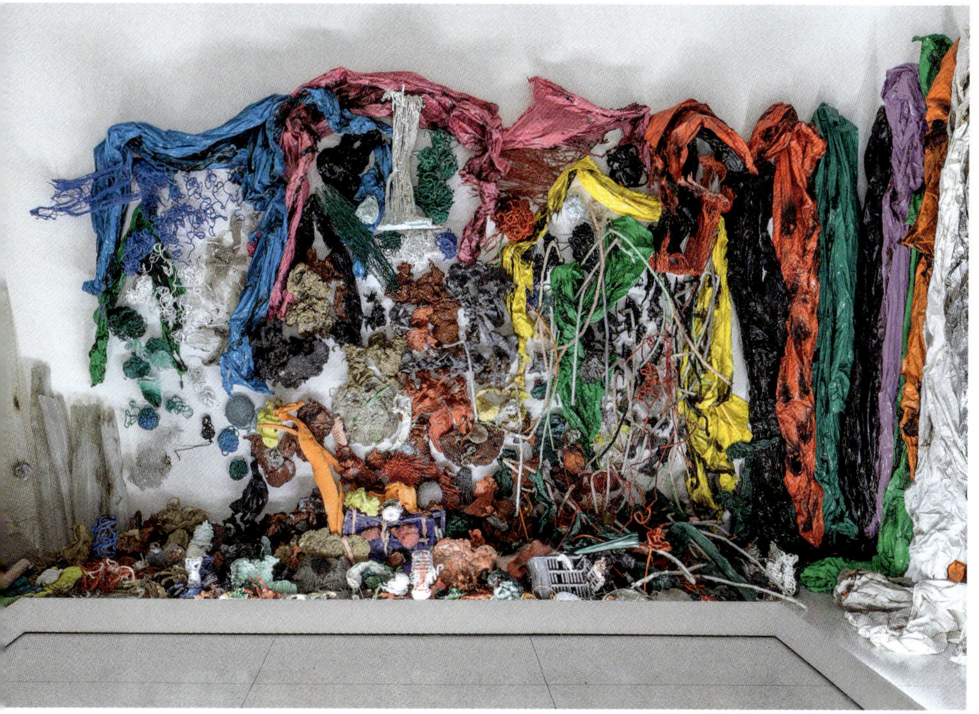

Figure 10 Gu Dexin, *Untitled*, 1989. Installation view, *The Allure of Matter: Material Art from China*, Smart Museum of Art, The University of Chicago, Chicago, 2020. Courtesy of the Smart Museum of Art.

The deterioration of *Untitled* is dynamic and active and is indicated by the embrittlement, distortion, cracking, stickiness, and odor of the plastic that composes the work, characteristics that were not present in 1989. Many of the plastic masses that have shattered as decay turned them brittle are thus smaller than their original state; the plastic sheets have become sticky and self-amalgamating and have fused into clumps. The inherently unstable pieces weakened, deteriorated, and incurred damage with each installation. The Musée d'art contemporain de Lyon understood well the work's active state of degradation but chose to favor the "message of the work," allowing for transformations in showing and lending the work.[22] This choice challenged each establishment exhibiting the work to solve not only how each component was to be installed, but also the work's final shape. Each installation was guided by the images from the Centre Pompidou and by cues from preceding shows, and drew upon a diagram containing the original gallery dimensions. With each reinstallation, alterations inevitably followed, as every manipulation or even handling of the work's components changed them and the installation still further: each occurrence and material transition is unpredictable, with a life of its own.

For the Smart Museum exhibition (for which I was the consulting conservator), the team carried out a great effort to reactivate the original 1989 manifestation by arranging individual pieces in their respective location and by matching the char marks that show where Gu directed the torch while assembling the work in Paris. This was similar to assembling a pictorial jigsaw puzzle but on a vastly different scale. This effort was done not only to maintain the physical traces of the process of creation, but also because the volume of pieces in the work necessitated a systematic approach for efficient installation and deinstallation. The approach also helped to identify needs for tackling actively deteriorating components for future exhibition, especially the two additional venues scheduled for *The Allure of Matter* exhibition.[23] Midway through the installation, however, the systematic approach imposed at the outset failed. It was impossible to distinguish and place each piece in its respective location: many pieces had transmuted and morphed to the point of being unrecognizable; others had broken into indistinguishable parts. Even when a piece could be identified, it could not always be hung as it had been in previous exhibitions; in many cases, the hole once used to hang the plastic sheet on a nail had torn, shredded, or shattered.

Once team members realized the impossible nature of their task, they were no longer bound by the structure that was imposed at the installation's onset. In fact, being forced to abandon the systematic approach activated independence and engaged consciousness in each participating member of the installation team, each of whom eventually contributed to the improvisations that culminated in the final installation. A dialogue between the work and each participant emerged. The physical touching sparked the participants' responsiveness, leading them to make autonomous decisions: they placed pieces in a way that made sense to them rather than simply copying the static images of the original installation. Their new approach also suppressed hierarchy, making way for equal contribution from each person involved (art installers, registrars, curator, and conservator) per Gu's vision: his philosophy deliberately rejects standards and normativity but also attempts to establish a parity between the artist, material, and viewer, as had the groups to which Gu belonged in the 1980s. In fact, at each venue where *Untitled* was installed, a sort of activation seems to have occurred with all parties involved. Installation team members became collaborators in the work—picking up pieces and carrying them into the exhibition space, where they paced, deliberated, and engaged with each piece before deciding on a final placement. In the act of reinstallation, they took on a part similar to those who carted away the rotting viscera, the wildlife that stole pieces of meat, or custodians who disposed of Gu's installation.[24] With *Untitled*, while not visually identical, each installation is recognizable as the same artwork, despite modifications of the work's spatial design, surrounding exhibition space, or diverse participants involved. Because of the material's fragility, each future installation will transform more pieces, eventually leading to the work's obliteration, perhaps within a decade or two. At a certain point of deterioration, installations could display simply what remains—piles of undefinable shapes—or the work could be put to final rest as was *2004-6-16*. The resulting decision would consider the opinions of each stakeholder involved. The work evolves through a combination of the various factors at play, active and passive, human and nonhuman.

CONCLUSION
A LIFE BEYOND THE ARTIST

Gu Dexin is a nonconformist who eschews conventional systems of form, structure, and hierarchy. He has a consistent understanding of the relationship between the impermanence of his works and the natural process of their transformations.[25] After Gu completes a work of art, it is turned over to its natural and inevitable material transformations; the materials in his works gradually decay, often turning into unintelligible, unrecognizable, indefinable substances with the passing of time, and these transformations may in turn activate viewer and stakeholder participation, as well as possible further transformation. His small-scale pieces, temporary site-specific works, and other installations create different possibilities for a work's life course, as exemplified by the two case studies discussed in this chapter. They demonstrate how nonhierarchical participation—whether by organisms, wildlife, or humans—is at the center of Gu's work and can lead to collaboration that transforms a work's trajectory.

Conservators responsible for the care of contemporary art face the difficult situation of tending to works that are often made from unstable materials or that are intangible. Traditional conservation approaches often do not apply. Even new models proposed for specific types of works may not necessarily fit for works like Gu's, which are difficult to categorize. Decisions may run counter to classic conservation principles associated with caring for a piece of art, such as reversibility or minimum intervention. Preserving the material substance of an artwork may be impossible, and the original material or materials might need to be replaced. Both of these steps conflict with the notion of respecting the original object's integrity, yet both are often pursued. Therefore, the approach taken for each work must be both unique and interdisciplinary.

In considering an approach to Gu's work more broadly, we must establish the foundations of a suitable decision-making process. These should include the examination and review of participation in Gu's body of work; knowledge of his views regarding his works and their preservation and presentation (gathered through manifestos and statements in interviews); and an understanding of Gu's participation, including nonparticipation, in his work. This body of knowledge will guide us to approach what is left of Gu's earlier installations in a way that adheres to his principles and philosophy: that after a work is created, it assumes its own life, involving material transformations and the participation of viewers and caretakers, and often leads to an outcome that is the result of its particular contingencies. Thus, a conservation approach that is faithful to his vision and work requires not an inflexible structure or a set of rules whose ultimate goal is preservation, but rather a negotiation between custodians, individual collectors, institutions, curators, and conservators, who work collectively to decide what is advisable for a given work. When a site-specific work cannot be removed, preservation practices can opt to protect its authenticity by assessing the idea it embodies, which is done by analyzing its significance and values according to the sanctions of its creator. In the case of *2004-6-16*, the decision making encompassed stakeholders who included the artist, the donor and his assistants, curators, conservators, and museum staff members, all of whom helped determine the best course of action for the artwork. These considerations apply also to works that can be more easily re-exhibited. While many of Gu's earlier installations were created for a particular environment and one appearance, a number of earlier installations, such as those noted in this chapter, have been shown repeatedly or restaged using new materials. However, there are also installations whose physical objects are actively deteriorating or cannot be replaced or reiterated, because they have been individually manipulated by the artist himself or will be further damaged with each installation, such as the case with *Untitled*. At times, the decision may result in the artwork's death. This is a choice inimical to conservation's traditional mission. But as David Lowenthal has argued, it is a fate that awaits all artworks in the end:

> Every inanimate object, like every living being, undergoes continual alteration ultimately perishing. . . . Things either morph into other entities, dismember into fragments or dissolve into unrecognizable components. . . . Gradual change maybe imperceptible within the span of a human lifetime or even longer, but it is eventually inexorable. Few things are made to last; evanescence is the *raison d'être* of the vast majority of artifacts.[26]

NOTES

1. Orianna Cacchione and Sara A. Moy, "Apples, Bananas and Meat: Re-Creating Gu Dexin's Artworks in His Absence" (presentation, College Art Association Annual Conference, Los Angeles, CA, February 22, 2018). Gu criticized the notion of a retrospective as "merely a habit formed by a market-driven system; a habit that he sees no reason to entertain." Karen A. Smith, *Nine Lives: The Birth of Avant-Garde Art in New China*, updated ed. (Hong Kong: Timezone 8, 2008), 194.
2. Problems in conservation can be complex, uncertain, and multifaceted, thus affecting a work's attributed value. Stakeholders in conservation can be defined as the parties making transparent decisions that are flexible to changing circumstances while bringing the knowledge and values to inform conservation decisions of a work. Stakeholders can include conservators, artists, estates, foundations, historians, curators, artist assistants, collectors, museums, etc.
3. On the conservation of performance and participatory art, see Hélia Pereira Marçal, "Conservation in an Era of Participation," *Journal of the Institute of Conservation* 40, no. 2 (2017): 97–104. On visual documentation, see Martha Buskirk, *The Contingent Object of Contemporary Art* (Cambridge, MA: The MIT Press, 2003); IJsbrand Hummelen and Tatja Scholte, "Capturing the Ephemeral and Unfinished: Archiving and Documentation as Conservation Strategies of Transient (as Transfinite) Contemporary Art," *Techné*, no. 24 (2006): 5–11; Harald Kraemer, "Art Is Redeemed, Mystery Is Gone: The Documentation of Contemporary Art," in *Theorizing Digital Cultural Heritage: A Critical Discourse*, ed. Fiona Cameron and Sarah Kenderdine (Cambridge, MA: The MIT Press, 2007), 193–222; and Salvador Muñoz Viñas, *Contemporary Theory of Conservation* (Oxford: Butterworth-Heinemann, 2004). On ethnological models or concepts in conservation, see V. E. J. P. van Saaze, "From Intention to Interaction: Reframing the Artist's Interview in Conservation Research," in *Art d'aujourd'hui patrimoine de demain*, ed. M. Stefanaggi and R. Hocquette (Paris: SFIIC /Institut National du Patrimoine, 2009), 20–28. On autoethnography in conservation, see Sanneke Stigter, "Autoethnography as a New Approach in Conservation," *Studies in Conservation* 61, no. S2 (2016): 227–32.
4. Smith, *Nine Lives*.
5. Peggy Wang, "Responding to the World: Contemporary Chinese Art, Exhibitions, and Criticism in the 1990s" (PhD diss., University of Chicago, 2010), 138.
6. Wang Luyan, "Tactile Art Statement," *Fine Arts in China* 35 (August 1988): 1.
7. Hou Hanru, "Beyond the Cynical: China Avant-Garde in the 1990s," *Art Asia Pacific* 3, no. 1 (1996): 51; Smith, *Nine Lives*, 205–6.
8. Hou Hanru, "Beyond the Cynical," 49–50; Wang, "Responding to the World," 137.
9. Smith, *Nine Lives*, 207.
10. Wu Hung with Wang Huangsheng and Feng Boyi, *Reinterpretation: A Decade of Experimental Chinese Art: 1990–2000* (Guangzhou: Guangdong Museum of Art, 2002), 306; Smith, *Nine Lives*, 201.
11. I do not discuss in this chapter Gu's later work using other organic media.
12. Gu Dexin, interview by Melissa Chiu, in *Between Past and Future: New Photography and Video from China*, ed. Wu Hung and Christopher Phillips (Chicago: David and Alfred Smart Museum of Art, 2004), 177–78.
13. "Collaboration," Cambridge Dictionary, accessed July 14, 2021, https://dictionary.cambridge.org/us/dictionary/english/collaboration.
14. Smith, *Nine Lives*, 194.

15. Cacchione and Moy, "Apples, Bananas and Meat."
16. Smith, *Nine Lives*, 207. Gu has also stated, "The date is also a way to avoid the influence of language on work." Heinz-Norbert Jocks and Gu Dexin, "Ein Sofa, gepolstert mit vergänglichem Fleisch" [A sofa upholstered with perishable flesh], *Kunstforum International* 194 (2008): 150–59.
17. Smith, *Nine Lives*, 208.
18. Sara A. Moy, "*2004-6-16* to *2014-8-15*: The Birth and Death of a Work by Gu Dexin," *Studies in Conservation* 61, no. S2 (2016): 137–41.
19. Sherri Irvin, "The Artist's Sanction in Contemporary Art," *Journal of Aesthetics and Art Criticism* 63, no. 4 (2005): 315–26.
20. Documentation based on written and visual elements produces a comprehensive archive similar to the conservation approaches used for traditional pieces. Such records help capture the overall viewing experience and enable future access. The information recorded also facilitates reconstruction efforts should future stakeholders decide to resurrect *2004-6-16*. This is especially useful for site-specific works re-exhibited in a museum context, where change or loss will inevitably occur. See Moy, "*2004-6-16* to *2014-8-15*."
21. Philip Tinari, "What Gu Dexin Left," *China File*, April 9, 2012, accessed March 3, 2021, https://www.chinafile.com/what-gu-dexin-left; and UCCA, exhibition wall text for *Gu Dexin: The Important Thing Is Not the Meat*, Beijing, 2012. How *Untitled* arrived at the museum in Lyon is a mystery, as no transaction record can be found. Charlotte Maday (registrar of the Musée d'art contemporain de Lyon), conversation with the author, January 28, 2020.
22. Charlotte Maday, in discussion with the author, 2020.
23. The work was scheduled to travel to two subsequent venues, but because of COVID-19, the exhibition ended in August 2020 at the Smart Museum.
24. This is based on my personal experience installing the work as well as the accounts of Charlotte Maday. Maday installed the work twice, first at LACMA and then at the Smart Museum with me, and experienced this activation at both sites.
25. Xiaoyu Weng, "Gu Dexin: Iconoclast," trans. Katy Pinke, *LEAP* Vol 14 (May 12, 2012), accessed June 20, 2021, http://www.leapleapleap.com/2012/05/gu-dexin-iconoclast/.
26. David Lowenthal, "A Sea-Change Rich and Strange," in *The Explicit Material: Inquiries on the Intersection of Curatorial and Conservation Cultures*, ed. Hanna B. Hölling, Francesca G. Bewer, and Katharina Ammann (Leiden: Brill, 2019), 17.

Immaterial Materiality

Song Dong's Multimedia Works with Water, Photography, and Video

Nancy P. Lin

In 1992 the Chinese artist Song Dong (b. 1966) created his first work using water, a material that would feature prominently in his artistic practice up to the present. *Frying Water* (*Chao shui*, 1992) (fig. 1), an early conceptual experiment, reveals several of the artist's key interests in and approaches to water. In this work, Song recorded on video his attempt to stir-fry water, an impossible performative act that caused the water to evaporate and leave only a thin film of oil in the empty wok. Song's treatment of water as an object that can be stir-fried revealed its intangible and ephemeral qualities. Remarking on this incredibly brief work, which lasted only one minute and forty seconds, Song noted, "I focused on the end which is Nothing."[1] The artist's actions resulted in an empty wok, rather than a stir-fried meal—he may as well not have done anything. Audiences might have assumed so if not for the video recording of this action, which serves as

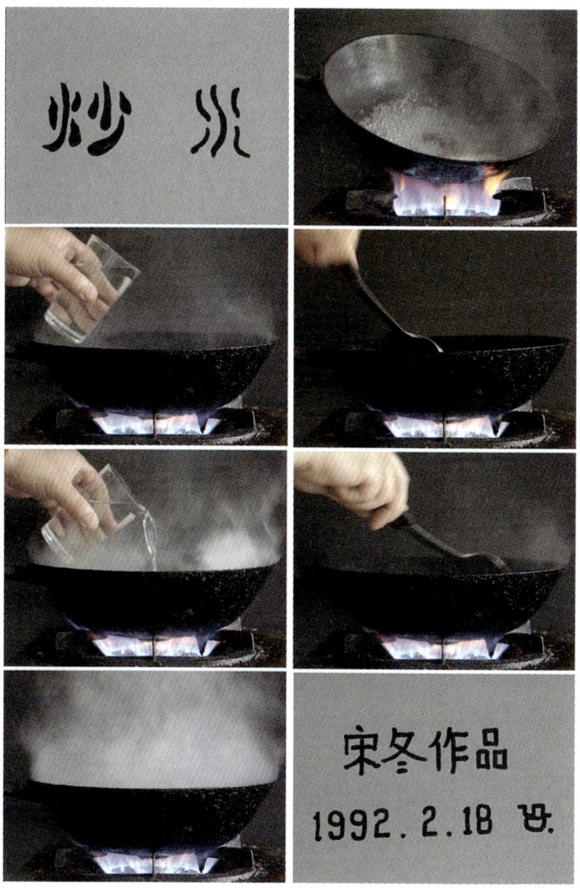

Figure 1 Song Dong, *Frying Water*, 1992. Single channel video, 1:40 minutes running time. Courtesy of Pace Gallery. © Song Dong.

the only evidence of the action's existence. As I have argued elsewhere, this seemingly absurd action illustrates several principles that Song would continue to explore in his water works up to the present.[2] First, attempts to treat water as a bounded concrete object often cause it to evade one's grasp and disappear. Second, any action with or upon water always *appears* futile, as if nothing happened at all. Finally, video or photo documentation of the water-based work often serves as a counterweight to the fugitive nature of water.

Song's extensive work with water since the early 1990s has been regarded by art historian Wu Hung as an example of "Material Art," an artistic tendency in China beginning in the late 1980s and 1990s featuring an artist's consistent use of one unconventional material to produce a broad range of works that foreground its materiality as central to artistic meaning.[3] Art historian David Clarke has also argued for a "watery turn in contemporary Chinese art," situating Song's works within a plethora of artworks that all appear to use water to symbolically and subversively contest state ideology.[4] Foregrounding the centrality of water, these accounts have nevertheless overlooked the ways in which Song's unique experiments with the material were deeply integrated with a set of parallel experiments with the material properties of video and photography, two developing modes of new media that the artist widely embraced throughout the 1990s. As I will argue, an understanding of the connections that the artist drew between the material of water and the mediums of video and photography offers new insights into Song's multimedial artistic approach and his contributions to broader artistic developments during this period.

Song's early adoption of video in this 1992 water-based work is significant within the development of video art, a relatively new art form first introduced to China in the late 1980s.[5] While a select number of contemporary Chinese artists began to work with video during this period, limitations in the accessibility of video equipment prevented a broader integration of the medium into contemporary art practice until the 1990s. As art historian Katherine Grube has pointed out, with the exception of a few artists, video was most commonly used during the 1980s as journalistic documentation of performance and art events commissioned by state-run television stations.[6] Many artists who sought to experiment creatively with video had to borrow large, unwieldy equipment from television studios or other professional photography studios. Not owning a video recorder himself, Song borrowed one from a wedding studio to create *Frying Water*. Fascinated by the new medium, he saved up all his money to purchase his own camcorder the following year for the enormous sum of 8,000 RMB. Song's acquisition of a Sony Hi8 camera, a compact handheld camcorder as opposed to the larger bulky professional equipment, offered the artist greater flexibility to incorporate the medium into highly intimate artistic experiments that blurred the clear-cut distinctions between performance and documentation, art and everyday life. In *Frying Water*, for example, the video documentation is the only evidence of the work's existence, and in fact, constitutes the artwork itself, which Song has also designated as his first video work.[7]

As Song's first attempt to combine the use of water with the video medium, *Frying Water* represented his preliminary understanding of the ephemeral material conditions under which the reproductive image might become an essential component of the artwork itself, rather than just a documentation of it. Many of Song's subsequent experiments with water further integrated video along with serial photography, using the three as analogous artistic mediums to think through one another. Beginning in the mid-1990s, Song's pioneering explorations coincided with the work of other multimedia video artists and conceptual photographers who sought to liberate video and photography from their role as mere documentations of reality. Within this milieu, Song's unique approach to video and photography, by way of his experiments with water, bridged material art's emphasis on materiality with video art and conceptual photography's focus on image.[8] Contrary to the materially specific connotations of the term "material art," the artist's works with water raised new issues surrounding the relationship between material reality and visual phenomenon.

Bringing together artist interviews and visual analysis, I examine the intersections between water, photography, and video in Song's practice to show how the artist intermedially combined each "material" to explore what he called their "immaterial" (*fei wuzhi*) qualities.[9] As I will demonstrate, Song understood the relationship between materiality and "immateriality" across multiple nested equivalencies between water, photography, and video. Not constrained within a static notion of materiality, the artist employed water's various transformations between solid, liquid, and gas, in combination with photography and video's material properties, to reveal the three mediums' intermedial potential. Exceeding an illustration of their basic physical properties, Song used water, video, and photography's material transformations and perceptual effects as metaphors for "immaterial" conceptual ideas. Exploring the metaphysical theme of transience, Song used water, photography, and video to materialize the continuity between presence and absence, visible and invisible, material and immaterial. Contextualized within the proliferation of artistic mediums during the 1990s, Song's fluid approach to materiality underscored his broad understanding of material as an artistic "medium" or, literally, an intermediary between two things or two states. By engaging photography and video through water, Song not only shed light on the medium-specific intersections between photography and video, but also illuminated the intermedial nature of all artistic media.

WATER AS MULTIMEDIA

Song's exploration of water's fluid material properties mirrored the breakdown of single-format art practices during a period when new art forms such as installation, performance, video, and photography were freely combined to create mixed-media (*zonghe meiti*) art. A student of oil painting in the Fine Arts Department of Capital Normal University (Shoudu shifan daxue) in Beijing, Song graduated in 1989 and quickly transitioned to working in installation, performance, and video art. Song's works from the early 1990s onward featured an assortment of everyday objects including used books, address plates, wooden windows and doors, and household items.[10] These works attest to Song's broad interest in the materials and subject matters of his own personal daily life and urban environment. According to the artist, his transition away from painting in the early 1990s was not so much a medium-specific rejection of painting, but rather a discovery of other more suitable media for conveying these concerns.[11]

While art academies in China continued to teach within the delineated confines of oil painting, traditional-style painting and calligraphy, and sculpture, artists had begun experimenting with new media and materials since the 1980s. Song's account is consistent with what Wu has described as the emergence of Material Art in the late 1980s when individual artists began to explore new forms of contemporary art beyond oil painting.[12] Whereas oil painting had been central to the generation of artists who participated in the '85 Art New Wave ('85 Meishu xinchao), a modern art movement deeply influenced by Western modernism and philosophy, by the late 1980s and 1990s its centrality was beginning to be eclipsed. Through the steady increase of information on global contemporary art practices and artists' own international travels, practitioners experimented with installation, performance, site-specific art, video, photography, and conceptual art. At the same time, inspired by materials found from their everyday lives, artists also began to use a plethora of unusual materials such as concrete, hair, and thread, among others. Some, like the artist Song, selected unique materials with which they would work extensively for long periods of time. No longer committed to one particular art form, however, artists in the 1990s worked fluidly across multiple formats.

While Song experimented with a wide range of found materials and artistic formats throughout the 1990s, water was singular in his practice as *the* multimedia material *par excellence*. Occurring naturally as a solid, liquid, or vapor, water offered a range of material manifestations for the artist to utilize. Rather than working with one material state, however, Song's process-based works with water highlighted the material's transition between states, pointing to its intermedial fluidity. In this way, Song honed in on water's transformational quality, using it as a root metaphor for broader conceptual ideas.[13] In two works from 1995, the artist used melting ice and evaporating water to explore themes of memory, secrecy, and erasure. For the site-specific installation *Secret Divulging (Leaking)* (*Xiemi*, 1995) (fig. 2), Song seized upon the thermodynamic principles of ice melting as a metaphor for the futility of containing political secrets. Subversively playing with the Chinese phrase *xiemi*, or "leaking secrets," the artist hung a row of white silk bags filled with ice on the perimeter walls of the residence of Hua Guofeng, the former chairman of the Chinese Communist Party. As the ice melted, these "secrets" eventually seeped out, leaving a trail of water that temporarily stained the wall and pooled in a dark puddle on the ground.

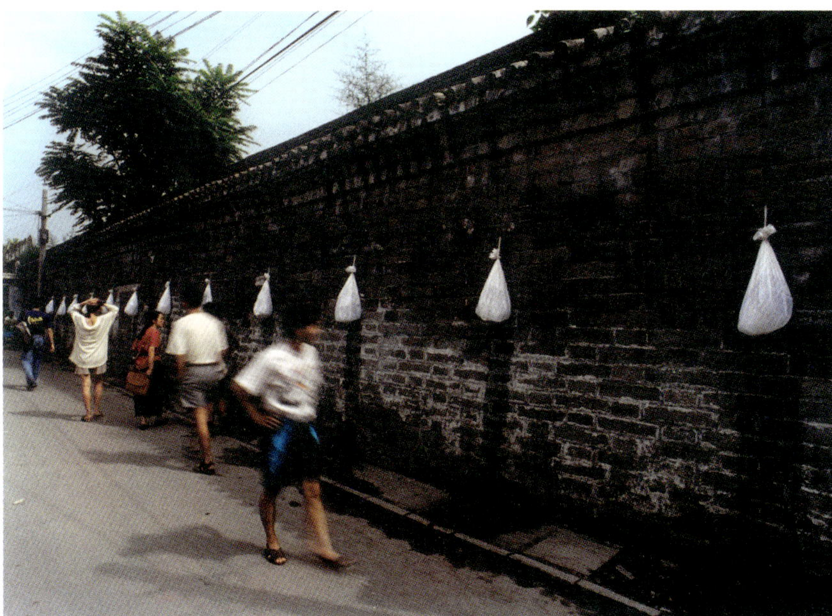

Figure 2 Song Dong, *Secret Divulging*, 1995. Silk, ice, rope, 90 × 30 × 10 cm. Courtesy of Pace Gallery. © Song Dong.

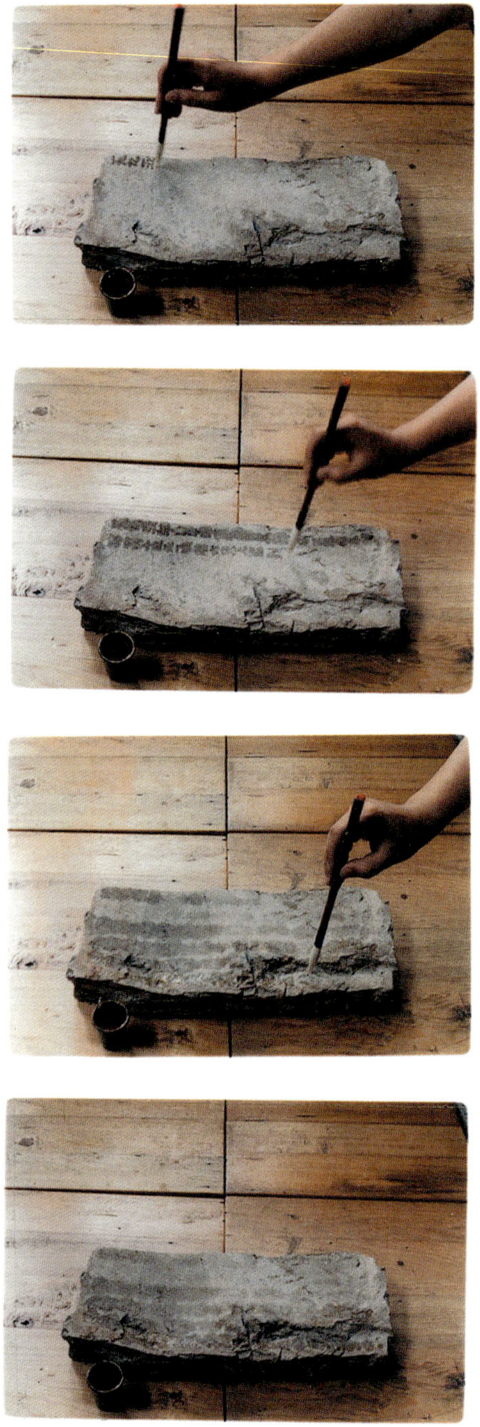

Figure 3 Song Dong, *Water Diary*, 1995–present. Private performance and experience, four color photographs, each 40 × 60 cm. Courtesy of Pace Gallery. © Song Dong.

In the work, water's transformational quality is shown to be difficult to control, even possessing its own agency.[14] This physical process thus alludes to the ways in which secrets often take on lives of their own, finding ways to seep out into the open and stain everything they touch.

If *Secret Divulging* used ice to evoke the exposure of public secrets, *Water Diary* (*Shuixie riji*, begun in 1995 and continuing to the present) (fig. 3) employed water as a vehicle for private expression and a means to safeguard personal privacy. According to Song, "You might not think about this generally but during the diary-writing process consider that someone else might be reading this someday. Since considering this I stopped writing a traditional diary."[15] *Water Diary* was based on a method of practicing calligraphy using clear water, which eventually evaporates. Recording his most intimate thoughts onto a stone slab, Song's brushstrokes left only a brief trace, like an invisible ink that betrays none of the writer's secrets. Exemplifying the artist's flexible approach to this malleable material, the work employed the same physical principle of water's tendency toward evaporation as *Secret Divulging* to suggest an opposite conceptual effect. While the former work was staged in a public environment, the latter work was done within the intimate context of the artist's own home. Whereas the former work demonstrated water's slipperiness as a metaphor for the leaking of state secrets, the latter work capitalized on its evasiveness to suggest the keeping of personal secrets.

An ongoing and deeply introspective work, the material transformations in *Water Diary* also served as a metaphor for transience and the passage of time. While the watery traces of writing attested to the artist's thoughts and expressive agency, their evaporative ephemerality also served as a humble reminder of the fleeting nature of memory and his own transience. As the serial photographs of the work show, each word written onto the stone slab slowly evaporated in the order of its appearance. Water thus visualized a continuum between presence and absence whose cycle is completed through the daily practice of writing, erasure, and writing again. Functioning as a medium between what is visible and what is invisible yet immaterially felt, water thus enacted an intangible transformation of the stone slab: steeped with layers of personal thoughts, it became more than simply an inert object, but rather an immaterial material laden with great significance.

In *Secret Divulging* and *Water Diary*, Song employed water's changing and elusive material properties as metaphors for secrecy, memory, and transience. In the latter work, however, water's role in mediating between presence and absence, visible and invisible, and material and immaterial foregrounds the very notion of "medium" (*meijie*) as precisely an *intermediary* between two things or two states. In this way, water's multimedial quality reflects Song's own fluid artistic approach to using various materials and artistic formats as intermediaries between the material world and the invisible, symbolic, and affective dimensions of the immaterial world.

BETWEEN PRESENCE AND ABSENCE

As Song's interest in the evaporative transformations of water suggests, water's intermedial materiality offered the artist a means to explore the relationship between presence and absence, a theme that he would continually return to throughout his career. Addressing this issue during a 2019 interview for *The Allure of Matter: Material Art from China* exhibition at the Smart Museum of Art, Song stated, "The allure of water is its formlessness, it lies in the communion between presence [*you*] and absence [*wu*]."[16] Elaborating on this further, the artist remarked:

> Actually, although the word "material" [*wuzhi*] contains the word "matter" [*wu*] it also contains non-material things [*fei wu*]. Whether you're talking about materiality or non-materiality, you can't get away from "matter," so [matter] becomes a kind of medium [*meijie*].[17]

While Song used the word "non-material" (*fei wu*), this term should best be translated as "immaterial" to reflect the ways in which the artist viewed the material properties of water as a medium to convey the conceptual, or "immaterial" theme of presence and absence.

In *A Pot of Boiling Water* (*Yihu re kaishui*, 1995) (fig. 4), Song integrated water and serial photography to visualize the dynamic between presence and absence, using water evaporation to suggest the ephemerality of his performance action and serial photography to stage a similar fluidity between the visual presence and absence of his physical body. For this work the artist walked along a neighborhood alleyway while continuously pouring a kettle filled with boiling water. This performance is documented through a set of black-and-white serial photographs. The figure of the artist first enters the scene in the upper left photograph as a small black dot in the distance. As he walks toward the camera lens in each progressive photograph, we begin to see greater details of his body. At the apex of this temporal progression, we see Song in greatest detail, yet part of his body—his face—is already out of the frame. In the next photograph he has

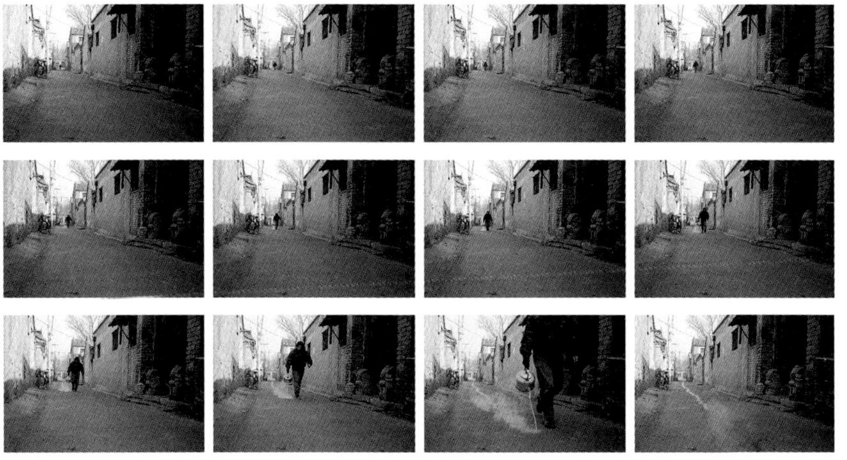

Figure 4 Song Dong, *A Pot of Boiling Water*, 1995. Twelve black-and-white photographs, each 33.3 × 50 cm. Courtesy of Pace Gallery. © Song Dong.

disappeared from the frame entirely, leaving only a cloud of steam and a trail of water soon destined also to dissipate. As the key photograph showing half of Song's body makes evident, presence already implies absence just as the set of photographs itself implies both the irrevocable passage of the action it documented and, paradoxically, its potentially limitless re-presentation.

In this work, Song's exploration of presence and absence through the confluence of water and photography is not only a metaphysical meditation on transience, but also a specific inquiry into the ontology of the reproductive medium.[18] *A Pot of Boiling Water* self-reflexively considers the material relationship between performance—an ephemeral and time-based format—and photography—a relatively more permanent format. While Song's performance might emphasize physical absence through the water's evaporation and the passage of Song's body, the reproductive photograph highlights visual presence through its ability to re-present transient actions. Commenting on the intermedial relationship between performance and documentation in his work, the artist has stated:

> . . . it's hard for me to say that my work is a record of performance, that is, even the act of recording is itself a component of the work, including the meaning captured by [the] image itself, which is also a very important component of the work. That is to say, what the image itself is talking about is not the thing that it captures, but rather the image itself already tells us the relationship between presence and absence.[19]

As the artist explained, rather than drawing a static distinction between performance art and the performance record, his artwork is constituted through the multimedial triangulation between the performance, the act of recording, and the photographic image.[20] Crucially, Song emphasized that in his works the resulting image of the performance did not just neutrally represent the thing that it captured, but instead possessed a self-reflexive capacity to disclose its own means of materializing presence and absence. The reproductive image, in other words, constituted a singular conceptual reality, or an immaterial reality located between material presence and absence.

MATERIALITY'S REALITY-PRODUCING EFFECTS

Increasingly fascinated by the relationship between material reality and the immaterial, conceptual reality of the artwork, Song's water-based works around the mid to late 1990s integrated performance and photography to assert the reality-producing effects of the multimedia artwork. In 1996 the artist was invited to Lhasa, Tibet, to participate in *Keepers of the Water* (*Shui de baowei zhe*), a series of site-specific environmental art activities around the sacred waters of the Lhasa River. Song's performance, *Stamping the Water* (*Yin shui*, 1996) (fig. 5), created in the Lhasa River, featured the artist sitting cross-legged in the river, repeatedly stamping the water with a large wooden seal carved with the Chinese character for "water."[21] According to Song, the dictionary definition of "water," a colorless, tasteless, odorless entity, is in fact an impossible conceptual ideal best embodied by the written character for water. By stamping the material water with the character for "water," Song juxtaposed water's written signifier with its material referent and signified concept. Although the artist performed the work continuously for one hour while the artist Yin Xiuzhen (b. 1963), his wife, took consecutive photos, at the end of this laborious effort, Song's actions ultimately made no physical mark. Asserting the conceptual efficacy of the symbolic action, however, *Stamping* became a way of imperceptibly purifying the water.

Song's insistence that material objects and actions can have extra-real effects was informed by his encounter with Tibet, where ritual culture offered a parallel model for how materials could pass intermedially between the material and spiritual realm. In his account of the trip, Song recalled the ways in which Tibetan spiritual beliefs were imbedded within everyday objects and materials.[22] The artist noted his fascination with the prayer wheel, a large device comprised of multiple cylindrical wheels inscribed with a Sanskrit mantra, that when rotated would conceptually "chant" the scripture. The prayer wheel thus enacts

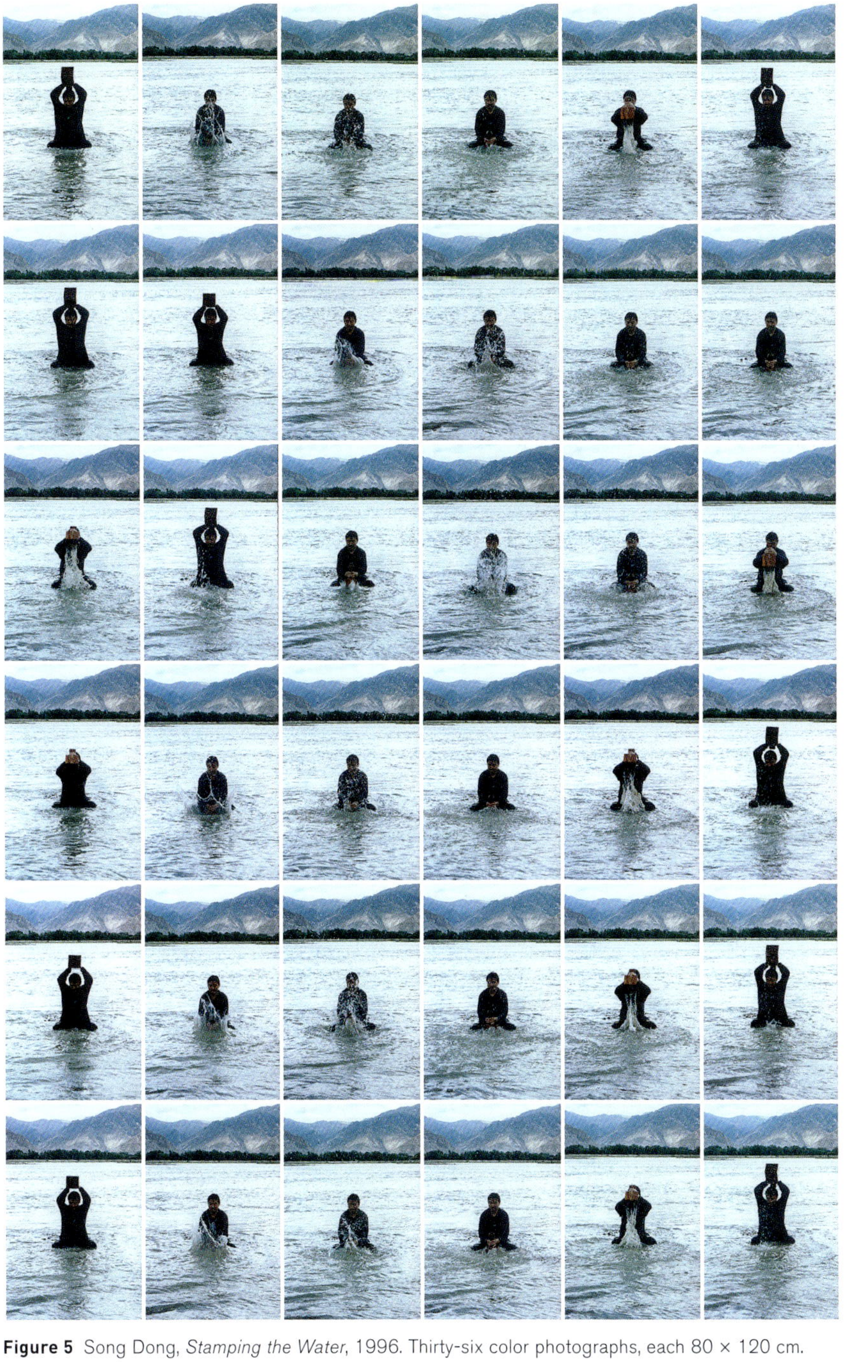

Figure 5 Song Dong, *Stamping the Water*, 1996. Thirty-six color photographs, each 80 × 120 cm.
Courtesy of Pace Gallery. © Song Dong.

a material transformation that substitutes the simple act of turning the wheels for the strenuous task of reciting countless scriptures.[23] Similarly, the artist recalled Tibetan uses of ghee, a type of clarified butter, for physical and spiritual sustenance. As food, ghee is a widely available staple of Tibetan cuisine; used as a butter lamp for the candles that light up temple interiors, however, ghee gains spiritual significance as a ritual medium, which in turn also imparts new meaning to eating ghee as both physical and spiritual nourishment. Song's fascination with the prayer wheel and the ghee are indicative of his conceptual interest in the reality-producing effects of these spiritual objects. For the artist, the conversion of one material into another paralleled the transformative effects that his own artworks enacted upon real phenomena.

Stamping was specifically inspired by another Tibetan ritual concerning the presence and the absence of the Buddha. The artist's trip to Lhasa coincided with Parinirvana Day, which commemorates the death of the historical Buddha and his simultaneous achievement of enlightenment, or the end of the cycle of life, death, and rebirth.[24] During this annual festival, religious practitioners would repeatedly dip a figurine of the Buddha into the Lhasa river to imbue the waters with spiritual essence. Interpreting the significance of this ritual, Song explained:

> When you put the Buddha in the water, the water has the Buddha, not the Buddha himself, but the shape of the Buddha in the water. In reality, this Buddha is the combination of these two intimately related things. Once the Buddha is lifted out of the water, the Buddha that is in the water disappears. Its form in the water is in a state of "absence", but it is also a state of "presence" [because] even when you take it out, it is still there. Here, the relationship between "presence" and "absence" is very fine.[25]

Stamping borrowed from this conceptual principle, substituting the figure of the Buddha with the stamp carved with the word "water." From the perspective of material phenomenal reality, viewers understand Song's stamping to be a futile act, where no amount of repeated stamping can ever make an impression on the water's surface. From the perspective of immaterial reality, or within the conceptual logic of the artwork, however, we are led to believe that the action does have an imperceptible effect that transforms the waters.

Stamping homes in on the question of the Buddha's material and immaterial presence or re-presence that is central to this Tibetan ritual practice. Just as *A Pot of Boiling Water* probed the material specificity of the photographic medium,

Stamping also integrated the performance photograph, connecting its formal properties with its capacity to conjure immaterial presences. Composed as a six-by-six grid of serial photographs, the visual representation of the performance—an essential part of this work—visually asserts the re-presentation of the artist's body thirty-six times.[26] The iconic repetition of Song's cross-legged figure in the water further evokes the Thousand-Buddhas motif, a depiction of rows of identical Buddha figures commonly found in Tibetan and Chinese Buddhist imagery.[27] Such motifs found in the Buddhist cave temples of western China have also been associated with methods of visualizing the Buddhist cosmos. Linking the artist's bodily movements of raising the stamp in the air and splashing down on the water, the rhythmic procession of images in the grid suggests the possibility of a perpetual re-presence of the past performance through the imaginative mental replay of the serial photographs. In this way, *Stamping*, whose thirty-six photographs referenced the typical number of exposures in a commercial roll of film, also implicates film's ability to animate static images through the consecutive cycling of multiple frames per second. Like the talismanic quality of the prayer wheel or the Thousand-Buddhas motif, *Stamping*'s multimedial orchestration of water, performance action, serial photography, and filmic imagination conjures up an immaterial reality that exceeds what is physically present.

THE CONCEPTUAL POTENTIALS OF THE REPRODUCTIVE IMAGE

Song's multimedial experiments with water, photography, and video and *Stamping the Water*'s investigations into materiality's conceptual potentials coincided with new directions in the development of conceptual photography and video art in the mid to late 1990s. Like Song's exploration of the ways in which water and photography bridge material and immaterial reality, contemporary photographers and video artists investigated the relationship between phenomenal reality and the filmic image to demonstrate the ways in which the reproductive image went beyond merely recording reality. While both photography and video had been used to document ephemeral artworks since the 1980s, they were initially understood as distinct from the actual artwork. Beginning in the 1990s, however, the outsize role that such images had in mediating non-extant performances or site-specific installations to subsequent audiences prompted new interest in its artistic potentials.[28]

Between 1993 and 1994 photography intersected with performance art in new ways at Beijing East Village (Beijing dongcun), an artist settlement where the photographer Rong Rong (b. 1968) collaborated with performance artists Zhang

Huan (b. 1966) and Ma Liuming (b. 1969), among others. Aesthetically composed as artworks in their own right, Rong Rong's performance art photography actively shaped the performance artists' artistic personas and influenced the visual interpretation of their ephemeral performances. As performance became increasingly inseparable from photography, some practitioners, such as Yan Lei (b. 1965) and Zheng Guogu (b. 1970), created performances fabricated entirely for the camera. In *Invasion–Face* and *Invasion–Back* (*Jinru*, both 1995), for example, Yan showed two color photographs of his battered face and backside, the results of a performance that was staged privately without an audience. Invested in the visual and affective effects of the photographic image, these works broke with the notion that performance was primarily an art form executed live for contemporaneous audiences. These "performed photographs" asserted that the photographic image *was* the primary site of the performance, ultimately challenging the assumption that photographs merely record reality rather than create it.[29] By the mid to late 1990s, conceptual photography had successfully divested the photographic medium of its former role as mere representations of reality to assert the validity of photography's conceptual reality.

Expanding the aesthetic possibilities of the reproductive image, video art practitioners in this period also moved away from the more limited medium-specific exploration of video popular in the late 1980s toward multimedia video works that combined multichannel video, performance, projection, layering, and installation. In *Image and Phenomena* (*Xianxiang-yingxiang*, 1996), the country's first exhibition dedicated exclusively to video art, organizers Qiu Zhijie (b. 1969) and Wu Meichun (b. 1969) foregrounded the relationship between video images and phenomenal reality as the thematic basis for the show. In the exhibition's catalogue, Wu provocatively asked, "What kinds of possibilities does the video medium bring to contemporary art? Does video art exist as images of phenomena, or is it a phenomenon that exists in the form of an image?"[30] Wu's question suggests that rather than merely serving as an indexical representation of an external phenomenon, the reproductive image might constitute its own kind of independent phenomenal reality.

Focusing on this issue, works chosen for the show pressed upon the complex relationship between image and phenomenon. In the eight-channel video installation *Focal Distance* (*Jiao ju*, 1996), for example, video artist Zhang Peili (b. 1957) sought to attenuate and ultimately sever the video image from its indexical reality (fig. 6). Displayed on a low bench, eight monitors show the same aerial view of a busy traffic intersection, except each of the monitors presents a progressively more pixelated version of the scene. Zhang achieved this visual effect by successively re-filming the scene depicted in each monitor at a fixed focal distance until the final monitor bears a fragmented image entirely abstracted from the original.[31] As Grube has observed, "The abstracted image is anchored spatially to its referent through a linear configuration of monitors, but the image's fracture and fragmentation in mediation points to the distortion of an empirical reality by technologies of representation."[32] Other works in the show employed multimedia techniques to create new perceptual effects.[33] Li Yongbin's (b. 1963) single-channel video work *Face 1* (*Lian 1*, 1995–1996) superimposed a video recording of his own face with that of his elderly neighbor's projected face to produce an uncanny visual juxtaposition (fig. 7). Wang Gongxin's (b. 1960) single-channel video installation *Baby Talk* (*Ying yu*, 1996) projected the faces of

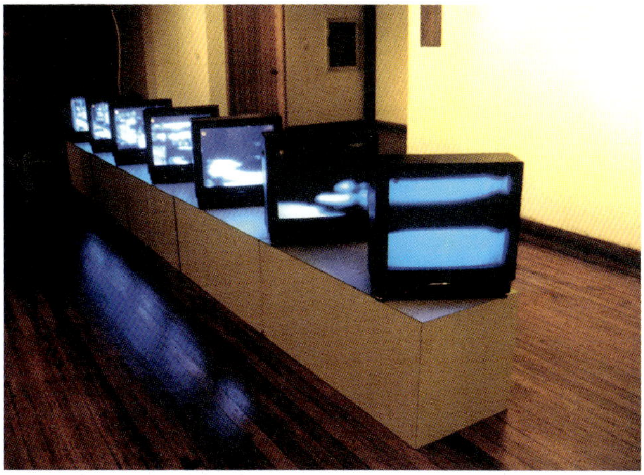

Figure 6 Zhang Peili, *Focal Distance*, 1996. Eight-channel video installation, 15 minutes running time. Courtesy of the artist. © Zhang Peili.

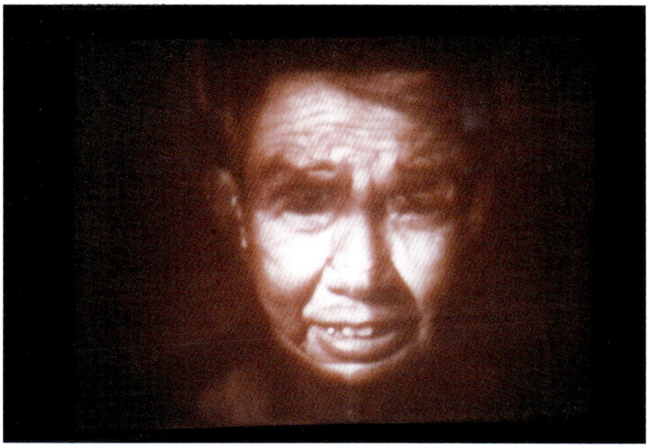

Figure 7 Li Yongbin, *Face 1*, 1995–1996. Video (color, silent), 36 minutes running time. Hans van Dijk Archive. Courtesy of Li Yongbin and Asia Art Archive.

six adults speaking to a baby onto the surface of a pool of milk fitted inside a baby bed. Creating combinatory images and perceptual effects that exceeded straightforward recordings of real phenomena, these new video works suggested that the artwork could conjure up its own independent kind of extra-reality.

Like Rong Rong's approach to performance photography, Song's attention to the specificities of the photographic medium—his use of framing, composition, and the serial format—in works such as *A Pot of Boiling Water*, *Water Diary*, and *Stamping the Water* mobilized photography as an integral component of the performance work. Paralleling the conceptual pursuits of photographers Yan Lei and Zheng Guogu and video artists Li Yongbin and Wang Gongxin, each of these three works combined different artistic mediums to materialize a conceptual reality that exceeded the work's individual physical components. Throughout the late 1990s and into the early 2000s, practices of conceptual photography and video would proceed to experiment with and foreground the importance of the reproductive image, whether in digital or analog form. Yet far from using photography and video as transparent mediums to achieve these conceptual effects, Song's unique approach to reproductive technology, through the lens of water and materiality, tied these seemingly dematerialized art forms back to their materiality. In Song's video works from the late 1990s and early 2000s, the artist would use video's intermedial intersections with water to more closely interrogate the medium's material basis.

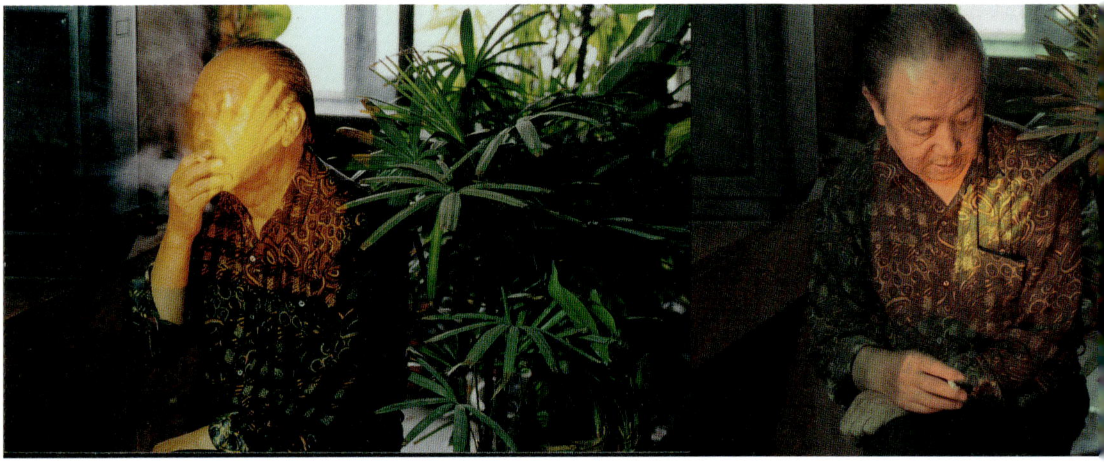

Figure 8 Song Dong, *Touching My Father*, 1997–2011. Photographs, video. Part I, 1997. Two photographs, each 80 × 120 cm. Courtesy of Pace Gallery. © Song Dong.

"A LIGHT YOU CAN SEE BUT NOT TOUCH"

Beginning in the following year, Song's exploration of the artwork's reality-producing effects was expanded upon in *Touching My Father* (*Fumo fuqin*, 1997–2011), a highly intimate three-part series concerning the artist's relationship with his father. Integrating water and video, the series reveals Song's insights into the two mediums' unexpected material and immaterial affinities. As the artist has pointed out:

> I like things like video and photography. If we regard it as a material, then I think its immateriality especially interests me. . . . Image, or video, which is a moving image, is a light you can see but not touch.[34]

Reminiscent of other statements the artist has made about water's immaterial materiality, here Song considers both photographic and video image in material terms, emphasizing their shared basis in light. Song reminds us that light, like water, possesses certain elusive properties: it can illusionistically suggest different material forms that ultimately can't be touched. In his invocation of light's paradoxical nature, the artist's comments also invoke light's peculiar physical properties as *both* a particle *and* a wave; while the former suggests a concrete materiality, the latter points to its dematerialized properties. In *Touching My Father* Part I (1997) and Part II (2002), Song employs these multimedial properties of video, later combining it with water in Part III (2011), to express and immaterially surmount the physical, temporal, and psychological distance between him and his father.

In *Touching My Father* Part I (1997), Song prerecorded a video of his own moving hand and projected the image onto the live body of his father sitting in his home (fig. 8). Through the superimposition of the projected image of his hand and its movements across the surface of the father's figure, Song was able to symbolically caress his father. This multimedial work drew from video projection and superimposition techniques that had been exhibited earlier at the 1996 *Image and Phenomena* show, yet foregrounded the material specificity of these visual devices. Whereas Li Yongbin's *Face 1* played with the perceptual indistinction between the two superimposed faces, Song's *Touching* made the two elements of the floating hand and his father's body clearly distinct from one another to draw out their physical juxtaposition. In this work, the father's body is physically touched by light, but not by the hand that the light describes. As the disembodied hand floats ghost-like over the surface of his father's body, viewers are at once cognizant of the perceptual conceit of communion and aware of the irreconcilable spatial and temporal disjuncture between Song's dematerialized hand and his father's material body.

An expression of closeness and distance, *Touching* was conceived as a reflection of Song's personal relationship with his father, which, according to the artist, had been characterized by fear and respect as well as the awareness of "a very deep generation gap" between the two.[35] In a bout of homesickness during the artist's first extensive artist residency abroad in Berlin in 1997, Song thought of his family in Beijing and longed to touch his father as an expression of his love. During this time, the artist had been experimenting with the perceptual effects of video projection in the work *Slap* (*Pai*, 1997), which he installed at the Ruin of the Arts (Die Ruine der Künste) art space. In this work, Song recorded his hand loudly slapping a hard surface and then enlarged it to room-size dimensions and projected it on the gallery floor. The video and sound installation created the uncanny sensation of a looming hand actually slapping the floor and any viewers caught below (fig. 9). Drawing from the life-like experiential effects of this work, Song used a similar projection technique in *Touching* when he returned to Beijing later that year. Unlike *Slap*, however, *Touching* possessed both a perceptual and an affective reality enhanced by Song's own physical proximity to his father

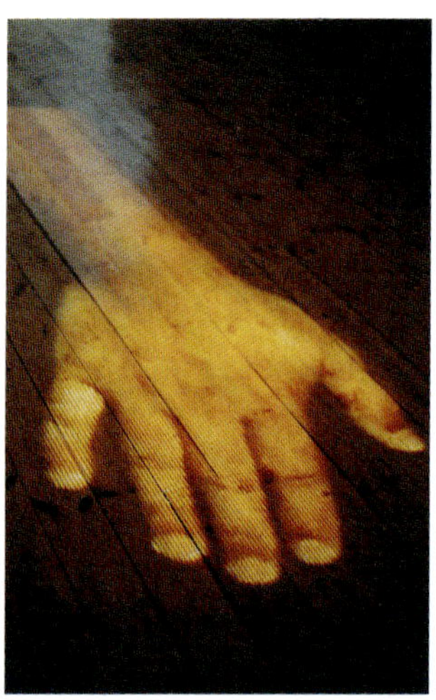

Figure 9 Song Dong, *Slap*, 1997. Video, installation, continuous loop. Francesca dal Lago Archive. Courtesy of Song Dong and Asia Art Archive.

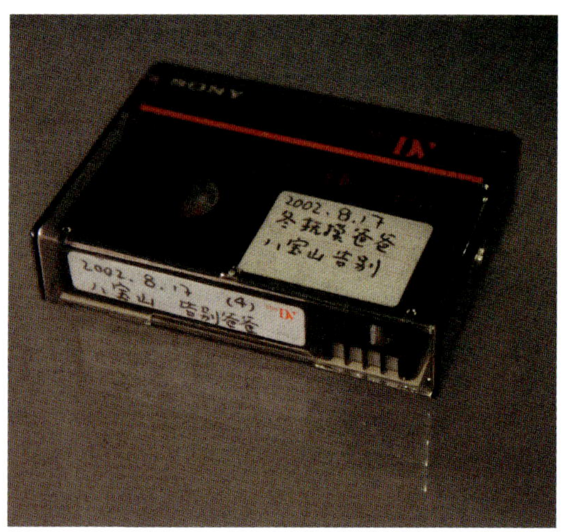

Figure 10 Song Dong, *Touching My Father*, 1997–2011. Photographs, video. Part II, 2002. Photograph of videotape and tape case, 18 cm × 12 cm. Courtesy of Pace Gallery. © Song Dong.

during the creation of the work. Compelled by the emotional impact of this virtual caress, Song's father spontaneously took off his shirt during the process, intensifying the intimacy of "contact" between the virtual hand and his bare skin. Despite the psychological distance between Song and his father and the unbridgeable material divide between the projected image and the real body, "my 'virtual hand' was breaching that invisible gap between us," according to the artist.[36] In this work, video's immaterial materiality served as a medium for a real emotional connection between the artist and his father.

Five years later, upon the death of his father, Song once again used the material properties of the video medium to symbolically express his feelings of loss and distance. *Touching My Father* Part II (2002) consisted of a video recording of Song touching his father's deceased body as a final farewell during his funeral ceremony. This intimate and grief-stricken physical contact was so painful for the artist that he subsequently sealed the recording so it could never be viewed again (fig. 10). The work, which exists solely as the physical videotape encased in its tape case, was exhibited in 2011 for the first time inside a plexiglass box with the accompanying artist statement:

> I was not brave enough to touch my father with my real hand until he passed away, but he could not feel me anymore. His body was cold and so was my heart. This has caused me constant sadness.
>
> I recorded my hand touching my father's body on video after he died. With my ongoing sorrow about his death, I have been incapable of watching it. I have sealed up the videotape and do not think that I will ever allow it to be viewed.[37]

Whereas previously video facilitated an immaterial connection between Song and his father's physical body, in this work the artist initiated a real physical connection, yet its material reality was permeated by intangible loss. No longer suggesting the possibility of connection, whether real or virtual, the video's material inaccessibility to viewers further heightened the sense of absence at the heart of this work. The videotape's small physical footprint—a reminder of the "dematerialized" technology's material basis—would seem to suggest its physical vulnerability, yet the video image's great psychological power is attested to by the need to physically sequester it away. By locking away the recording, Song attributes a talismanic quality to the videotape, suggesting that by doing so, he could also bury his emotional pain. Juxtaposing the lightness of video's materiality with the heaviness of its affective immateriality, *Touching My Father* Part II points to video's immaterial materiality.

In 2011 Song returned to the memory of his father for the third and final time. Bringing together video projection and water, *Touching My Father* Part III (2011) used light and water's elusive material qualities to evoke the spectral presence and absence of his father (fig. 11). In this work, Song projected a video of his father onto a dark pool of water and sought to touch the image of his father. Taken while he was still alive, the video showed his father animatedly playing a game with his niece. The affective image of a deceased loved one brought to life, as it were, invited Song's hands to reach out and longingly touch his father once more. Yet each time Song's hands breached the water's surface as if to confirm the reality of this visual illusion, the resulting ripples distorted and erased his image. The work illustrates a simple material principle: in a state of undisturbed stillness, water can function as a screen upon which the projection of varied light beams can produce convincing visual illusions; yet, disturbed by the slightest physical contact, such representations are shown to be entirely immaterial and fleeting. Through this material metaphor, the work expresses in tangible terms the slipperiness of memory and the delicate balance between presence and absence on which longing depends. To resummon the image of the father, Song only has to wait patiently for the water to recover its reflective stillness. In this way, *Touching My Father* Part III concludes the series much more optimistically than the previous work, preserving the hope, no matter how tentatively, of connecting with his father's presence through the mediums of light and water. Crucially, like *Stamping the Water*'s virtual re-presence of the artist's body through serial photography, *Touching My Father* asserts that video's reality-producing capacity is conditioned precisely on a profound faith in the medium's immaterial materiality.

THE ALLURE OF IMMATERIAL MATERIALITY

Song's multimedial art practice represents the work of a generation of Chinese artists active from the 1990s onward who seized upon the liberatory possibilities that conceptual art and new media offered to produce works that defied the rigid boundaries of genre or medium. Focusing on the material of water, Song explored its various physical transformations as a metaphor for the themes of immateriality and transience. At the same time, his initial use of photography and video to document ephemeral water-based works, and his later use of them as essential parts of the artworks themselves, prompted a deeper reflection on

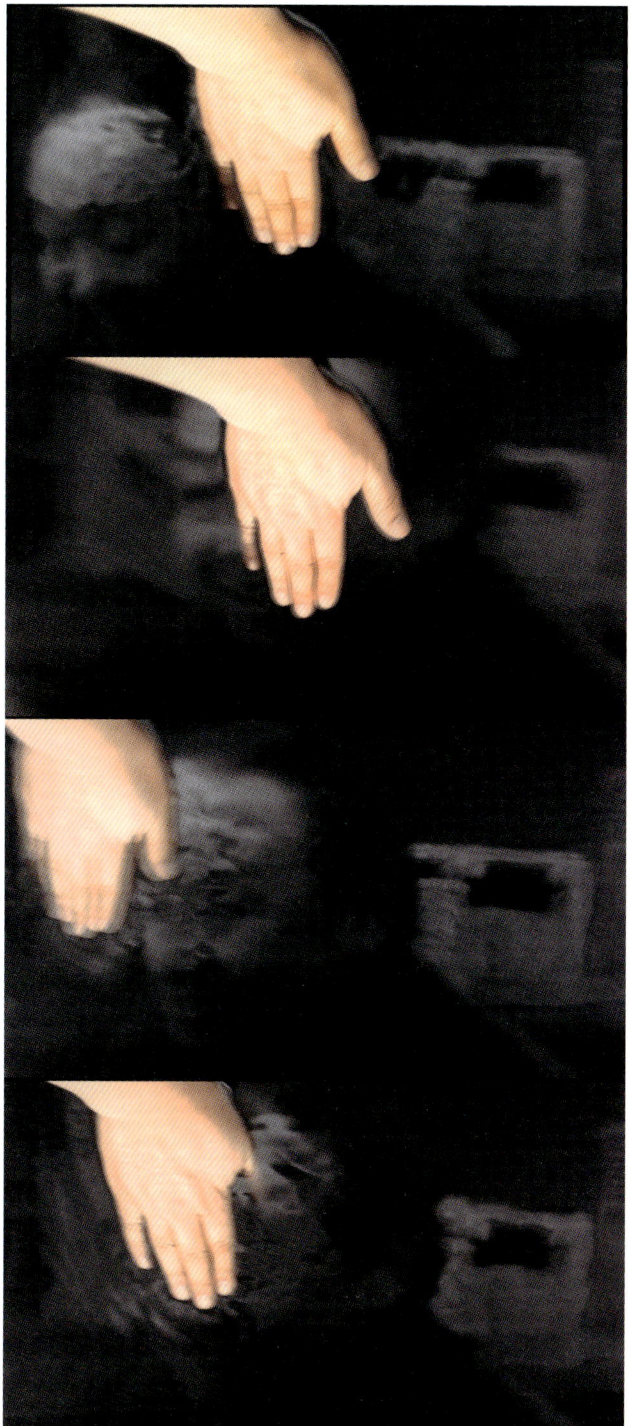

Figure 11 Song Dong, *Touching My Father*, 1997–2011. Photographs, video. Part III, 2002–2011. Video.
Courtesy of Pace Gallery.

the shared properties of these three intermedial mediums. Song's exploration of water's multimedial qualities thus became a means through which to interrogate the multimedial potential of artistic mediums, namely photography and video, and the ways in which their very materiality could be used to make meaning. Song's oeuvre of water-based works not only speaks to themes that continue to be central to Song's artistic practice—transience, presence and absence, reality and illusion, family—but also constitutes a broader self-reflexive meditation on the role of medium within art making itself.

Thinking through water, photography, and video as analogous mediums, Song demonstrated how artworks could combine physical and visual effects to produce their own conceptual reality. Song's works with video and photography contributed to a watershed moment in the mid-1990s when the two reproductive technologies took off as independent forms of artistic expression in their own right, rather than as ancillary tools for mediating installation and performance. What is significant in Song's singular approach to conceptual video and photography, however, is that despite growing artistic interest in the power of the image in conceptual video and photography since the second half of the 1990s, Song's works reasserted visuality's inextricable connections with materiality. Offering an expansive vision of art and materiality, the artist has stated, "whether it's water . . . or any multitude of things, they are all fluid and changing. They are not constrained by any particular material; rather they are ways of thinking that radiate outward on the basis of material."[38] These insights suggest that the more one plumbs the depths of material reality, the more one approaches a kind of immaterial reality. In Song's works, the allure of immaterial materiality lies in its paradoxical passage between the real and the symbolic and this, perhaps, is also the allure of art.

NOTES

The author wishes to thank Song Dong for his insightful conversations; Pace Gallery and Asia Art Archive for their assistance with archival materials; H. S. Sum Cheuk Shing at the University of Chicago for his insights on Buddhist and Daoist practices; and Orianna Cacchione for her helpful editorial suggestions.

1. Song Dong and Barbara London, *Song Dong*, ed. Sabine Wang (Groningen: Groninger Museum, 2015), 8.
2. Nancy P. Lin, "Song Dong: Water," in Wu Hung and Orianna Cacchione, *The Allure of Matter: Material Art from China* (Chicago: David and Alfred Smart Museum of Art, 2019), 186–91.
3. Wu Hung, "Material Art from China: An Introduction," in *The Allure of Matter: Material Art from China*, 15–41.
4. David Clarke, "The Watery Turn in Contemporary Chinese Art," *Art Journal* 65, no. 4 (Winter 2006): 56–77.
5. Orianna Cacchione, ed., *Zhang Peili: Record. Repeat.* (Chicago: The Art Institute of Chicago, 2017); Juxing He, *Moving Image in China, 1988–2011: la piu completa retrospettiva sulla videoarte cinese* [The most complete retrospective on Chinese video art] (Cinisello Balsamo: SilvanaEditoriale, 2012); Wu Hung and Christopher Phillips, *Between Past and Future: New Photography and Video from China*, 1st ed. (Chicago: David and Alfred Smart Museum of Art, 2004); Katherine Grube, "Image and Phenomena: The Development of Video Art in China, 1988 to 1998," Asia Art Archive, accessed November 1, 2020, https://aaa.org.hk/en/resources/papers-presentations/image-and-phenomena-the-development-of-video-art-in-china-1988-to-1998.
6. Grube, "Image and Phenomena."
7. Song and London, *Song Dong*, 8.
8. The critic Zhu Qi has suggested that artistic interest in installation art and found materials characterized by the first half of the 1990s and the interest in video and photography characterized by the latter half of the 1990s constituted two separate phases in the development of contemporary Chinese art. Zhu Qi, "1990s Conceptual Art and Artistic Conceptualization," in *Reinterpretation: A Decade of Experimental Chinese Art: 1990–2000*, ed. Wu Hung, Huangsheng Wang, and Boyi Feng (Guangzhou: Guangdong Museum of Art, 2002), 20–34.
9. Although "*fei wuzhi*" can be translated as "non-material," I have translated it as "immaterial" throughout this chapter for reasons which I will explain later on. My interview with the artist, June 28, 2019. All translations are my own unless otherwise indicated.
10. For a discussion of Song's broader art practice and its concerns with everyday local culture see, Wu Hung, "'Vernacular' Post-Modern: The Art of Song Dong and Yin Xiuzhen," in *Chopsticks: Song Dong and Yin Xiuzhen*, ed. Song Dong, Yin Xiuzhen, and Christophe W. Mao (New York: Chambers Fine Art, 2002), 9–23.
11. "Yong yishu gandong shijie: guangyu 'wujin qiyong' de tanhua," *Art Gallery Magazine*, no. 127 (June 2009): 34–41.
12. Wu Hung, "Material Art from China: An Introduction."
13. Sinologist Sarah Allan has argued that premodern Daoist philosophy used water and plants as "root metaphors" to formulate broader abstract concepts and philosophical worldviews. Allan's framework of the metaphor can be used to understand the idiosyncratic ways in which Song also used water to develop his own artistic and conceptual ideas, which include, but are

not limited to, Daoist concepts. Sarah Allan, *The Way of Water and Sprouts of Virtue* (Albany: State University of New York Press, 1997).

14. Wu has suggested that in this work water becomes the sole "actor" of this performative process. Wu Hung, "Material Art from China: An Introduction," 34.

15. Julie Walsh, "Song Dong Diary Keeper," in *Chopsticks*, 12.

16. Song Dong, interview with the author, June 28, 2019.

17. Song Dong, interview with the author, June 28, 2019.

18. The subject of photography's ontology has been widely debated. I draw from art historian Joel Snyder's recent unpublished rereading of André Bazin's seminal essay "The Ontology of the Photographic Image," as not a literal assertion of photography's indexical relationship to reality, but rather "analogies [that] are meant to capture something fundamental about the character of our compulsion to believe photographs are identical with their models." Joel Snyder, "Photography, Ontology, Analogy, Compulsion" (unpublished paper).

19. Song Dong, interview with the author, June 28, 2019.

20. Recent art practice and scholarship have emphasized the essential role that visual documentation plays in the performance work. See Martino Stierli and Mechtild Widrich, *Participation in Art and Architecture: Spaces of Interaction and Occupation*, vol. 19, International Library of Visual Culture (London: I.B. Tauris, 2016); Thomas J. Berghuis and Keith Wallace, eds., "Action-Camera: Beijing Performance Photography," in *Action-Camera: Beijing Performance Photography* (Vancouver: Morris and Helen Belkin Art Gallery, 2009), 67–80; Tracey Warr, "'Image as Icon: Recognizing the Enigma,'" in *Art, Lies and Videotape: Exposing Performance*, ed. Adrian George (London: Tate, 2003), 30–37.

21. Song Dong, in interview by Cici Wu and Jane DeBevoise, November 4, 2017, Asia Art Archive in America.

22. Song Dong, in interview by Cici Wu and Jane DeBevoise.

23. This ritual transformation of one material substance into another has parallels in the Christian practice of transubstantiation, where bread and wine are converted into the body and blood of Christ during the Eucharist.

24. Song's understanding of Buddhist concepts is general rather than doctrinal. For an overview of the concept of "Nirvana" and "enlightenment" see Donald S. Lopez Jr. and Robert E. Buswell Jr., *The Princeton Dictionary of Buddhism* (Princeton: Princeton University Press, 2013), 1096–97.

25. "Move the World with Art: Discussion About the Work 'Waste Not,'" Yong yishu gandong shijie, 37.

26. Song has insisted that serial photographs of his performances, including *A Pot of Boiling Water* and *Stamping*, must be presented as composed sets of twelve or multiples of twelve because the number alludes to a complete cycle. Song used the terms "the cycle of life and death" (*lunhui*) and "cyclical" (*zhouer fushi*), which have specific Buddhist connotations. In personal communication with the author on February 19, 2019, via WeChat.

27. Lokesh Chandra and Sushama Lohia, *Iconography of the Thousand Buddhas* (New Delhi: International Academy of Indian Culture and Aditya Prakashan, 1996).

28. For a historical account of developments in contemporary photography, see Wu and Phillips, *Between Past and Future*.

29. Using the artist Yves Klein's *Leap into the Void* (1960) as an example, performance scholar Philip Auslander defines "performed photography" as a work that is "staged solely to be photographed or filmed and had no meaningful prior existence as autonomous events presented to audiences . . .

[wherein] the space of the document . . . thus becomes the only space in which the performance occurs." Philip Auslander, "The Performativity of Performance Documentation," *PAJ: A Journal of Performance and Art* 28, no. 3 (2006): 84.

30. Wu Meichun and Qiu Zhijie, "Xianxiang yingxiang zhanlan jihua" [Image–Phenomena], 1996.

31. An earlier 1993 work, *Continuous Reproduction 25 Times* (*Fanpai 25 ci*), demonstrated a similar principle by re-photographing a photograph taken from a Chinese pictorial magazine twenty-five times. For more on this work, see Cacchione, *Zhang Peili*.

32. Grube, "Image and Phenomena."

33. Curators Wu Meichun and Qiu Zhijie highlighted these techniques in the exhibition, remarking that "works in the exhibition may be divided into two parts according to the trends exhibited. First, the works that were introspective in regard to the medium itself and were generally simple in structure. Second were the intricately structured scenes, which pushed at the boundaries of the video's image by adding rich layers and a finer perception." Wu Meichun and Qiu Zhijie, "The Rise and Development of Video Art and the Maturity of New Media Art," in *Reinterpretation: A Decade of Experimental Chinese Art: 1990–2000*, 54.

34. Song used the words "*fei wuzhihua*," which can be translated as "non-materialization." To capture the suggestion in his following sentence that this "non-materialization" is a property that inheres to photography and video, I have translated it as "immateriality." Song Dong, interview with the author, June 28, 2019.

35. Song Dong, "Touching My Father," in *Song Dong*, 71.

36. Song, "Touching My Father," 71.

37. Song, "Touching My Father," 71.

38. Song Dong, interview with the author, June 28, 2019.

The Fugitive Luxury of Porcelain in Contemporary Chinese Art

Alex Burchmore

Porcelain, like many creative media that blur the boundary between art and craft, resists singular definition. Elegant vessels of the finest clay sell for millions at auction and take pride of place in museums across the world; mass-produced cups and plates, on the other hand, are among the most inexpensive yet indispensable household essentials. Those who work with porcelain are equally diverse: amateur potters, factory laborers, studio ceramicists, artisan-entrepreneurs, and, increasingly, contemporary artists. The origin of porcelain manufacture in China, a nation so tied to this material that the two are synonymous in the Anglophone world, has been dated to the Tang dynasty (618–907), expanding in subsequent centuries to encompass an awe-inspiring range of clays, glazes, vessel forms, motifs, and styles.

Despite this illustrious pedigree, porcelain did not attract significant interest from contemporary Chinese artists until the 1990s. One explanation for this could be the stigma of its association, on one hand, with the quotidian and industrial and, on the other, with the imperial and aristocratic. For those seeking to reject the socialist realism of the Maoist era as well as the elitism of the dynastic past, porcelain may have seemed too close to the laborer and landowner. Compared with European and North American forms of art in vogue in the 1980s, it may also have seemed too Chinese to sustain a "contemporary" voice. In a 1983 account of his contact with China's new artists, *New York Times* reporter Fox Butterfield captured these connotations of refinement and convention with great alacrity, recalling "an old Qing dynasty vase . . . emblazoned with dragons and flowers" presented to him by sculptor Wang Keping (b. 1949), on his departure from Beijing in 1980:

> . . . the gaudy glaze was chipped and there was a jagged piece missing from the . . . mouth. Wang had scavenged it in the Cultural Revolution. "It is broken, I know," he said, handing it to me with both hands . . . . "Consider it a symbol of our broken culture."[1]

Porcelain, it seems, was regarded as a suitable gift and emblem of the past, but not as a medium for artistic expression. On a practical note, the issue could also have been one of access: many artists were constrained in the 1970s and 1980s by dire economic circumstances, forced to adapt their ambitions to suit the materials on hand.

Porcelain remains an anomaly in the field of contemporary Chinese art and materials-centered art in general. An emphasis on material over symbolic or stylistic dimensions of meaning usually prompts a turn toward the unconventional.

Artists who are now identified with Arte Povera, Gutai, and Mono-ha—three canonical materialist tendencies—for example, tend to value the humble and abject over the beautiful and refined. Yet work in porcelain by globally renowned artists Ai Weiwei (b. 1957), Liu Jianhua (b. 1962), and Cai Guo-Qiang (b. 1957), among others, rests on a reversal of these terms, foregrounding the sensuous appeal, formal perfection, and enviable luxury of a time-honored medium.

Like Wang, before these artists sought to test the creative limits of porcelain, they knew it above all as a material of elegiac refinement and historical prestige. Liu, for example, the most prolific contemporary porcelain devotee, inaugurated his ongoing relationship with this medium in July 1977, when he took up an offer of employment at a factory in Jingdezhen, Jiangxi province, once renowned as the global "Porcelain Capital" (Cidu).[2] He has recalled that he felt drawn to ceramics even while growing up in nearby Ji'an, seizing an opportunity to train with his ceramicist uncle, Liu Yuanchang.[3] After a two-year apprenticeship, he put the skills he had acquired to the test on the assembly line, creating socialist realist and classical-style sculptural tableaux that attracted official attention: when he was just 19 years old, he received several awards for his tableau of dancers performing the Tang dynasty *Raiment of Rainbows and Feathers* (*Nishang yuyi wu*).[4] Yet his role offered little prospect of advancement: no matter how accomplished he became, he could only aspire to replace an older colleague. The reopening of universities seemed to promise a different path, so Liu sat the entrance exam for the Jingdezhen Ceramic Institute (Jingdezhen taoci xueyuan), gaining a place in the sculpture department in 1985. He rejected his professional training, determined to reinvent himself as a contemporary artist:

> I was quite tired of porcelain when I left the factory, because I had been dealing with that material for such a long time . . . I could see what my life would be until I retired. . . . After I got accepted by the university, I just thought that I would never touch this material again. I'd even given away all [my] tools.[5]

> I felt it wasn't really art . . . I was certain that I could never go back.[6]

These comments exemplify the general attitude toward porcelain in the 1970s and 1980s, when it would have seemed unthinkable to forge a career as a contemporary porcelain artist.

Ai Weiwei also received some instruction in ceramics-making in the summer of 1977—two years before his participation, with Wang Keping, in the inaugural

Stars (*Xingxing huahui*) exhibition—at the historically renowned Cizhou kilns in Handan, Hebei province.[7] Over three months, he created a selection of relatively conventional pieces that included his first published work: a tawny-glazed statuette of a winking owl, perhaps a nod to the infamous painting of the same subject by senior arts stateman Huang Yongyu (b. 1924).[8] Yet, unlike Huang's officially denigrated painting, Ai's owl has largely escaped notice among his biographers, dismissed perhaps as a youthful dalliance. For critics and artists alike, porcelain has long seemed too artisanal and so unsuitable for contemporary artistic expression. An aura of the quotidian and of the past has proven difficult to shake, leading many to regard this medium as an aspect of material heritage to be overcome on the path to more experimental visions.

By the 1990s, however, as the transition to a market-based economy and international interest in Chinese art brought opportunities to experiment, porcelain gained fresh appeal. Some critics might identify this shift in attitude with a general move toward "traditional" materials and a desire to interrogate the Chineseness with which these are associated—and such historical, cultural, and political connotations were certainly an important contextual factor. Yet it is the specifically *material* qualities of this medium that take precedence in works by Ai, Liu, and Cai: the sensuous visual and tactile appeal of a thickly applied glaze, the resonance of vitrified ceramic, the perilous allure of an impossibly thin surface or exposed fracture, inviting caress yet rewarding affection with the quickening of blood. Seductive yet dangerous—these are the marks of luxury, defined by design historian Peter McNeil and historian Giorgio Riello as that which is "*extra*-ordinary . . . which goes beyond the everyday, the affordable, and the mundane . . . uplifting both spiritually and materially [yet] 'unproductive' and therefore useless."[9] For Ai, Liu, and Cai, the attraction of porcelain emerges from its association with and subversion of such categories: in their work, the patina of the antique takes on a tangibly material rather than symbolic significance, the allure of the exotic gives way to a more considered reflection on mobility and precarity, and the mystique of a branded identity blurs the boundaries separating the personal from the national or cultural. These qualities escape straightforward categorization and reveal a flexible materiality defined by movement between organic, social, political, and cultural states. The luxury of porcelain, in their hands, becomes a distinctively *fugitive* luxury, in which it is "a material's ability to permutate and transform, not its essence or persistence," that takes precedence.[10]

PATINA AND PROVENANCE

By 1998, Ai and Liu had moved past their earlier doubts, finding a new fascination with the allure of porcelain and the interface it can create between past and present, embodied sensation and visual spectacle. These material qualities recall those of *patina* and *provenance*, defining traits of a luxury that McNeil and Riello have identified as "the greatest . . . of them all": the antique, and the opportunity "to play with time" that this affords, reviving glories of the past and arresting the threat of change.[11] Leading historian of Chinese art Jonathan Hay also draws attention to patina in his foundational study of Ming and Qing dynasty decorative arts, arguing that "the single most obvious characteristic of a luxury object [was its] sensuous surface." Bronze, lacquer, ivory, porcelain, and other such media were valued, he explains, for their ability to "connect us visually and physically to the world . . . to weave us into our environment."[12] Porcelain held comparable appeal for Ai and Liu, both of whom were drawn to return to the medium in their search for a material that could fuse the ancient and contemporary, imagination and sensation, eye and hand. The first works they created following this shift in perspective accentuate the luxury of patina and provenance yet draw attention at the same time to purely physical qualities of surface texture, variety, and luster, emphasizing the extent to which luxury can signify much more than antiquity and lineage.

Following his return to Beijing in 1993, after twelve years in New York, Ai Weiwei embarked on his first substantial body of work in porcelain. Rapid urban redevelopment and the transition to a market-based economy had transformed the city, yet this pursuit of the future had in turn accelerated an unearthing of the past as construction disinterred long-forgotten artifacts, many of which resurfaced in Beijing's antique markets. Ai spent many hours in these markets, where he discovered an enduring fascination for ceramics of the Yuan (1271–1368), Ming (1368–1644), and Qing (1644–1911) dynasties. Above all, it was the "definition of shape, colour, [and] marking" distinguishing various eras and places of production that captivated his interest, testifying to both generations of artisanal accomplishment and the longevity of China's ceramic heritage.[13] Another quality he valued was the extent to which the familiarity of ceramics could foster intimacy across centuries, revealing "what a certain people in a certain time and location were . . . thinking and making."[14] This intimacy points to an understanding of patina distinct from that to which many collectors subscribe: a record not of time in the abstract, but of the palimpsest of traces left by multiple hands and fingers—an anonymous provenance of tactile materiality, rather than a lineage of eminent names.

Inspired by this proximity to the past, Ai created several works in which he attempted to extract the materiality of patina and provenance from the cultural and historical record with which they are customarily associated, and by which they are frequently overshadowed. To accomplish this aim, he followed the logic of the counterfeit. During his trips to Beijing's markets, Ai had often encountered fakes disingenuously displayed alongside bona fide antiques, their similarity to the untrained eye revealing the ease with which tradition could be fabricated if the correct material formulae were followed. In 1996, Ai commissioned a workshop in Jingdezhen to create several reproduction Ming and Qing dynasty vessels for display in his name as works of art, blending conceptual subterfuge and artisanal skill.

These early works in porcelain, now grouped as the *Blue and White* series (fig. 1), have been framed as a play on the value attached to antiquity by connoisseurs, dealers, and collectors.[15] Ai himself has endorsed this interpretation, clarifying

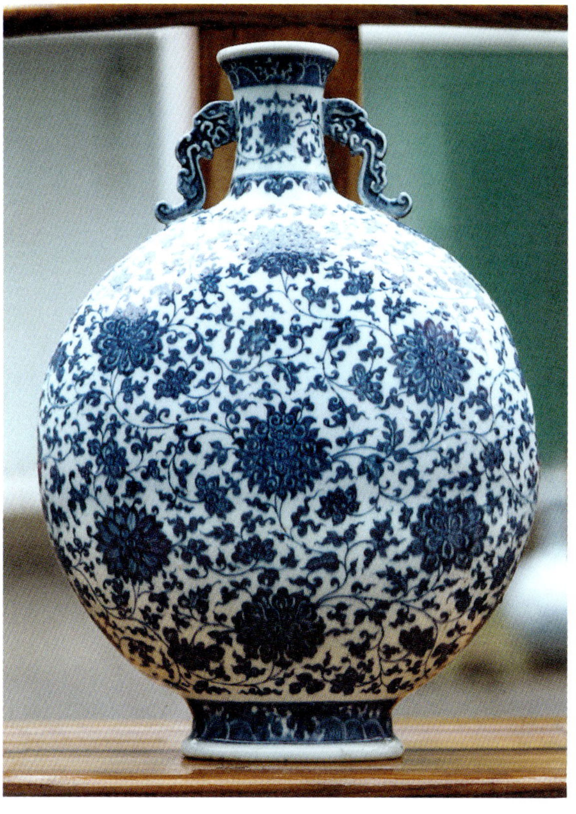

Figure 1 Ai Weiwei, *Blue and White Moonflask*, 1996. Replica in style of Qing dynasty, Qianlong reign era (1736–1795). Porcelain with underglaze decoration in cobalt blue, 53 × 36.8 × 7.6 cm. Courtesy of Ai Weiwei.

that "the central issue [of the series] is [that] of authenticity. What is real and what is fake . . . ?"[16] Yet these vessels are much more than an artful deception or tongue-in-cheek nod to the skill of those who make their living producing imitation antiques. In the same breath, Ai also made sure to observe that his counterfeits represent "the highest quality [work] of imperial *guan* [official] standards."[17] This boast points to another motive: a desire to showcase China's ceramic tradition, to elevate that which had been denigrated as a quotidian craft to the rarefied realms of high art simply by accentuating the material beauty of porcelain and its luxurious appeal, even in the absence of a certified antiquity.

Liu Jianhua has also sought to accentuate the luxury of porcelain. In 1998, after working almost entirely in fiberglass throughout the decade, he returned to the medium that initiated his artistic training in search of a vehicle for his desired aesthetic. He had established his reputation with the fiberglass sculptural series *Concealed* (*Yinmi*, 1993–94) and *Disharmony* (*Buxietiao*, 1994–97), in which Sun Yat-sen jackets are juxtaposed with exposed women's thighs, arms, and genitals, skillfully carved and painted to imitate life. In his subsequent *Obsessive Memories* (*Milian de jiyi*, 1997–99, also *Infatuated Memory*) (fig. 2) series, also in fiberglass at first, Liu heightened the contradiction between these elements with the addition

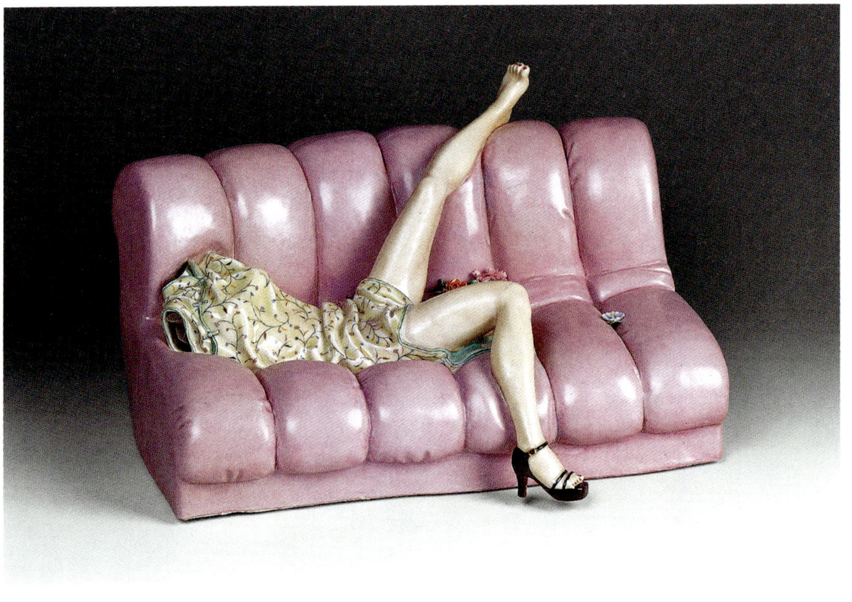

Figure 2 Liu Jianhua, *Obsessive Memories*, 1997–1999. Porcelain with overglaze polychrome decoration, 60 × 42 × 41 cm. Courtesy of Liu Jianhua.

of a 1930s-style *qipao*. The coarseness of fiberglass seemed unsuited for such a hyperfeminine article of clothing, however, when compared with "the soft, satiny smoothness" of glazed porcelain, a sensuous surface-scape animated by "a current of desire" arousing fantasies of ecstatic possession.[18] These qualities of a medium Liu had formerly abandoned now seemed perfectly suited to capture the languid beauty of the dismembered yet sexualized women who play a starring role in this series, reclining in overstuffed armchairs and voluptuous bathtubs.

The suitability of porcelain for these images of voyeuristic seduction is evident in the affect-laden comment inspired by *Obsessive Memories* and the subsequent *Games* (*Xixi*, 1999–2000, also *Play* or *Merriment*) (fig. 3), in which plates replace furniture. In both series, brightly colored *qipao* are arranged in poses that follow the curves of a stereotypically attractive woman's body yet adorn only a pair of long, elegant legs, with apertures in place of head and arms revealing little more than an empty shell. Fabric-like folds of ceramic cling tightly to the breasts and stomachs of these fragmented women, who sit, lay, or kneel in coquettish poses, dresses raised to expose parted thighs, painted toenails, or glossy high-heeled shoes. Writing about these series on their initial showing in Hong Kong, curator Pi Li and gallerist Johnson Chang lingered over

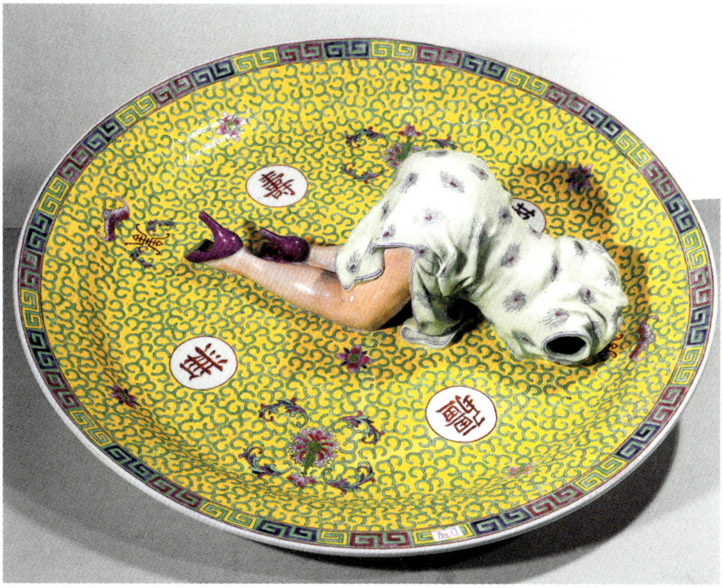

Figure 3 Liu Jianhua, *Games*, 1999–2000. Porcelain with overglaze polychrome decoration, 58 × 19 cm. Courtesy of Liu Jianhua.

"milk-white thighs and pert breasts," relishing this chance to enjoy "the old dynamics of seduction and conquest," while art historian Zhang Hongxia later recounted feeling "hesitation and fear . . . uneasiness and anxiety," when confronted by these "plump but incomplete, gorgeous but empty, sexy but stiff, seductive but refusing" *femmes fatales*.[19] Zhang's unease points to the unsettling consumerist lust that Liu has identified as his primary inspiration and subject of critique, both communicated by and concealed beneath their superficial allure:

> The [*qipao*] will arouse the imagination and a desire for possession. Meanwhile, the sofa reminds us of modernity, power, money, sex, comfort, and the West. . . . In recent years, the Chinese economy has developed in stride [yet] I doubt if the inner world of individuals has proceeded in such a pace. . . . Superficial beauty [cannot] conceal the loneliness and frailty of . . . an unstable, insecure and highly sensitive materialistic world.[20]

Obsessive Memories and *Games* are animated by a similar disparity, their enchantment failing to distract from the desolation of their voiceless subjects. Lacking heads and arms, Liu's women are little more than objects of desire, ultimately unfulfilling in the absence of human connection. Porcelain, "[a] beautiful yet . . . fragile material, with a lustre . . . ideally suited to the representation of superficial prosperity, [but] susceptible at any moment to evaporate into nothingness," is central to this fusion of attraction and repulsion.[21]

In 2004, Ai Weiwei embarked on another series of works in which superficial allure supersedes cultural or political connotation. Like his reproductions, these are remarkable for their technical brilliance, while the dexterity with which his models have been recreated affords the delight of a skillful *trompe l'oeil*. At first glance, these models are absurdly quotidian—a watermelon, a *prêt-à-porter* dress, a pool of crude oil. Yet they offer an ideal showcase for the "chameleon-like ability [of porcelain] to convincingly disguise itself," an ability appreciated by generations of ceramicists dedicated to the art of the skeuomorph.[22] *The Wave* (2005) (fig. 4) exemplifies the extent to which Ai's sculptures sustain this tradition, even while their unorthodox subjects push the boundaries of possibility. Critics have identified this as a sculptural rendition of Katsushika Hokusai's (1760–1849) iconic *Under the Wave off Kanagawa* (c. 1830–32), arguing that Ai intended to compare the commodification of the print with the typecasting of his own work.[23] Maxwell K. Hearn, Chairman, Department of Asian Art at the Metropolitan Museum of Art, has extended this comparison with historic works of art even

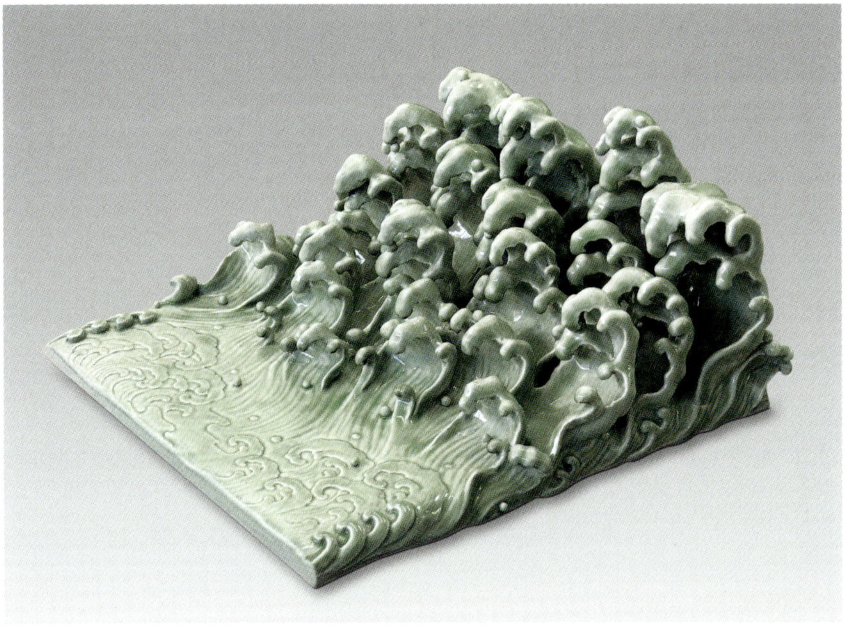

Figure 4 Ai Weiwei, *The Wave*, 2005. Porcelain with celadon glaze, 25 × 40 cm. Courtesy of Ai Weiwei.

further, identifying scholar-artist Ma Yuan's (c. 1160/65–1225) seascapes and the carved ornament of Song dynasty celadons as additional sources.[24] Yet these anachronistic parallels distract from the sheer facticity of *The Wave* as a showcase for the malleability of clay and the sheen of a vitrified glaze, here used to evoke a shimmering cascade of water.

Liu has also tested the skeuomorphic potential of porcelain. In *Trace* (*Jixiang*, 2011), echoing the fluidity of *The Wave*, he created the impression of ink seeping down the walls of the Ullens Center for Contemporary Art in Beijing. Like Ai's earlier work, *Trace* exaggerates the plasticity of porcelain and the tension between organic expression and artisanal control inherent to its shaping. It is a product of Liu's shift from the gaudy to the monochrome, a transition inaugurated by a pair of exhibitions at Beijing Commune: *Untitled* (2008) and *Horizon* (2009–10). The works created for *Horizon* are comparable with Ai's skeuomorphs in their derivation from quotidian models, yet their shrouding in a monochrome glaze removes any ties with the history of the skeuomorph and instead accentuates material qualities. Liu's focus on the material is clearest in *Blank Paper* (*Baizhi*, 2009–12) (fig. 5), a series of porcelain tiles so thin that they resemble sheets of paper, one corner slightly turned to create the illusion of flexibility. Their appeal derives not only

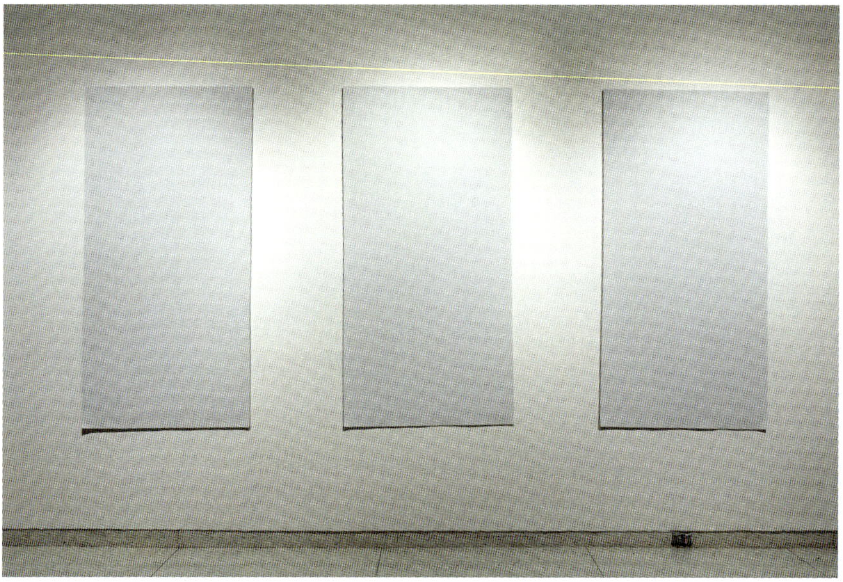

Figure 5 Liu Jianhua, *Blank Paper*, 2009–12. Porcelain, each 201 × 103 × 0.8 cm. Installation view, *The Allure of Matter: Material Art from China*, Smart Museum of Art, The University of Chicago, Chicago, 2020. Courtesy of the Smart Museum of Art.

from verisimilitude, but, above all, from a foregrounding of the material in its most unadulterated form, and from an awareness of the skill required to achieve such delicacy, drawing attention to the durability, fluidity, malleability, and, of course, luxury of a sensuous porcelain surface.[25]

NEW EXPORT CHINA

In addition to the merging of past and present, sensation and spectacle, McNeil and Riello have identified a blurring of boundaries between self and other and a collapsing of the distance between sites of production and consumption as comparably defining characteristics of luxury. These qualities, they argue, were most visible in a European context in the eighteenth century, when an influx of goods from China, India, and Japan enticed consumers to indulge in the exotic. Market expansion sparked a debate between the leading European philosophers of the time, some of whom sought to curb consumption to prevent a forecast decline in morals while others argued that profligacy should be encouraged to stimulate economic growth. From this debate, "luxury as we know it was born: a phenomenon that not only interested just the few, but . . . involved entire societies," fostering commercial contacts that spanned the globe and crossed cultural boundaries.[26] This discourse of mobility, precarity, and exoticism has greatly inspired expatriate Chinese artists like Cai, while Liu, although he has remained in China, has artfully exposed the lines of descent linking the China Trade with contemporary consumer capitalism.

Cai's first work incorporating porcelain, *Reflection—A Gift from Iwaki* (2004) (fig. 6), commissioned for the Smithsonian Institution, Washington, D.C., marked the culmination of an ongoing dialogue with residents of Iwaki in Japan's Fukushima prefecture. His first stay in this city in 1994 coincided with the community-led salvaging of a local fishing vessel, the remains of which had been submerged for 20 years. Collaborating with local carpenters, Cai used the ship's timbers to create two installations for the Iwaki City Art Museum: *Kaikou—The Keel (Returning Light—The Dragon Bone)*, for which he installed the ship in the museum with a mound of local sea salt; and *San Jō Tower*, a pagoda-like timber structure intended to reflect the historic role of the city's beacons for those lost at sea.[27] In 1997, Cai adapted *San Jō Tower* for the 47th Venice Biennale, suspending it from the gallery ceiling and attaching thirteen Chinese flags to the base, rendered flame-like by electric fans

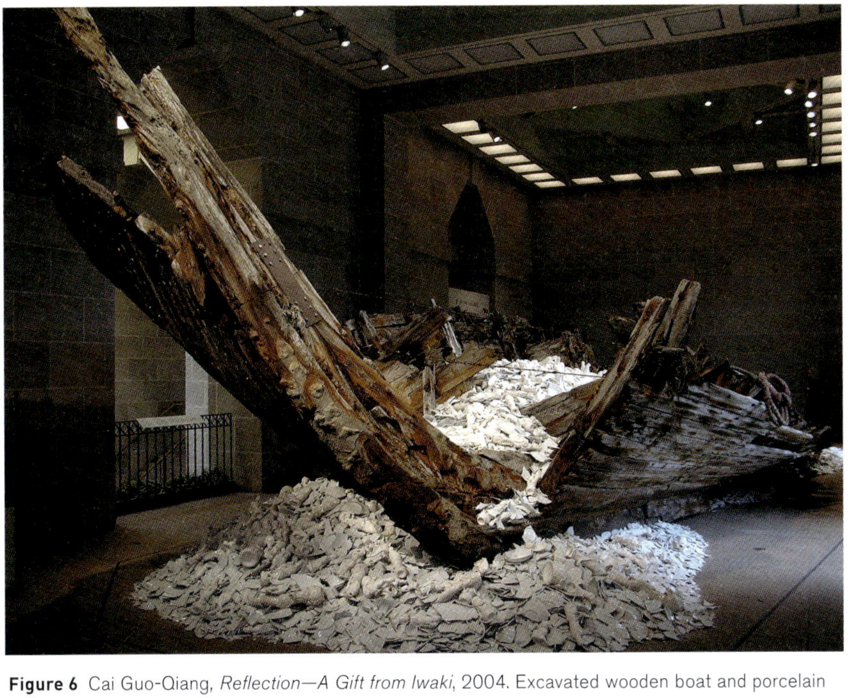

Figure 6 Cai Guo-Qiang, *Reflection—A Gift from Iwaki*, 2004. Excavated wooden boat and porcelain figurines, 500 × 500 × 1500 cm. Installation view, *Cai Guo-Qiang: Traveler*, Arthur M. Sackler Gallery, Smithsonian Institution, Washington, D.C., 2005. Photo: Cai Guo-Qiang. Courtesy of Cai Studio.

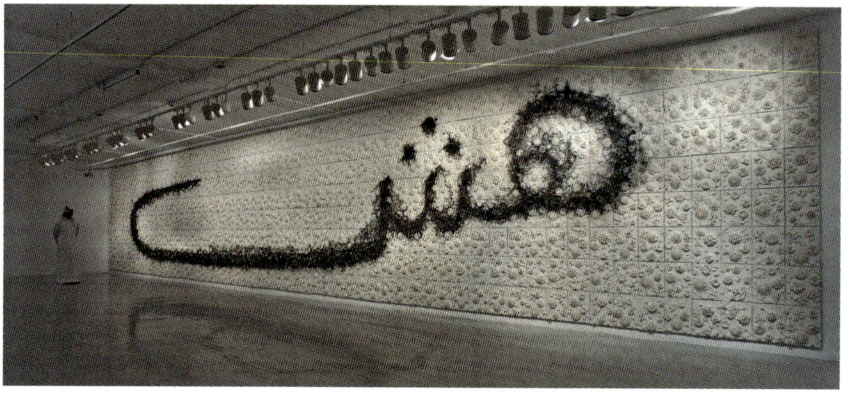

Figure 7 Cai Guo-Qiang, *Fragile*, 2011. Gunpowder on 480 porcelain relief panels, 318 × 1800 cm. Installation view, *Cai Guo-Qiang: Saraab*, Mathaf: Arab Museum of Modern Art, Doha, 2011–12. Photo: Lin Yi. Courtesy of Cai Studio.

and red lights. He has explained this version, *The Dragon Has Arrived!*, as a response to the burgeoning "China Threat" narrative provoked by tensions with the U.S.[28]

Reflection, on the other hand, for which Cai repurposed the ship's frame, drew inspiration from a less antagonistic narrative of cultural contact. Cai had conceived his 1994 installations as arguments for the local when "the Japanese were concerned with 'going global' . . . creating a Western-style super economy [even while] forgetting their own history."[29] His 2004 installation, on the other hand, emphasises the symbolic role of the ship as a mode of transport rather than an artifact of life in a coastal community:

> I love boats. I don't know how many future projects I will do with boats, but it's a recurring image. . . . [It] symbolises my current life of travelling to many places [yet] encompasses so much more. It's a vessel, it's a carrier . . . more an idea than just an object.[30]

To further emphasize this association with "travel as a physical, geographical, and cultural activity," Cai chose to replace the sea salt used in *Reflection* with a cargo of porcelain figurines, filling what remains of the hold and spilling over exposed beams.[31] Manufactured in Dehua, Fujian province, a kiln city almost as ancient as Jingdezhen and almost as renowned, these figurines are remarkable not only for their quantity but their modeling in the likeness of the Buddhist deity Guanyin.[32] As the bodhisattva of compassion and patron of those whose professions compel them to live at sea, Guanyin's presence reinforces the theme of travel while introducing a note of pathos: even a hold overflowing with such talismans cannot guarantee protection against the ocean's violence. Ornamenting the remains of the wreck, these shattered icons and the salvation they embody stand in vain against the currents of time and fortune.

Yet Cai frames this precious cargo as a "gift" from Iwaki and Dehua, the places of production for his salvaged ship and ceramics, respectively, to the chosen site of the installation in Washington, D.C.—as such, the figurines become a cipher for the global trade in ceramics. Cai returned to this theme in *Fragile* (2011) (fig. 7), an installation of white porcelain panels at Mathaf: Arab Museum of Modern Art in Doha, Qatar, ornamented with an Arabic translation of the title in a calligraphic flourish of gunpowder residue staining their otherwise unblemished surface. In contrast to the anxieties of geopolitical conflict and parallels between human impermanence and ocean travel provoked by *The Dragon Has Arrived!* and *Reflection*, *Fragile* appears to strike a more celebratory tone. Cai's use of porcelain as a support for his signature "gunpowder drawing" is central to this shift—gunpowder is, of course, a core ingredient in fireworks, while events of note in China are often commemorated with a porcelain plaque.[33] Cai's panels are ornamented with an applied design of flowering vines that mimics the "arabesques" used to decorate Chinese ceramics for Islamic markets. They are miraculously undamaged by the explosive force of the gunpowder, transforming the tension between opposed elements into a union of complementary forces. Yet the word "fragile" implies that this may be a fleeting truce, and an air of danger is evident in the implied contrast between the durability of porcelain and volatility of gunpowder.

The frailty of porcelain and the movement between worlds evoked by the China Trade are central as well to a series of installations by Liu Jianhua that reveal the parallels between the circulation of mass-produced commodities, economic cycles of planned obsolescence, and natural processes of decay and renewal. Liu started work on the first of these, *Regular-Fragile* (*Richang-Yisui*, also *Daily-Fragile*) in 2002, when news of several plane crashes prompted him to reflect on life's vulnerability:

> [Those crashes] had a profound effect on me, leading me to question the permanence of a lot of everyday things. I started to contemplate the fact that [our] dreams and even [our] lives are so fragile. I also wanted to use the specific material traits of ceramics, which also seem solid but are . . . extremely fragile, so I combined these properties with my ideas.[34]

Coverage of these tragedies, and especially an image of a child's toy floating in the Taiwan Strait with the wreckage of China Airlines Flight 611, prompted Liu to reflect on the health of his son, who had suffered since birth with a medical condition requiring regular hospital visits.[35] With these thoughts at the forefront of his mind, Liu created a series of replicas in porcelain of a teddy bear, plane, and skull. These were followed by other symbolic yet prosaic objects, including a motorcycle helmet, hammer, gun, boxing glove, and a set of weights, chosen for the absurdity of their association with violence and strength when rendered in fragile ceramic. Liu then expanded his repertoire to include mass-produced commodities—hairdryers, bottles and cans, thermos flasks, hats, shoes, and handbags—apparently notable only for their homely familiarity. He used molds taken from a sample of each category to produce slip-cast replicas, pouring liquid clay or "slip" into each one to form a microscopically thin shell of porcelain, just enough to retain the shape when air dried. Applying this method with exacting skill, Liu created forms of such delicacy that they warp when fired, cracking under the strain of their own weight.

Liu's production methods mimic those developed by the manufacturers responsible for the goods he replicates, satirizing their pursuit of profit, yet the similarities end when his replicas leave the workshop. Unlike their prototypes, the latter are not distributed in global networks of exchange or priced for sale to eager buyers, only to wear down until they become dysfunctional or obsolete. Reproduced in a more durable and valuable material that removes function while extending shelf life, his replicas are destined—like Cai's salvaged ship—for re-use in various configurations. They gained their first public display in 2003, in an installation planned for the ill-fated Chinese Pavilion at the 50th Venice Biennale but ultimately installed at the Guangdong Museum of Art, Guangzhou province, when SARS prevented their export.[36] Liu restaged this installation many times in subsequent years, arranging his commodities on gallery floors, mounting them on the walls, suspending them from the rafters, even displaying them on steel-and-glass shelves that mimic those of a high-end boutique.[37] Nevertheless, despite prosaic subject matter and flawed production, the *qingbai* glaze with which Liu covered his replicas imbues them with an otherworldly idealism comparable to that evoked by Cai's *Reflection*. He has explained that this glaze is intended to eradicate fixed meaning, preparing a *tabula rasa* for the projection of new narratives and thereby "inspiring a wide range of viewer experiences [and] affective sensations—joy, pain, excitement, fantasy, secrecy, [and] fear."[38] Faced with a mass of familiar yet sterile commodities, we are compelled to "fill in the blanks" by drawing on our reserves of memory and fantasy, fulfilling the promise of the ideal contained within the materiality of the real.

CHINA™

In the current century, luxury is defined by the marketing of certain products and experiences as more desirable than others. Faced with an expanding field of consumption, in which rarities once available only to a privileged elite are now enjoyed by millions, those who desire to retain a sense of distinction must turn to a constellation of certified luxury brands. The chosen few are distinguished from their commercial competitors, McNeil and Riello explain, by an ability "to convey exclusivity and excellence [in] the quality and the look of their products," orchestrating extravagant promotional campaigns to draw attention to "high quality or novelty of materials [or] detailed workmanship," manufacturing product lines in limited quantities, and closely guarding their "allure and prestigious image" with legal and other protections.[39]

Recent studies by scholars of marketing and promotion trace a parallel trend in the reception of contemporary art, noting the increasing need for artists to cultivate a personal brand if they wish to stand apart from their competitors.[40] The use of a material like porcelain offers one pathway for the achievement of such distinction, yet it can risk exposing an artist's work to appropriation by other entities, individual and otherwise, who seek to develop a brand of their own. The revival of traditional forms of artistic practice, for example, has long been a central conceit of "soft power" campaigns intended to shift international attention away from the ethos of quantity over quality associated with the pejorative label "Made in China," and toward the promise of design innovation and brand leadership suggested by the official slogan "*Created* in China." Porcelain, as a historically Chinese invention and a material of globally acknowledged elegance and refinement, is an ideal ambassador for such aims.[41] Yet, as noted in the opening line of this chapter, it resists singular definition. The same material qualities of artisanal skill and superficial allure deployed in national branding campaigns to obscure the complexities of the present beneath the "allure and prestigious image" of the past can serve radically different ends in the hands of an artist seeking to consolidate a personal brand.

Ai Weiwei has used porcelain to advance his reputation as dissident and activist with increasing frequency over the past decade, often at moments of pivotal significance in the development of this reputation. Two explicitly political works created following the confiscation of his passport and surveillance of his studio, for example, *Free Speech Puzzle* (2014) and *Remains* (2015), have been framed as a response to his experiences of incarceration and censorship. *Free Speech Puzzle* is a jigsaw-like arrangement of tablets adorned with the "hundred flowers" (*baihua buluodi*) motif popular in the Qing dynasty, each bearing the characters for *yanshuo*, meaning "speech," painted on their surface in enamels. The title and design are likely intended to recall the Hundred Flowers Campaign (Baihua qifang) of 1956–57, when intellectuals were encouraged to voice their criticism of the government, only to be detained, exiled, even executed in the ensuing Anti-Rightist Movement (Fanyou yundong) of 1958–59. This persecution is the subject of *Remains*, a scattering of bones allegedly exhumed on the site of a former labor camp and recreated in porcelain with incredible verisimilitude.[42]

Like Ai's earlier *Blue and White* series, these works draw attention to the artisanal skill involved in porcelain manufacture, recalling traditions of skeuomorphic imitation and polychrome enamel ornament much admired by collectors and connoisseurs. Yet Ai does not use the prestige of these traditions to distract from contemporary realities but rather to draw attention to those realities through an aesthetic strategy of hyperbolic juxtaposition. In *Free Speech Puzzle*, the delicacy and fragility of porcelain expose the ease with which the eponymous right can be denied, while the corresponding quality of material endurance, also typical of porcelain, is emphasized in *Remains* as a warning to those who perpetrate such injustices that their crimes will not be forgotten. Five years earlier, Ai emphasized the same qualities, as well as the tradition of the skeuomorph, in his most successful porcelain installation, *Sunflower Seeds* (2010) at the Tate Modern in London, the central conceit of which was the imitation of the eponymous seeds in unglazed ceramic and their reproduction in a quantity massive enough to occupy 1,000 square meters of the Tate's Turbine Hall.

In contrast to the official promotion of porcelain as a coveted inheritance of China's classical past, *Sunflower Seeds*, like Cai's *Kaikou—The Keel (Returning Light—The Dragon Bone)* or Liu's *Regular-Fragile*, drew attention to the humility and humanity of clay and so endorsed Ai's artistic brand as a man of the people. As such, it has been read as an ode to the humble snack food that Ai chose to recreate in this humblest of materials:

> When we grew up, we had nothing. . . . But for even the poorest people, the treat or the treasure we'd have would be the sunflower seeds in everybody's pockets . . . we always had this secret friend and we could always eat it . . . we'd all talk and eat them.[43]

With *Sunflower Seeds*, Ai had intended to recreate this camaraderie by allowing visitors to walk, stand, even sit among the seeds, picking them up to feel the rough ceramic and to hear the resonance of porcelain on porcelain beneath their feet. For marketing and entrepreneurship scholars Daniel Hjorth and Robin Holt, this relational function of the work placed consumers and producers "in proximity [in an] undulating grey sea of possibility, a speaking space from which further speech may take place."[44] Ironically, however, the very tactility that imbued the seeds with an affective charge ultimately curtailed any such spontaneous union when it was discovered that the dust they produced posed a health risk, forcing curators to cordon off the installation.[45]

Nevertheless, *Sunflower Seeds* remains one of Ai's most popular projects, perhaps inspiring his return to the combination of porcelain, plants, and protest with a sculptural series created in 2014. In this series, Ai turned from the germinal promise of seeds to the fleeting beauty of flowers in bloom, reflecting a shift in concept from a meditation on collective solidarity to an affirmation of the value of hope for those whose movements are restricted by surveillance or incarceration. *Bicycle Basket with Flowers* (2014) (fig. 8), for example, commemorates a social media trend in support of Ai's cause. In November 2013, Ai announced on Twitter that he would mark each day following the confiscation of his passport with a bouquet of fresh flowers in the basket of a bicycle outside his Beijing studio, encouraging followers to share images of their own bouquets using the hashtag #flowersforfreedom until he had regained the right to travel. Neither flowers nor porcelain are usually considered political, yet the fragility of Ai's ceramic bouquet belies a potent critique of the limits placed on his movement. Ceramics and floral motifs are often disdained as a subject and material compromised by delicacy and superficiality, yet these qualities equally serve the expression of deeply sincere political statements. There is a certain strength in the fragility of a new blossom, or the equilibrium of a tapering vase. What some might denigrate as an indulgent luxury can be an invitation to tolerance or declaration of self-confidence.

Beyond these relatively superficial dimensions of meaning, flowers and porcelain also possess a limitless symbolic depth. As products of natural forces—the generative potential of organic life and the metamorphosis of raw clay into vitrified ceramic—they offer a concentrated metaphor for the cyclical rhythms of birth, death, decay, and renewal. Shaping clay into complex forms or arranging colorful blossoms provides a calming reassurance of our ability to manipulate these cycles as emblems of shelter and domestic comfort. In 2014, imbuing these dimensions of meaning in *Bicycle Basket with Flowers* with universal significance,

Ai created a more resolved statement of floral resistance in porcelain for the exhibition *@Large: Ai Weiwei on Alcatraz* (2014–15). From his confinement in Beijing, he arranged for the sinks, bathtubs, and toilets of the hospital ward in the former penitentiary to be filled with flowers recreated in undecorated porcelain, the purity of the clay made luminous by a transparent glaze. Several writers, including the exhibition co-curator David Spalding, identified this piece with the comparably arrested potential of the Hundred Flowers Campaign. As such, *Blossom* (2014) can be read, like *Free Speech Puzzle* and *Remains*, as a memorial to those who lost their lives or liberty for speaking truth to power.[46] Yet rather than an elegiac monument, these ornate floral encrustations celebrate the endurance of beauty and innocence, even in degrading conditions. Their installation in a section of the prison set aside for convalescence, "planted" in fixtures of the same material, imbues the sterility of these vessels intended for bathing and waste disposal with the transcendence of the divine.[47] In each of these installations, as in *Sunflower Seeds*, the material qualities of fragility,

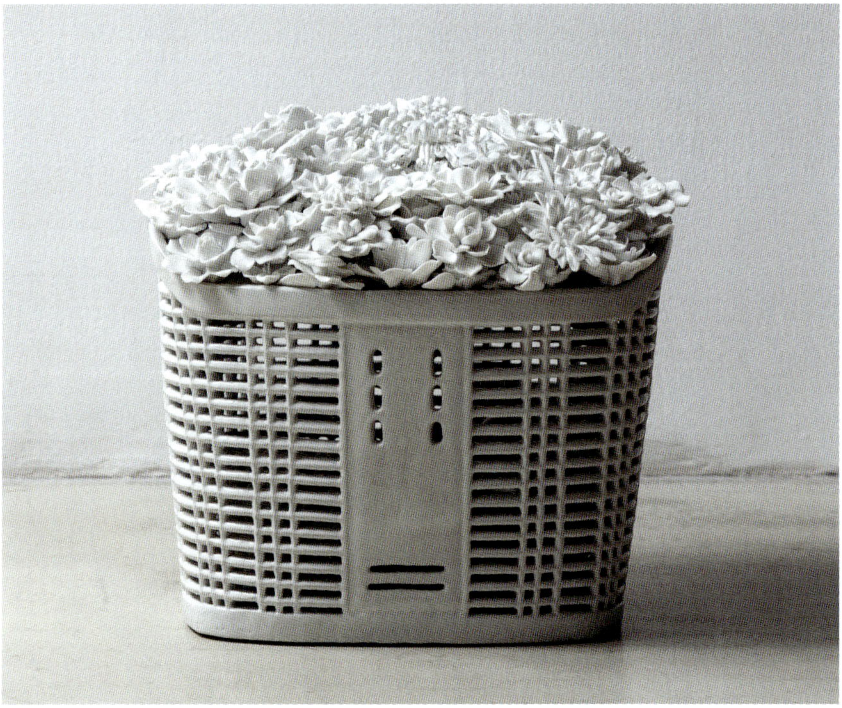

Figure 8 Ai Weiwei, *Bicycle Basket with Flowers*, 2014. Porcelain, 34.3 × 36.8 × 27.9 cm. Courtesy of Ai Weiwei.

delicacy, and endurance contribute to the promotion of Ai's personal brand as an artist-dissident, offering a counterpoint to the parallel use of porcelain by national brand makers as an emblem of refined antiquity.

Cai Guo-Qiang, like Ai Weiwei, is frequently associated with the branding of Chinese national and cultural identity. While Ai has been routinely hailed as a heroic voice for those suffering under authoritarian rule, however, Cai has been accused in equally reductive terms of endorsing Chinese Communist Party-sponsored visions of Chinese ascendancy. Media and culture scholars Lin Zhang and Taj Frazier have identified Cai's role in the spectacle of events like the 2008 Olympics as a primary vector for censure.[48] Cai ensured that the opening ceremonies of the Olympics—the first in China—were the most spectacular since its revival at the turn of the previous century. For an audience of 91,000 and an estimated 1.5 billion television viewers, he illuminated the skies over Beijing with a series of awe-inspiring incendiary displays, including a projection of the *Five Olympic Rings*, a cascade of *Blossoming Peonies*, and his celebrated *Footprints of History*. Zhang and Frazier also note that Cai has been accused of "flaunting exotic, stereotypical cultural and political symbols . . . for commercial profits and career advancement."[49] Yet much of the responsibility for this lies not with the artist but with critics who have persistently associated his work, alongside that of other expatriates, with stereotyped sources as diverse as Daoist cosmic principles, the Confucian ideals of the scholar-gentry, and Maoist maxims.[50] Although not as widely recognised and discussed as his use of gunpowder, Cai's small yet growing body of work in porcelain draws on many of the same philosophical sources while also introducing a specifically material form of cultural and political symbolism. Rather than an "off-brand" deviation from his established artistic approach, it could therefore be equated with the initiation of a new product line, expanding Cai's brand while unintentionally supporting China's officially endorsed national image at the same time.

Accusations of a veiled promotion of the national narrative could be leveled, for example, at a pair of porcelain installations commissioned for *Cai Guo-Qiang: The Transient Landscape* (2019), a recent survey of new work at the National Gallery of Victoria (NGV) in Melbourne, Australia. Seeking to draw a parallel between Cai's spectacular creations and the comparably awe-inspiring remains of China's ancient past, curators installed his work in porcelain alongside—even within—*Terracotta Warriors: Guardians of Immortality* (2019), a parallel display showcasing several of these figures as well as bronze, gold, and jade artifacts of the Zhou, Qin, and Han dynasties.[51] In the exhibition text for *The Transient*

Landscape, Cai admits some resistance to the proposal, mindful perhaps of the accusations of complicity with soft power strategies that might ensue: "I am personally not very fond of exhibitions of ancient artifacts [or] cultural tourism."[52] Such parallels do carry a risk of reductive stereotype, potentially endorsing an anachronistic vision of Chinese art and culture that privileges the inertia of the past over the momentum of the present.[53]

Yet the gunpowder-blackened porcelain installations that Cai created for the NGV—*Murmuration (Landscape)* and *Transience I (Peony)*—recall his earlier combination of these materials in Doha, countering the vaunted immortality of the Terracotta Army and the ancient past it embodies with an unsettling impermanence. *Murmuration (Landscape)* (fig. 9; see also pages 304–5) is comprised of 10,000 porcelain starlings manufactured in Dehua and exposed by the artist to a controlled explosion that has left them stained with gunpowder. For the exhibition in Melbourne, these were suspended from the ceiling of the gallery in an undulating formation with which Cai hoped to recall the mountains of an ink landscape. In the exhibition text, Cai framed his porcelain birds as ghostly emissaries for "the lingering spirits of the underground army, or . . . the haunting shadow of China's imperial past," and imagined Qin Shi Huangdi watching starlings in flight,

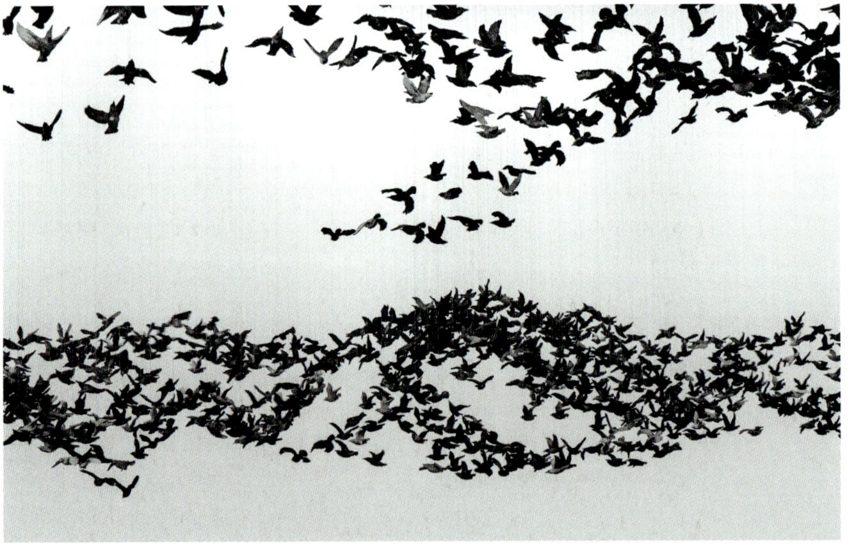

Figure 9 Cai Guo-Qiang, *Murmuration (Landscape)*, 2019. Gunpowder on porcelain, dimensions variable. Collection of the National Gallery of Victoria, Melbourne. Photo: Tobias Titz. Courtesy of Cai Studio.

“empathizing with the hero’s ambition and innermost solitude.”[54] Standing beneath the blackened porcelain, however, this writer felt neither uplifted nor transported; the overriding impression, like that provoked by Ai’s *Sunflower Seeds*, was one of unbearable mass, poised to collapse and smother those standing below.

The same themes reoccur in *Transience I (Peony)*, an installation of porcelain blossoms produced, perhaps, by the same ceramicists commissioned to create *Fragile*, their ethereal whiteness once again embellished with (or scarred by) Cai’s incendiary inscriptions. No longer confined to a single calligraphic flourish, these blooms of explosive potential saturate the *blanc de chine* petals and leaves, piled in an untidy heap on the gallery floor. In the exhibition text, Cai recalls a trip to Luoyang, Henan province, for the peony festival held there every year:

> It was late in the season [and so] many had already begun to fall . . . but the scene touched me deeply. . . . Why do Chinese painters always portray these flowers either in bud or in full bloom? . . . If we say the peony is a symbol of China, it is only interesting if we also incorporate the flower’s decay and withering return to the earth in our representations.[55]

Cai intended *Transience I (Peony)* to convey something of this pathos, “the delicate . . . petals and leaves, infused with colored gunpowder [to] convey the ephemerality of their short lives [and] the lustre of a dark gem.”[56] Crystalized relics, perhaps, of the heavenly blossoms with which he illuminated Beijing ten years earlier, their transubstantiation portending the ensuing collapse of the internationalist ambitions commemorated in *Fragile*. Cai had foreshadowed this downfall even earlier with *Black Peony* (2008) (fig. 10), created for his retrospective at the Guggenheim Museum: a lone ceramic flower that exemplifies the hope for a better future, or a more peaceful realm beyond this one, so central to *Fragile* and *Transience I (Peony)* but obscured in these installations by a patina of gunpowder residue marking the explosive passage of events beyond our control. Each work casts doubt on the purity of porcelain and the anticipated renewal implied by the bouquets we present to the bereaved—connotations also championed in Ai’s *Bicycle Basket with Flowers* and *Blossom*—seeking instead to expose the impermanence of all such ideals. Yet they also create a tension between each artist’s brand and the narratives of national ascendancy with which their medium is associated, marking a path beyond the ready-made appeal of a stereotyped antiquity by harnessing material qualities of porcelain that simultaneously underlie and transcend its historical, cultural, and political connotations.

Nevertheless, for Cai Guo-Qiang as for Ai Weiwei and Liu Jianhua, the allure of porcelain is not confined to the mutability of clay or fragility of broken ceramic. These qualities have a place in their work, yet their affective charge is secondary to an affiliation with the discursive dynamics of luxury. Unlike the typical contemporary materialist, neither Cai nor Ai nor Liu expose the abject, raw, unprocessed, or un-aesthetic. On the contrary, they cultivate the luxurious allure of antique patina and time-honored provenance, the fragile mystery and mobility of the exotic, and the confidence inspired by a trusted brand. At the same time, they also practice a distinctly fugitive approach, transgressing established conventions and striving to remain independent in their open-ended exploration of novel material possibilities.

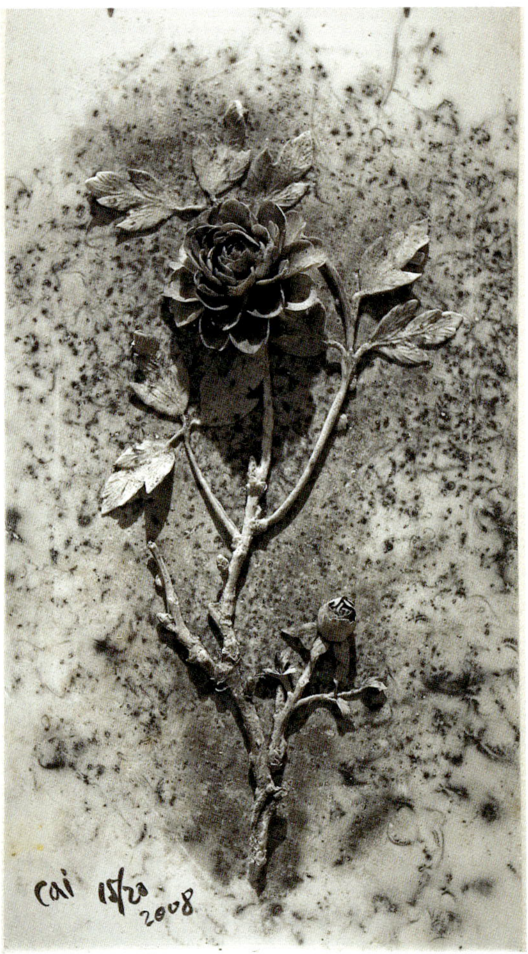

Figure 10 Cai Guo-Qiang, *Black Peony*, 2008. Gunpowder on porcelain, 66.83 × 37.31 × 5.72 cm. Photo: I-Hua Lee. Courtesy of Cai Studio.

NOTES

1. Fox Butterfield, "Serving the Workers and Peasants: Wang Keping," in *China: Alive in the Bitter Sea* (London: Coronet, 1983), 597.

2. For more on Jingdezhen, see Maris Boyd Gillette, *China's Porcelain Capital: The Rise, Fall and Reinvention of Ceramics in Jingdezhen* (New York: Bloomsbury, 2016); and Anne Gerritsen, *The City of Blue and White: Chinese Porcelain and the Early Modern World* (Cambridge: Cambridge University Press, 2020).

3. Luise Guest, "Translation, Transformation and Refiguration: The Significance of Jingdezhen and the Materiality of Porcelain in the Work of Two Contemporary Chinese Artists," *Journal of Contemporary Chinese Art* 6, no. 2/3 (2019): 213.

4. Jin Simeng, "Liu Jianhua: Gei yishu zuo jian qu" [Liu Jianhua: an art of subtraction], *L'Officiel Art China* (January 2013): 89.

5. Liu Jianhua, in Guest, "Translation, Transformation and Refiguration," 214.

6. Liu Jianhua, in Pi Li, "Polychrome Ceramics, Cheongsam and Chinese Porcelain," in *Porcelain-Like Skin*, ed. Zhu Qi and Pi Li, trans. Trevor Morris (Hong Kong: Hanart TZ Gallery, 2001), 17.

7. Philip Tinari, "Postures in Clay: The Vessels of Ai Weiwei," in *Ai Weiwei: Dropping the Urn (Ceramic Works, 5000 BCE–2010 CE)*, ed. Gregg Moore and Richard Torchia (Glenside, PA: Arcadia University Art Gallery, 2010), 31.

8. An image of Ai's porcelain owl appeared in *Renmin huabao*, no. 4 (1979) alongside an article detailing the state-led revival of the Cizhou kilns. In 1974, Huang Yongyu's *Winking Owl* (1973) was chosen as one of many "counter-revolutionary" works included in the notorious *Black Painting Exhibitions (heihua zhanlan)* staged by Jiang Qing and her allies to kindle the flames of revolutionary ardor.

9. Peter McNeil and Giorgio Riello, *Luxury: A Rich History* (Oxford: Oxford University Press, 2016), 4–5.

10. Wu Hung, "Material Art from China: An Introduction," in Wu Hung and Orianna Cacchione, *The Allure of Matter: Material Art from China* (Chicago: David and Alfred Smart Museum of Art, 2019), 33.

11. McNeil and Riello, *Luxury*, 11–13, 38–40.

12. Jonathan Hay, *Sensuous Surfaces: The Decorative Object in Early Modern China* (London: Reaktion Books, 2010), 12–13.

13. Ai Weiwei, in Ai Weiwei and Charles Merewether, "Changing Perspective," in *Ai Weiwei–Works: Beijing 1993–2003*, ed. Charles Merewether (Hong Kong: Timezone 8, 2003), 28.

14. Ai Weiwei, in Ai Weiwei and Brendan McGetrick, "Ai Weiwei: Cultural Evidence," *Flash Art International* 43, no. 275 (November–December 2010): 57–58.

15. Garth Clark, for example, noting that these works "could easily just be regular forgeries," imagines Ai "slipping them quietly into the marketplace," with "destabilising [sic] and seditious" consequences, while Danielle Shang defines the *Blue and White* series as one of many projects in which Ai has destroyed or defaced allegedly antique ceramics, forcing viewers to question the value of such artifacts as well as the authority of those who claim to measure such value. Garth Clark, "Mind Mud: Ai Weiwei's Conceptual Ceramics," in *Ceramics in America*, ed. Robert Hunter (Lebanon, NH: Chipstone, 2011), 64–65; Danielle Shang, "Multiply It and Fake It: On Ai Weiwei," *Yishu* 11, no. 2 (March/April 2012): 42–44.

16. Ai Weiwei, in Ai Weiwei and Robert Bernell, "Ai Weiwei with Robert Bernell," in *Chinese Art at the End of the Millennium*, ed. John Clark (Hong Kong: New Art Media, 2000), 176–78.
17. Ai and Bernell, "Ai Weiwei with Robert Bernell," 176–78
18. Liu Jianhua, in Yan Yuting and Liu Jianhua, "Shanbianzhong de Liu Jianhua: Yishu zhuanbian de neizai luoji—Yan Yuting duihua Liu Jianhua" [The evolution of Liu Jianhua: Internal logic for art transformation—Yan Yuting in dialogue with Liu Jianhua], *Dongfang Yishu*, no. 3 (2009): 41; Liu Jianhua, in Liu Jianhua and Zhu Qi, "Ruguo mimang dehua, wo hui buzhi suo cuo—dui Liu Jianhua de fangtan" [If you're confused, then I have no idea—an interview with Liu Jianhua], ShanghART Gallery (March 23, 2001), accessed March 3, 2021, http://www.shanghart.com/texts/LJH-interview-c.htm.
19. Pi, "Polychrome Ceramics," 16; Johnson Chang, "Flesh in Porcelain: Liu Jianhua," in *Three Artists from Kunming*, ed. Marcello Kwan (Hong Kong: Hanart TZ Gallery, 1999), 3; Zhang Hongxia, "Body of Desires Beneath Porcelain Skin," *Ceramics: Art and Perception*, no. 99 (2015): 74–75.
20. Liu Jianhua, "Infatuated Memory," in *Three Artists from Kunming*, 15.
21. Liu, in Liu and Zhu, "If you're confused."
22. Garth Clark, review of *Ai Weiwei: Dropping the Urn (Ceramic Works, 5000 BCE–2010 CE)* at Arcadia University Art Gallery, Glenside, PA, February 24–April 28, 2010, *ArtAsiaPacific*, no. 70 (September/October 2010): 159.
23. See, for example, Sue-an van der Zijpp, "Unbreakable," in *Ai Weiwei*, ed. Mark Wilson and Sue-an van der Zijpp (Groningen: Groninger Museum, 2008), 11.
24. Maxwell K. Hearn, *Ink Art: Past as Present in Contemporary China* (New York: Metropolitan Museum of Art, 2013), 170–71.
25. For further discussion of sensuous surfaces in porcelain art by Ai Weiwei and Liu Jianhua, see Alex Burchmore, "The Visual and Tactile Experience of the Monochrome: Mapping Surfacescapes in Ai Weiwei's *Colored Vases* and Liu Jianhua's *Container* series," *TAASA Review* 28, no. 1 (March 2019): 4–6.
26. McNeil and Riello, *Luxury*, 97–103.
27. Dana Friis-Hansen, "Towards a New Methodology in Art," in *Cai Guo-Qiang*, ed. Dana Friis-Hansen, Octavio Zaya, and Serizawa Takashi (New York: Phaidon, 2002), 60–62; Michelle Yun, in *Cai Guo-Qiang: I Want to Believe*, ed. Thomas Krens and Alexandra Munroe (New York: Solomon R. Guggenheim Museum, 2008), 194.
28. Cai Guo-Qiang, "On Venice's *Rent Collection Courtyard*," translated by Philip Tinari, in *I Want to Believe*, 280. For further discussion of the "China Threat" polemic and its implications for the reception of Chinese art, see Alex Burchmore, "*La maladie de porcelaine*: Liu Jianhua's *Regular/Fragile* (2007) at Oxburgh Hall and the History of Massed Porcelain Display in English Aristocratic Interiors," *Oxford Art Journal* 42, no. 3 (2019): 257–63.
29. Cai, "Octavio Zaya in Conversation with Cai Guo-Qiang," in *Cai Guo-Qiang*, 18.
30. Cai Guo-Qiang in Sarah Tanguy, "Fire Medicine: A Conversation with Cai Guo-Qiang," *Sculpture* 24, no. 4 (May 2005): 36.
31. Tanguy, "Fire Medicine: A Conversation with Cai Guo-Qiang," 34.
32. In the years between the creation of *Kaikou—The Keel (Returning Light—The Dragon Bone)* and *Reflection—A Gift from Iwaki*, Cai established a comparable connection between Dehua and the mountain village of Tsunan in Niigata Prefecture with *DMoCA: Dragon Museum of Contemporary Art*, the first work in his "*Everything Is Museum*" series. Following a pattern of community consultation and collaboration comparable to that which he had initiated six years earlier in Iwaki, Cai directed

the dismantling of a characteristic "dragon kiln" in Dehua—first built in 1956 and so a relic of the same era as the fishing boat—which he then shipped to and reconstructed in Niigata as an exhibition space for use during the inaugural Echigo-Tsumari Art Triennial. After the conclusion of the Triennial, Tsunan residents assumed responsibility for the custodianship of the kiln/museum, which remains a popular venue for both the Triennial and other community-based arts events. Reiko Tomii, in *I Want to Believe*, 242.

33. Following the transfer of sovereignty over Hong Kong from the United Kingdom to the People's Republic of China on July 1, 1997, for example, the Jiangxi Provincial Government presented the Hong Kong Conference Centre with a commemorative porcelain plaque measuring over two meters in width and inscribed with the unambiguous title, "Return to the Fatherland." Feng Guoping, Hu Yinjiao, and Shao Jimei, *Jingdezhen: A City with Kiln-fire Burning a Thousand Years* (Beijing: Intercontinental Press, 2006), 90.

34. Liu, in Yan and Liu, "The Evolution of Liu Jianhua," 42. The three ill-fated flights were: Air China Flight 129, which crashed in Busan, South Korea, on April 15, 2002, killing 129 passengers and crew; China Northern Airlines Flight 6136, which crashed near Dalian, Liaoning province, on May 7, 2002, killing all 112 onboard; and China Airlines Flight 611, which disintegrated above the Taiwan Strait, killing all 225 onboard. The four American Airlines and United Airlines flights hijacked to commit the September 11 attacks in the previous year, as well as the notorious Hainan Island incident of April 1, 2001, may have provided further inspiration, conscious or otherwise.

35. Yan and Liu, "The Evolution of Liu Jianhua," 42. For further discussion of *Regular-Fragile*, see Monica Dematté, "Projecting Dreams: Liu Jianhua's Spiritual Things," *Yishu* 9, no. 1 (January/February 2010): 19, 28.

36. For further discussion of *Regular-Fragile* and the 2003 Chinese Pavilion, see Meiqin Wang, "Officialising the Unofficial: Presenting New Chinese Art to the World," *Modern Chinese Literature and Culture* 21, no. 1 (Spring 2009): 102–40.

37. For further discussion of some of these subsequent iterations of *Regular-Fragile*, see Alex Burchmore, "Smashing Vases: Ceramics and the Aesthetics of Destruction in Works by Ai Weiwei and Liu Jianhua," *Espace Art Actuel*, no. 122 (Spring–Summer 2019): 36–45.

38. Liu Jianhua, "Siwei de lianguanxing: Guanyu wo zhexie nian de zuopin" [Collected thoughts: about my work over the years], *Suzhou gongyi meishu zhiye jishu xueyuan xuebao*, no. 2 (2014): 77.

39. McNeil and Riello, *Luxury*, 257–61. The phrase "allure and prestigious image" was used in a ruling by the European Court of Justice in 2009 to define the protection of an intangible "aura of luxury" in a dispute between brands.

40. See, for example, Chloe Preece, "The Authentic Celebrity Brand: Unpacking Ai Weiwei's Celebritised Selves," *Journal of Marketing Management* 31, no. 5/6 (2015): 616–45.

41. Some idea of the extent to which the luxurious allure and historical significance of porcelain have played a key role in government-endorsed soft power initiatives can be gained by noting the transformation of Jingdezhen from an ailing post-industrial city to a thriving hub for heritage tourism. This transformation was initiated in 1979 with the construction of replica Ming-dynasty workshops in preparation for the naming of Jingdezhen in 1982 as one of twenty-four National Famous Historical and Cultural Cities (*Guojia lishi wenhua mingcheng*), and the opening in 1984 of the Jingdezhen Ceramics Museum. The culmination of these and subsequent programs of urban redevelopment and "museumification" was attained in 2014 when UNESCO named Jingdezhen a

Creative City of Crafts and Folk Arts, in recognition of both its historic prestige and contemporary rejuvenation. For further discussion of Jingdezhen as a tourist destination, see: Alex Burchmore, "Drifting through the Porcelain Capital: Art Residencies and the Enforced Continuity of an Illustrious Past in Jingdezhen, China," *Kunstlicht* 39, no. 2 (2018): 39–49; and Zhang Xinmin, Xie Hualin, Zhou Caihua, and Zeng Bindan, "Jingdezhen: The Millennium Porcelain Capital," *Cities* 98 (March 2020): 1–9.

42. Adrian Locke, ed., *Ai Weiwei* (London: Royal Academy of Arts, 2015), 197.

43. Ai Weiwei, Juliet Bingham, and Marko Daniel, "A Conversation," in *Ai Weiwei: Sunflower Seeds*, ed. Juliet Bingham (London: Tate Publishing, 2010), 79.

44. Daniel Hjorth and Robin Holt, "It's Entrepreneurship, Not Enterprise: Ai Weiwei as Entrepreneur," *Journal of Business Venturing Insights* 5 (June 2016): 52.

45. Mike McKiernan, "La maladie de porcelaine," *Occupational Medicine*, 61, no. 3 (2011): 146.

46. David Spalding, *@Large: Ai Weiwei on Alcatraz* (San Francisco: FOR-SITE Foundation, 2014), 98; David Raymond Bell, "Aesthetic Encounters and Learning in the Museum," *Educational Philosophy and Theory* 49, no. 8 (2017): 779; Erika Doss, "Public Art, Public Feeling: Contrasting Site-Specific Projects of Christo and Ai Weiwei," *Public Art Dialogue* 7, no. 2 (2017): 217–18; Mary Thomas, "Beyond Bars and Broken Wings: A Review of *@Large: Ai Weiwei on Alcatraz*," *American Quarterly* 68, no. 1 (March 2016): 143.

47. For further discussion of *Blossom*, see Alex Burchmore, "Floral Resistance to Authoritarianism and Incarceration in Porcelain Installations by Ai Weiwei and Cai Guo-Qiang," *Esse Arts + Opinions*, no. 99 (April 2020): 70–77.

48. Lin Zhang and Taj Frazier, "'Playing the Chinese Card': Globalisation and the Aesthetic Strategies of Chinese Contemporary Artists," *International Journal of Cultural Studies* 20, no. 6 (2017): 571–72.

49. Zhang and Frazier, "'Playing the Chinese Card,'" 566–67.

50. See, for example, Abdulwahed al-Mawlawi, "*Saraab*: A Constant Negotiation with the Invisible," in *Cai Guo-Qiang: Saraab*, ed. Wassan Al-Khudairi (Doha: Arab Museum of Modern Art, 2012), 367–73; Friis-Hansen, "Towards a New Methodology," 40–42; and Alexandra Munroe, "Cai Guo-Qiang: I Want To Believe," in *I Want to Believe*, edited by Thomas Krens and Alexandra Munroe (New York: Solomon R. Guggenheim Museum, 2008), 27–29. Cai has, to a certain extent, encouraged such associations with his frequent reference to the same traditions. Consider, for example, the following two statements published in 1988 and 2002: "Through my work, I explore my inherited culture. . . . Being a proud son fostered on 5,000 years of culture, I . . . find myself in direct communion with my forefathers who, laying their mighty palms upon my shoulders, endow me with a sacred strength." Cai Guo-Qiang and You Jindong, "Painting with Gunpowder," *Leonardo* 21, no. 3 (July 1988): 253. "My father is a calligrapher [and] my home was always full of traditional artists and a love for traditional Chinese art; my family was always talking about the grandeur and accomplishment of Chinese art and civilisation. . . . Now, looking back, I see I've inherited some of my father's scholarly thinking; Chinese cultural tradition is a part of me." Cai, "Octavio Zaya in Conversation with Cai Guo-Qiang" in *Cai Guo-Qiang*, 10.

51. Wayne Crothers, ed., *Terracotta Warriors: Guardians of Immortality* (Melbourne: National Gallery of Victoria, 2019). This was not the first time that such a comparison had been drawn—*Chaos: Cai Guo-Qiang* (1994) at the Setagaya Art Museum in Tokyo was timed to coincide with a display of Qin dynasty artifacts that included several conscripts from the ancient battalion. Two of the works Cai created for the exhibition, *Grave Robbing* and *Elixir of Immortality*, were intended as a direct response to this anachronistic pairing. Lesley Ma, "History in a Flash," in *Cai Guo-Qiang: The Transient Landscape*, ed. Lesley Ma (Melbourne: National Gallery of Victoria, 2019), 18–20.

52. Cai Guo-Qiang, "Shadow of the Empire," in *Cai Guo-Qiang: The Transient Landscape*, 41–44.

53. For further discussion of these stereotypes in *Cai Guo-Qiang: The Transient Landscape* and *Terracotta Warriors: Guardians of Immortality*, see Alex Burchmore, "The factory-assemblist and the scholar-artist in the historiography of Chinese art," *Art Monthly Australasia*, no. 319 (October 2019): 46–53.

54. Cai, "Shadow of the Empire," 50.

55. Cai, "Shadow of the Empire," 48.

56. Cai Guo-Qiang, in *The Transient Landscape*, 77.

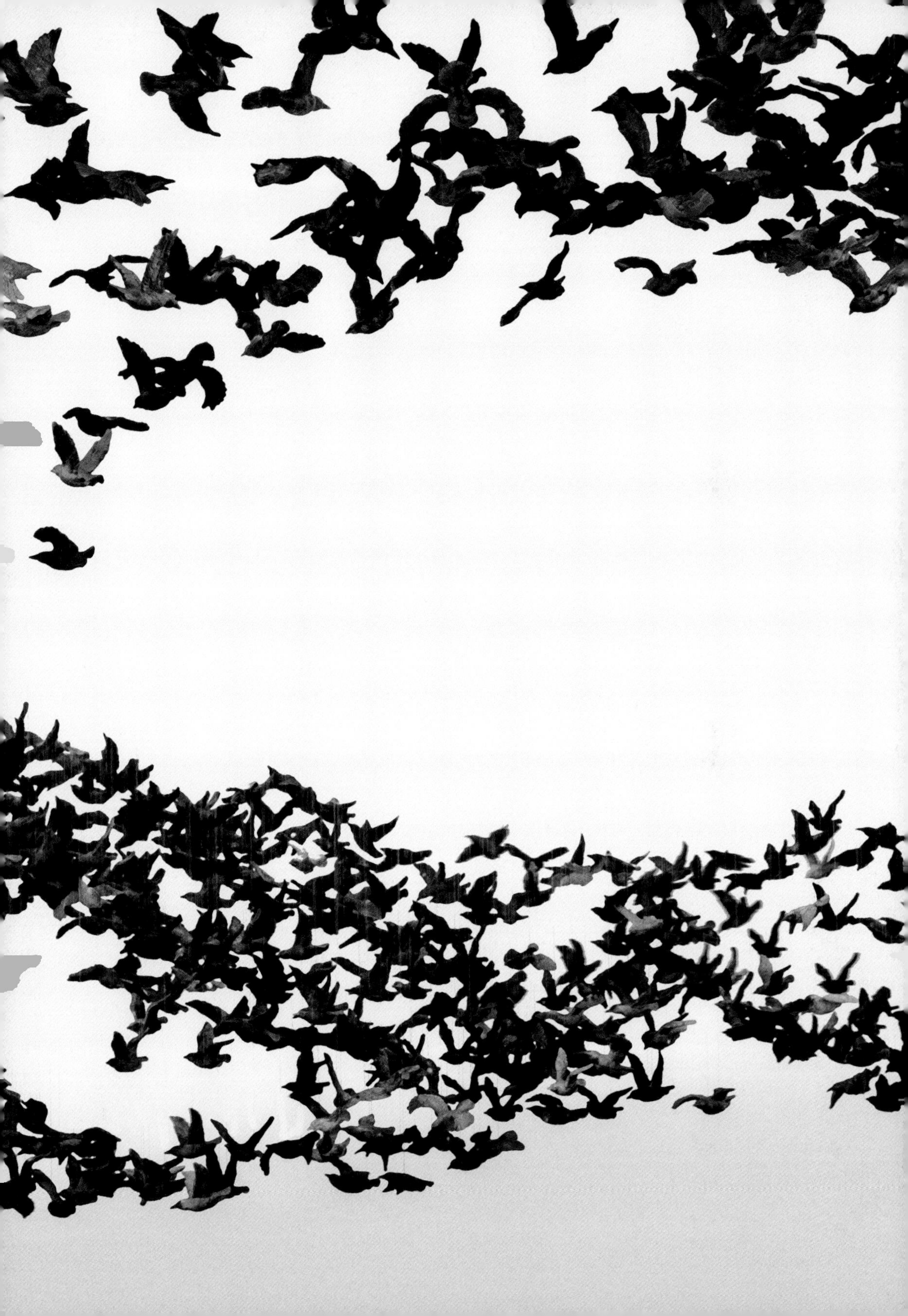

GLOSSARY OF CHINESE TERMS

'85 meishu xinchao　'85 美术新潮
'85 meishu yundong　'85美术运动
Ai Weiwei　艾未未
babaohuidi　八宝灰地
baibaoqian　百宝嵌
baihua buluodi　百花不落地
Baihua qifang　百花齐放
baishi　白石
Baiyun guan　白云观
baojuan　宝卷
Beihai　北海
Beijing dongcun　北京东村
beizi　褙子
[bi]chun wannian youjin
(笔)醇晚年尤谨
biliuli　璧流离
bian　变
boli　颇黎
bolisheng　玻璃声
Boxing　博兴
Cai Guo-Qiang　蔡国强
caihua tiejin　彩画贴金
caizhi yishu　材质艺术
Cangzhou　沧州
Chang Bei　长北
Changju　长沮
chaoshi de shouduan　潮湿的手段
chaoshou　抄手
Chaozhou　潮州
Chen Hongshou (Mansheng)
陈鸿寿(曼生)
Chen Wenshu　陈文述
Cheng Jingben　成景本
chengni　澄泥
chi　尺
Chongyang jie　重阳节
Chujue yishu　触觉艺术
chun　纯
chunjin qiangong bugou yanxiao
醇谨谦恭不苟言笑
Chun Zaifeng　醇载沣
Cidu　瓷都
Cishi pusa luexiu yuqie niansong fa
慈氏菩萨略修瑜伽念诵法
Cixi　慈禧
cuhao zhibi　粗豪之笔
cun　寸
Da baoji jing　大宝积经
Dacheng zaoxiang gongde jing
大乘造像功德经
da fachuan　大法船
Daju gui　大巨鬼
Daliang　大良
Da Ming Yongle nian zhi　大明永乐年制
Dashi ye　大士爷
Da song chuan　大送船
Da Tang xiyu ji　大唐西域记
Daxingguosi　大兴国寺
Dazhuangyansi　大庄严寺
Dai Kui　戴逵
Danxia Tianran　丹霞天然
Dao　道
Dao'an　道安
Daofa huiyuan　道法会元

Daoguang 道光
Daoguang wushu xia liuyue Kuisheng fanggu 道光戊戌夏六月葵生仿古
Daoxing bore jing 道行般若经
Daoxuan 道宣
Dehua 德化
Dizang 地藏
diao 雕
diaoqi hua 雕漆画
diaoqi 雕漆
Dingyou 丁酉
Dingzhou 定州
Donghuamen 东华门
Dongxin xiansheng 冬心先生
Dong yin 栋印
duanwen 断纹
Duanwu jie 端午节
er manyue li fachuan 二满月礼法船
Fachuan jing 法船经
Fachuan jing yijuan 法船经一卷
Fachuan pai 法船派
Famensi 法门寺
fashen 法身
Fayuansi 法源寺
Fayuan zhulin 法苑珠林
fan 范
Fanyou yundong 反右运动
fang 仿
Fangbi 方弼
fanggu 仿古
fang Song Xuanhe neifu zhi 仿宋宣和內府制
fang Tang jinglan 仿唐井栏
fangxiang 方相
fei chuangtong cailiao 非传统材料
feihuo fachuan 飞火法船
fei wu 非物
fei wuzhi 非物质
fei wuzhihua 非物质化
fenshao 焚烧
Fenshao Xiamen dada zhanchu zuopin yishu huodong 焚烧厦门达达展出作品艺术活动
Fengquansi 凤泉寺
Fuchengmen 阜成门
Fuhai 福海
Fuping 富平
Ga De 嘎德
gaizhuang 改装
ganying 感应
Gao Shiqi 高士奇
gaoya tonggu 高雅通古
Ge Hong 葛洪
gengzi 埂子
Gaige kaifang 改革开放
Gaochang 高昌
Gu Dexin 顾德新
Gu Guangqi (Qianli) 顾广圻 (千里)
gupu yajie 古朴雅洁
guyi 古异
Guyu shuwu 古榆书屋
Guanfo sanmei haijing 观佛三昧海经
Guangxu 光绪
Guangyi ji 广异记
Guanyin 观音
guanyin zhi 观音纸
guan 官
Guan Yi 管艺
Guan Yi yishu wenxianguan 管艺艺术文献馆
guikemu 龟壳墓
Guojia lishi wenhua mingcheng 国家历史文化名城

Guozhou 虢州
Haimen 海门
He Chou 何稠
Hejiacun 何家村
Hetaoyuan dazhuangyansi yihaota
核桃园大庄严寺一号塔
Heibai wuchang gui 黑白无常鬼
heihua zhanlan 黑画展览
Hongloumeng 红楼梦
Hong Mai 洪迈
Hongyesi 弘业寺
Hou Hanru 侯瀚如
huachuan 华船
huachuan 画船
huajiang 画匠
hua lianchuan 化莲船
Hu Meier 胡媚儿
Hualin xinyong 画林新咏
Hua Yan 华岩
Huang Cheng 黄成
Huang Ping 黄平
Huang Rui 黄锐
Huang Tingjian 黄庭坚
Huang Yong Ping 黄永砅
Huang Yongyu 黄永玉
Huihuiguan yiyu 回回馆译语
huihuai 毁坏
huojing 火精
huoyao 火药
huozhu 火珠
jijie xinsi 既竭心思
Ji Naijin 紀乃進
jiachu 夹紵
Jiading 嘉定
Jiaqing 嘉庆
jiansheng 监生
Jiangnan Songjiangfu Huatingxian Baishacun Xiaoxiu huilang baojuan
江南松江府华亭县白沙屯孝修回郎宝卷
Jiang Shoucheng 姜守诚
Jiao Yaoming 焦耀明
Jiaozhou 交州
Jieni 桀溺
jindiwen 锦地纹
Jin Heshang 金和尚
Jin Nong 金农
jinren 金人
jintong xiang 金铜像
jinxiang 金像
jingbei Jin hua 镜背晋画
Jingdezhen 景德镇
jingshi miaowu 精识妙悟
jingxin fodao yiwei zhu mucai
净心佛道以为诸木材
Jingzhisi 静志寺
juan hua 绢画
juanjian 捐监
juzhi xiang 俱胝像
Kangxi 康熙
kehuiqi 刻灰漆
kesi hua 缂丝画
Kusang ge 哭丧歌
kuancai 款彩
Kuisheng zhiyin 葵生之印
Kunming hu 昆明湖
Laiwen 来文
Laomu 老母
Lichun 立春
Li He 李贺
Li Xiang 李翔
Liyang 溧阳
Li Yaonian 李跃年

Li Yongbin 李永斌
Lianggezhuang 梁各庄
liangting 凉亭
Liang Shaoji 梁绍基
Liang Tongshu 梁同书
Liaozhai zhiyi 聊斋志异
Lin Chun 林春
Lin Jiahua 林嘉华
Linyi 林邑
lingmei 灵媒
Liu Jianhua 刘建华
liuli 琉璃
Liuqiuguo hua 琉球国画
Liu Yiling 刘一菱
long 龙
Longyu 隆裕
lüci 绿磁
luding fanghan 盝顶方函
Lu Dong (Kuisheng) 卢栋 (葵生)
Lu Shenzhi 卢慎之
Lu Yingzhi 卢映之
lunhui 轮回
Luoshengbai re 罗生柏热
Luoyang 洛阳
maki-e (J) 莳绘
Ma Liuming 马六明
Ma Yuan 马远
man(sheng) hu 曼(生)壶
Mao Zedong sixiang xuanchuan dui 毛泽东思想宣传队
mei 美
meijie 媒介
Meishu sichao 美术思潮
Meishu xinchao 美术新潮
Mianran dashi 面燃大士
Mianran guiwang 面燃鬼王
Mianran gui 面燃鬼
mihua 米画
Mingbao ji 冥报记
mingliao 冥料
mingqi zhizha 冥器纸扎
mingqi 明器
mo 模
mobu biju yijin qibian 莫不毕具以尽其变
Mogaoku 莫高窟
moyu 墨玉
Muling 慕陵
Nanhai jigui neifa zhuan 南海寄归内法传
Nantong 南通
neiwai tongche 內外通彻
neiwai yingche 内外应澈
niuli 牛李
penjin hua 喷金画
Peng Yuncan 彭蕴璨
Pi Li 皮力
Pingcheng 平城
Pingsha xiying 平沙息影
Puming 普明
Pu Songling 蒲松龄
puti ruixiang 菩提瑞像
Puxian 普贤
qibaoxiang 七宝箱
qipao 旗袍
qipidiao 漆皮雕
qisha 漆砂
Qishayan ji 漆砂砚记
qixi fachuan 七夕法船
Qizhou 岐州
qia hua 掐画
Qianlong 乾隆
Qiantang 钱塘
Qian Yong 钱泳

Qinhuangdao 秦皇岛

qinzi duzao ruya mingliao shenliao wucai zhipin fashou 亲自督造儒雅冥料神料五彩纸品发售

qingbai 清白

Qingming jie 清明节

Qinglongxian 青龙县

qingshi 青石

qiongjie bujin 穷劫不尽

Qiu Zhijie 邱志杰

Qiu Zhong 裘钟

Quyang 曲阳

Quanzhou gaojia xiju tuan 泉州高甲戏剧团

Quanzhou 泉州

Renmin huabao 人民画报

renru rouruan yinian wei ding 忍辱柔软忆念为钉

Ribenguo hua 日本国画

Ronger 荣儿

Rong Rong 荣荣

ru liuli 如琉璃

ru shuijing 如水精

ruixiang 瑞像

sajin jianzhi 撒(洒)金笺纸

sangyi 丧仪

Shancai 善财

Shanghai meishu yongpin chang 上海美术用品厂

Shanghai xiju xueyuan 上海戏剧学院

Shangyuan jie 上元节

shaozhi 烧纸

sheli rongqi 舍利容器

Shendesi 神德寺

Shen Kuo 沈括

shenliao 神料

Shenxiao qianwen songchuan yi 神霄遣瘟送船仪

Shenxiao qianwen zhibing juefa 神霄遣瘟治病决法

shenzhi 神纸

Shen Yuan 沈遠

Shen Zhou 沈周

Shi Hui 施慧

Shibao 实报

Shijiamouni 释伽牟尼

shike Han hua 石刻汉画

shishi yitan 施食一坛

shiwu pintie fudiao 实物拼贴浮雕

Shoudu shifan daxue 首都师范大学

shuijing 水精

shuise ningjie 水色凝结

Shunde 顺德

Song Di 宋迪

Song Dong 宋东

Songfengge shi 松风阁诗

songwen chuan 送瘟船

Songzhuang yishuqu 宋庄艺术区

Suzhou 苏州

Sui Renqian 眭仁倩

Sun Guoxin 孙国信

Sun Guoxin yin 孙国信印

Sun Wen 孙温

Tang Peng 汤鹏

tangyang 烫样

Tao Qian 陶潜

ti 剃

tihong 剃紅

Tian Xilai 田喜来

tiehua 铁花

tie hua 铁画

tiehua ge 铁画歌

Tingli guan 听鹂馆
tuokong xiang 脱空像
tuomo nixiang 拓摸泥像
tuo 拓
tuo 脱
wanquan kong de nengzhi 完全空的能指
Wang Bomin 王伯敏
Wang Gongxi 王功新
Wang Keping 王克平
Wang Luyan 王鲁炎
Wang Qi 王琦
Wang Shixiang 王世襄
Wang Xianzhi 王献之
Wang Xuance 王玄策
Wang Yikun 王以坤
Wang Yun 汪鋆
Wei Qianheng 卫谦恒
Weituo 韦陀
Wei Yingwu 韦应物
Wenchuan pai 瘟船派
Wen jin tu 问津图
Wenshen 瘟神
wenshou 吻兽
Wenshu 文殊
Wen Zhengming 文徵明
Wen Zhenheng 文震亨
Wenzhou 温州
wu 无
wu 物
wu biaoli 无表里
wucai 五彩
Wuhu 芜湖
Wu Meichun 吳美纯
Wu ren xiandai yishu zuopin zhanlan 无人现代艺术作品展览
wuse zhi 五色纸
wushen xia liuyue, Kuisheng fu Linglingsi Tang jingwen zhiwei chaju 戊申夏六月葵生撫零陵寺唐井文制为茶具
Wu Wei 吴伟
wuwu 无物
Wu Yanping 吴燕萍
wuzhi 物质
Wuzhong 吴中
xihe 羲和
xi fachuan 习法船
xiji 袭击
Xiyang hua 西洋画
Xiamen dada 厦门达达
Xiamen dada – xiandai yishuzhan 厦门达达 – 现代艺术展
Xiamen meixie 厦门美协
Xiamenshi qunzhong yishuguan 厦门市群众艺术馆
xianchangpin pintie 现成品拼贴
Xianxiang - yingxiang 现象–影像
xianghao juzu 相好具足
xiangjiao 像教
xiang 相
Xiao Yuncong (Chimu) 萧云从 (尺木)
xiaojin 销金
xiaoshen 孝慎
Xin jiexin xiaozu 新解析小组
Xin kedu xiaozu 新刻度小组
xingxiang 行像
Xingxing huahui 星星画会
Xiudesi 修德寺
Xiudingsi 修定寺
xiu hua 绣画
Xiushilu 髹饰錄
xiyu Han hua 西域汉画

Xizang hua 西藏画
xu yi shan ye 絮一苫也
Xuanhe 宣和
Xuantong 宣统
xuanzhi 宣纸
Xuanzang 玄奘
xuejin xuan 雪金宣
yahua jianzhi 砑花笺纸
yan hua 烟画
yanhuo fachuan 烟火法船
Yankou guiwang 焰口鬼王
Yan Lei 颜磊
yanqiao 妍巧
yanran Da Mi shanshui yifu
俨然大米山水一幅
Yanzhou 兖州
Yang Jian 杨坚
Yangzhou 扬州
Yangzhou huayuan lu
扬州画苑录
Yaozhou 耀州
Yecheng 邺城
Yiheyuan 颐和园
Yijian zhi 夷坚志
Yijing 义净
Yijing 易经
Yixing 宜兴
yin 印
yinsha fo 印沙佛
Yinsha fohui 印沙佛会
yinshou 引首
Yin Xiuzhen 尹秀珍
yingwu 映物
Yingzao si 营造司
Yonghegong 雍和宫
you 有
youse 有色
you wendu 有温度
Youzhou 幽州
yu hua 雨画
yujin xuan 雨金宣
yulan 盂兰
yulan daochang 盂兰道场
yulan daochang yanhuo fachuan
盂兰道场烟火法船
Yulan shengmu 盂兰圣母
yuxiang 玉像
Yu Xiaogang 俞晓刚
yuxue xuan 雨雪宣
Yuanchun 元春
Yuan Mei 袁枚
Yuanmingyuan 圆明园
Yuezhi 月氏
zangli 葬礼
zao fachuan 造法船
Zengyi ahan jing 增一阿含经
Zhang Cining 张赐宁
Zhang Huang zhuan fu Zhang Menjin
xiansheng xingzhuang
章潢撰附张门津先生行狀
Zhang Huan 张洹
Zhang Peili 张培力
Zhangwu zhi 长物志
Zhang Ziwen 张子闻
zhang 丈
Zhejiangsheng bowuguan
浙江省博物馆
zhenrong 真容
zhenxing 真形
Zheng Guogu 郑国谷
zhi hua 纸画
zhi hua 织画

zhihu 纸糊

zhihu chuan 纸糊船

zhijin huayang duanzi 织金花样段子

zhima 纸马

zhi mingqi 纸明器

zhiren zhima 纸人纸马

zhizha 纸紮/纸扎

Zhongguo meishuguan
中国美术馆

Zhongguo meishujia xiehui
中国美术家协会

Zhongguo xiandai yishuzhan
中国现代艺术展

Zhongyang meishu xueyuan
中央美术学院

Zhongyuan jie 中元节

zhongyuan li fachuan
中元礼法船

Zhou Benyi 周本义

zhouer fushi 周而复始

Zhou Lianggong 周亮工

zhu 铸

Zhuchen 铸臣

Zhuchen ke 铸臣刻

Zhu Yizun 朱彝尊

zigong qian shishi yingyong fachuan
梓宫前施食应用法船

Zilu 子路

zisha 紫砂

zonghe meiti 综合媒体

Zuo fo xingxiang jing 作佛形像经

INDEX

Note: Page numbers followed by "f" reference figures.

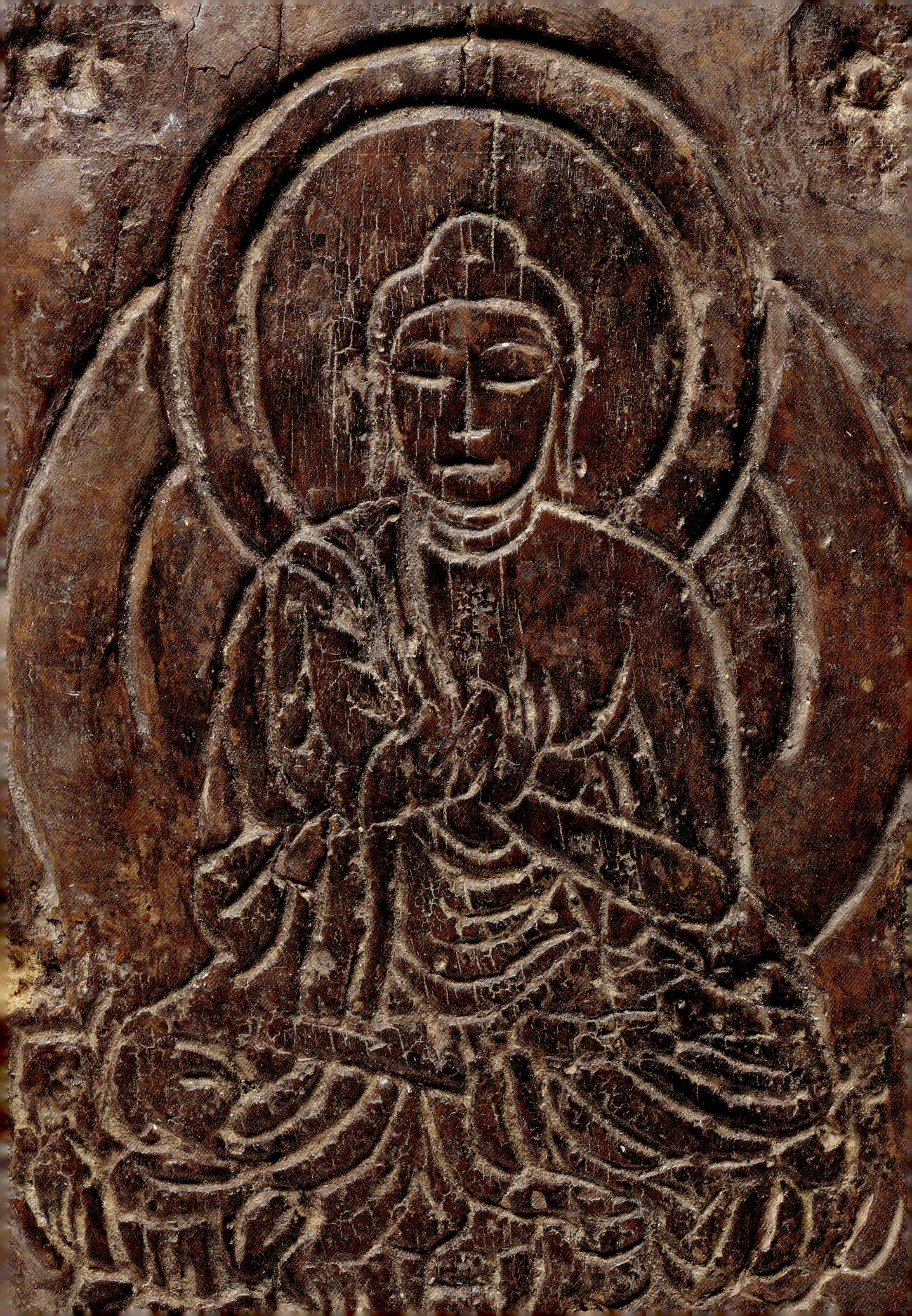

CONTRIBUTOR BIOGRAPHIES

ALEX BURCHMORE is an art historian based in Canberra, Australia, specializing in the study of Chinese art of the past and present, with a particular focus on ceramics, trade and export, and the interweaving of personal and material identities. He received his PhD from the Australian National University in 2019 and joined the faculty of the University of Sydney's Museum and Heritage Studies department in 2021. His doctoral dissertation traced the extent to which Chinese artists have used porcelain to shape their personal, historical, and cultural identities, from the 1990s to the present. He has published widely on Chinese contemporary art, most recently receiving, in 2018, the Art Association of Australia and New Zealand's annual award for the Best Scholarly Article in the *Australian and New Zealand Journal of Art*, and, in 2019, the inaugural *Oxford Art Journal* Essay Prize for Early Career Researchers.

ORIANNA CACCHIONE is Curator of Global Contemporary Art at the Smart Museum of Art, The University of Chicago. Her curatorial practice is committed to expanding the canon of contemporary art to respond to the global circulations of art and ideas. At the Smart Museum, she curated the exhibitions *The Allure of Matter: Material Art in China* (with Wu Hung); *Samson Young: Silver moon or golden star, which will you buy of me?*; and *Tang Chang: The Painting that Is Painted with Poetry Is Profoundly Beautiful*. At the Art Institute of Chicago, she organized *Zhang Peili: Record. Repeat.* A specialist in contemporary Chinese art, she holds a PhD in Art History, Theory, and Criticism from the University of California, San Diego. Her writing has been published in the *Journal of Art Historiography*, *Yishu*, the *Journal of Contemporary Chinese Art*, and numerous edited volumes and scholarly catalogues.

ANNE N. FENG is Assistant Professor of Chinese Art at Boston University. Her research interests include visual and material cultures of the Silk Road, theories of vision and meditation, mural painting, and representations of the Western Pure Land. She is currently preparing a monograph that explores the impact of an aquatic imaginary on immersive architectural schemes of the Buddhist cave complex Dunhuang, located in northwest China. Her writings are featured in *Archives of Asian Art*; *Studies in Late Antiquity*; *Journal of Silk Road Studies*; and edited volumes on Chinese art and architecture. She is the recipient of the East Asia Studies Career Development Professorship at Boston University. Her work has been supported by the Dunhuang Foundation, the Franke Institute for the Humanities, and the Fulbright-IIE Fellowship. Anne has also worked at the Palace Museum, Beijing, the Metropolitan Museum of Art, and the Art Institute of Chicago.

YUHANG LI is Associate Professor of Chinese Art in the Department of Art History at the University of Wisconsin–Madison. She received her PhD from the University of Chicago and was awarded several postdoctoral and research associate positions by Yale University, Grinnell College, and the Women's Studies in Religion Program at Harvard Divinity School. Her research interests cover a wide range of subjects and mediums of visual and material cultures in late imperial China, such as the cult of Guanyin and gendered image making; mimesis and devotional practice; and textile and paper arts. She is the author of *Becoming Guanyin: Artistic Devotion of Buddhist Women in Late Imperial China* (Columbia University Press, 2020) and was co-curator of *Performing Images: Opera in Chinese Visual Culture* (presented at the Smart Museum of Art in 2014) and co-editor of the exhibition catalogue. She has also published articles on Empress Dowager Cixi dressing up as Guanyin in paintings and photographs, as well as articles on theatricality and garments.

NANCY P. LIN is a PhD candidate specializing in modern and contemporary Chinese art and architecture at the University of Chicago. Her dissertation, "Making Spaces: Site-based Practice in Contemporary Chinese Art, 1990s–2000s," focuses on the intersection of art and urbanism in examining locally situated, yet globally oriented, spatial and site-based artistic practices in China. From 2019 to 2020, she was an Andrew W. Mellon Graduate Curatorial Intern at the Smart Museum of Art, where she worked extensively on the exhibition *The Allure of Matter: Material Art from China* and its innovative, archival-based online platform, theallureofmatter.org. Her publications include contributions to the exhibition catalogue for *The Allure of Matter*, a chapter in the edited volume *Visual Arts, Representations and Interventions in Contemporary China: Urbanized Interfaces* (Amsterdam University Press, 2018), and a forthcoming article in the *Journal of Contemporary Chinese Art* (Intellect, Winter 2021).

WEI-CHENG LIN is Associate Professor in the Department of Art History at the University of Chicago. He specializes in the history of Chinese art and architecture, with a focus on the medieval period; his research on Buddhist and funeral art and architecture of medieval China has been published extensively. His first book, *Building a Sacred Mountain: Buddhist Architecture of China's Mount Wutai*, was published in 2014 by the University of Washington Press. He has also written on topics related to traditional architecture in modern China. He is currently working on two book projects: *Performative Architecture of China*, which explores architecture's performative potential through history and the meanings enacted through such architectural performance; and *Necessarily Incomplete: Fragments of Chinese Artifacts*, which investigates fragments of Chinese artifacts, as well as the cultural practices they solicited and engaged, to locate their agential power in generating the multivalent significance of those artifacts, otherwise undetectable or overlooked.

SARA A. MOY is an independent conservator whose work centers on the preservation of modern and contemporary objects and installations and on the material behavior of complex composite objects. As the founding conservator for Hong Kong's M+ Museum, she developed the new museum's conservation policies and workflows and advised on the design of conservation laboratories, storage spaces, and galleries. Her previous affiliations include the Peabody Museum of Archaeology and Ethnology at Harvard University; Straus Center for Conservation and Technical Studies of the Harvard Art Museums; the Brooklyn Museum; and the Art Institute of Chicago. She holds a BA in visual arts from Bennington College in Vermont and an MSc in conservation from University College London.

RACHEL RIVENC is the Head of Conservation and Preservation at the Getty Research Institute (GRI). Prior to her current position, she worked at the Getty Conservation Institute (GCI) as part of the Modern and Contemporary Art Research Initiative, through which she researched the materials and processes used by contemporary artists and the conservation challenges that they pose. Before coming to the GCI, she taught paintings conservation at the University of Malta and worked as a conservator in private practice in France, Spain, and the United Kingdom. She holds a master's degree in paintings conservation from Paris I-Sorbonne and a PhD in Cultural History of Contemporary Societies from the Université de Versailles Saint-Quentin-en-Yvelines. She authored the book *Made in Los Angeles: Materials, Processes, and the Birth of West Coast Minimalism* and is currently writing a book on the artist Cai Guo-Qiang.

CATHERINE STUER is Associate Professor of Asian Art History and Visual Culture at Denison University and a scholar of Chinese visual and material culture. Her current work explores the role of maps, landscape images, and photographs in place making and in constructions of selfhood and identity. She has published on uses of landscape as an autobiographical medium in nineteenth-century pictorial books and on the role of photography in early field archeology and art history. She is currently writing a book on the visual imagination of Nanjing in Imperial and early Republican China. Her contribution to this volume is part of her recent research focus on nineteenth-century visual culture and comes out of an ongoing interest in transmedia relations and craft-based approaches to material and image making.

WU HUNG, a recipient of a Harvard University honorary degree in arts and a member of the American Academy of Arts and Sciences, currently holds the Harrie A. Vanderstappen Distinguished Service Professorship in the Department of Art History at the University of Chicago, and is also the director of the Center for the Art of East Asia and an Adjunct Curator at the Smart Museum. He sits on many international boards and chairs the Steering Committees of the OCAT Museum Group. His research interests include both traditional and contemporary art. Regarding contemporary art, he has curated more than sixty exhibitions since the 1980s. In addition to the catalogues that he compiled for them, he has published many books and anthologies, including *Making History: Wu Hung on Contemporary Art* (2008), *Wu Hung on Contemporary Chinese Artists* (2009), *Contemporary Chinese Art: Primary Documents* (2010), and *Contemporary Chinese Art: A History* (2014), among others.

YUSEN YU is Junior Research Fellow in Comparative Aesthetics and Art History at Corpus Christi College, Oxford. His areas of interest span the fields of Islamic and Asian studies, including book history, material culture, history of technology, and circulation of people, objects, and ideas across Eurasia.

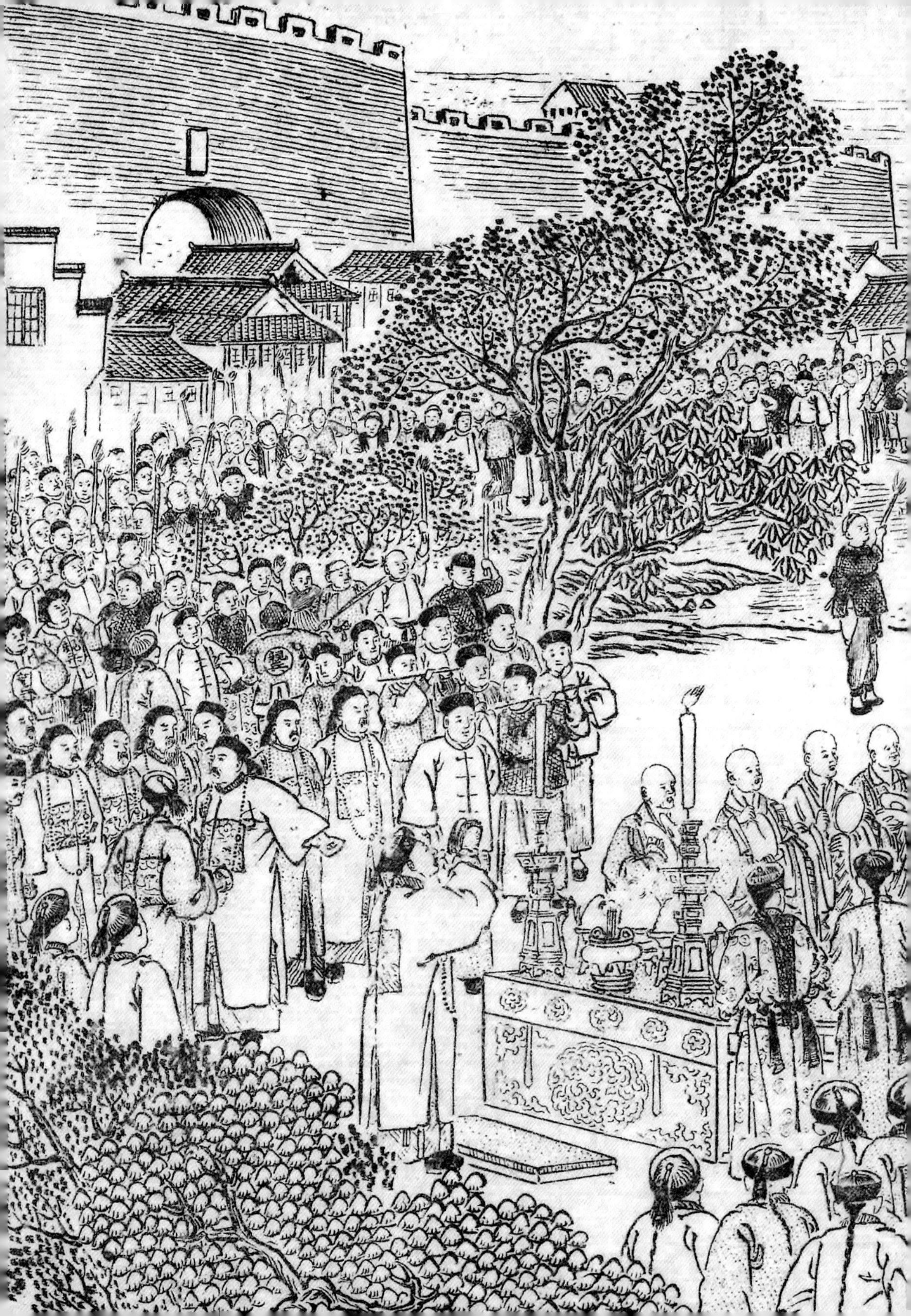